GOD ON THE BIG SCREEN

God on the Big Screen

A History of Hollywood Prayer
from the Silent Era to Today

Terry Lindvall

June 15, 2022

To Steve, our brilliant legal counsel, may the good Lord overwhelm you with grace, your friend
Terry Lindvall

NEW YORK UNIVERSITY PRESS
New York

NEW YORK UNIVERSITY PRESS
New York
www.nyupress.org

References to Internet websites (URLs) were accurate at the time of writing. Neither the author nor New York University Press is responsible for URLs that may have expired or changed since the manuscript was prepared.

Library of Congress Cataloging-in-Publication Data
Names: Lindvall, Terry, author.
Title: God on the big screen : a history of Hollywood prayer from the silent era to today / Terry Lindvall.
Description: New York : New York University Press, 2019. | Includes bibliographical references and index. | Includes filmography.
Identifiers: LCCN 2018043711| ISBN 9781479886746 (cl : alk. paper) | ISBN 9781479892617 (pb : alk. paper)
Subjects: LCSH: Prayer in motion pictures. | Motion pictures—Religious aspects.
Classification: LCC PN1995.9.P6575 L56 2019 | DDC 791.43/682—dc23
LC record available at https://lccn.loc.gov/2018043711

New York University Press books are printed on acid-free paper, and their binding materials are chosen for strength and durability. We strive to use environmentally responsible suppliers and materials to the greatest extent possible in publishing our books.

Manufactured in the United States of America

10 9 8 7 6 5 4 3 2 1

Also available as an ebook

CONTENTS

Introduction

Give honor unto Luke Evangelist;
For he it was (the aged legends say)
Who first taught Art to fold her hands and pray.
—Dante Rossetti

Amistad's depiction of the mutiny and liberation of captive Mende people aboard a Spanish slave ship springs from the historical episode of
1839 (Steven Spielberg, 1997). The film dramatizes the legal and moral
controversy of the status of these captives as they face a trial that will
either send them back into slavery or liberate them. A key character,
Yamba (Razaaq Doti), sits waiting in a prison and looks at an illustrated Bible. His friend, Joseph Cinque (Djimon Hounsou), tells him
that he need not pretend to be interested in it. Yamba replies that he's
not pretending, but beginning to understand. Cutting away, we watch
Judge Coglin (Jeremy Northam), who is responsible for overseeing the
court proceedings, entering a church to pray for wisdom and guidance.
Returning to Yamba, we see him observe that the people of the Bible
had suffered more than his own people. Turning to an illustration of the
Nativity, he says, "Then he was born and everything changed."
    "Who is he?" asks Cinque. Yamba says he doesn't know, but everywhere
he goes, he is followed by the sun, by a light that shines around his head.
Looking at images of Jesus healing a man, defending Mary Magdalene,
and holding children, he continues, "Here he is healing people with his
hands, protecting them, being given children." Seeing Jesus walking on
water, Cinque asks, "What's this?" Yamba answers, "He could also walk
across the sea. But then something happened. He was captured, accused
of some sort of crime. He must have done something." Yamba continues,
keenly questioning the scene. "Why? What did he do? Whatever it was, it
was serious enough to kill him for it. Do you want to see how they killed
him?" He shows an illustration of the crucifixion of Jesus.

1

Cinque says, "This is just a story, Yamba." But Yamba protests, "Look, that's not the end of it." Pointing to a picture of the disciples taking Jesus's body down, he says, "His people took his body down from this . . . thing . . . this . . ." and draws a cross in the air. Then "They took him into a cave. They wrapped him in a cloth, like we do."

Coming upon illustrations of the Resurrection and the Ascension, Yamba points out, "They thought he was dead, but he appeared before his people again and spoke to them. Then, finally, he rose into the sky. This is where the soul goes when you die."

Juxtaposed with the two captives reading the Bible, the Roman Catholic Judge Coglin prays in the background. Yamba concludes, "This is where we're going when they kill us. It doesn't look so bad."

Spielberg crosscuts the exegesis of the illustrated text with depictions of the praying judge, suggesting an intimate relationship between the Gospel and the trial, mediated by the prayers of Coglin, one man seeking to do what is just and right. However, Spielberg also uses humor to characterize those who pray. Congregational abolitionists huddle outside the prison gates as the *Amistad* refugees parade out. One of the prisoners asks who the sullen protestors are as they begin to kneel and pray. Cinque thinks that they "are going to be sick." As they start singing, "Amazing grace, how sweet the sound," the first man laughs and says, "They're entertainers!" As they keep singing, "that saved a wretch like me," Cinque asks, "But why do they look so miserable?"

Spielberg's film suggests that spectators learn religion visually. They learn about the Cross, about grace, and about freedom through images that speak eloquently. Like the illustrated Bible that the captives read, so the prayers of a nation depicted by Hollywood function as cinematic catechisms. They teach as exemplary and revelatory models for people to see, and perhaps imitate.

Winston Churchill once observed that after we shape our buildings, they begin to shape us. Scholars have debated how Hollywood films construct and reconstruct human identity, influencing our conceptions of race, ethnicity, and gender. So, too, they have inquired about how films in various eras have shaped the evolving nature of religious identities, particularly those from Jewish and Roman Catholic traditions that were assimilated into the greater American culture.

The practice of prayer has historically been shaped and reshaped by scripture, liturgical tradition, classic works of piety, and personal and communal rituals. While a recent poll by Barna Research indicated that only one out of six Americans finds guidance for their lives from the Bible, a *US News and World Report* indicated that about two-thirds of Americans pray more than once a day.[1] As biblical influence wanes, popular culture waxes, inculcating millions with its own secular models of religious habits and customs. Religious critic Neil Hurley once quipped that movies are for the masses what theology is for the elite, which makes one wonder what kind of theology of prayer films offer.[2]

This volume evolved out of a recognition of how many prayers have populated Hollywood films and a contemplation of their far-reaching effects on their viewers. When film critic Roger Ebert became too ill to attend the Virginia Film Festival in Charlottesville several years ago, I was invited to present a mediated lecture presentation on prayers in film. I gathered hundreds of clips to show the unexpected presence of such moments of prayer in an enormous range of popular films across all genres.[3] Indeed, these secular films often appeared more religiously attuned than many church activities.

Prayer is defined as spiritual communication with God, a mode of discourse expressed through speech, music, contemplation, journaling, poetry, music, and other arts. Historians Philip and Carol Zaleskis surveyed how individual saints and communities approached the practice of prayer, outlining four archetypal models: the refugee who clings to God with requests and petitions, the devotee, the ecstatic, and the contemplative, who "tastes ultimate reality."[4]

This book examines how films may have shaped popular ideas about prayer, not only reflecting but also prescribing how one is called to pray. The primary goal of this work is to survey the landscape of those Hollywood films that employ prayers in their narratives. Various questions guide this research. First, this book asks what kinds of themes are represented by groups of cinematic prayers during various time periods.

Second, it examines particular aspects of the presentation of prayer and worship, such as demographics (the race, gender, or age of the person praying), function (adoration, confession, thanksgiving, supplication), salience and valence in the context (how important is the prayer to the storyline and what is the attitude toward it?), and efficacy (is the prayer answered?). The valence of prayers reveals its positive or negative aspects as used in the films. For example, does the prayer offer a sacramental view of communication with God or an instrumental one? Is it said sincerely, hypocritically, or ironically? Is the prayer answered in the affirmative or in silence? Remarkably, as we will see with efficacy, prayers are frequently answered in films in supernatural ways with impeccable timing.

Finally, this book seeks to place the use of these religious expressions in film into a general historical context, exploring what was going on in church history and in the larger society during each decade over the past hundred years as films evolved. This volume seeks to tease out general correlations between film history and church history, as Hollywood has incorporated bits of piety into its productions, and these representations of worship have both reflected and, simultaneously, shaped a cultural understanding of prayer.

The gap between the secular Hollywood establishment and the potential religious market was best captured in an apocryphal tale told by biographer Bob Thomas about Columbia Studio's legendary Cohn brothers. The two producers debated the prospect of making a religious film. Harry challenged his brother Jack, claiming that he knew nothing about religion.

"What the hell do you know about the Bible, Jack? I'll bet you fifty bucks you don't even know the Lord's Prayer," said Harry.

"Oh, yes I do," boasted Jack.

"Well then, let's hear it."

"Now I lay me down to sleep . . ."

"Okay, okay, you win," Harry said, and handed over the fifty bucks.[5]

This comic anecdote in which Jack mistakes a common children's bedtime prayer for Jesus's instructions on prayer in the Gospels offers two insights. First, that Hollywood did not know much about praying and, second, that it nevertheless knew that religion in film mattered. Cinematic prayers would come to be significant elements of film, intentionally scripted and embedded in Hollywood narrative paradigms, almost like religious product placements.

This book examines how films have sought to shape popular ideas about the religious practice of prayer over the past hundred years. It argues that these depictions of prayer have not only reflected but also sometimes worked to instruct viewers on how one is called to pray. Tracing the confluence of film and this liturgical ritual of communication from the era of American silent film to the present day, it explores how films have constructed modes of religious piety for both American culture and global consumption.

Previous scholarship has chronicled key shifts in religious trends in the United States, placing them in cultural perspective. Sydney Ahlstrom's *A Religious History of the American People* provided an anthropological reading of the moral and spiritual development of the United States, while Lary May's *Screening Out the Past* laid out the cross-fertilization of American society's and American films' two distinct social histories.[6] So, too, the social church histories of Martin Marty and Robert Wuthnow have provided fresh perspectives on theological currents. For example, Wuthnow's *After Heaven* marked a shift in American spirituality, tracing a move from what he called spiritual dwellers to spiritual seekers. Wuthnow argues that up through the 1950s, congregants coalesced within communities, remaining in one tradition mostly in the same sacred places, such as churches, synagogues, and homes.

Attending to the communal and private voices of prayer throughout a century of Hollywood films opens a treasure chest of gems and fool's gold. One discovers several basic facts. First, these films embed practices of prayer on a fairly regular basis. They are more pervasive than most viewers realize, as both incidental and salient moments in film narratives. In addition to Roman Catholic and Protestant petitions, they include Jewish prayers (for example, Steven Spielberg's *Raiders of the Lost Ark*, 1981, and the Coen Brothers' *A Serious Man*, 2009), Muslim prayers (Mikael Håfström's *Escape Plan*, 2013), Hindu prayers (Ryan Murphy's *Eat Pray Love*, 2010), and Mormon prayers (Alfred Hitchcock's *Family Plot*, 1976). Second, mediated images of prayer provide models, however superficial or satiric, of ways people communicate with God. They show the postures, modes of communication, and range of forms that are recognizable and familiar to young and old spectators alike. Unlike literary and poetic models, however, they are succinct.

Third, while they circumscribe what the typical practice of praying looks like and sounds like, they also present alternative examples. For example, the independent and groundbreaking *Easy Rider* (Dennis Hopper, 1969), which attacked the American dream, surprisingly celebrated the sincere improvised prayers of Hispanic and hippie communities, showcasing what "true" prayer ought to look like. Fourth, mediated images of prayer are rhetorical events, which can help to shape spectators' attitudes toward God, religious rituals, and prayer itself.

Writers often construct prayers as key parts of the narrative design of films. Someone, usually the scriptwriter, consciously plants prayer in the arc of the story. It either slips in comfortably and unobtrusively or it interrupts the flow of the narrative like a pie in the face. Prayers can reveal aspects of the prevailing theological and religious trends in specific eras, such as the desperate prayers of a country slogging through a Depression or world war or the liberal prayers of a Death of God movement. The peculiar Zeitgeist of a historical period shapes the writers and directors of a film so that the spirit of the culture can intentionally or unconsciously leak into the film's narrative and dialogue.

If true piety is caught and not taught, it will be seen and imitated, not merely memorized. But can piety come from seeing it through a glass darkly, watching it in moving images on a screen, finding the practice embedded in an entertainment medium? As revelatory signs, movie prayers work like slanted mirrors to show us what we do and what we might look like when we pray. Rhetorical scholar Richard Weaver's classic adage that "ideas have consequences" suggests a logical and provocative extension, namely, that "cinematic portrayals of prayer have consequences." This book illuminates those portrayals and potential consequences, placing the use of expressions of prayer in film into historical context. It explores what was going on in church history and in society during each decade of the past century in order to shed light on America's broader relationship with religious currents during these time periods and how filmic depictions of prayer have both reflected and sought to influence religious practice.

1

Silent Prayers (1902–1927)

American society rushed into the early twentieth century, with trains, a few planes, and automobiles moving people quickly from one place to another. A suggestion that Americans suffered from neurasthenia, a nervous restlessness, seemed credible. Even entertainment moved more frenetically, with nickelodeon movies supplanting and speeding up old vaudeville acts of singers, comics, magicians, and dog tricks, all of which had been trundled slowly off the music hall stages.

Moving out of the Victorian era into the early twentieth century, the American Protestant church split into fundamentalists and modernists. Classical liberal theology that had permeated German universities began to shape American approaches to faith and practice. The American Roman Catholic Church had swollen with waves of immigrants from Ireland, Italy, and other European countries and remained culturally isolated and entrenched since the *Kulturkampf* in Prussia. It would not be the last of the culture wars between religious groups and mainstream society in the coming years.

Prayers in the post-Victorian era, a time when public agnostics and atheists like Mark Twain and H. L. Mencken took to the stage and newspapers, were vestiges of social religious rituals. Many Americans habitually said grace at meals or insisted that their children say bedside prayers. For some of the devout, these acts kept them tethered to a tradition of faith or introduced them into a communion with God. For others, they became a ritual without meaning. Some used prayers for personal or national gain. In his "War Prayer," Twain mocked sanctimonious congregations praying for the destruction of their enemies. He scoffed at what he believed was the self-delusion of man, who thinks "he is the Creator's pet."

He believes the Creator is proud of him; he even believes the Creator loves him; sits up nights to admire him; yes, and watch over him and keep him out of trouble. He prays to Him, and thinks He listens. Isn't it a quaint idea?[1]

However, while Twain satirized religious piety, the fin de siècle augured an optimism about social progress and global missions. The 1893 World Parliament of Religions brought dozens of faiths together in Chicago to celebrate the march of civilization in an "elaborate display of religious cosmopolitanism."[2] Protestant modernists would embrace the new century with all its innovative possibilities, including moving pictures, which they championed as a panacea for societal ills. Religious language would become more inclusive. Rather than praying "in Jesus's name," prayers addressed God with more elastic and generic apostrophes.

With the turn into a modern age, the answered prayer became a modern evangelical apologetic. For the liberal Protestant establishment, belief in divine immanence led to a fresh devotional, practical approach to piety, with a revived belief in prayer, healing, and intercession.[3] In 1902 psychologist William James published his *Varieties of Religious Experience* and offered his reflections upon hearing a "great deal of discussion about the efficiency of prayer." "Why do we pray?" he asked, to which he quickly responded, "Simply we cannot *help* praying."[4]

During this time, progressive religion and Victorian morality competed for dominance in movies, with the latter trying vainly to maintain a pastoral idyll in the midst of urban progress. Decorum, respectability, and propriety all dictated behavior. By focusing on the Victorian films of D. W. Griffith and the emergence of the American spunk and ecumenical spirit of America's sweetheart, Mary Pickford, we can see that traditional prayers from the Victorian era dominated the screens of the 1910s. Silent film comedians picked up the ordinary ritual of saying grace before meals and made comedy out of divine conversations of gratitude, yet within circumscribed postures and language. By the end of the decade, however, modernist Cecil B. DeMille was promoting the universal prayer of American civil religion. In essence, the models of prayer offered to the American public on celluloid in the early twentieth century carried on a Victorian propriety rooted in a knowledge of scriptures. The standard prayers were rote, but were on the verge of slipping into more comfortable conversations with the Almighty. One notable film portended with sly humor this transition from an old, biblically based culture to an American civil religion.

In Marshall Neilan's *Rebecca of Sunnybrook Farm* (1917), Mary Pickford plays the spunky eponymous character, for which she maintained the sobriquet of America's sweetheart. In Francis Marion's clever adaptation of Kate Douglas Wiggin's 1903 children's novel, her matronly Victorian aunt punishes Rebecca by denying her dinner and orders her to take the dishes into the kitchen. There one tin plate contains a cherry pie, tempting the hungry girl. She lingers over the delicacy, smelling its aroma, running her finger along the edge of the pie, and lifting it to her mouth until she looks up and espies a wall sampler that reads, "Thou Shalt Not Steal." The Mosaic commandment lays the law down, and Rebecca lays down the pie and ruefully retreats, hands folded prayerfully, from the succulent temptation.

But as she shuffles toward the door, she spots another homespun sampler. This one announces, "God Helps Those Who Help Themselves." She weighs the two competing laws, nods thankfully toward the latter, picks up a slice of cherry pie, and gobbles it down with thanksgiving.

The ironic juxtaposition of the two messages is that the second maxim does not come from the Bible. It is an American proverb, from the rascally Benjamin Franklin, and reaffirms the underlying principle of the Hollywood classical narrative film paradigm—namely, that a protagonist makes things happen. An individual American is an action-oriented, causal agent who propels the narrative. It is not biblical law that informs Hollywood films as much as the self-reliant initiative of the American citizen. Mary has left the land of the Victorian tradition and biblical morality for the dynamic independence of the American way and Hollywood hegemony. In the eating of the pie, Mary still shows signs of her gratitude in enjoying something she did not deserve, but the emphasis is on the American way rather than biblical law. The two were becoming more closely aligned through the propaganda of the movies. In their 1929 study of small-town America, cultural sociologists Robert and Helen Lynd saw a link between civic patriotism and religious life.[5] And almost everyone in Middletown went to the movies.

The key theme here is how a biblically based culture was being transformed into an American civil religion, but such a transition met with resistance. Generally, the moving pictures' depictions of prayer during the first three decades of the twentieth century continued a pious tradition of folded hands and bowed heads. Roman Catholics would cross themselves and Protestants would say grace at meals.[6] What is remarkable is that any sacred canopies constructed by various denominations during this era would be undercut by the ecumenism of the movies. The image of the religious American, whether Protestant, Roman Catholic, or Jew, blended into one cinematic cipher, that of the person who prays.

Silent Religious Photoplays

Victorian society foregrounded the powerless, generally saints, women, and children, as those whose prayers were heard by God. The Gospel rescued the weak and the perishing. Such Sunday school stories of struggling against evil dominated early nickelodeons. The anguish of wrestling over temptations in one's personal devotions is the focus of American Mutoscope and Biograph's silent production of *The Temptation of St. Anthony* (1902). The film's story harks back to Saint Athanasius's hagiography, in which Saint Anthony struggles with the desires of the flesh. During his contemplation of sacred writings and a skull, the latter, unfortunately for Saint Anthony's piety, mutates into a vision of a nude woman. Yet his desire for her is quickly quenched when she metamorphoses again into a skeleton. The shock of seeing the wages of his sinful desires awakens him from temptation. Such films confronted Victorian hypocrisy, and the prayer to be "not led into temptation" by a visual erotic delight became more frequent.

We see similar issues depicted in Ferenc Molnar's adapted play about marital infidelity, *The Devil* (1921). Director James Young shows a devilish and suave Dr. Muller (George Arliss) seeking to manipulate two couples as his puppets, demonstrating that goodness can be led astray by temptation. The trusting wife Marie is lured to Muller's apartment. As she is stripped to her undergarments (with a cross strategically placed over her private parts), she desperately prays for help. Her prayer to overcome temptation is answered when a shining cross appears and flames conveniently consume the devil. The post-Victorian prayer highlights a moral battle in the midst of supernatural and even occult spiritualism. Prayers worked like magic and efficiently chased away dangers.

In addition to such paranormal fascinations, sentimental prayers of the era valorized children (especially poor and neglected ones) and their closeness to God. In Biograph's 1910 film *A Child's Faith*, a young woman marries a poor tradesman. They have a child, but the overworked husband dies. The grandfather of the child refuses to help, caring only for his wealth, which he hoards and hides in a wall. The curly-haired granddaughter prays with her mother, folding her hands, kneeling, and earnestly entreating God for help. The grandfather's money happens to drop through a hole in the wall down into the girl's lap as an immediate answer to her prayer. When the grandfather retrieves it, the little girl prays once again at her mother's knee. Conviction strikes the old man and he is reunited with his small family in a hug. The film sets the ritual of prayer as a practice of innocent children, not modern adults. Prayers are the rhetorical means of the powerless to effect change.

Prayers function to restore goodness and virtue, to soften the heart of a greedy grandfather, or to save the lost. In the Pickford vehicle *To Save Her Soul*, Mary, a playful woman, jumps into the lap of a young minister and plays the piano. A musical manager sees potential in the talented young beauty and takes her to the big city, where she becomes involved with a dazzling new set of fast friends. The young minister tries to dissuade her, but to no avail. Her triumphs in the city notwithstanding, the distraught curate resolves to bring her back, and, after various misadventures with unsavory characters, he does. Back at the church organ, they kneel and pray together, pointing to the cross. Subtlety was not an early cinematic practice.

In 1912 French filmmaker and magician George Melies released a film entitled *Forgive Us Our Trespasses*, in which little Danny, living alone with his father, is taught to say the Lord's Prayer every night. When a kind neighbor takes Danny to town one evening to see a dramatic troupe, the lead actress recognizes Danny as her son. She had abandoned the family years ago, but now repents and seeks to be reconciled. However, Danny's father sternly rejects her appeals, until Danny repeats the line, "forgive us as we forgive," and the family is reunited. This notion of forgiveness as dictated by religious decree is a model that recurs throughout silent films of this era.

The social gospel advanced by Congregationalists Walter Rauschenbusch and Washington Gladden was widely influential at the turn of the century, with its religiously motivated commitment to social services and concern for the urban poor. In particular, holiness movements led to the formation of groups like the Salvation Army, which provided fodder for silent film scenarios. In D. W. Griffith's 1909 *Salvation Army Lass*, Mary Wilson (Florence Lawrence) can't pay her bills and is taken in by a prostitute, then abducted by a gang of thieves, but is rescued by the Salvation Army. As she witnesses to others in a saloon, Mary rediscovers her old boyfriend stuck in crime and tries to get him to pray with her. He initially rejects her, but seeing a banner proclaiming, "God is My Light; God is my Salvation," he submits, kneels, repents, prays, and ultimately hugs her. Showing support for the social gospel, Griffith sets forth prayer and charity as major weapons of the temperance movement.

Griffith views prayers, rather than the evangelism of do-gooders, as more effective in promulgating social change. In *The Drunkard's Reformation* (1909), gospel thumpers do not reform an alcoholic and abusive husband and father. Yet the mother's prayers for her husband are answered when he and their daughter go to a temperance play. He is convinced not by the Gospel, but by the art of the theatre, a bit of self-promotion by Griffith of the virtuous power of his own dramatic art. What is significant is that the Victorian Griffith gives women (and children) the power of prayer. Melodramatic prayers of the era are feminine.

A more complex plot underlies *The Converts* (1910), Griffith's temperance melodrama on hypocrisy, which again uses a woman's prayers to effect change. The Biograph film begins with a carefree young gentleman disguised as a minister, possibly influenced by Max Beerbohm's story "The Happy Hypocrite." An intertitle promises spectators that "The Word rings Truth though uttered by false lips," an indication that the earthen vessel may not be trustworthy, but the message is. The masqueraded clergy pretends to preach abstinence to those who walk in darkness—saloon frequenters and loose women. Unexpectedly, his artificial preaching persuades a saloon girl, who repents. Drunk jokesters mock her, calling for her to shout "Hallelujah." When an intertitle declares, "Forgive them for they know not what they do," she kneels. The scene dissolves to a crucifix on the wall where she has become a settlement house worker to protect abused women, seeking to carry the "Word that restores me" unto "the fallen." When she encounters the hypocritical preacher, she preaches Christ's love back to him. Haunted by his guilty conscience, he repents and begins to help others. What he pretended to be, he has become. A woman's prayers are remarkably efficacious.

Griffith uses fewer prayers in his 1915 racist *Birth of a Nation*. He orchestrates flag-waving battles, gun-blazing, desperate charges by Confederates toward a well-established Union line, inserting scenes of weary parents and their two daughters praying for the boys fighting in the battle; the mother holds a letter from the front while the father clasps his hands over the giant family Bible. Griffith's crosscutting juxtaposition between home and hearth and the carnage of the war reveals that many prayers were not answered, as the victorious North vanquished its brothers and cousins of the South.

In her Dickensian films, America's movie saint Mary Pickford was the very model of sheer spunk and virtuous mischief. In Pickford, goodness rarely wilted into saccharine bromides. Silent actress Julia Marlowe wrote, "It takes a greater artist to make a good woman sympathetic and thrilling than to make a base woman sympathetic and thrilling." Pickford made goodness exciting and prayers compelling.

Showing ethnic and religious diversity in the slums, Mary Pickford plays the title character in *Little Annie Rooney*, William Beaudine's 1925 urban dramedy. At home with her father, an Irish cop, and her rambunctious brother, Annie prepares the meal and seeks to civilize the men. She takes the paper from her father while her brother fixes his tie. When he grabs a piece of bread, she gets her father to pray before eating, slapping the over-eager grasping hand of her brother.

After her father is shot, Roman Catholic Annie is invited across the hall to have dinner with her Jewish neighbors. Abie Levy (Spec O'Donnell) brings her into their home and pulls out a chair for her to sit. She finds her place beside his younger brother, Jake. Abie's father reminds him to put on his head covering, a yarmulke. Davening, the bearded father recites the prayers. As they all dig in to the steaming food, Annie bows her head and crosses herself. Her Jewish neighbors serve her an "extra-special" non-kosher meal, ham, for which she gratefully smiles. While the film previews an ecumenical practice of prayer and generosity of spirit that will mark later decades, it still focuses upon marginalized people seeking God and thanking Him.

In John Robertson's 1922 remake of the melodrama *Tess of the Storm Country*, the aptly named landowner and Protestant elder Elias Graves seeks to rid his property of squatters, primarily the Skinner family. Tess Skinner, played by Pickford, befriends Graves's daughter Teola, who becomes pregnant out of wedlock. When Tess takes care of the baby, the community is scandalized, thinking that the child is hers. Tess finds the baby sick and wants to baptize him before he dies. With a strong dose of Augustine's notion of original sin, the film emphasizes the necessity of infant baptism. The dramatic denouement takes place during a formal church service, as Tess, bundled up in an old winter coat and boots, trudges decisively down the center aisle of the great cathedral. The congregation stands aghast at such a brazen sight. She moves immediately to the baptismal font while the Episcopal priest watches in silence. The real mother of the child, Teola, stands with the others, but with pained grief.

Tess addresses the cleric: "I brought ye a dyin' brat, preacher, what's got to be sprinkled." Graves stares at her with disdain and ironically protests, "The presence of that girl is an insult to every woman in this church!"

With pathos, Tess responds, "But the poor little cuss air dyin'. He's got to be sprinkled or he won't never see the face of God." Undeterred, Tess moves quickly to the font, touches the child's forehead with water, and looks heavenward. Looking at the baby, she kneels, with the priest following her example, bowing his head in prayer. So too does almost all the congregation except the patriarch. Teola prays with great suffering.

As Tess offers the child to God, kisses him one last time, and prays, Teola clasps her hands in desperation, but the child is dead. Such an emotional scene illustrated the place of prayer at the moment of death. Prayers for the life of a child resonated with a culture in the early 1900s in which infant mortality rates ran around 10 percent. Martha May Eliot had established the Children's Bureau in 1912 to curtail such deaths, but their frequency made the fictional story more salient and distressing for many families. While the film again placed the act of praying into the hands of women, it also challenged the tradition of the Book of Common Prayer as the necessary model for praying, as Tess extemporaneously expressed her grief and hope in the vernacular.

Mary Pickford's most resilient performance occurs in director Beaudine's brilliantly conceived *Sparrows* (1926), a masterful Sunday school story in the style of Dickens's best melodramas of children. Running an

Shepherding a flock of orphans in *Sparrows* (William Beaudine, 1926), Molly (Mary Pickford) instructs them to pray for deliverance in the beginning and give thanks at the end.

illegal orphanage, a "baby farm" in a southern swampland, villainous Mr. Grimes traffics in lost and stolen children. In one deliciously wicked iconic moment, Grimes receives a gift of a rag doll for one child, which he promptly tosses into the quicksand. The willful destruction of the toy reflects his malice toward the hapless children.

However, the eldest is teenage Molly (Pickford), whose maternal instincts, pluck, faith, and sheer grit keep the family of orphans intact and safe. She steals potatoes for them to eat and reads the story of the Good Shepherd from an illustrated book. She schemes to escape, sending out messages attached to the tails of kites. They write, "Please come and take us away from the Grimses cause they are awful mean to us . . . we can't get out the gate and the swamp is full of mud. Molly and 7 orphans and 1 baby. PS Bring something to eat."

As she sends out their kite-plea, she summons the children to kneel and pray with her beside the edge of the swamp. All kneel, including the lame boy with a makeshift cane, fold their little hands, and close their eyes as Mary speaks for them, looking heavenward: "Lord, our other kite done no good 'cause I guess Your angel had his mind on his harp. Couldn't You tend to this one *personal*?"

The film cuts to the tattered kite entangled in a tree, as if to test the providence of God. However, an intertitle explains, "But He, in His infinite wisdom, had other plans."

Prayers dot the narrative as the dangers of the swamp threaten from all sides. The sadistic Grimes and his ferocious dog keep the infant inmates corralled. Denied food, the children suffer hunger pangs. When one boy hears of how God watches over the sparrows, giving the film its title, he questions why the Almighty doesn't look after them rather than the birds.

Molly holds a sick baby in her lap, slipping into a weary reverie. She dreams that the barn door dissolves and there in the pasture among a flock of sheep sits the Good Shepherd. He rises, turns toward her, and comes over, carrying His crook with His left hand on His breast. He touches Molly on the head, leans down, and picks up the ailing child. He walks out back to His flock, carrying the infant. The pasture dissolves back to the barn door. As Molly wakes, she looks at the child and realizes that he has died. Her reflective gaze at the child and toward the heavens conveys tender, heartrending, and wistfully joyous emotions.

After a fearless escape from dog, quicksand, and alligators, the nursery of children are about to run off down the road, but Molly gathers them together and counts to make sure that they are all safe. Once she retrieves the last stray, she again commands that they kneel and give thanks, pointing to the God who delivered them from their dangers. "Thanks, Lord," she says. "We won't never forget Your kindness." The action completes the circle of prayer. Their deliverance, the film suggests, came not only through the ingenuity and courage of Molly, but through the divine intervention of God Himself.

The film punctuates their escape with one last comic reminder. As they are kneeling, eyes closed, beside the perilous waters they had just traversed, an alligator appears and opens his toothy jaws at them, at which they all rise and run away, except for the one rascally stray, who returns to mock the reptile with fingers on his nose.

Films of the post-Victorian era emphasized the role of women as primary agents of prayer and the place of prayer in bringing about social and personal change. Prayer worked, especially in transforming drunken husbands and fathers. It helped rescue desperate children, re-affirming biblical principles that God's eye is upon the little sparrows. For a sentimentalist like Griffith, effective reform stemmed more from personal prayers than social protests. Film prayers reassured viewers that the prayers of righteous women and children would be heard by God. Society held on to these hopes even as it began to find diversions in modern amusements.

Silent Laughter and Prayer

While staid mainline churches did incorporate the use of stereopticons, slides, and motion pictures in their sanctuaries, church decorum kept worshippers in solemnity. However, the emergence of energetic evan-gelists like Billy Sunday unleashed comedy in the pulpits, as the former Chicago White Stockings baseball player ridiculed Satan and saloons. If there could be comedy in his revivals, why could there not be prayer in silent film comedies?

During this era, prayers were depicted in benignly humorous ways. In *The Cohens and the Kellys* (Harry Pollard, 1926), the secularized duo of Jew and Roman Catholic ride a runaway motorcycle in Atlantic City. Fearful for their safety, Kelly shouts, "You better say your prayers." To which Cohen responds, "I forgot the words." The phrase "Now say your prayers" would be shouted on many intertitles, such as with Charlie Chaplin in *The Floorwalker*, when the villain prepares to pummel him. "Now, say your prayers!"

Each of the four major comedians of the silent era employed the rit-ual of prayer for comic effect. Charlie Chaplin, Buster Keaton, Harold Lloyd, and Harry Langdon found uses for common religious rituals that would evoke laughter, and for Chaplin, poignant sentimentality.

Chaplin combined the act of prayer with his customary touch of pa-thos in *The Kid* (1921), a remarkably affecting film in light of the recent death of his three-day-old son. An opening title card promises "A picture with a smile, and perhaps a tear." As the caretaker for an abandoned child left in an alley, Charlie becomes the reluctant adopted father of the en-dearing child actor Jackie Coogan as the waif. He tends him and teaches him to survive with a life of petty crime and hard work. The two create a sense of family as they make a haven for themselves in a tenement loft.

Jackie Coogan as *The Kid* (Charlie Chaplin, 1921) pleads desperately for divine help as social service workers abduct him from his adopted father.

Charlie makes a stack of pancakes in their little idyllic hole-in-the-wall apartment, and the kid eagerly starts to eat his breakfast. Charlie hushes him and begins his prayer. The kid bows his head into the pancakes, while Charlie looks up and chats with God before saying, "Amen." Then they both dig in. These two companions share bread and emotional bonding, with the poor and the meek of the kingdom of God being brought together for good.

In an emotionally wrought scene, an official from social services comes to Chaplin's atelier to retrieve Jackie for the orphanage, as Charlie has no visible means of support or legitimate claim on the child. The heartless official and the cop struggle with Charlie until they abduct the kid and throw him into the back of a truck. Jackie's sad and desperate face looks heavenward; he calls out to God, asking for help. Charlie escapes the police and runs across the rooftops to save his kid. The answer to the kid's prayer thus comes from above, as Charlie descends to rescue the boy and chase off his institutional kidnappers.

Later, when Charlie sneaks Jackie into a flophouse to sleep for the night, the boy kisses his adopted father good night, but then wants to kneel beside the bed to say his prayers before going to sleep. In a richly comic sequence of Chaplin trying to hide the kid under the covers and the bed, it is the prayer that draws the suspicion of the proprietor, especially as he approaches the pair and Charlie continues to say the prayer with his little companion, who has disappeared.

In the Hal Roach production of *Bumping into Broadway* (1919), Harold Lloyd introduces his glasses-wearing character as a would-be writer trying to escape the clutches of his overbearing landlady. Harold hangs outside his upper-story apartment, feet dangling. The film then exploits the efficacy of a minor character's prayer as a complement to the hero's own journey. Living one floor below, unawares, is the ugliest-looking spinster (with Gus Leonard playing the desperate woman in drag), who prays with arms outstretched, "O Lord, send me a man!" Harold falls into her clutches; she pulls him in by the leg, claiming him as the answer to her prayer. The film slyly points to the irony of answered prayers, showing that one may be unwittingly (and unwillingly) the answer to someone else's prayer.

The "Great Stone Face" comedian, Buster Keaton, set a paradigmatic pattern with his comic scene around the dinner table in *Our Hospitality* (John Blystone, 1923). As an eastern college boy returning to his southern roots, Willy McCay (Keaton) strikes up a friendship on the train with a lovely girl, Virginia (Natalie Talmadge), who turns out to be the daughter of his family's nemesis, the Canfields. She invites him for dinner as both are oblivious of the clans' long-standing feud. When her father and brothers discover his identity as a McCay, they are set to kill him. However, southern hospitality forbids them from harming anyone actually in their house.

McCay discovers his dilemma during dinner. The family and their guest sit suspiciously, wary of each other's every move. The mustached father leers with malice as Keaton rolls his eyes heavenward. In a classic visual scene, the innocent Virginia asks the visiting elderly parson to pray over the meal. He folds his hands with fingertips touching, bows his wrinkled face, and begins.

McCay peeks with one eye as the two brothers squint at him, giving new meaning to the admonition to "watch and pray." The coup de grace comes when the patriarch opens his beady eye to assess the situation, which climactically closes with the "Amen" and the waiter dropping a

dish behind skittish McCay. The prayer serves to unite, however pre-
cariously, opposing groups, but the comedy also sets a pattern for future
table scenes of saying grace. Christian journalist G. K. Chesterton observed that "it is the test of a good religion that you can joke about it,"
suggesting that the assurance of God's grace gave one the freedom to
laugh in His presence. Thus, one could pray with laughter as much as
with solemnity, even as one could pray in Dutch as much as in Japanese.

Directed by Roman Catholic Frank Capra, *The Strong Man* (1926) features Harry Langdon playing a naïve Belgian soldier, Paul Bergot, seeking his pen pal, a blind girl named Mary Brown (Priscilla Bonner). He
makes his way through America in his quest to find her, working as the
assistant to the Strong Man, Zandow the Great. When the Strong Man
gets knocked out, the twerpish Bergot must perform his act in a disor-
derly saloon. Meanwhile, church reformers, led by "Holy Joe," Mary's
minister father, march around the saloon as if it were Jericho, seeking
to bring it down. As they sing and protest, bar rowdies mock the hymn
singers. Bergot, however, thinks it is a funeral march (and in a sense, for
the saloon itself, it will be) and takes off his hat in respect.

The crowd waits for its entertainment in the smoke-filled tavern, waving their hats boisterously and shouting for the performer to get shot
out of a cannon. Bergot tries to shush the unruly crowd to respect the
funeral. One heckler, holding his mug of beer, mouths off: "The Kid's
right! Let's bow our heads and pray for poor old 'Holy Joe'!" He takes off
his cap, and Bergot does the same, bowing his head in reverence. Lifting his glass, the heckler shouts, "And if 'Holy Joe' must sing, get him an
ukulele!" Bergot is stunned at such sacrilege, even while other bar denizens feign religious piety while scoffing and laughing. Snapping his fingers futilely, Bergot tries to restore order and some decorum. However,
the drunk continues, and mocks someone more sacred than God: "and
may we soon have the honor of entertaining Mary Brown in our midst!
A-*men!*", even as he baptizes the marching saints outside with his beer.

The mocking of prayer by this disruptive saloon gang marks a turning
point in Bergot's actions. He mounts a trapeze, conks out the obnoxious
drunk, and then proceeds, however unintentionally, to bring down the
walls and house of the Jericho bar. The uttering of the sacrilegious prayer
wakens the meek fool and transforms him into an unintentional avenging angel.

Comic prayers during the silent film era came to humanize the image of religious actions. Chesterton, known for mixing serious Christian themes with buffoonery, quipped, "It is not funny that anything else should fall down; only that a man should fall down. Why do we laugh? Because it is a gravely religious matter: it is the Fall of Man. Only man can be absurd: for only man can be dignified."[7] His cheerful Christian perspective celebrated the humility and humor of the slapstick comedies, providing a theological basis for religious laughter. For Chesterton, one need not be solemn and ponderous, but could be light and playful in the worship of God. Such honest laughter seemed more inviting to those who felt oppressed by moral laws. Victorian respectability gave way to comic authenticity, as men could confess to being fools. Along with the athletic outreach of the YMCA, Protestant churches fostered the ecumenical Men and Religion Forward movement, which sought to evangelize men and involve them in church life. Other genres, like the adventure film, would also draw men into a vibrant and virile religion, depicting a representation of muscular prayer warriors.[8] Not only clowns and chumps would see the power of prayer, but handsome, dynamic heroes would bow the knee to the Almighty.

Masculine Prayers

The fin de siècle unleashed a slew of inspirational literature for men, from Charles Sheldon's *In His Steps* (1896) and Lew Wallace's *Ben Hur* (1880) to religious western novels like Ralph Connor's *Sky Pilot* (1899). Their masculine religion emphasized action over prayer, but by the time they were adapted for the screen, they would call men to the Benedictine motto *Ora et labora*, to both pray and work. A frontier tradition of tough men would show prayers as words preceding tough, sacrificial actions.

By 1916, western actor William S. Hart had emerged as the top movie star, according to the Quigley Poll, which measured box office profits. In part his status was due to his phenomenally popular moral western, *Hell's Hinges* (Charles Swickard, 1916). Starring as good/bad guy Blaze Tracy, Hart represented the muscular Christianity that countered what the Victorians presented as a meek and mild Jesus. *Hell's Hinges* begins with the ordination of the Reverend Robert Henley (Jack Standing) from an East Coast seminary; however, after his sermon at the Mission of Saint John's,

The good/bad cowboy Blaze Tracy (William S. Hart) prays for Faith (the virtue *and* the woman) while smoking his cigarette and drinking his whiskey in *Hell's Hinges* (Charles Swickard, 1916).

he is considered not-yet-prime-time material for the church. His sister, aptly named Faith (Clara Williams), possesses the character her brother woefully lacks. She serves God faithfully, while he is a weak and selfish youth, utterly unfit for the calling that a devout, love-blinded mother persuaded him to pursue. He is sent west to establish a church on the prairies and be made a man, with his sister accompanying him.

Henley arrives into that den of iniquity known as Hell's Hinges, where neither law nor religion exists. This "Gospel shooter" starts his church in a barn. As he arrives, the villainous saloon owner, Silk, mockingly says, "I reckon it's a sin to shoot a parson, so I'll just scare him to death." Discerning the clergyman's weak nature, he invites him to hold a service for the dancehall girls. The pimp Silk gets him to drink with the girls and he falls asleep in the bed of a prostitute, spurring the crowd to mock religion. "He's like the rest of them, a low-down hypocrite and liar. There ain't no such thing as real religion."

Meanwhile, Faith runs the mission church. When a mob invades the barn service, Blaze recognizes her piety and his own impiety. He wrestles with his conscience. As Henley slides into sin, Tracy moves toward Faith. He sits at a bare table with a bottle of whiskey. Putting down his mug, he puts a cigarette in his mouth and earnestly reads Matthew 21:22: "And all things, whatsoever ye shall ask in prayer, believing, ye shall receive." He closes the good book, reflects, and prays, "God, if You mean what You say here, I'm askin' for her." (The title card shows a sunset with an illuminated cross in the background.) After this conversion, Blaze will become both an angel of judgment in purging the town with fire and a disciple of Faith. His prayer marks his conversion from villainy to ministry, as he "wins" Faith. The film introduces a vigorous, masculine mode of praying, one that reflected the aforementioned Men and Religion Forward movement, an ecumenical trend emerging around 1912 that sought to reclaim male leadership in Protestant churches. It stressed a religious model of strength and action and decried emotional and sentimental appeals. The religious western offered prayers for such heroic saints.

The great swashbuckler Douglas Fairbanks, the movies' version of evangelist Billy Sunday, prays with fervor.[9] *The Gaucho* (Richard Jones, 1927) offers an Argentinean version of the American cowboy, unleashing the frenetic energy of Douglas Fairbanks as the eponymous character who rides the Argentinean Andes. His devil-may-care persona makes him an enemy to the corrupt state and a hero to the people. The first prayer in the film occurs when a shepherd girl (Joan Barclay) falls from a cliff trying to rescue a lamb. After her traumatic tumble beside a pool of water, a radiant vision of the Virgin Mary (Fairbanks's wife, Mary Pickford, in an ironic cameo) appears, heals her, and invests her with healing powers. With hands folded and luminous face, she whispers a prayer. Poor peasants gather to marvel, kneel, remove their hats, cross themselves, and pray. One grieving mother pleads for her dying child, and, as the girl quietly prays, the miraculous occurs. As she blesses the child with holy water from the spring, the infant is restored to robust health. A panning shot of the amazed and worshipful peasants thanking God highlights this astonishing opening.

Upon these holy waters a shrine is built that welcomes pilgrims. A humble padre collects money to distribute to the poor. Both the government's representative, Ruiz-the-Usurper, and the bandit Gaucho arrive at the City of the Shrine, setting up a battle between forces of institutional evil and the Gaucho's own bandits. Winning control of the city,

the Gaucho holds court at a banquet. When the city's criminals are pa-
raded before him, he becomes their judge. The priest seeks forgiveness
for all these sinners. A leper, a victim of the Black Doom, refuses mercy
from the priest. The Gaucho tells him to go and kill himself; however,
the leper infects the Gaucho with his disease. Losing feeling in his left
hand, he prepares to follow his own advice and kill himself over his affliction. The girl of the shrine (now grown into a pious woman, played
by Eve Southern) stops him. Citing Matthew 21:22, she tells him, "All
things whatsoever ye shall ask in prayer, believing, ye shall receive."

The dashing but doubting Gaucho shows his diseased hand and asks,
"This?" Looking kindly upon him, she asks, "Do you believe?" He confesses that he doesn't really know about God, but he trusts her. She leads
the doubting cowboy to the pool of the shrine carved into the mountain's rocks. Amid the candles and crosses, she kneels and prays. He
watches and looks at the shrine, bows his head, and weakly kneels in the
background. He entreats her, "Teach me to pray." As he places his good
hand on his breast, and his leprous hand in the pool, both his mountain
girlfriend (Lupe Velez) and the leper eavesdrop on them. A vision of the
Madonna reappears, opening her arms in benevolent charity. As the girl
continues to pray, the Gaucho suddenly realizes that his hand is clean.
He has been healed! His joy becomes infectious as his girlfriend thanks
God. Even the leper raises his own hands in exuberant amazement and
praise. As the Gaucho rushes to thank the girl, she points to God. "No,
thank Him," she instructs. The prayers, both during the preface and at
this climactic point, alter the narratives and draw characters to God in
gratitude and sheer delight. The inspired prayers of the Gaucho matched
the manly prayers of the Men and Religion Forward movement.

Melodramatic Prayers

More cynical and ambiguous treatments of prayer kept pace with pious
depictions as the Roaring Twenties revved into high gear. The post–
World War I and influenza era sizzled with new fashions and fads.
Churches divided along liberal and fundamentalist lines over doctrinal
beliefs and critical approaches to hermeneutics. Prayers in films held
on to much moral baggage from the post-Victorian era, but they also
expressed a restlessness of flaming youth. The modern era wanted to

leave the bluenoses behind, giving way to a cynical view of prayer. *Manslaughter* (1922) fairly represented what director DeMille thought of this emerging audience, which wasn't much. When spoiled Jazz Age flapper Lydia Thorne (Leatrice Joy) speeds around at fifty-five miles an hour, she epitomizes the immorality of the era. A crusading district attorney (Thomas Meighan) denounces a dancing party, "with its booze and license," as "no better than a feast of Bacchus." DeMille flashbacks to Roman-era orgies, with the district attorney as Attila the Hun bringing judgment down on the revelers. In this overwrought melodrama, Lydia tries to bribe a cop with a bracelet of diamonds, only to find herself handcuffed with steel. She prays the old prayer desperately, "Forgive us our trespasses as we forgive those who trespass against us." DeMille was notorious for sneaking sin into his biblical spectaculars while still holding a religious pose. He would tantalize with titillating sex and sin and then disapprove with a "tsk tsk." Prayers could cover a multitude of sins.

* * *

In W. S. Van Dyke's *The Pagan* (1929), a brutal, manipulative trader, Brother Slater, oversees his young, half-caste ward Tito (Dorothy Janis). Henry Shoesmith (Ramon Novarro), a lazy native plantation owner, pursues her. Tito must attend to Bible reading lessons, stumbling over the verse "for the heart is dee-ceet-ful above all things and des-pair-ate-ly wicked." Praying and hymn singing ("Yes, Jesus loves me") occur in the church, but Tito is more interested in the nature religion of Henry. During a service, Slater preaches interminably, but the lush outdoors distract Tito as she yearns for the heavenly sunshine. When the minister calls for prayer, even those who fell asleep during his sermon awake to join in. When Tito asks a bare-chested Henry, "Why not go to church?," he answers, "Too hot in church. God is everywhere, so why go to church?" Unlike the Griffith pieties, these 1920s prayers function as mere rhetorical decoration in the film and express an emerging skepticism about praying. While prayers reminded spectators of religious traditions, they also suggested that they may not be sufficient to keep people from trespassing into more carnal temptations.

Married to an elderly millionaire, Theodora (Gloria Swanson) prays with her hands clasped before her face, seeking deliverance from the temptation of the dashing Lord Bracondale (Rudolph Valentino) in *Be-*

yond the Rocks (Sam Woods, 1922). She dare not trust herself in his presence and so kneels beside her bed in an anguished posture of prayer.
"Lead me not . . ." At a Whitmonday pageant, she wrestles between marital fidelity and this illicit romance. While on a northern African expedition, her elderly husband, a selfish, ailing old duffer, intercepts a letter
addressed to her from Bracondale and realizes that his existence keeps
them apart. He dies so the kids can marry and be happy. While her
prayer is answered, so are her desires, as Theodora is kept from temptation until her husband conveniently sacrifices himself. Jazz Age prayers
focus on the unfulfilled needs of the plaintiff, seeking wish fulfillment
more than right behavior. The appearance of Freudian wish fulfillment
and a focus upon sexuality began to crowd into religious life.

Two versions of British author Somerset Maugham's novella *Rain*
take place in the exotic world of a Far East British colony. Raoul Walsh's
Sadie Thompson with Gloria Swanson and Lionel Barrymore appeared
in 1928, and four years later, Lewis Milestone's sound adaptation of *Rain*
featured Joan Crawford and Walter Huston. Both films followed the narrative pattern of threat, repentance, rape, and suicide as reformer Alfred
Davidson tries to convert prostitute Sadie only to experience his own
spiritual disintegration through sexual obsession. The films are packed
with prayers that sound as hypocritical as the missionary, and yet also
have a potency that alters Sadie's life.

Professional reformer Davidson uses the words of prayer without
power. He preaches incessantly with bromides that "the knife of reform
is the only hope of a sin-sick world" and "a righteous man will not hesitate to renounce evil." His encounter with Sadie upends his insincere
posing. She tells jokes about the farmer's daughter and playfully pinches
and gooses the marines of Pago Pago. She lives by the motto "Smile,
bozo, smile, for no matter how tough it is today, it's bound to be worse
tomorrow." Reformers in the film do not smile; only genuine, natural
people do.

Wearing a dark suit in the tropical climate, the stern Davidson smol-
ders in the heat. After he first says grace, standing with his hand covering
his face as if in anguish, and symbolically indicting his own blindness
to spiritual needs, he tells the governor of the island that the morals on
the island must be cleaned up. He finds the natives so depraved that, he
confesses, "I actually have to teach them what sin is."

In Sadie's hut, on a torrentially rainy evening, Davidson confronts Sadie, who desperately worries what might happen to her: "Repent, Sadie, and you will have no cause for fear." She sits on her bed and Davidson pulls up a chair, looking down at her as he says, "Pray, Sadie Thompson, yield your soul!" Wiping her brow and wringing her hands, she cries out from her vulnerable position, "I don't know how to pray." With an odd gleam in his eye, he exclaims, "Poor child! Repeat after me."

She glides with seductive openness and gazes back up at him. "Put your hands together like this." She complies and he cites the Hebrew prophet Isaiah, "O God—though my sins be as scarlet—, wash me in the blood of the Lamb—, save me from Thy awful vengeance—." She grows calmer, but wearies and faints. Davidson leaves her room with his arms raised in prayer, thanking God for her conversion.

After three tortured days of loneliness, repentance, and redemption, she is tamed, which her marine boyfriend sees as hypnotism. Davidson leers menacingly, telling her that Satan has tested her. Yet as he prays, lust overtakes him. He dreams about Sadie and rubs his hands with guilt even as he tries to fold them to pray. He comes into her room and confesses that he has been "seeing things in the dark—flaming-hot eyes— Aphrodite—Judas!" An ellipsis suggests that he commits suicide in the morning tide, his unbridled lust and hypocrisy exposed. His prayers did not even save his own soul.

The sound version of *Rain* follows the same plot of the dour, legalistic moralist trying to redeem the woman. In offering her a free key to salvation and trying to feed her the bread of the spirit, Davidson gives her a chance "to be saved." He comes on with unrelenting ferocity: "You are an evil woman, liar. Kneel, Sadie Thompson, kneel and repent." She retorts that such a mealy-mouthed reformer like Davidson "ain't a minister; you don't fool me," a sop for religious audiences to divide the authentic minister from its counterfeit.

Davidson blackmails her with threats of deportation, entreating her to pray for forgiveness. She responds, with wretched and despairing emotions, "I am bad, but I want to be good, but I don't know how." Davidson responds, "You got to serve your time." Out of frustration she shouts, "Your God and me could never be shipmates. Tell Him that Sadie Thompson is on her way to hell." She accuses him of believing in torture: "You know you're big and you're strong and you have law on your side.

You hang me and be damned." Just as she accuses him of not understanding, he begins to recite the Lord's Prayer as a mantra to block out her pleas and accusations. Then he interrupts his own performance to proclaim, "O Lord, hear Thou my prayers for this lost sister. Close Thy ears to her wild and heedless words." He continues to recite the Our Father as she kneels, weeping copious tears. She begins to say the prayer with him. "Thy will be done, on earth as it is in heaven. Lead us not into temptation, but deliver us from evil." She kneels humbly as he hovers above her, and the rain keeps coming down and the native drums beat loudly and incessantly.

Back from the brig, her marine finds a subdued Sadie: "What's he been doing [with Sadie]?" The answer is "Praying. Praying." In spite of her claims that he's a holy man, the marine counters that "this hyena's got you so hypnotized, it's like dope." When Davidson is found drowned in the morning, Sadie is liberated from his sanctimony. In both versions of the film, prayer finds itself a victim to the stronger desires of the flesh. Freudian psychology trumps evangelical self-control, and even earnest prayers cannot save a modern man from his own passions.

Other directors were inspired to express their religious convictions on the screen. Where Griffith saw "man made in the image of God" but ruined by Satan, another young, naïve director, King Vidor, opted for an optimistic view of human nature as fundamentally good. His early exposure to Mary Baker Eddy left him a lifelong adherent of Christian Science. In the January 1920 issue of *Variety*, Vidor published his filmmaker's "Creed and Pledge," promising not to produce anything that would injure anyone, nor anything "unclean in thought or action," nor to "deliberately portray anything to glorify mischief, condone cruelty or extenuate malice."[10] Such principles of "goodness" would guide his filmmaking. Fifty years later, Vidor confessed his hypocrisy: "I might have been stupid enough in my first few pictures to put out a creed that I wouldn't make pictures with violence or sex. It was an advertisement, you know.... Right after it came out in the paper, I got arrested for playing poker."

Publicizing a moral creed of forgoing sex in his films may have stirred nary a ripple in a religious periodical, but for a virile film director to shout from the headlines of a trade magazine was a burst of misguided idealism. This passion for virtue may have been subverted in his shooting of his religious adventure, *Sky Pilot* (1921), not so much regarding the moral content of the film, but in Vidor's extramarital affair with his star, Colleen Moore. As one wag put it, "Sinning has a way of changing one's view of sin." As seen in the Somerset Maugham adaptations, sinning also had a way of eviscerating the power of prayers. Modern men and women of the 1920s found themselves depicted in cinema as victims to unbridled ids.

The Miracle Man (George Loane Tucker, 1919) starred the incomparable Lon Chaney as the Frog, part of a gang of hoodlums exploiting a local faith healer called the Patriarch (Joseph Downing). Eventually, each criminal, converted by his charity, vows to carry on the Patriarch's good works.

One extant clip of this film movingly contrasts the bogus miracle of the Frog and an authentic miracle of a crippled boy. After the Frog fakes his performance, a young boy receives faith to walk without crutches. One can easily understand why it was "the most highly praised and successful picture of 1919."[11] Historian Benjamin Hampton saw *The Miracle Man* as enhancing the prestige and power of directors as "audiences everywhere gave their heartiest approval to the production, and the powerful cult of the Christian Science Church welcomed it as propaganda for Mrs. Eddy's teachings."[12] But such prayers brought more attention to a biblical model for both spiritual and physical healings. In the same period, the emergence of a Pentecostal movement, with more orthodox denominations like the Assemblies of God, also emphasized spiritual gifts such as faith healing through prayer.

Lon "Man of a Thousand Faces" Chaney starred in *Shadows* (Tom Forman, 1922) as the Chinese laundryman Yen-Sin. A young minister arrives at a fishing village at the same time that Yen-Sin washes ashore from an apparent shipwreck. The minister proceeds to marry a local widow and tries to convert Yen-Sin to Christianity, but Yen-Sin dismisses the hypocritical faith of the minister's congregation. A rival suitor attempts to dishonor the minister by blackmailing him. Yen-Sin, however, exposes the culprit's schemes. Yen-Sin fully expects the minister to take revenge on the blackmailer, but instead the minister forgives him in an act of Christian charity. Witnessing a sincere act of forgiveness convinces Yen-Sin of the truth of Christianity. In response, he accepts the minister's God as his own.[13] What was remarkable about these last two conversion stories is how they suggested that the life of a Christian, rather than his prayers and preaching, influenced evangelism. The grace of such clergy was the miracle.

Religious films waned in popularity in the consumerist society of the 1920s, except for DeMille's biblical blockbusters. He was wily enough to insert sufficient naughty bits to attract the sinners and to combine biblical dramas with contemporary parables. For example, in his 1923 spectacle *The Ten Commandments*, DeMille co-opted the Jewish history of the Exodus for a modern morality tale of a mother whose two sons take different paths: John obediently keeps the commandments and becomes a carpenter, while Danny breaks them. In particular, Danny spurns the commandment to not steal, using inferior materials to build a church with shoddy materials, building "upon sand." One rainy night, the mother preaches to her agnostic son about the fear of God and prays for his compliance. John, however, emphasizes the New Testament story of Jesus healing a leper, a sign of grace and mercy. Danny ignores his mother to his own disaster when his work comes crashing down, killing his mother, who finally recognizes that she should have taught him more of the love, rather than the law, of God.

In one of the last silent/sound film hybrids of the decade, director Michael Curtiz exploits DeMille's technique of parallel narratives in his spectacular *Noah's Ark* (1928). Starting with a shot of the ark beached on Mount Ararat, haloed by God's rainbow covenant, the film unleashes a blast of judgment upon the wicked who scheme to build a tower whose top may reach unto heaven. When God orders Noah to build the ark of gopher wood, His servant utters the prayer of Jesus, "Thy will be done, on earth as it is in heaven." With gold becoming man's only god, evidenced in the anachronistic golden calf, Curtiz presciently structures his film to condemn the profit speculators in the days before World War I, such as the power-hungry and lascivious sadist Nickoloff (Noah Beery). Ironically, on the eve of the Wall Street market crash, Curtiz juxtaposes greedy investors and the wicked hubris surrounding the Tower of Babel, with his story of the imminent world war by focusing upon an international caravan traveling the Orient Express run.

Curtiz includes a Chaucerian collection of types in his cavalcade. One businessman ridicules a pious minister and prates, "The Bible won't work nowadays; science is god." A sarcastic Frenchman mocks, "There

is no God, gentlemen. There is only a Goddess. Her name is woman—
and she's a Devil." Nickoloff barks out that Soviet military might is the
only god. To all of these, the devout cleric responds, "Only with the eye
of Faith can we see God's eternal plan." The comrade condescendingly
adds, "Faith is food for fools and invalids. If there is a God why doesn't
He show Himself?" The final word comes from the Bible reader: "Peace
brother, lest He show Himself in wrath." Immediately the dramatic denouement unfolds with a horrendous accident.

The minister/chaplain reads, "The Lord hath said, 'measure not thy
wrath against thy child.'" Then he prays, "O God, have mercy on Thy
children! They know not what they do!" Immediately, as some are rescued and sinners are killed, the minister compares the flood of blood to
the inundation during the wicked times of Noah. "As the Ark prevailed
upon the flood waters, O God, so let Thy righteousness prevail in this
Deluge of Blood!"

After God destroys those who worship the false gods, the film ends
with the rainbow of a new covenant, along with the armistice, celebrating that war shall be no more. God seems to answer prayers; however, it
is a theologically and politically optimistic hope that will not prove true,
no matter how many silent prayers were uttered throughout the first
decades of Hollywood movies.

The era of silent films charted a trajectory of church life from Victorian traditions of the effective prayers of women and children in Griffith
films, leading to a feminization of church life, to a more dismissive approach to religion during the Roaring Twenties. Women not only took
a more active and dynamic role in providing religious education for the
young, but also demonstrated leadership in the temperance movement,
women's suffrage, child labor, global mission work, and other social
and religious concerns (even in promoting moving pictures for children in churches).[14] In the beginning, films often depicted prayers as
playing central roles in converting sinners or restoring families. Men
and women would confess their sins and pray that they be kept from
temptation.

With energetic evangelists like Billy Sunday modeling a masculine
vitality, a men's movement developed, with westerns and film comedies
showcasing virility and humor practiced in the presence of God. Virtues of honor, courage, sacrifice, and humor attracted more men back to

church than had attended in the Victorian age, with candid and comic prayers offered by actors like Hart and Chaplin respectively.

This silent film era introduced prayers to innumerable spectators, even teaching them the words on the intertitle cards. Such intertitles not only taught immigrants to read, but taught them words to pray. Some were pious exemplary models of a child's or mother's petition for a father or husband to be transformed. Prayers in westerns and comedies demonstrated that one could be a man of God and speak candidly or humorously with God. But then some films raised questions about the efficacy of prayers.

However, in the early 1920s, with the church dividing into fundamentalist and progressive camps, churches found themselves divided by culture as much as theology. Conservatives began to retreat from cultural engagement and liberals found themselves out of step with the new hip morality. Ironically, Cecil B. DeMille, the filmmaker of religious spectaculars, privileged sin over sanctity in his Jazz Age melodramas, squeezing the religious element out of prayers. Religious concerns took on less significance in a culture of prosperity. Prayers that did appear showed the hypocrisy of religious figures. In an era of plenty and pleasure, one went to a "petting pantry" (a movie theatre) not to see religion but to watch "whoopee." But an economic disaster on Wall Street altered this trend of easy, libertine living. By the 1930s, moving pictures attracted more spectators, but also drew religious protests from conservatives and liberals alike against their rampant immorality. Curiously, a clamor for national censorship would spark an ecumenical agreement among diverse religious leaders. Protests against sin in movies and the ridicule of religious figures would unite Roman Catholic, Protestant, and Jewish leaders to censor celebrity characters like Mae West and to hold Hollywood accountable for how they represented prayers. With impending hardships on the horizon, spectators would look back to God, and films would speak more gingerly in addressing the divine.

2

Censored Prayers (1927–1939)

The 1930s generated desperate prayers in America as the Depression, the Dust Bowl, unemployment, and poverty plagued the land. However, most films during this golden age of Hollywood did not reflect the need for jobs, food, and rain. From gangsters and Broadway musicals to screwball comedies and Mickey Mouse cartoons, crowds were amused to distraction. FDR's radio homilies sought to assure the American public that the only thing we had to fear was fear itself.

In his history of the liberal Protestant magazine the *Christian Century*, Elesha Coffman outlined how the journal's editorial convictions paralleled many cultural dilemmas facing Americans.[1] Caught up in the rift with fundamentalists, the journal emphasized its concern for the social gospel and for the tools of modern reason. Tackling such topics as race and immigration, it promoted what it saw as civil rights for the common good; yet it remained wary of the Roman Catholic Church. For all its liberal leanings, the periodical revealed a cultural conservatism, mostly in its relation to movie censorship. Its religious moralism exposed a frustration with Protestantism's own moral czar, Presbyterian elder Will Hays, as it soured on his impotence in the face of the entertainment industry. Disturbed about the consequences of the film industry's effects upon the moral conscience, it admitted that while it preferred "clean movie makers to censors," it did "not fear censorship as much as film filth."[2] The periodical constructed an ordered and meaningful cultural identity centered upon the teachings of Jesus that shaped liberal Protestant thought in the early twentieth century. Up through the 1920s, major religious traditions looked askance at one another. However, change came in the 1930s. As historian Garry Wills argued, a new Jewish/Catholic/Protestant puritanism arose during the Depression, one that renounced the "binge morality of the Roaring Twenties," the flamboyant desire for pleasure and speed.[3] Hard times required religious discipline.

During this time, Hollywood colluded with censorship boards and religious organizations to keep its films showing. The Breen Code, following the toothless Hays Code, sought to establish a national morality in entertainment. Led by energetic Roman Catholic laity like Joseph Breen, the Code dictated screen content.

The Motion Picture Association of America (MPAA) laid out its rubric for the "Don'ts and Be Carefuls" in 1927, resolving that the screen should not ridicule clergy or use profanity ("hell," "damn") or the name of God ("Lord," "Jesus," "Christ") "unless used reverently in connection with proper religious ceremonies." However, enforcement was quite lax. Only when an amendment to the Code established the Production Code Administration under the leadership of Breen in 1934 did Hollywood provide teeth for the agreement. Until then, however, religion and sexuality were often shared themes.

One safe realm outside the then-vigilant eyes of the Motion Picture Production Code Board was representation of African American and marginal forms of worship, such as Pentecostalism, as sensitivities to racism and respect for black religious traditions had not yet equaled concerns for ridicule of mainstream religion. The invisible institution of the slave church may have been overlooked in the church history records of the day, but it appeared publicly in the movies.

Race Prayers

Race movies in the silent era had addressed hypocrisy among the black clergy in films like Oscar Micheaux's *Body and Soul* (1925). In his film debut, Paul Robeson plays both the malevolent Reverend Isaiah Jenkins and his good brother Sylvester. The prayers and preaching of Jenkins hark back to the sham religion of the adaptations of Somerset Maugham's *Rain*. Micheaux sharply reaffirms that not only good people pray.

Director King Vidor sought to depict realistic black melodrama in his early sound film *Hallelujah* (1929), with dollops of enthusiastic religion. Prayers infuse the narrative as ordinary parts of the cultural life of poor black cotton workers. Children pray at night for one another, a precursor of the television Walton family prayers.

Sharecropper Zeke (Daniel Haynes) falls for a juke-joint girl, Chick (Nina Mae McKinney), and loses his money. Meanwhile, his mother senses that something is wrong and implores the Lord to "have mercy on my soul." Implicated in the death of his brother, Zeke repents to his father, who points him toward heaven. Contrite and inspired, Zeke preaches on God's grace and forgiveness: "The Lord done showed me the light. The Lord done revealed the truth of His creation. . . . Come, O Lord. Come to that land of green pastures and clean waters. Come to the Lord." He is transformed into a charismatic preacher.

At one revival baptismal service, Zeke's impassioned preaching about a train to heaven puts Chick under religious conviction. The entire congregation "gets on board" the train to glory, with even Chick crying out to God. But even filled with the Holy Ghost, the seductive Chick leads Zeke astray again, suggesting that prayer may not be sufficient to keep one from temptation. Scholar Judith Weisenfeld has identified prayers, the Ten Commandments, Bible reading, and singing spirituals as essential elements of southern faith, but also sees sexualized religion underlying some enthusiasm.[4] Both religious ecstasy and sexual passion are inextricably linked in Vidor's film, where former blues singer Chick can belt out "Give Me That Old Time Religion" and simultaneously fuel her tempting allure. The intimacy of prayer and worship was frequently intertwined with physical attraction in southern revivals.

In Hal Roach's *Our Gang* episode *The Little Sinner* (1935), Spanky plays hooky from Sunday school with Buckwheat and Porky. Wandering into the woods, they encounter a black Pentecostal baptism ceremony, replete with praying, hallelujahs, singing, and the most charismatic worship shown on film to that point, enough to send the boys quivering back to public school. Like the prayers offered at other Pentecostal and marginal religious groups, the prayers of African Americans were depicted as emotionally charged and treated with ambiguity. The exposure of such prayers on film brought charismatic rituals from the backwoods margins into the mainstream, showing more staid denominations how others worshipped.

What these portrayals of church people did reveal was a rediscovery of both the embodiment of worship, with the body praying as much as the mouth, and the power of sin in religious lives. Liberal theology, with its optimistic hope in progress, contrasted with real lives of churchgoers who struggled with their own sins, with some interpreting the Depression as a sign of God's judgment. Movies would also reveal that religious fallibility was not confined to race movies.

Humanized Ministers

While the Production Code Administration kept Hollywood from ridiculing the clergy, it didn't forbid making them human. Clergy struggled throughout the Depression, economically and professionally. As Methodist ministers were transferred from parish to parish and evangelists wandered across the country, clergy had to adapt to the harsh times as much as anyone else. The Oklahoma Land Rush formed the backdrop for Wesley Ruggles's Academy Award–winning *Cimarron* (1931), one such story of an itinerant minister/lawyer/editor/sheriff, Yancey Cravat (Richard Dix), who transports his wife, Sabra (Irene Dunne), and family to settle in the boomtown of Osage. Based on Edna Ferber's bestselling novel, the epic story compares the settling of the territory to the biblical narrative of Creation. The charismatic Cravat brings order to Osage, preaching his first sermon in the rudimentary gambling casino, Great-Gotcha's-Hall-of-Chance, with the announcement that all are welcome. In fact, all come, including Indians, whom Cravat defends as victims of persecution and injustice. Even the town's lone Jew, Sol Levy (George Stone), is welcome. (When told by an old biddy that one of her ancestors signed the Declaration of Independence, he quips, "That's all right. A relative of mine, a fellow named Moses, wrote the Ten Commandments.") So, too, the church welcomes disreputable women who swagger in and sit up front.

When asked whether he feels nervous, Cravat tells his wife that he would rather "plead to a Texas jury than preach a sermon to this gang." Nevertheless, looking at a congregation that looks "as queer at church as a mule does in the front parlor," Cravat conducts the "first meeting of the Osage Methodist, Episcopalian, Presbyterian, Congregationalist, Baptist, Catholic, Unitarian, and Hebrew Church." He acknowledges that as a lawyer he has experience convicting horse thieves, but "while I know my Bible from cover to cover, this is the first time I have been requested to speak the word of God in His temple; for any soul, no matter how humble or sordid, becomes, when His word is spoken in it, His temple."

He takes his text from Proverbs, "There's a lion in the street," and his allegorical interpretation aims at a murderous ruffian standing menacingly at the back of the meeting. He is the lion, or "I might say 'jackal' or 'dirty skunk,' which wouldn't be sacrilegious," which threatens the good people of the town. The killer draws his gun, but Cravat shoots him, explaining that "under the circumstances, we will forgo the sermon and conclude the service with a brief word of prayer: 'Bless this community, O Lord. Amen.'"

The remarkable aspect of the film is the plethora of prayers that dot its landscape. When Cravat goes traveling abroad, his long-suffering wife, Sabra, publishes a newspaper called the *Wigwam* and emerges as a congresswoman in her own right. She leads the family in prayers as well; sitting at a table with her two children, and an empty chair set for Cravat, she tearfully prays, "We thank Thee for Thy blessings, O God, and we pray that You will watch over us all while we are separated. Spare our dear ones and bring us all together again in safety and happiness. Amen." Immediately, her husband reappears. Women, men, and children pray, and the efficacy of their prayers is astounding. So too, the country at large found itself in need of prayers as migrations of family members seeking work separated loved ones.

In Alfred Santell's whimsical melodrama *Polly of the Circus* (1932), a cheeky and spoiled trapeze artist, Polly (Marion Davies), falls during a performance and is sequestered in the parish home of Rector John Hartley (Clark Gable) to recuperate from her fractures and fever. Their verbal sparring leads to the inevitable romance. As protests against immorality in Hollywood films mounted, this film slyly raised subversive issues of censorship, with bluenoses protesting the figure of Polly on advertising posters. What makes the film clever is the incorporation of prayers and religious discourse on the side of the titillating circus vamp.

The handsome and witty Hartley makes clergymen appear urbane and suavely sophisticated (well, he is the nephew of an Episcopalian bishop). Polly flirts with him, saying, "Didn't you break the Fifth Commandment in college?" Hartley responds, "No, that would be ingratitude." "Well, what is the Fifth Commandment?" she asks, thinking it has to do with sex. "Honor thy father and thy mother." "Oh."

In their courtship, Hartley brings Polly an illustrated Bible and copies of *True Confessions*. She chooses to look at some of the Bible's "hot stuff." Talking about whether he would get married, she says, "All your wife would have to do is learn her catechism and you'd give her a kiss every Ash Wednesday. And she would have to sleep in the woodshed during Lent." He laughs.

Her coup de grace, however, occurs when she reads to him from the book of Ruth, "Whither thou goest, I will go; your people will be my people; your God will be my God." It is the best pickup line she could have used. However, when they marry, the vestry will not accept their rector having a circus girl (read foreigner in the Ruth story) as his wife. He calls the congregation to confess their sins, pointing out their own manifold sins as recorded in the Book of Common Prayer. As an exemplary model of church leaders, Hartley prays and lives out his prayers. As the Depression leveled social and economic strata, so the respectable rector weds the itinerant entertainer.

The alloy of church and entertainment reflected the growth of radio ministries and religious showmanship in the 1930s. Sinclair Lewis had penned his satire *Elmer Gantry* about bogus religious leaders in the mid-1920s. Gantry's exploits, however, were mild compared to the antics of Pentecostal evangelist, divine healer, and pioneer in religious broadcasting Aimee Semple McPherson, who went through three husbands before settling in to her center of welfare services and evangelism in 1923. She incorporated a network of churches into the International Church of the Foursquare Gospel.

Despite her shady scandals, her preaching reached out to the dispossessed and lost, expressing the fullness of God's love and joy. Her services made spellbinding use of vaudeville and theatrical showmanship, with scenery, costumes, props, drama, choirs, and an aggressive public relations machinery.[5] They offered therapeutic blessings to those who came. In Frank Capra's *The Miracle Woman* (1931), Barbara Stanwyck, in a bravura performance, plays Sister Fallon, a not-too-subtle allusion to McPherson, whose Angeles Temple satirist Mencken would describe as the wildest nightlife in southern California. Gospel preaching joined with superb showmanship and sparked the religious followings of growing celebrities like McPherson.[6]

Quoting Matthew 8:15 ("Beware of false prophets that come to you in sheep's clothing"), the film offered an onscreen "rebuke to anyone who, under the cloak of Religion, seeks to sell for gold, God's choicest gift to Humanity—Faith." As the film opens with the congregation singing "Holy, Holy, Holy," Fallon enters the church and takes her father's pulpit. Fallon delivers a powerfully riveting sermon, blasting the hypocrites who underpaid her father and abetted his premature death. Recognizing her talents, Hornsby, an unscrupulous promoter passing by, persuades her to hit the road to make some money as a freewheeling evangelist. Her religious work expands into a radio ministry, and the film cuts to an impeccably dressed blind veteran and music composer, John Carson (David Manners), who writes a suicide note that ends with "forgive me." He stands by the window of his fourth-floor apartment and prepares to leap out. Providentially, across the apartment building, a poor woman rocking her child is listening to the radio and the voice of Sister Fallon wafts over to him, arresting his act as he attends.

> The trouble with most people is that they're quitters, they're yellow and the moment there is any sort of test, they cave in. The difference between a man and jellyfish is the fact that a man has backbone. What did God give him a backbone for? To stand up on his feet. That's what real men do. Beethoven wrote his greatest symphony when he was deaf. Oscar Wilde wrote his greatest poem in jail. And Milton, a blind man [John laughs], gave us *Paradise Lost*. It is easy to forgive sinners, but it hard to forgive quitters.

As the sermon fades off, he laughs and chooses to live. With his sweet and nosy housekeeper, Mrs. Higgins, he attends one of Sister Fallon's sermons. Sister Fallon stands in a cage with several lions, American and Christian flags mounted, wearing a flowing white gown, in prayer posture with arms raised: "The grace of our Lord be with you all. Amen."

A loud "Amen" resounds from the congregation. Then she begins her spiel to invite those who doubt to join her in the cage of lions. "Isn't there one among you who trusts the Almighty? Didn't my Lord deliver Daniel? Why not every man?" At the film's finale, Sister Fallon realizes how others exploited her, turning her evangelism into a circus. She chooses to expose the sham sideshow. In her farewell sermon, she again attacks hypocrites, adding, "You're not a hypocrite if you admit it," which is what she does. The film paralleled the questionable exploits of the female evangelist, yet it affirmed the efficacy and power of prayer, even from sinners. Religious leaders were exposed both as human sinners and God's ordained. Such is the fictional character of Casy, created by John Steinbeck in his 1939 novel *The Grapes of Wrath*, who transforms from a preacher weak with the women to a union organizer, paralleling many Roman Catholic priests and others who join labor unions and the

church. Their prayers for justice were put into action, even as President
Roosevelt adopted Pope Pius XI's 1931 encyclical *Quadragesimo anno*,
which promoted economic justice and helped shape the New Deal.

Another charismatic woman of tremendous faith appeared on screen
the following year. In director John Cromwell's *Spitfire* (1934), Katharine
Hepburn plays Trigger Hicks, an independent hillbilly country girl who
sings, "At the Cross, at the Cross, where I first saw the light" to her black
cat and talks to toad-frogs. As she steals a page from a magazine, she
sings "Jesus, Lover of My Soul."

Welcoming an engineer (Ralph Bellamy) whom she thinks is a doctor coming to fix up someone she beaned with a rock, she says, "Reckon
doctors must pray. If they didn't, folks would die before they got there."
Then she prays over the fellow she stoned. "Lord, let [the masher] live.
I'll even let him kiss me, if he wants to."

The man asks, "Who taught you so much about praying?"

"God," she answers unashamedly.

When Trigger comes upon that engineer, Fleetwood, and another,
his married friend Stafford (Robert Young), building a dam, they marvel at her spirit and pluck. Bright and defiant, she combines guileless
simplicity and a literal faith with superstitious backwoods skills in faith
healing that some view as witchcraft. She is just an ordinary Christian
who follows the biblical sayings on her illustrated Sunday school Bible
verse cards.

Kneeling beside an old granny's bed, Trigger prays, "Good Lord, I
know Granny ain't much account, but she does help folk sometimes with
her herb doctrine. Don't let her die there, please, Lord." Then reading a
Bible picture card about Jesus and little children that quotes Matthew
7:7 ("Knock and it shall be opened to you"), she focuses on the phrase
"knock." "I wonder why ya knock? Well," she says, and knocks on a
bench several times and looks back up to God, "Thank ya, good Lord,
and amen." Her prayers follow a simple, literal formula. But when the
granny is seemingly raised from the dead through her prayers, Trigger
is viewed with both awe and suspicion. Astoundingly for Hollywood,
the one who prays and heals has the most common sense and good reason. She is human in the best sense. When Aeta, her slow-witted single neighbor, wants God to give her a husband, she asks Trigger, "You
reckon Mr. Simmons would take me to a picture show if I ask God?" To

Trigger Hicks (Katharine Hepburn) converses directly with God in John Cromwell's *Spitfire* (1934), literally obeying the scriptures to ask, seek, and knock, especially knock.

which Trigger dismissingly says, "Don't bother Him with such things." Then she continues to intercede for her friend: "Good Lord, I didn't want to trouble You about it, but what could I do? Please give her a little more sense, for Jesus's sake. Amen." Trigger's prayer recognizes that God cares for little things like sparrows, but sees that human folly does not know how to pray.

When an adulterous Stafford tells Trigger that she is beautiful, she retorts that she will have to pray for his eyesight. She holds to a rule of prayer that one "can't pray for yourself." Thus, when she discovers that Stafford, who had kissed her, is married, and she has to give up a baby that she rescued from near death, she looks up to God, pulls out another Bible picture card, and reads, "Blessed are they who do hunger and thirst after righteousness, for they shall be filled." Having suffered deception and calumny, with tears in her eyes, she struggles to understand righteousness: "I reckon if you're full of righteousness, you don't need anything to eat, or somebody to love."

As she separates the laundry, she prays for the little baby and quotes an appropriate prayer for the clothes she is washing: "Good Lord, though your sins are as scarlet, they shall be as white as snow." However, when the ill-used baby grows sicker, she chooses an illustrated card that promises, "If you ask anything in my name, I'll do it." In Christ's name, she explains, means in the way He asks. "God knows if we don't." When the baby dies due to his own parents' neglect, the mother accuses Trigger of witchcraft.

Even the resurrected Granny is after her, but she declares to all her persecutors, "The baby is dead. Don't know why I prayed for ya. Jesus says love your enemies; do good to those that hate ya. Love ya and pour coals down on ya." Sensing failure in her ministry, and feeling that her prayers have been selfish, she burns her cards, except for one. She reads it and it brings assurance with the words of Jesus: "I am the Resurrection and the life. He that believeth in me, though he were dead, yet he shall live. Nothing," she affirms, "can kill that life." The prayers of uneducated hill people were the ones that Mencken found across the river in the Hills of Zion as real religion. The fervent Pentecostal prayers of common people had a passion and purpose to them. It is this most human of saints who emerges as an exemplary model for praying—direct, candid, and comic.

In *The Little Minister* (Richard Wallace, 1934), Babbie (Katharine Hepburn), the feisty, eccentric daughter of a Scottish noble, frequently disguises herself as a "gypsy" (the term used in the film) to interact incognito with the commoners. A new minister, Reverend Dishart (John Beal), arrives at Thrums' Auld Licht Church to serve the rural congregation (accompanied by his mother). The adaptation showcased the pious charm of J. M. Barrie's play as a secret romantic liaison builds between the scampish Babbie and the mother-dominated little minister. Suspecting illicit behavior in their pastor, the congregation conspires to chase him out of town.

When they first arrive, his mother orders, "Not another word do we utter," until, with hands clasped and kneeling, they say a prayer. The congregation views the little minister as too young, but "he prays like one giving orders." When a woman is about to be evicted, he prays, publicly shaming her landlord for his lack of compassion.

Near the climax, the little minister becomes a man as he takes a knife meant for another parishioner. Babbie kneels outside his door, interceding. "Please, God, he's so good; he really deserves Your help. I need him too." As she prays, the rest of the "kirk" watches and then begins to kneel. As the minister is restored to health, his mother gives up her pious son to the spirited Babbie, acknowledging, "You might say my prayers have ever been for his happiness" (in finding such a wife). For what else would a good Scottish mother pray?

By the end of the Depression, several clergy expressed gratitude for God's blessings. Pastor Ethan Wilkins (Walter Huston) exhibits good character through his prayers in Clarence Brown's film *Of Human Hearts* (1938). "We thank Thee, Father, for this and all Thy bounties. Teach us to avoid the pitfalls of prejudice, pride, and vanity. Make us thought-ful of the weak, the sick, the needy, and the unfortunate, and make our humble lives a reflection of Thy goodness. We ask these things in Thy name. Amen." His prayer reflected the growing gratitude of churches as the Depression waned. Nevertheless, his son, Jason (Jimmy Stewart), who wants to become a doctor, would "rather save bodies than souls any day."[7] The crisis of an impending war would require both prayer and action.

The Grapes of Wrath (John Ford, 1940) closed the Depression-era films with its stark adaptation of John Steinbeck's novel.[8] Adapted by Nunnally Johnson, the film featured Henry Fonda as Tom Joad and John Carradine as Casy, the sepulchral preacher. Standing over Charley Grap-win's grave, Casy mutters an unconventional eulogy:

This here ol' man jus' lived a life an' jus' died out of it. I don't know whether he was good or bad, an' it don't matter much. Heard a fella say a poem once, an he says "all that lives is holy," but I wouldn't pray for jus' a ol' man that's dead, because he's awright. If I was to pray, I'd pray for folks that's alive an' don't know which way to turn. Grampa here, he ain't got no more trouble like that. He's got his job all cut out for 'im—so cover 'im up an' let 'im get to it.

Prayer in this view is useless for the dead and inadequate for the living.[9] Though this implicit critique of prayer could stand, the Motion Picture Production Code stopped Ford from using Steinbeck's "Yes, sir, that's my Savior, Jesus is my Savior, Jesus is my Savior" parody of "Yes, Sir, That's My Baby," in Casy's singing. The Production Code had banned the words "God" and "Jesus" unless they were used reverently.

The hapless and hopeless Casy could have been a good preacher, but he "seen things clear. He was like a lantern. He helped me to see things clear." Casy's inadequacy as a preacher comes about more from the temptation of women than from any intellectual or spiritual struggles during the Depression. Telling Tom Joad about his churching, Casy confesses, "Why, at my meetings, I used to get the girls so gloried something that they pass out, then I go to comfort them. And always end up by loving them. I'd feel bad and pray and pray, but it didn't do no good; next time, do it again. I figured I just wasn't worth saving."

Tom, laughing and rubbing his cheek, says, "Pa always said you was never cut out for no preacher."

Casy smiles back. "I'd never let one get by me if I could catch her," he says as he pulls out his whiskey bottle. "Have a snort?" Continuing, he explains to Tom, "But you wasn't a preacher! A girl was just a girl to you. To me they were holy vessels. I was saving their souls." Then he took a swig of the bottle. Prayers, it seemed to Casy, were to be blocked if one were taking advantage of those holy temples of flesh. Ford's film, with its shameless sentimentality, pointed back to the struggles of the Depression with its American virtues of resilience and hardiness. Ironically, while both Hitler and Stalin allowed its exhibition, as it showed American workers as oppressed and weak, it suggested to the Soviet proletariat, as critic Richard Corliss points out, that even the poorest Americans have cars. Americans and their clergy may have problems, but they have a buoyant faith.

The prayers of ordinary ministers, ones frequently consigned on screen to the backcountry or frontiers, were of little concern to the Breen office of censorship. Yet they represented a devout and committed pastoral leadership during the severe days of need. These religious leaders prayed with fervor, but also were gifted with the common sense needed for such desperate times. They were God's human beings, male and female, called to serve and pray.[10]

Seeking God in Tribulation

With many people unemployed and bankrupt, one might expect church attendance to swell during this bleak period, but there was only a slight increase. Liberal churches called for an end to the scourge of capitalism through the Federal Council of Churches in a well-articulated social creed, while conservative congregations denounced individual sins of dancing, sexual license, card playing, and Hollywood movies.[11] While ministering to poorer communities, holiness groups equaled the size of the Episcopal Church by 1939, with their emphasis upon praying, hymn singing, and sermons on personal sanctification.[12] All religious groups struggled with understanding the judgment of the Depression.

Films like *Sea Bat* (Lionel Barrymore, 1930) spurred the call for censorship from conservatives and Roman Catholics for revealing wet-bloused Nina (Raquel Torres), a West Indies soul-torn temptress whose brother was killed by the titular creature. The watery adventure is more about religious struggles than catching a deadly manta ray. A convict (Charles Bickford), escaping from Devil's Island, disguises himself as a minister, Reverend Sims, who speaks platitudes such as "God works in mysterious ways" to Nina, who neither wants nor needs such a Christian God. She stands on a rocky shore and shouts to the heavens, "You liar. I'm not afraid of you. I don't believe in you. I hate you!" She throws her brother's cross to circling sharks. Nina offers herself to whomever will kill the monster, and several sponge divers die in their attempts. Sims performs their funeral rites, marking a pivotal point in the narrative, as Sims emphasizes that Jesus is the Resurrection and the life and whoever believes in Him will never die. But "whoever shall be ashamed of me and my words, of him shall the Son of Man be ashamed. God have mercy upon us. Amen."

The rough crowd responds with "Amen!" Sims, however, is spiritually troubled, confessing that the reading stirred his own hypocritical soul. Nina also confirms that the reading "talked to her."

Sims replies, "I'm no good. When I spoke I knew I was more rotten than the corpse I buried. The sermon hit me harder than any liquor or woman." Yet they read together. "Come now and let us reason together. Though your sins be as scarlet, they shall be whiter than snow." Sims strips off his religious pretense and asks whether it was an accident that he swiped a minister's garb, or was it God's way? "We think we're smart and He outsmarts us." By the end, he repents and returns to Devil's Island to make restitution. The remarkable aspect of prayer in this pre-Code production is its brazen honesty of Nina challenging God, wrestling with theodicy and her own soul. Hers was a defiant prayer that

looked to God during a Depression, asking Him where He was when all
was lost. For conservatives, theological questions that arose during times
of tribulation pointed to a deficiency in personal sanctity. Judgment,
economic and social, was deserved, but could be resolved by repentance.

Prayers set in the past captured questions of America's plight during
the hard times of the Depression, with many wondering whether God
answers prayers. Frank Borzage adapted Hemingway's *Farewell to Arms*
(1932) as an overwrought melodramatic tearjerker, featuring ambulance
driver Frederic Henley (Gary Cooper) and his illicit and ill-fated romance with Red Cross nurse Catherine Barkley (Helen Hayes). With the
Armistice of World War I just announced, deserter Henley sits alone at
a café, eating bread and praying for his beloved Barkley: "Don't let her
die. O God, please, don't let her die. I'll do anything for you if you don't
let her die. You took the baby; that was all right, but don't let *her* die." He
seeks to make deals with God to save what is treasured on earth.

He holds her tearfully, looks into the heavens, and tells her, "I'll never
stop loving you. Not even if I die," with Wagner's funereal *Tristan and
Isolde* theme playing. They promise that "in life and death, we'll never
be parted." According to theologian Jerald Brauer, churches during the
Great Depression grew in their understanding of "the meaning of suffering and sacrifice in the Christian life." Understanding began with questions of why God does not seem to answer some prayers. As doves fly
and bells toll for Armistice, one wonders not "For whom do the bells
toll?" but how prayers are not heard in Hemingway's world as well.[13]

The angst of seeking God in prayer occurred in other exotic spots.
Leading a cast of notables in *Shanghai Express* (Josef von Sternberg,
1932), Marlene Dietrich plays Shanghai Lily ("It took more than one
man to change my name to Shanghai Lily"). She jumps aboard a train
journeying from Peking to Shanghai, but there are various secrets and
conspiracies among the passengers. Chinese rebels hijack the excursion.
Their leader, Henry Chang (Warner Oland), mixes among the passengers incognito. Complicating Lily's trip is the presence of her former
lover, an English medical officer, "Doc" Harvey (Clive Brook), along
with her companion and fellow courtesan (Anna May Wong), and a
seemingly meddlesome Christian missionary, "Doctor of Divinity in
the Service of Mankind," Mr. Carmichael (Lawrence Grant). The reverend's initial condemnation of the two fallen women alters dramatically

when he discovers their sacrificial actions in saving others. When Chang threatens to blind Harvey, Lily appeals to Reverend Carmichael to do something. He says that all he can suggest is that she get "down on your knees and pray."

Lily reflects and says, "I think that you're right, if God is still on speaking terms with me," to which Carmichael responds, "God remains on speaking terms with everybody." In one of cinema's most ravishing images of prayer, Lily clasps her pale elegant hands to plead for Doc. As the scene slips into darkness, Sternberg's shadows and butterfly lighting illumine her with a mystical presence.

When Doc discovers that Lily had prayed for him and then had offered herself to Chang, he cannot reconcile the two actions: "If you did pray for me, which I doubt, do you mind telling me why?" She tells him, "I would have done that for anybody, Doc. Good night," leaving him confused, as piety and immorality seem to conflate. Later she confesses, "When I needed your faith, you withheld it. And now, when I don't need it, and don't deserve it, you give it to me." To which Carmichael speaks the final sermon of the film: "Love without faith, like religion without faith, doesn't amount to very much." The film preaches that God remains on speaking terms even with His wayward children who find themselves in dire straits. Reflecting the concern of religious people was this pressing issue of why some prayers were answered and others did not seem to be.

Rowland Lee's *Cardinal Richelieu* (1935) stars George Arliss as the crafty, power-wielding cleric serving Louis XIII (Edward Arnold), who ruled France over the titular royalty. When his lovely young charge Lenore (Maureen O'Sullivan) asks what he is doing, he whispers that his life is a contradiction: "I pray for peace and salvation and send men to their death. I serve a king, amass worldly wealth, and tax the poor and pray God to be merciful and make men hate me." His calling was to be ruthless for the king. Aware of his hypocrisy, Richelieu works for France, even inveigling the papacy.

His enemies ridicule Richelieu as one who can only "count his beads and pray" when he performs a wedding. When they come to assassinate him, he kneels at his private altar and then tricks them by playing dead. Ultimately, the cardinal prays for the interests of France, that God would make him "merciful and strong, kind and just" for God and country. The film subversively views the prayers of national leaders with suspicion, but the Breen Code scrutinized historical scenarios with less concern. Yet what this film implicitly revealed was that America itself needed the prayers of its churches that interceded faithfully for the nation's leaders, with the 1928 revised Book of Common Prayer providing a liturgical model.[14] Churches wrestled with God's apparent absence during this difficult time, but also found their priorities moving from building new edifices to taking care of the needy. As conservative churches did not trust welfare coming from the government, many set up their own charities.

Distrust over authority and its religious posturing appeared as well in the archetypal sea adventure, Frank Lloyd's 1935 *Mutiny on the Bounty*. The tyrannical and cruel Captain Bligh (Charles Laughton) offers an official morning deck prayer and demands that a dead sailor be flogged. The prayers have an evocative sublimity, promising grace but not delivering. Bligh prays that the eternal God who rules the raging seas might preserve them from danger, so that we "may return in safety to enjoy the blessings of the land."

As soon as the prayer is over, Bligh tells his men, "Perhaps you are not aware that the articles of war invest in me the authority to order punishment." He orders half-rations. In spite of his despicable behavior, his prayer for safety is amazingly answered, showing that God answers all sinners. The film hints at the exploitation of prayers for political purposes, of prayers being used as means to an end. The mix of religion and politics, as with the strange bedfellows of demagogue Louisiana governor Huey Long and Father Charles Coughlin, suggested that despotic leaders could use religion for less savory political purposes. It would culminate with the Nazi Party in Germany commandeering a national Lutheran church for its own nefarious plans.

The apotheosis of classic films dealing with the anguish of hard times was reached with Margaret Mitchell's epic *Gone with the Wind* (Victor Fleming, 1939). Prayer does not appear until nearly an hour into the film, when Ashley, Scarlett's true love, explains that the South needs all of the prayers it can get as the war is coming to an end. However, one sees prayers only in the actions of a priest praying over fallen soldiers in the hospital. As Sherman marched toward Atlanta, its beleaguered citizens prayed. And in one of the most dramatic prayers of self-assertion, Scarlett avers, "As God is my witness, as God is my witness, they're not going to lick me! I'm going to live through this, and when it's all over, I'll never be hungry again—no—nor any of my folks! If I have to lie, steal, cheat, or kill! As God is my witness, I'll never be hungry again." It is not really a prayer to God, but a waving of a white puny fist against all the forces of the Yankee North. Yet in 1939 Lulu Morris sang with her chorus a song that captured the worries and hopes of a troubled nation, "The United States Needs Prayer, Everywhere." Its sentiment would continue as prayers pleading for rescue from the domestic economic tribulation were to be directed overseas in response to a more destructive foe.

Roman Catholic Rescue

In W. S. Van Dyke's drama *San Francisco* (1936), Blackie Norton (Clark Gable) has little to do with religion. For him, faith "gets hold of people that are all right and makes monkeys out of them." "What I believe isn't up in the air, it's here," he says, pointing to his head. "What more do I need?" Yet he realizes that he needs more after the catastrophe of the great San Francisco earthquake of 1901. He pleads with his childhood friend, Father Tim Mullin (Spencer Tracy), to help him after the devastating disaster upends his world and ruins his club, the Paradise (pair-of-dice) saloon. Father Mullin and an opera/saloon singer, Mary Blake (Jeanette MacDonald), the daughter of a minister, stand ready to help him.

Blackie's earthquake conversion occurs at a makeshift Salvation Army camp after the catastrophe. Blackie and Father Tim search for Mary throughout the flotsam and jetsam until they come upon people singing "Nearer My God to Thee" (even as Blackie gets nearer to Mary). They find Mary leading the singing as she tends to the victims. Blackie, overcome with the grace given him, tells the priest, "Tim, I want to thank God. What do I say?" Mullin responds, "Just say what's in your heart." Norton kneels with back turned, and prays simply: "Thanks, God, thanks, I really mean it." Immediately, Mary sees him kneeling, and comes to him; they touch and then hear "The fire's out," but it's just beginning for them. The film highlights the influence of Roman Catholicism upon the film industry during this golden age of film, with the prayers of priests shaping the hearts of capitalists and scoundrels for good.

Tracy reappears as Father Flanagan in *Boys Town* (Norman Taurog, 1938). In an early scene with a convict on death row, the priest hears of the condemned man's life as a juvenile delinquent, sent to reformatory, where he fell from bad to worse. He sobbingly confesses to Flanagan, "I am sorry for my mistakes. I am sorry," but explains he wasn't given a chance as a boy. Working to establish a community for the orphaned boys, the priest is compassionate but tough. When one kid suggests a criminal caper on Christmas Eve, he admonishes him, "Bob, you should get down on your knees and ask pardon for a thought like that."

Tough kid Whitey Marsh (Mickey Rooney) enrolls in the school. In the dining hall, he sees boys praying before their meal, with prayers such as "I thank Thee, O Lord, for these Thy gifts, which we receive," and "Heavenly Father, I thank Thee for this food," as well as a Jewish prayer. One kid tells Whitey that each boy can say the kind of grace he wants to say. Unmoved, Whitey rejects such prayers until one young boy is struck down by a car.[15] Father Flanagan quietly prays (in silhouette) while lines of boys kneel and hold a prayer vigil outside the hospital room; even Whitey kneels sobbing for his little friend. The populist film reiterates the motto of the Nebraska Boys Town throughout, that "There is no bad boy," and witnesses to priests' pioneering social ministry to juveniles as well as their determination to teach the children how to care for and pray for others. The film preached that piety and social action belonged together, even as the Roman Catholic Church became deeply committed to justice for forgotten people.

In *Angels with Dirty Faces* (Michael Curtiz, 1938), James Cagney stars as notorious racketeer gangster Rocky Sullivan, with Pat O'Brien as his conscience and opposition, Father Jerry Connolly. Delinquent boys idolize Rocky and tell "Fadder" Jerry, "We don't fall for that pie-in-the-sky stuff." They prefer to follow Rocky, a path leading the wrong way in Hell's Kitchen. Yet Rocky exhibits vestiges of the Roman Catholic faith as he tells his gang to "say your prayers, mugs."

Father Jerry entreats Rocky to sacrifice his reputation for the good of the kids, calling on him for one favor: "Act the coward when you die." As Rocky is about to be executed, the priest counsels him to "straighten yourself out with God. Outside of that—I can't ask for anything else." Rocky sacrifices his tough-guy pride, letting the boys believe that he is a coward. In the last line of the film, after Rocky has forfeited his dignity to dissuade the boys from following his life of crime, Father Jerry tells the boys, "All right, fellas, let's go and say a prayer for a boy who couldn't run as fast as I could." Echoing the sermon of *Boys Town*, the film depicts the Catholic doctrine of *ora et labora*, praying and working to redirect the lives of young men by establishing houses of refuge. The film inspired worker priests in rescuing young men from lives of crime while also critiquing other, harsher reform houses of the time. Churches, especially Roman Catholic parishes, responded to the need to help the unfortunate. Priests not only modeled fervent praying, but inculcated the general public on how to pray.

Populist sentiments prevailed during the decade, so that even prayers reflected a folk tradition, triggering more ordinary prayers of the people than formal discourse with the divine. The great populist director of the decade was Roman Catholic Frank Capra. In his penultimate film of the 1930s, *You Can't Take It with You* (1938), Capra adapted the Moss Hart/ George S. Kaufman Broadway play, which juxtaposed the wealthy but unhappy Kirbys with the madcap Sycamores, poor, eccentric, and fun. By the end of the film, the voluble Grandpa Martin Vanderhof (Lionel Barrymore) mumbles the final communal prayer at dinnertime, bringing the two families together in a playful communion:

> Well, Sir, here we are again. We've had quite a time of it lately, but it seems that the worst of it is over. Course, the fireworks all blew up, but we can't very well blame that on You. Anyway, everything's turned out fine, as it usually does. Alice is going to marry Tony. [They look at each other.] Mr. Kirby, who's turned out to be a very good egg, sold us back our house— he'll probably forget all about big deals for a while. [Everybody winks.] Nobody on our block has to move; and, with the right handling, I think we can even thaw out Mrs. Kirby here. [She looks up incredulously.] We've all got our health. As far as anything else is concerned, we still leave that up to You. Thank You. Bring it on, Reba!

Mrs. Kirby is slapped heartily on the back, making her one of the motley company. Capra united the wealthy and the common people during the Depression and blessed them with one last populist generic prayer. While most of the classic prayers of this decade entreated God for help, as the Depression warranted, Capra's film summarizes the grati-

Grandpa Vanderhof (Lionel Barrymore) leads all the people in thanksgiving in Frank Capra's *You Can't Take It with You* (1938).

tude of Americans by the end of the decade, thanking God for putting food on the table and for helping everything to "turn out fine."

So, too, Roman Catholic priests extolled the virtue of hope. The phrase "Win one for the Gipper" became a celebrated catchphrase in Lloyd Bacon's 1940 Notre Dame football biopic, *Knute Rockne, All American*. Showcasing the quintessential Roman Catholic, Pat O'Brien, the film, which starred future president Ronald Reagan as George Gipp, offered this enduring slogan, which could symbolize a rallying cry for intervention into the war. On the eve of crisis, Hollywood took religion seriously. Warner Bros. researchers sought to find the right last words and necessary props for the Roman Catholic baptismal service, ending it with the blessing "Go in peace and the Lord be with you," after which the college men's chorus sings, in both Latin and Greek, "O my people, what have I done to thee or in what have I afflicted thee? Answer me! Because I have led you out of the land of Egypt, you have prepared a cross for your Savior. O holy God! O mighty God!"[16]

When Rockne confides to his priest, Father John Callahan, that he had decided to take up coaching as his life's work, the priest quietly says,

"Hmm." "You think I'm making a mistake, don't you?" he asks. To which Callahan responds, "Anyone who follows the truth in his heart never makes a mistake." The Church prepared people to make difficult choices in the coming year, blessing vocations outside the formal ministry.

Teaching Children to Pray

Before becoming a member of Our Gang, child actor Dickie Moore appeared kneeling beside the bed with his mother in *Passion Flower* (William DeMille, 1930). She entreats him to say his bedtime prayer. He tells her, "I don't remember, Mommy."

She coaxes him and he recites, "Now I lay me down to sleep." When he forgets, she prompts him with "I pray." He continues, "I pray the Lord my soul to keep." When he pauses again, she starts: "If" and he quickly takes up the hint and says, "If he hollers let him go, Eeny meeny miney mo."

"No, that's not quite right. Say it again."

"If I should die before I wake, I pray the Lord my soul to take."

"There, that's right."

Parents, especially mothers, sought to pass on pious bits of their faith tradition, and movies with children and for children reaffirmed that spiritual calling. Films not only showed this practice, but also employed children to teach spectators how to pray with thanksgiving and in times of trouble.

Amidst the slapstick of the Little Rascals, one finds holy bits. In *Little Daddy* (Robert McGowan, 1931), an orphanage tries to take Stymie (Matthew Beard) away from his "guardian," his brother Farina (Allen Hoskins), when their father is in jail for running a bootleg still. Farina must watch over Stymie (and rub goose grease on his neck if he gets sick).

Going to church and singing, "Swing low sweet chariot, coming for to carry me home," the boys take the offering, only to find that cheap parishioners give buttons rather than coins. After church, Farina kneels and prays,

Dear Lord, I'm asking You something. Stymie boy gets in a heap of trouble. I don't think one guardian angel gonna be enough to watch him, and so if You all have extra around, please put them on. Watch him at night, 'cause he keeps the clothes off and gets whooping cough, and if he do get whooping cough just rub his soul with cold oil on his neck and put fried onions on his chest and I'll do the same for You sometime.

Stymie asks Farina to tell him another Bible story, the one about the "boat with all the animals on it." So Farina tells his version of the story of Noah's ark and the flood to his little brother, a precursor of Madea's prayers of tall tales. In a routine equal to "Who's on First?" the boys misunderstand each other as to who built the boat, Noah or Yeah. "Who's this man Yeah?" "Noah's brother?" "Make up your mind." "Ain't Noah, man." Farina continues and says that Noah puts out a rattrap and catches lots of animals, including two skunks, but then reconsiders, since "one skunk would be plenty."

Farina leans on a fence with eyes heavenward and asks the Lord for help. Stymie's own prayers are more specific: "I wish my Pappie was out of jail. I wish I had some chicken." Spanky appears, rubs his lamp, and says, "I wish I had a monkey. I wish I had a monkey." Prayers and wishes are interchangeable for the kids. During the 1930s, religious education for children made the transition to Sunday mornings, with children receiving more instruction on Bible study and prayers. Children receiving religious teaching would culminate in Marc Connelly's 1936 *Green Pastures*, with curious, wide-eyed children inquiring about Adam and Eve, Noah, and various Bible stories. Children needed to be taught the Bible and how to pray.

Manuel Fidello (Spencer Tracy) teaches a rescued, spoiled Harvey (Freddie Bartholomew) about fishing in *Captains Courageous* (Victor Fleming, 1937). When Harvey asks whether they really fish in heaven, Manuel says, "Sure, they fish in heaven. What else they do?" Manuel then tells him that the apostles were all fishermen and reminds him how Simon Peter could catch no fish in the Sea of Galilee until the Savior told him to throw "your net on the right side . . . and he catch so many fish his net almost break. Oh, I think the Savior, He the best fishman."

Manuel reminisces about his own father's conversations with God as he was dying:

Savior, He see my father all tired and wet down there in the water. So, He light the harbor buoy and He say, "Come on up, old Manuel. I am happy you come up here to help us." And my father, he say, "Thank You. I am very happy to come up to help You. Maybe I show You something about fishing up here, huh?" And then they all laugh. And the Savior He put His arm around my father and He give him brand-new dory to fish in.

At the end, after the Roman Catholic Manuel has sacrificed himself, Harvey goes into a church, lights a candle, and prays, thanking God for all the fish in heaven. The culmination of Harvey ultimately entering the church echoed the goal of Catholic leaders during the Great Depression to keep every "Catholic child in a Catholic school" so that they might learn their catechism fully.

Shirley Temple became the one cinematic child who prayed the Depression away. In *Dimples* (William Seiter, 1936), a pickpocket grandfather raises a motherless child, Dimples, and teaches her that when things are low, she must pray that God "show her the way." In *Heidi* (Allan Dwan, 1937), Temple plays the titular character, who is stuck with the evil Fraulein Rottenmeier. Church bells summon forth her desire to pray and she asks God to be reunited with her grandfather. Shirley Temple's films reinforced the importance of the emerging Sunday school movement and taught young children the importance and almost "magical" efficacy of prayers; yet some of her prayers would go unanswered, reflecting real-life hardships.

Seeing no hope in the orphanage in *Little Miss Broadway* (Irving Cummings, 1938), Betsy Brown (Temple) recites a little prayer and finds her troubles immediately removed. In *Rebecca of Sunnybrook Farm* (Allan Dwan, 1938), her prayers are translated into songs, but her self-reliance and good works supplant prayer. A Pelagian theology underlies her insight that "goodness can only bring the happiness." As long as she "is good, God will watch over her" in *The Littlest Rebel* (David Butler, 1935). Like the American civil religion of Mary Pickford in the 1920s, one finds it a matter of attitude and pluck rather than dependence upon God that marks most of the little darling's prayers. One only needs to be bright and sunny on the good ship *Lollipop*.

The Littlest Rebel pulled out all the stops in garnering sympathy for the pint-size star Shirley Temple. While scouting for the Confederacy, Virgie Cary's father is captured. In a long conversation on prayer, she questions her mother on why her father has not come home. "I say my prayers every night and I say a special prayer for Daddy to come and see us, but it doesn't seem to do any good, so yesterday, I started praying in the daytime too. I prayed twice yesterday and I prayed three times today. I'm sure it will work now, Mommy." Her prayers for her father's return are answered, but ironically, her mother dies. Hardships and death required religious leaders in the 1930s to wrestle with the value of unanswered prayers. During this era, Anglican cleric Albert Richardson penned a popular and influential book entitled *The Kneeling Christian* that raised questions about whether God always answered prayers; Norwegian Lutheran Ole Hallesby also published his *Prayer*, advising that one should not look "upon painful experiences too pessimistically," but truthfully recognize our weakness in prayer, admitting that "we are faced with a problem which cannot be solved by our own efforts." Both the church and movies posed these same concerns; however, both also ardently affirmed the value of prayer. Both works sought to teach parents the value of prayer, that they might pass it on to their children.

In *The Little Princess* (Walter Lang, 1939), Sara Crewe (Temple) is stuck in the prestigious Minchin Seminary for Girls, while her father, Captain Crewe, has been away fighting in the Boer Wars in Africa. Though he was reported missing in action, she does not give up on him. Sara appears in her bedclothes, fingers piously intertwined, eyes open, and prays, "I know soldiers are supposed to stand a lot, and my daddy is a good soldier, but they've waited so long for help, please do something about Mafeking right away. They'll all be lost and my daddy won't come back." Suddenly she hears military band music. Rushing out onto the balcony, she sees Union Jack flags waving and hears people shouting, "The army at the siege of Mafeking is relieved." Amidst the rousing patriotism, presented strategically in 1939, she rejoices over her father's imminent return. As she starts back into the room, she stops, turns back to the balcony, folds her hands, and exclaims, "Oh, thanks for being so quick about it this time." Prayers for her father's safe return (and miraculous recovery) rank as some of the timeliest propaganda of hope in light of the impending clouds of war. Reassuring a country on the brink of war, Shirley Temple's films provided a tonic of hope, a reminder to be good and say your prayers.

Children and their prayers dotted the landscape of the Depression era. In George Cukor's *David Copperfield* (1935), Charles Dickens's young hero (Freddie Bartholomew) walks many miles alone, praying, "Our Father who art in heaven, hallowed be Thy name for bringing me here, and please, God, please, may I have a home now?" The prayer, not so subtly, changes events in his life, leading to the Victorian happy ending.

An odd little parable of a film appeared during the cinematic *annus mirabilis* of 1939, Wilhelm Thiele's *Bad Little Angel*. If Shirley Temple had a darker and more Baptist Bible-reading side, she might have starred in this story of a runaway orphan. Instead, Virginia Weidler, as Patsy Sanderson, learned to go to the Bible for answers, not as a fortune-telling book, but as a guide to life. Her favorite story is of Samuel, called by God when he was a child.

Her Sunday school literacy is spotty but endearing. She warns a snarky young friend that "pride goeth before a fall." When he trips, she allows, "I am glad he wasn't hurt." Turning to God, she asks, "Did you have to trip him?" Then she tells him that in the Bible "even a sparrow doesn't fall without Him knowing." "Does it keep them from falling?" he asks. "No," she assures him, "but it keeps them from being afraid when they fall."

Accused of bringing bad luck to families (she lived with a minister and they were reading 1 Corinthians 13:6 when "he up and died"), Patsy worries that she might be a jinx. When her kind elderly guardian, Mrs. Perkins, dies, and she fears going back to the orphanage, she consults the Bible, using John Wesley's plunk method (opening the Bible at random to find a verse) for seeking divine will, which directs her to "flee to Egypt." She sets out for Egypt, New Jersey, where she inveigles herself into a new family, the Creightons, headed by the father, Jim (Ian Hunter), the editor of the local paper, who is trying to expose the dangerous conditions of a local paint factory. When she sits at the table praying quietly before the meal, she stirs her guardian's family to pray. They join her silent prayers until the father says, "Amen." As he confesses to his wife, "I guess it wouldn't do me any harm to start praying. I've got a lot to be thankful for: you, the children, my job." When he loses his job and Patsy feels she has jinxed him, he suggests that she ask the Lord what He wants her to do. She looks in the Bible for a message from the Lord and finds a call to "fight the good fight, of faith."

The self-absorbed "skinflint" (Guy Kibbee) who owns the factory had put pressure on the *Sentinel*'s publisher to fire Creighton for his editorials. An emboldened Patsy goes to confront him. "If the Lord can shut the mouths of lions, I am sure He can take care of an old skunk." She first quotes the Gospel to the wealthy manufacturer to convince him that he should forgive Creighton: "The Bible says we should forgive our enemies 70 times 7; that is, let's see, 490. So you have 489 times to go." When he complains and orders her to stop quoting the Bible, she responds, "The only real sense comes out of the Bible."

To demonstrate, she plunks it open for him and finds, "If thou afflict any widow or fatherless child and they cry at all unto me, I surely hear their cry; and I will not withhold mine anger" (Exodus 22:22). She looks at him and says coyly, "You better read this. I think it is for you."

He calls her a sanctimonious little hypocrite, to which she sportily quips, "I hope the Lord gets good and mad at you." Just as she leaves, an explosion rocks his paint-manufacturing factory. When Creighton arrives at the scene of the disaster, he is seriously injured. Worried, Patsy asks the Lord what to do. In this dire moment, she opens the good book and reads, "I am the Resurrection and the Life. He that believeth in me, though he were dead, yet shall he live." She announces with total faith, "He's listening to me right now and Father Jim is going to live." This little child planted the hope of new life in an America about to experience death. *Bad Little Angel* explicitly dealt with the faith of children that Jesus recognized in Matthew 18, admonishing sophisticated followers that they must become like little children.

The peculiar combination of children teaching others about death, prayer, and hope continues in *Five Came Back* (John Farrow, 1939). Gangster Pete (Allen Jenkins) puts his boss's son, Little Tommy (Casey Johnson), into bed: "All right now, Tommy, let's go to sleep." "Well," responds the pajama-clad boy, "we have to say our prayers first." "What do you mean *we*?" Tommy asks whether Pete says his prayers every night. "Well, sure, sure I do," says the gangster. "Shall we say your prayers or mine? Well, I'm kinda sick of my prayers. Let's say yours."

Tommy bows his head and folds his hand. "Now I lay me down to sleep." He then looks up and tells Pete to repeat the words after he recites each phrase: "I pray the Lord my soul to keep. If I should die before I wake, I pray the Lord my soul will take." Tommy continues, "Please take good care of my Daddy. It's personal right here. You don't have to say it if you don't want to. Please take good care of my Daddy and help us to get back together again. Soon as You think You can. Thank You. Amen."

One of the most poignant prayers occurs in *Judge Hardy and Son* (George Seitz, 1939), in which Judge Hardy (Lewis Stone) and Andy (Mickey Rooney) pray aloud over Andy's mother's deathly illness. The judge reflects upon "how strange it is. We thoughtless, selfish human beings must have tragedy come to our lives to make us call on God for help. I don't think I'd have been able to stand it the past two hours, alone here, without that faith, without that solace." In his research on MGM, critic Bosley Crowther recounted the story of MGM tycoon Louis B. Mayer's contribution to the film's emotional prayer.[17] Mayer, representing middle America, motherhood, and virtue, scolded scriptwriter Carey Wilson about his effete prayer. Mayer then acted out the scene. With tears streaming down his cheeks, he fell to his knees and fervently cried out, "Dear God, please don't let my mom die, because she's the best mom in the world. Thank You, God!" Mayer's intuitive sense of showmanship and wholesome moral instruction resonated with audiences, as he taught his writers how to teach families to pray.

Children expressed the most basic but most compelling prayers during the decade. With the Breen Office alert to any ridicule of religion, the safest way to convey prayers in a humorous or direct way was through children. Children were not only able to demonstrate faith, but could also voice doubts. The decade showed that out of the mouths of infants came wisdom and hope. Filmmakers used children as vehicles to promote the power of prayer to endure and to triumph. But stranger, darker prayers ran in a subterranean current alongside such ingenuous conversations with God.

Final Notes

Certain genres offered escape during the Depression. Musicals and screwball comedies offered spectators a diversion from hard times. But the horror genre also offered those who wanted to bolt from everyday problems an opportunity to go to darker places. For many members of the audience knew that something was amiss. Churches that preached about love and faith were missing something more sinister about the human condition—namely, sin.[18] Horror movies portrayed evil in recognizable tropes that would cause even the most thoroughgoing atheist to consider praying.

Robert Louis Stevenson's *Strange Case of Dr. Jekyll and Mr. Hyde* put flesh onto the Apostle Paul's writings in his letter to the Romans, uncovering a primitive tension in his own soul. When the raging spirit of hell wakes in Mr. Hyde, he gleefully mauls an unresisting body until his lust for evil is gratified. The image of Hyde singing and drinking over a dead man contrasts with the scene of Henry Jekyll waking with pangs of remorse, falling upon his knees, and lifting his hands to God. Ready to scream aloud from the horrors he has committed, Jekyll seeks "with tears and prayers to smother down the crowd of hideous images and sounds with which my memory swarmed against me."

So in Rouben Mamoulian's 1931 adaptation, Jekyll (Fredric March), after reading of the brutal murder of a streetwalker in Soho by "Hyde," leans on a Bible, looks up to the heavens, and cries out, "I saw a light [science]. I could not see to what it was leading. I trespassed on Your domain. I've gone further than man should go. Forgive me. Help me." Crying that he is in hell, he begs forgiveness from his fiancée. He dies as Hyde, but turns back to Jekyll; however, a bubbling cauldron of fire symbolizes his damnation. Some fundamentalist theology would easily consign the carnal Hyde to hell, whether he said his prayers or not. Roman Catholics would see the hope of Purgatory, a refining fire in which his prayers were answered.

James Whale's classic *Bride of Frankenstein* (1935) reveals the poignancy of prayer. When Frankenstein's monster has fled the doctor's castle, he wanders into a cabin in the woods, inhabited by a blind man who offers to get him some food. The monster grunts, and then recoils from a flame, but the hermit brings a bowl of soup and gives him bread to eat. "We should be friends. I have prayed many times for God to send me a friend."

The monster groans, "Yes, yes, now you must sleep." The hermit takes the monster's hand, bows, and prays, "Our Father, I thank Thee that in Thy great mercy Thou hast taken pity on my great loneliness and now out of the silence of the night hast brought two of Thy lonely children together and sent me a friend to be a light to my eyes and a comfort in a time of trouble. Amen." As the hermit weeps, the monster sheds a single tear, with a glowing cross in the candlelight strategically placed in the background. In sweet gratitude for the prayer and the kindness, the monster pats the hermit on the back. While respectable churches neglected these marginalized characters, the hermit and monster would find the presence of God in their need, hinting of a greater sympathy and community among sinners outside the mainline churches. Ironically, the prayers in these horror films exposed needs that churches were not yet willing or able to address.

The 1930s, shackled by the institution of the Production Code with its concern to prevent the ridicule of religion, tended to secularize the film industry. Films like *The Green Light* tiptoed around the Breen Code, with its theological blandness revealing an evisceration of the power of prayer. With a few exceptions, religious behavior became the province of children, women, minorities, and the clergy. To avoid controversy with its publics, Hollywood provided generic prayers. Yet many prayers still reflected the deep soul searching of a nation trying to come to grips with its economic tribulation and wondering whether God heard their prayers. But this era of asking God for daily bread would be altered as an impending global crisis emerged, with the imminent threat of war rousing a need for desperate prayers that God deliver us from the evil one.

3

Foxhole Prayers (1939–1945)

Many Americans eschewed foreign entanglements in the late 1930s; the isolationist bloc, represented by such notables as Charles Lindbergh and Henry Ford, thwarted active intervention against the policies of Nazi Germany and its Axis allies. Some film studio executives, especially MGM's Mayer, stayed away from war subjects, hoping to keep their lucrative markets in Germany and the rest of Europe open. Profits dictated film content. Not so for the Warner Bros. studio. As a vanguard of moral forces, it was itching for a fight, and it would make it a holy propaganda war.[1]

As Germany invaded neighboring nations, it supplied the symbolic villain for the allegorical melodrama *Strange Cargo* (Frank Borzage, 1940), with the coldhearted and cynical German, Hessler (Paul Lukas), as one of the escapees from a Devil's Island prison. Hessler would be the only fugitive who does not ultimately accept the film's Christ figure, Cambreau (Ian Hunter). Sinners Verne (Clark Gable), a fugitive convict, and Julie (Joan Crawford), a saloon "entertainer," are seeking to escape the penal colony on Devil's Island (using a getaway map tucked inside a Bible—the film flaunts its symbols with unabashed chutzpah). At one point of respite in the jungle trek, Verne opens the Bible at random and starts reading from the Song of Solomon for a moving, comic, and poignant effect. He has dragged Julie through the jungle brush, as she loses her high-heeled shoes and hat, gets mud on her legs, and has her hair mussed. Around a campfire, he reclines among the vines and ferns, amidst jungle animal sounds, as Julie peers into a tin can top, primping with no makeup. Then he begins to read from the Song of Solomon, with the words becoming both a pickup line and a prayer:

> Behold, thou art fair, my love, behold, thou art fair. Thine eyes are as doves behind thy veil. Thy lips are like a thread of scarlet and thy mouth is comely. . . . Thou art all fair, my love, and there is no spot in thee.

"How do you like that, baby? Great stuff, huh? I guess nobody ever said anything like that to you before, did they? Does that put me out in front or not?"

"Listen," he continues.

> Thou hast ravished my heart, my sister, my bride. Thou hast ravished my heart with one of thine eyes. . . . How much better is thy love than wine and the smell of thine ointments than all manner of spices. Thy lips, O my bride, drop as the honeycomb. Honey and milk are under thy tongue and the smell of thy garments is like the smell of Lebanon.

Julie sobs. The words capture the ironic juxtaposition of the flawed reality of the woman, like a blemished bride of Christ, and the glorious beauty that the bridegroom sees. Later, she would confront the Christ figure, Cambreau, as he seeks to educe true love and kindness from her. She recoils and tells him, "Don't give me any of that Sister-come-to-Salvation. Look, I'm not buying any. I know the routine. It starts out with a prayer, and ends up with a Bible in one hand and me in the other!" In this retort, she gives one of the most insightful lines for any woman being seduced by a religious poser.

Cambreau, however, sees more hope for the ravaged and suspicious outcast. He sees redemption. As she languishes in the bottom of the boat, during a cessation of the wind, thirsty and hopeless, Julie confesses her heart, her worries, fears, and hopes, and then wishes she knew how to pray. Cambreau answers gently that that is exactly what she has been doing all along. Few films reached the ideal of prayer as conversation with God as adroitly as this one did, as it modeled how to talk to God during moments of despair, danger, and death. As a harbinger to men in uniform serving in the midst of war, it allowed both cynicism and faith in one's dialogue with the Almighty, especially in seeking guidance through the valleys of the shadow of death.

In *White Cargo* (Richard Thorpe, 1942), a cynical rubber plantation owner mocks both a padre and a doctor. The latter recommends that when a patient finds serenity, it would be like "morphine beginning to take effect." The padre counters that one might discover "the peace of the heart after prayer." The businessman quips that both of them "sound like a couple of commercial traders advertising your wares." Indeed, cinematic advertisements for prayer would multiply after a decade of reticence on spiritual matters. With an impending world war on the horizon, the movies of the 1940s would bend a knee and seek divine help.

Finding Protection

As Europe plummeted into war, William Wyler's 1939 *Wuthering Heights* captured the impending horror of mental and physical cruelty. The tragic Heathcliff (Laurence Olivier) grieves over the dead Catherine (Merle Oberon), a love unrequited due to his lower social class:

> What do they know of heaven or hell, Cathy, who know nothing of life? Oh, they're praying for you, Cathy. I'll pray one prayer with them. I repeat till my tongue stiffens: "Catherine Earnshaw, may you not rest so long as I live on. I killed you. Haunt me, then! Drive me mad. Haunt your murderer! Take any form, drive me mad; only do not leave me in this dark alone where I cannot find you. I cannot live without my life! I cannot die without my soul."

Heathcliff's animosity toward Catherine's husband stands as a warning against hatred; yet even more pressing reasons for anger and acrimony are to come when the Nazis unleash their evil and German churches collaborate with Hitler. Charlotte Brontë's work, adapted by Aldous Huxley, contained a different message. The film version of her gothic novel *Jane Eyre* (Robert Stevenson, 1943) chronicles the coming-of-age of the eponymous heroine Jane (Jane Fontaine). The opening line portends ill for such hypocritical religions as the contaminated Nazi Reich Church: "Money and position seemed all that mattered. Charity was a cold and disagreeable word. Religion too often wore a mask of bigotry and cruelty."

A destitute Jane suffers physical, emotional, and spiritual abuse growing up in her uncle's home and at an institution for poor orphan girls. Religious authorities exploit the Bible and the Book of Common Prayer in demanding obedience from young women, rather than in communicating grace. Jane is told to "pray over dying, child." It is no wonder that she learns to prefer a cynical sinner to a religious zealot, as she is beat up with the Bible and prayers: "Remember your prayers, [and say] 'Thy will be done.' If you work hard, God will help you."

The harsh headmaster, Henry Brocklehurst (Henry Daniell), preaches penitence and humility, and keeps the school at insufferably cold temperatures so as not to "pamper the body, but to strengthen the soul." A good doctor rebukes him, saying, "I should not have thought that a bad cough was any aid to salvation, but then I'm not a theologian." Nevertheless, Jane is told, "You must pray God to take away your heart of stone and make you meek and humble and penitent. We will collaborate with the Almighty."

Her friend Helen Burns (Elizabeth Taylor) suffers pneumonia and is forced to stand outdoors in the rain, due to her "vanity" about having curly hair. When she grows perilously ill, the doctor tries to nurse her to health, but Brocklehurst offers a sham prayer: "Almighty God, look down upon this miserable sinner and grant the child respite of her weakness; give strength to her faith and seriousness to her repentance." When she dies, he avers with a cruel Calvinist determinism that the ways of Providence are inscrutable. The doctor responds tersely, "You murdered her." Helen becomes a martyr of grace. The film contrasts bogus praying and acts of love. It is not enough to look religious; one must love one's neighbor.

Prayers at the formal institutional dinner are similarly counterfeit. The girls sit in rows, with one potato each. An older girl steals Jane's during a prayer: "O merciful Providence who doth give us the abundant fruit of the field, then make us duly and properly grateful of Thy generous plenty, of earthly food that our hearts may be more heavenly fixed." When the school's housekeeper tries to turn the begging Jane away, Jane tells her that "if you are a Christian, you ought not to consider poverty a crime."

Becoming the ward of Edward Rochester (Orson Welles), Jane prays in candlelight to the Holy Virgin that God would bless Monsieur Rochester so that he would like her and she could "stay forever and ever. Amen." Jane frequently prays, imploring God to assist her, particularly in her dealings with Rochester. Curiously, this Roman Catholic appeal, rather than an Anglican note, enables her to find true Christian piety: "Virgin Mary, may God bless me so he will stay with me." Both filmed novels by the Brontë sisters critique the moody cruelty of a past Victorian era and the present grim darkness of war; yet both yearn for goodness, desperately hoping that prayers will make a difference.

In the opening of *The Hunchback of Notre Dame* (William Dieterle, 1939), Chief Justice Claude Frollo (Cedric Hardwicke) is wary of a Gutenberg printing press, a device that can create a Bible in only weeks for a reasonable price, enabling common people to read the holy word. Frollo also asserts that Gypsies do not have the right to pray for the intercession of the Virgin Mary, but Quasimodo (Charles Laughton) knows that the cathedral provides sanctuary for those in need. A debate between the cold-blooded, thin-lipped lecher Frollo and the earnest Esmeralda (Maureen O'Hara) essentially concerns whether God hears the prayers of Gypsies.

> FROLLO: What are you doing in Notre-Dame?
> ESMERALDA: But ... I was praying.
> FROLLO: You wouldn't know to pray here, heretic.

The priest demands that she obey, but Esmeralda challenges him. He accuses her of profaning the stones on which she kneels because her public dancing has awakened impure and sacrilegious desires. As he threatens to have her hanged, she sees him with the mark of the devil and prays, "Mother of the Savior, don't let me be hanged. Protect me! Protect me!"

Frollo counters that her prayers are useless, as she is from a cursed race who abandon themselves to witchcraft. Esmeralda asserts with faith that "the Mother of the Savior will hear." Issues of religious hypocrisy, iron obedience, torture, and the threat of death shape the debate. Esmeralda still hopes that Frollo will turn from his meanness and show love. Even if that doesn't happen, God will "show me how to help my people. Mother of the Savior, you know that Gypsies are chased everywhere." The cripple Quasimodo seeks to rescue her with sanctuary. During the Nazi oppression as well, thousands of Roma, along with millions of Jews and other outcasts, would be chased down. The secret hope and prayer that hovered was that God would deliver a persecuted people.

Adapted from Johnston McCulley's 1920 serialized book, the swashbuckling *The Mark of Zorro* (Rouben Mamoulian, 1940) features the champion of justice Zorro/Don Diego (Tyrone Power). Lolita (Linda Darnell) prays to the Virgin to "send someone to take me" from this place of tyranny. Zorro, a masked avenger, is the answer to her prayers and rescues her. As if on divine cue, Zorro also enters the church just as Friar Felipe (Eugene Pallette) is leading the people in prayer, as an immediate answer to their prayers. Later, in the climactic battle, when Felipe is bonking Spanish soldiers over the head with his club, the good friar repeats a prayer of contrition: "God forgive me!" [*Whack.*] "God forgive me!" [*Whack.*] "God forgive me!" Felipe's prayer offers a comic hope, but the churches in the early 1940s were desperately seeking more powerful divine intervention.

Hollywood's literary choices employed prayers that focused upon the need for rescue and protection. Yet they also warned of religious hypocrisy. If America was going to war, it needed to do so with pure hearts and clear minds.

Under the guise of writing the history of World War I hero Alvin York, Warner Bros. attacked American pacifism with bravado. In Howard Hawks's 1941 *Sergeant York*, Gary Cooper plays the eponymous hero, whose prayers and spiritual struggling give way to a bold endorsement of fighting for country and God.

York, a Tennessee country boy, is a hell-raiser and a darn good shooter. Yet at home with his Ma and his younger brother and sister, he sits obediently for the grace before a meal, head bowed, but eyes open. Fire blazing in the background, Ma prays, "The Lord bless these vittles we done got and help us to beholding to no one. Amen." Then Ma gives York salt for his meal. The idea of being "beholding to no one" instills a sense of independence, as well as stubbornness.

While Alvin is plowing away with his old mule Noah, struggling against the elements and removing as many rocks as he can from his land, Pastor (Walter Brennan) walks beside him, prodding him to take account of his spiritual travails. He berates Alvin for letting Satan get him by the shirttails, trying to "yank" him down to hell. Pastor encourages Alvin to "rassel him like ya would a bar. You and the Lord could throw him out. Well, twixt the two of you you'd have old Satan down in a jiffy." Alvin argues that he prayed until "I was black in the face, but it warn't no use." Pastor answers that it's "not just praying, Alvin, it's believing."

Alvin York (Gary Cooper) gets down on his knees to seek that old-time religion in Howard Hawks's *Sergeant York* (1941).

Human works contrast vividly with grace in Alvin's efforts to make it on his own. His crisis of faith comes after he has gotten drunk and heads out in a storm to kill a man who cheated him. On his way, he is almost struck by lightning, providing him a virtual Damascus-road experience. His near-death encounter leads him to a small country church. Inside, the praying and singing congregation, including his devout, ever-praying mother (like Saint Augustine's mother, Monica), brings him into the fold.

When he converts, he becomes a stanch fundamentalist, reading the Bible literally. Where it commands him not to kill, he holds to it, and when drafted for World War I, he refuses combat service. His commanding officer allows him to go home and search out his conscience. Finally, he comes across Jesus's words that one is to render unto God what is God's and unto Caesar what is Caesar's, which he interprets as duty to country. His sharpshooting skills thus lead him to become a daring hero of the war.[2] Hawks's film portrays prayer as the means to understand the workings of God during a war, a way of listening for guidance.

The Academy Award–winning *Mrs. Miniver* (William Wyler, 1942), about an ordinary stalwart British family during the war, sparked tremendous support for the Allied cause, with Churchill proclaiming, "The film helped Britain more than a fleet of destroyers." President Roosevelt had leaflets of its stirring final speech air-dropped over Europe. (On the evening he won an Oscar, director/pilot Wyler was allegedly flying a bombing mission run over Germany.) Anglican prayers and hymns (such as "Onward Christian Soldiers") play a major role in the film in uniting the beleaguered British people, blending patriotism with traditional faith.

As the war went badly during its early stages, Tay Garnett directed the realistic *Bataan* (1943), an inoculation against false hopes. A squad of American soldiers left behind enable others to escape and nobly give their lives. After the death of their captain, the remaining soldiers dawdle about, waiting for his burial. One green trooper prepares to play taps on his trumpet, but is quickly hushed, lest it draw attention to their position. Another soldier suggests that someone ought to say a few words. Okay, says Sergeant Bill Dane (Robert Taylor), "Speak your piece." "Not me, Sergeant," he responds, "Epps here could do it better."

They ask the one black soldier, demolitions specialist Private Wesley Epps (Kenneth Lee Spencer) whether he was a preacher back home, and he allows that he was studying to be. They take off their helmets; one leans on the shovel over the makeshift grave as the shirtless soldier prays,

> Heavenly Father, Captain Lassiter was our captain. He was a good captain. He did his job and kept on doing it as long as he could. He died a long ways from home. His folks probably won't ever know where he is buried, but I reckon he was prepared for that. As long as we know that what comes out of the grave is the best part that goes into it, we know that he's all right. Blessed are the pure in heart, for they shall see God. Amen.

"Amen," say the others, and then the tough sergeant concludes, "Okay, break it up." The dedication of the captain to his men and his mission kept him pure in heart, but it is the theological recognition of the power of the Resurrection that forms the heart of the prayer, and the only hope of these soldiers doomed to die. With so many fatalities reported back home, the prayer reaffirms the substance of faith and reassures anxious spectators of the blessed hope of a new life. Prayers in film contended with the war by seeking to provide meaning and hope in God.

Prewar Optimism

The Office of War Information (OWI) censored films that did not positively contribute to the war effort. Films like Preston Sturges's luxurious farce *The Palm Beach Story* portrayed the overindulgence of insouciant Americans while men died on the battlefield. The OWI worried that such luxury would stir resentment that "would gladden Hitler's heart."[3] Another smart set of selfish, pampered people appeared in George Cukor's theatrical *Susan and God* (1940). Written by the witty Anita Loos, the film, as Ida Lupino quipped, gave Joan Crawford as Susan top billing over God. The intrusive and self-indulgent socialite Mrs. Susan Trexel has a religious conversion in Europe; when she returns home, she demands changes in everyone around her, including her pitiful husband, Barrie (Fredric March).

At the beginning of the film, Barrie hides drunkenly in a movie theatre watching a Minnie Mouse cartoon. Susan seeks to expose the truth in God's name, meddling in the affairs of her pampered wealthy friends. She attempts to promote spirituality by cramming her religion down their throats. Neglecting her husband and their daughter, Blossom, she leaves human wreckage in her wake as she marches about "reforming" others. When someone asks, "What is Lady Wickstaff's movement?" they are told, "She's found God in a new way."

Susan confesses that she had once talked about sacred things flippantly, but now, on a mission from God, she tells her friends, those "poor miserable unhappy things" and vapid Long Island hedonists concerned about dinner cocktails and divorces, that they are not happy. She preaches that there is only one way to fill up their emptiness or to stop quarrels and wars. She advises her husband to pray. "Tell God. He knows what you've done. If we're sorry and want His help, we can be made over." Against her cloud of sentiment, her "spiritually lazy" friends protest, "Don't probe around my soul."

The film, filled with sentimentality and cynicism, stops to make a key point about the power of prayer as Barrie responds, "You believe what you just said; I believe it too. You think He could do something about me? What you just said could change the whole rotten world." Barrie avers that one could be made over if he asks God for help. He points out, however, that Susan should start as God's servant at home, with her husband and daughter.

Barrie has a quieter, more substantial religion. Strategically, on the eve of war, the film suggests that love for country is a sign of spiritual health; he has it; she doesn't. Her external needs for prayer, requiring fifteen minutes of quiet time before eating her muffin, does not discipline her soul, as she still sneaks a bite before finishing her prayer.

By the end of the film, husband and wife confess their lack of knowledge about God and admit that they have made a mess of their lives and those of others. Susan concludes, "Oh, Barrie, I've failed you so miserably." As they repent and apologize to each other, Susan's revelation becomes clear: "If only I had done myself what I told others. God couldn't help myself because I wouldn't dig to get to the rotten inside of me." The film's last line cries out for help, the first step toward personal and marital recovery: "O dear God, don't let me fall down again."[4] This prewar film preaches the need for humility and contrition, but warns against excessive religion.

Additional instruction in enlightened religion occurs in John Ford's Academy Award–winning *How Green Was My Valley* (1941). Philip Dunne's screenplay introduced the Welsh mining community's local preacher, Mr. Gruffydd (Walter Pidgeon), who preaches love over judgment and damnation. He lectures the thirteen-year-old crippled boy Huw (Roddy McDowall) as they sit under a spreading oak tree. He straightens out the boy's mangled legs and reduces prayer to positive thinking. However, his twaddle on luck over grace, on transcendental drivel over divine petitions, slips into long-winded prattling:

You've been lucky, Huw, lucky to suffer, lucky to spend these weary months in bed. For so God has given you a chance to make the spirit within yourself. And as your father cleans his lamp to have good light, so keep clean your spirit. . . . By prayer, Huw, and by prayer I don't mean shouting and mumbling and wallowing like a hog in religious sentiment. *Prayer is only another name for good, clean, direct thinking.* When you pray, think. Think well what you're saying, and make your thoughts into things that are solid. In that way, your prayer will have strength, and that strength will become a part of you in body, mind, and spirit.

And, Gruffydd explains, "The first duty of these new legs is to get you to chapel on Sunday." To which his young charge responds, "Indeed they will, sir."

Reflecting a passing Age of Reason and portending a secular age of material prosperity, *How Green Was My Valley* extols the enlightened supremacy of human reason, will, and virtue. Romantically set in a picturesque location under the spreading chestnut trees, the good reverend's instruction revels in exalted feelings and "good, clean, direct thinking," a precursor to the positive thinking of Norman Vincent Peale after the war. Gruffydd elevated thought over the old-time Methodist enthusiasm; unfortunately, the irrational reality of a world war burst in upon its tranquility, and prayers had little effect on the blitzkriegs that were to follow. Such prayers echoed the rational and isolationist posture of liberal Protestantism and Unitarianism. For more realistic and prophetic theologians like Reinhold Niebuhr, moral men could become brutish in immoral societies. Reason was insufficient to save humans in collectives from egoistic behaviors. As Niebuhr became more convinced of the power of sin, he rejected the "Promethean illusion" that one can achieve goodness alone. Thus prayer had to be more than just "good, clean, direct thinking."

The Sins of Men

Subtexts of horror films often alluded to the effects and impact of the horrors of the war. When a werewolf bites Lon Chaney Jr., he must struggle with his brutal nature in *The Wolfman* (George Waggner, 1941). Whenever anyone mentions werewolves, a village legend is spoken: "Even a man who is pure in heart / and says his prayers by night / may become a wolf when the wolf-bane blooms / and the autumn moon is bright." All men are sinful, and some, even German Lutherans, may become monsters and murderers.

In *I Walked with a Zombie* (Jacques Tourneur, 1943), Betsy (Frances Dee), a comely Canadian girl, travels to the Afro-Caribbean island of St. Sebastian to nurse Jessica, the ailing wife of a morbid and moody plantation owner, Paul Holland (Tom Conway). Holland and his brother have been raised by a missionary father and a mother who is a voodoo priestess who mixes Christianity and voodoo, the cross and the drums. The brothers share a dark family secret, seemingly cursed through their possessed mother, Jessica, who had bargained with witchcraft for spiritual powers.

Trying to understand the syncretism, Betsy asks a young native boy, "How do you ever expect to get to heaven with one foot in voodoo and one foot in church?" The question remains unanswered. When the zombie-like Jessica dies, the Houngan high priest sounds like an Anglican:

> O Lord God, most holy, deliver them from the bitter pains of eternal death. The woman was a wicked woman, and she was dead in her own life. Yea, Lord, dead in the selfishness of her spirit, and the man followed her. Her steps led him down to evil. Her feet took hold on death. Forgive him, O Lord, who knowest the secret of all hearts. Yea, Lord, pity them who are dead, and give peace and happiness to the living.

Prayers ring forth from American churches asking mercies for the dead and hope for the living. The syncretism of the traditional German Lutheran Church and the National Socialist Party raised similar concerns for the evangelical Church of Germany, asking how one could serve two masters, Jesus Christ and Adolf Hitler.

As a challenge against a satanic cult, two diverse characters employ the Lord's Prayer to fight demonic evil in horror icon Val Lewton's production of *The Seventh Victim* (Mark Robson, 1943). An unlikely pair, consisting of a psychiatrist, Dr. Louis Judd (Tom Conway), and a poet (Erford Gage), combines forces to help Mary Gibson (Kim Hunter) look for her older sister, and then to thwart the insidious influence of the cult to manipulate a young woman to kill herself.

The poet mocks "the devil worshippers, the lovers of evil," and calls them a "joke, a pathetic little joke." He ridicules the diabolical cult as a poor, wretched group of people who took a wrong turn.

"Wrong!" retorts the leader with Nietzschean bombast, "who knows what is right or wrong? I prefer to believe in satanic majesty and power. Who can deny me? What proof can you bring that good is superior to evil? One proof!"

The doctor remembers certain evocative phrases from childhood, namely, the simple words of the Lord's Prayer. He argues that no learned person has equaled it as a rule for human relationships. Nothing can substitute for "Forgive us our trespasses as we forgive those who trespass against us." The poet adds that there follows one sentence for "you people from that same prayer: 'Lead us not into temptation, but *deliver us from evil.*'" He cleverly indicates that they are the evil from whom deliverance must come. The topic of the evil incarnate in popular theology blazoned across the cover of *Time* magazine. Oxford don C. S. Lewis introduced the world to his devil Screwtape, whose satirical commentary alerted the world to the unremitting presence of sin and evil.[5]

Spiritual Battles

Petunia Jackson (Ethel Waters) prays that God save her craps-playing husband, "Little" Joe Jackson (Eddie Anderson), from the devil (Rex Ingram Jr.) *and* from a sultry Sweet Georgia Brown (Lena Horne), in Vincente Minnelli's *Cabin in the Sky* (1943). Though it indulges in racial stereotyping, the dreamscape film also captures some of the energy and sheer joy of African American Christianity. Opening the musical track is "The Prayer, or Take a Chance on Love," followed later by "Amen." The Pulitzer Prize–winning theatrical production translated into film is itself a prayer, particularly with the enormous talent of Ethel Waters. At Joe's bedside, Petunia in a teary close-up pleads,

> Lord, please don't take Little Joe from me. I know how sinful he's been lately, but I love him. Please forgive me for loving him so much, but Little Joe ain't wicked, he's just weak. So if You just let him get well, I promise You he'll mend his ways and give You no more trouble.

Still, the devil, Lucifer Jr., comes for the shiftless, no-account man, readying his asbestos chariot. Petunia cries, "O Lord, something's wrong down here, I can feel it. You're not going to let him die, are You?" Little Joe's spirit sees the spiritual warfare going on and shouts, but is not heard: "That's right, Petunia! Pray! Pray harder! Keep plugging away!" The good and faithful servant continues, "If Little Joe die, I ain't got nothing to live for neither. I know You hear me up there, Lord." Later, she adds her own query: "Lord, why'd You let me love him so much? It hurt me so bad. Why?"

When Little Joe is shot for a gambling debt at Jim Henry's Paradise Club, Petunia implores God for his life. She chases off her husband's diabolical nemesis and calls out to God, "O Lord, please forgive me for backsliding, but sometimes when you fight the devil, you've got to jab him with his own pitchfork!" The devil listens in and admits, "Dat is terrific prayin'!" The Angel Gabriel arrives and Lucifer Jr. asks him what he is doing there. He answers, "We received the most powerful prayer from Petunia, most powerful prayer in a long time."

When it appears that she has lost Joe and that Lucifer Jr. has won, Petunia beseeches God to "hear her prayer" and "destroy this wicked place!" Remarkably, thunder resounds and a tornado comes swirling through (recycling a bit of the tornado footage from *The Wizard of Oz*) to cleanse the barroom. Both Petunia and Little Joe are shot and end up wearing heavenly white robes. Little Joe finally repents. "O Lord, I know I ain't got no right asking for forgiveness, but Lord, You know I was doing all right until I had that falling-out with Petunia. Excuse me, Lord." Petunia pleads with the Lord for Him to receive the rascal. As the balance sheets are checked, a repenting Georgia Brown tilts Little Joe's account to the good, and he makes it to heaven on a technicality. A choir of angels sing "Hallelujah" and the Lord opens up the Stairway to Heaven for them both, until Little Joe wakes, revealing that it was all a dream. While emphasizing a theology of works, the film highlights the importance of intercessory prayer for those facing death. The film stressed the urgency of praying for servicemen and servicewomen overseas, for making petitions to God for life.

Other prayers on the home front, especially those that dealt with death, sought to bolster morale and to remind America's citizens why they were fighting evil. The frontier prayers of director Clarence Brown's naturalistic *The Yearling* (1946) offer both the halting, hick prayers of old men who stutter and that of the pioneer farmer soldier Ezra "Penny" Baxter (Gregory Peck), who had some "Christian learning." However, he adapts to the situation. At the dinner table, he prays, "Dear Lord, thanks again for the vittles. Amen."

"That's a mighty skimpy prayer," says his wife.

"Well, I'm mighty hungry."

When Penny goes to trade a hunting dog for a gun at his neighbors', the brood of brothers invite him to eat. The matriarch tells all the men to sit down and then, turning to her husband, she barks, "Pa, it won't hurt you to say the blessing once in your life."

He stutters, "O Lord . . . O Lord . . . We . . . We . . . [He looks up as if for help.] O Lord, Thou hast seen fit to bless our sinning and souls and with the . . . with the . . ." Penny steps in and finishes the prayer "all the vittles."

"Thanks," says the old man. And everyone says, "Amen."

In this touching and tender story of the fragility of life on the frontier, Penny and his wife, Orry (Jane Wyman), tend to their last surviving child, Jody. Orry's fear of losing a fourth child isolates the boy from her motherly affection. He thus adopts a fawn that his father tells him must someday be let go. The pathos of prayers reaches its climax when a crippled friend of Jody's dies. Penny delivers the eulogy:

> It ain't for us ignorant mortals to say what's right and what's wrong. Was any one of us to be doin' of it, we'd not have bring this poor boy into the world a cripple, and his mind teched. But in a way o' speakin', Lord, You done made it up to him. You gave him a way with the wild critters, gave him a sort of wisdom. . . . The birds come to him, and the varmints moved free about him, and like as not he could of takened a she wild-cat right in his poor twisted hands. Now You've done seed fit to take him where bein' crookedy in mind or limb don't matter. But Lord, it pleasures us to think now You've done straightened out them legs and that poor bent back and them hands. It pleasures us to think on him, movin' around as easy as anyone. And Lord, give him a few redbirds and maybe a squirrel and a 'coon and a 'possum to keep him company, like he had here. All of us is somehow lonesome, and we know he'll not be lonesome, do he have them little wild things around him, if it ain't askin' too much to put a few varmints in heaven. Thy will be done. Amen.

The prayer indirectly addresses a complementary theme of wounded veterans returning home. It prepares the home front for the amputees and psychologically scarred, and even more, it sets a hope for those who die and those who remain. The vacuum left by those who would die would make "all of us somehow lonesome." And above all, the prayer sets a vision of heaven as a better earth, with a few varmints for Jody's friend to chase.

The cinematic version of Hartzell Spence's biographical story of his Methodist father's itinerant ministry, *One Foot in Heaven* (Irving Rapper, 1941), followed the family through challenging and comic events during the early part of the twentieth century. From getting a new church built to teaching tolerance, the chronicles of a modern parish minister fit the times of the imminent war, even planting seeds of hope about the impending conflict. Studio researchers inquired about the "theological interpretation" of Luke 22:36, "He that hath no sword let him sell his garment." They received an answer from Jesse Bader, an executive evangelist of the Federal Council of Churches, that twisted the scriptural context and suggested war preparedness: "From sermons I have heard I would say that because of conditions that would follow the Crucifixion, the followers of Christ would have to fight for their faith and they should not hesitate to do so."[6] The words of the Man of Peace strategically became a call to arms.

To create verisimilitude, producers for the film investigated stained glass windows, took note of signs outside churches announcing sermon titles, and studied six editions of the *Discipline of the Methodist Episcopal Church* (1904–1924), hymnals for the fin de siècle period, and a copy of the Bible Quotation Game. Looking at the script, author Spence challenged several bits: first, an evolutionary heresy trial; and secondly, and more importantly, the impression that his wife doesn't know what her husband has done. "A Protestant minister's wife ALWAYS knows what he is doing." He argued that Methodist people do not run away from trouble. "They stand like the old hymn: 'Bless the rock, I stand upon it.' They have faith, even when they don't understand it. And that's got to be in this movie." Spence demanded that the saints be shown as more Christian; in other words, Spence required that the film accurately reflect biblical Methodism.

Many wrote letters of commendation to Warner Bros., thanking them for *One Foot in Heaven*. One Protestant praised it as "so thoroughly American and refreshing after the deluge of crosses, candles, and Latin chants which is the usual lot of the moviegoer."[7] However, even among those deeply touched and inspired, one Lutheran clergyman, "faithful to all the Confessions of my Church," complained that he could not "subscribe to all the theology that filtered thru the picture. One thing was not emphasized, the most important tenet of all and one which justifies the existence of the Protestant Church: emphasis upon the redemption of the individual through the substitutionary atonement of Jesus Christ." When the church fails to stress this central doctrine, he averred, "it is no longer Protestant!"[8] Additionally, one Methodist minister attacked Warner Bros. for a most egregious oversight: they hired the Baptist Reverend Daniel Polling as a consultant for a Methodist movie.[9] However, almost all Christian traditions, from Roman Catholic to Baptist, praised the film.[10]

The film provided ministry itself to a war-threatened audience. One Methodist layman died shortly after seeing it, and his wife reported that he passed after spending one of the most enjoyable times of his life and that he couldn't have spent his last moments on earth in a better way. "Little did he realize when he entered the theatre that one of his feet was already in Heaven and the other was soon to follow."[11] Churches seeking to comfort those with heartache found an ally in the cinema.

In Paramount's *The Shepherd of the Hills* (Henry Hathaway, 1941), Harold Bell Wright's novel was adapted to tell the story of dysfunctional moonshiners living superstitiously under a curse. A mysterious stranger, Daniel Howitt (Harry Carey), arrives at a beleaguered backwoods community in the Missouri Ozarks. Howitt takes a sick girl's hand and prays, bringing healing. One of the denizens, an angry young man, Matt Matthews (John Wayne), blames an absent father for his mother's death. Yet when Matthews discovers that Howitt is his father, who had not abandoned his family but had been in prison, he also discovers that Howitt is the good shepherd who returned for his lost sheep, his son.

Other characters simmer with bitterness and hate, as one shrew sits in her rocking chair and curses life. When the doctor brings healing to a blind woman, removing bandages from her eyes, she sees the green mountains and blue skies, and then her granddaughter, a "mighty pretty thing." Her first words are "Thank You, God!" with tears of joy. The film reminded spectators to be grateful for those common blessings one took for granted. Prayers of thanksgiving were the completion of the healing process.

To keep his son from making the mistake of shooting a wicked person, the crime he had committed years ago, Howitt shoots and wounds his own son. Realizing the love and grace of his father who visits him in his recovery bed, Matthews confesses that it's "kinda like being born all over again, from the inside." Director Henry Hathaway (later to direct comic prayers in John Wayne's *True Grit*) focuses on the larger issues of reconciliation and of prayers used to heal rather than to hex. Wright's novel preached a necessary sermon for a country on the edge of war. Whatever internal conflicts may exist, the time for forgiveness and unity was now. External conflicts demanded internal cohesion and *The Shepherd of the Hills* modeled it.

Director Lloyd Bacon drew up two other models of faith for audiences. In *Brother Orchid* (1940), the gangster Little John Sarto (Edward G. Robinson) seeks refuge from a rival gang and hides in a monastery. The brother superior (Donald Crisp) quietly cultivates the pigheaded mug by putting him to work in the garden, teaching him to fulfill the Benedictine rule *Ora et labora*, praying and working. In *Captain Eddie* (1945), a biopic of ace Air Force pilot and Medal of Honor winner Captain Eddie Rickenbaker (Fred MacMurray), Bacon reifies habits of piety, as Rickenbacker, struggling to stay alive on a tiny rubber raft, endures when he reads the Bible and prays.[12] Such examples reiterated the sermons of churches, teaching congregations to work and pray.

During wartime, prayers in film were frequently depicted in rural communities, suggesting that most vigorous faith existed in the Bible Belt churches. In Clarence Brown's poignant *The Human Comedy* (1943), adapted from William Saroyan's heart-wrenching novel of the war years, Homer Macauley (Mickey Rooney), the fatherless telegraph messenger of the fictional town of Ithaca, must deliver telegrams and death notices to families who have lost sons in the war.

As Homer sits down to lunch with his older sister and their widowed mother, all bow their heads in silent prayer. His sister asks what he said in his prayer. He answers, "What I always say" and speedily recites, "Lord, be present at our table. Lord, be here and everywhere adored. The creatures bless and grant that we may feast in paradise with Thee." He then adds a postscript, asking for help in winning a 220 low hurdles race.

When his sister taunts that he doesn't know what he is praying, he responds that he prays "swiftly because I'm hungry, but I can say it slowly too." He protests that it's the spirit of the whole thing that matters. His sister persists: "And what do the words mean, Homer?"

He slowly unravels his prayer:

> Well, "be present at our table, Lord" means a lot of things and I guess all of them are good. "Be here and everywhere adored" means to love the good things here and everywhere else. "The creatures"—creatures, that's you and Mom and myself and everybody. "Bless" means to bless, bless, well, bless may be to forgive or love or watch over. And "grant that we may feast in paradise with Thee"—Mom, doesn't that mean that if you're right, every time we sit down together we feast?

His mom asks, "What about the 220 low hurdles?" "Well, I just gotta win in the track meet."

The town is all-American, patriotic, and sentimental, with picnics, parades, and Easter Sunday, when a large congregation sings Charles Wesley's "Christ the Lord Is Risen Today" beneath stained glass windows. The war story highlights Homer's brother Marcus (Van Johnson) as he prepares to go to war. On the troop train, Marcus is squeezing his portable accordion and a fellow comes up and confesses that he would like to hear "Leaning on the Everlasting Arms."

Men playing chess, writing letters, and chatting take notice. They all begin to join in: "What a fellowship, what a joy divine, leaning on the everlasting arms." All gather and sing robustly and prayerfully that they would be "safe and secure from all alarms!"

Later, after Marcus has told his friend Tobey George (Tom Craven), an orphan, all about his small, friendly hometown in California and invited him to return with him someday, they sit on artillery guns on the moving train and Tobey asks, "Do you pray?"

"Always, constantly," Marcus replies.

"We were forced to pray at the orphanage," Tobey says.

"That's the one thing you can't force. It's not a prayer if you do."

"I know. I know. That's why I quit. But I'm beginning all over again."

Marcus begins to pray,

> Get me to Ithaca if You can, but get me home. Anything You say, but get me home. Protect everybody and keep them from pain. Send the home-

less to their homes. Get me to Ithaca and keep the town. Don't change a stick of it. Let me walk through its streets; let me see it as it is. Keep the Macauleys, all of them. Keep Bess [Donna Reed], let her know I love her. . . . Keep Ma. Keep the harp, the piano, the songs, everything, the empty lot next door. Save everything for me. Get me to Ithaca if You can. That's all, I guess. Amen.

"Yeah, that's a good prayer. I hope it's answered."
"What do you pray for, Tobey?"
"Same things you pray for, the very same things."
Marcus will make the ultimate sacrifice during the war, and Homer receives the telegram with the bad news he must take home, just as Tobey walks up to the porch.

Prayers focus on normalcy, on keeping things the same, "if at all possible." With the war, it is not possible. Home-front prayers want everything to return to the way they were. Nostalgia reigns, but realism, even in the movies, intrudes. The discussions of praying among the various characters help suggest ideas for prayers to those who aren't quite sure how to pray, or what it means. *The Human Comedy* becomes a religious catechism.

In *Since You Went Away* (John Cromwell, 1944), the battle for the home front, and its shortages, rationing, and uncertainty about a father missing in action, centers on Anne Hilton (Claudette Colbert) and her family. Her charity to immigrant Zofia Koslowska demonstrates sacrificial kindness. On the voyage to America, Zofia read to her young son Janka and then "we'd pray together that God would let us go to the fairyland across the sea." But Janka did not make it to see the Statue of Liberty. Zofia tells Hilton that "you are what I thought America was—what I meant when I prayed with little Janka."

In a journal voice-over, Hilton confides, "And, as in my own small way I help here in the shipyards, I hope I may be worthy of her words, just as each night I pray that always I may be worthy of those other thrilling words . . . the first time and every time since that you've said, 'I love you.'" Continually, she and the family pray for their father, missing in action.

Gary Cooper, an actor whose persona represented all that was good and noble in classic American mythology, filled roles in Frank Capra's

Mr. Deeds Goes to Town and *Meet John Doe* at the end of the Depression. He stands against oppression by corrupt powers culminating in William Wyler's *The Westerner* (1940), where, as Cole Harden, he sides with struggling homesteaders against his friend Judge Roy Bean (Walter Brennan) and greedy cattlemen. The ruthless judge pronounces a perfunctory prayer, "May the Lord have mercy on your soul," to a man who shot a steer (he should have hit the man he was aiming at rather than the bovine, mutters the judge), just before hanging him.

In contrast, the goodness of the common people is reflected in the prayer of Caliphet Mathews (Fred Stone), the father of the defiant heroine, Jane Ellen Mathews (Doris Davenport). In a long shot, viewed from a high angle, the entire community of men and women, old and young, gather before their fields ripe for harvest and kneel, as a bearded Caliphet leads them in prayer over their crops:

> Almighty God, we offer Thee thanksgiving for Thy help and Thy divine bounty. Thou hast poured Thy blessing on our land. Thou has visited the earth and made it plenteous. Thou hast made it soft with drops of rain, and the land that was desolate has become like a garden, and the waste places are fenced and become inhabited. Thou hast made the tree and field yield her fruit and the earth her increase. Thou broke the bonds of our yoke and delivered us out of the hands of our enemies so that we dwell here safely and none shall make us afraid. And for this Thy divine bounty, O Lord, we thank Thee. Amen.

After the hundred people join with an acclamation of "Amens," the harvest fiddling music erupts with dancing and festivity. However, it is all short-lived because the judge's henchmen start a major conflagration in the fields, and Caliphet is killed in the process. His daughter reads from a charred Bible over his gravesite, "Man that is born has a short time to live, cut down like a flower." But she is resolved not to be moved or leave. With time, Cole Harden will bring about justice, restore peace and security for the homesteaders, and fulfill the prayer of Caliphet.

Hollywood's imagined peace on the home front did not isolate spectators from the dire conditions of the world war or the deep need to pray. The films gently prodded people to pray, recognizing that many loved ones already had one foot in heaven. In contrast to the nostalgic desire for things to stay the same, many of the prayers not only prepared the people for loss, but provided healing of body and soul.

Detecting God's Presence

Films reflected both the providence of God and His incognito presence. One may not be able to see God's direct intervention into the affairs of His people, but there were clues and hints that He was quietly working behind the scenes. As Albert Einstein once quipped, "Coincidences are God's way of remaining anonymous."

In the costume melodrama *All This and Heaven Too* (Anatole Litvak, 1940), Henriette (Bette Davis) serves as a governess for a French duke (Charles Boyer). Her joie de vivre and warmth with the children cause resentment in the duke's wife. When the duchess is murdered and the duke commits suicide, Henriette is sent to prison, but ultimately released. Seeking refuge in America working with seminary students, she reveals her "tainted past" and finds hope with her confessor, the Protestant Reverend Henry Field (Jeffrey Lynn), who promises her a "heaven upon this earth."

In discussing the prayers in the film, screenwriter Casey Robinson wrote to producer Hal Wallis and suggested that "Henriette's 'Bless you' is a little too familiar. I think 'God bless you' is more in keeping."[13] He also raised questions about the "prayers that children in France would say on going to bed." Robinson sought to emphasize the presence of God in one's prayers, indirectly challenging the liberal idea of prayer as good thinking.

In one particular scene, a Roman Catholic priest prays off screen: "Oremus Deus cui uncta adolescunt et per quem adula firmantur extende desteram." Then he appears and continues: "Let us pray. O God, through whom all things grow and through whom the grown are strengthened, extend Thy right hand to Thy servant who is at a tender age, so that he may unceasingly offer faithful service to Thee all the days of his life, through our Lord Jesus Christ." What is remarkable about this adaptation of Rachel Field's biographical novel of her great-aunt is the concern for religious accuracy. The novel and film reflected the specific Christian words of ordinary people. It was the way people prayed, using the name of Jesus as the entrance into God's presence. The Warner Bros.

research team not only investigated the construction of a small shrine for the priest, including a kneeling stool and the image of a patron saint, but sorted through old Protestant hymns and hunted up biblical quotations such as "Suffer the little children to come unto me."[14] The film summoned forth sympathy for the children of France, but not so much for the dysfunctional French aristocracy, who lacked the love and faith necessary to survive.

The apotheosis of religious films during this time was Henry King's inspirational *Song of Bernadette* (1943), about the nineteenth-century French saint from Lourdes. Jennifer Jones dramatized the hagiography of Saint Bernadette of Lourdes and her vision of the "beautiful lady" (Linda Darnell) adorned with a pearl rosary, inhabiting a dump on the outskirts of town. The film essentially cross-examines Bernadette's claims to the visions of the Virgin, with a formal investigation dotted with prayers, faith, and skepticism.

Trying to elude the Nazis, author Franz Werfel and his wife had escaped to Lourdes to hide out. Numerous citizens sheltered them at their own risk and told him the story of Bernadette. He vowed to write that inspirational story as a novel once he escaped, and in 1941 it was published and immediately opted by producer Darryl F. Zanuck for the film. The almost unbelievable prayers and visions of the saint resonated with spectators who saw little hope in the war effort. Something transcendent was needed, and what better than a suffering saint?

Diagnosed with tuberculosis of the bone, Bernadette endures her pain with peace and equanimity. Jealous of Bernadette's piety, Sister Marie (Gladys Cooper) asks forgiveness for her treatment of the adolescent peasant girl: "O God, I've tried to storm the gates of heaven by sacrificing myself. I know now that we must be chosen, that we must be graced as You have graced this child. God, forgive me. . . . God, help me to serve this chosen soul for the rest of my days. God help me. "

Doubting that she will ever see the Holy Mother again, Bernadette lies on her deathbed. The Virgin does appear, holding out her arms in welcome and smiling. Bernadette cries out in joy, "I love you! I love you! Holy Mary, Mother of God, pray for me" and dies, entering heaven.

The film alters the character of the prosecutor, Vital Dutour (Vincent Price), whose skepticism revolves around his suspicion that the young woman is hallucinating. In the film, Dutour is dying of cancer of the larynx and, at the end, he kneels at the gates of Lourdes shrine and entreats the saint, "Pray for me, Bernadette." Throughout the war, the prayer would be repeated. Both *All This and Heaven Too* and *The Song of Bernadette* focused attention on France, connecting American faith tradition with its historic Catholic roots. No films celebrated German Lutheranism at this time; only American allies were depicted as keeping the faith. Ultimately the films argued that God was on the Allied side.

War Prayers

Military films to bolster the home front usually included prayers that connected familiar traditions with ever-present death. Chaplains, like Father Donnelly in Lewis Seiler's *Guadalcanal Diary* (1943), are present on the front lines with their prayers. In *Air Force* (1943), director Howard Hawks inserted a brief scene where a chaplain conducts the hasty burial of a soldier while the battle rages on. He told his writers that the denomination of the soldier is unknown and the service would therefore be nonsectarian. As earth was cast upon the body, the chaplain prayed,

> Almighty God, we commend the soul of this soldier departed and we commit his body to the ground. Earth to earth, ashes to ashes, dust to dust; in sure and certain hope of the Resurrection unto eternal life, through our Lord, Jesus Christ, at whose coming . . . the corruptible bodies of those who sleep in Him shall be changed, and made like unto His own glorious body; according to the mighty working whereby He is able to subdue all things unto Himself.

The chaplain closed with the following prayer: "O God, whose mercies cannot be numbered, accept our prayers on behalf of the soul of Thy servant departed, and grant him an entrance into the land of light and joy, in the fellowship of Thy saints, through Jesus Christ, our Lord. Amen."[15] There is a certain authenticity in the prayer, which enables it to resonate with a devout audience, one who could recognize the reality behind the cinematic façade. What is unique is its use of the name of Jesus, which most generic prayers eschew. Hawks included it as an element of religious realism, noting how most Protestants prayed.

One conversation in Delmer Daves's *Destination Tokyo* (1943) between a doubting sailor and his submarine mate, Pills, affirmed the efficacy of prayers: "Do you think prayers do any good?" Pills answers, "Yes, they do. I *know* they do."

This affirmation of faith was echoed in *God Is My Co-Pilot* (Robert Florey, 1945), with Dennis Morgan playing Flying Tigers pilot Colonel Robert Lee Scott Jr. In their mission to bomb Tokyo, Big Mike (Alan Hale) recites the poem "They Speak of God" by Dan Blanding as a prayer:

> For those who only lean on their own strength find that fear can
>   sabotage the bravest heart, crying out: "Help us, Oh God."
> Then silence lets the Silent Voice be heard
> Bringing its message like a spoken word,
> Believe. Believe in Me. Cast out your fear.
> Oh, I am not up there beyond the sky, but here,
> Right here in your heart. I am the Strength you seek.
> Believe.[16]

The prayer sought to infuse the warrior with courage; however, the film drew the attention of the Motion Picture Producers and Distributors of America (MPPDA) and its Roman Catholic watchdog, Breen. Breen wrote to Jack Warner that certain expressions in the film were objectionable: the use of the phrase "hell on high," the expression "you setting son of a . . . ," and "May God roast your soul in Hell" were entirely unacceptable.[17] In trying to make prayers authentic, the filmmakers inserted the vernacular language of soldiers, but censors thwarted their intent.

Warner Bros. felt that it included sufficient doses of religion in its flag-waving propaganda, but wanted to keep Chinese allies mollified and not offend their religious traditions. When Colonel Scott sees the beautiful, benign face of a woman carved in stone, he asks who she is. Researchers suggested that an old Chinese doctor reply, "That is YanYin, the Chinese Goddess of Mercy." Whereupon Scott would say, through teeth clenched with pain, "God has a way of speaking in many languages, hasn't he?" The researchers suggested that the goddess could be "repeated with a Christian parallel when we later get to

Big Mike's chapel. Here I think we could show a figure of the Virgin Mary with an inscription which one frequently sees below it—'Mother of Mercy, Pray for us.'" For the filmmakers, "the religious note comes over without preaching."

Screenwriter Jack Moffitt added that they rather liked

> the idea of including the Chinese as children of God in the picture's phi-losophy and not limiting the spiritual message to a purely denominational Christian dogma. So Colonel Scott articulates the Studio's syncretistic philosophy: "Whether we worship by burning candles to the Virgin Mary or incense to YanYin, whether we follow the words of Moses, Jesus, or Budah [sic], or whether we have no formal religion and believe only in God as he is expressed in the good within us, the division remains the same. It is the good people against the bad people. We are on God's side and we know that he is on ours.[18]

This propaganda is similar to the kind of prayer that Mark Twain satirized at the beginning of the century, as he ridiculed the arrogant attitude of those who claimed God as their ally.

When the patriotic film was released, *New York Times* reviewer Bosley Crowther complained that the "pious injection of the spiritual in an otherwise noisy action film is patently ostentatious and results in maudlin effect."[19] The overreaching Universalism of the Warner Bros. film struck him as treacly. The colonel's climactic triumph felt contrived by the scriptwriters and arranged "in a suspenseful moment as an answer to prayers." The conflation of the war effort and religious fervor gave opportunity for filmmakers to show faith, to quote prayers, and to demonstrate that "God was on our side."

Alfred Hitchcock's *Lifeboat* (1944) isolates a group of survivors whose ship the Nazis torpedoed. Charles Rittenhouse (Henry Hull) tries to pray for the burial at sea of Mrs. Higley's (Heather Angel) baby. After the death of the child, he asks whether "anyone knows words for burial at sea." Another passenger mutters, "Well, I—I suppose any prayer would do. Er, let me see now. The Lord is my shepherd. I shall not want. He maketh me to lie down in green pastures. He . . . er, . . . He . . . er—"

Joe Spencer (Canada Lee), the black steward, finishes the psalm that the others had forgotten:

He leadeth me beside still waters. He restoreth my soul. He leadeth me in paths of righteousness for His name's sake. Yea, though I walk through the valley of the shadow of death, I will fear no evil, for Thou art with me. Thy rod and Thy staff they comfort me. Surely goodness and mercy shall follow me all the days of my life, and I will dwell in the house of the Lord forever. Amen.

Joe also functions heroically as the one who rescues a woman at sea. When a German tries to board their lifeboat, he steps forward to disarm him. He remains the only compassionate person of faith in a raft of bickering allies. Throughout the crises, we see Joe looking heavenward and keeping the balance. Racial harmony on the home front would not be so easily kept, with Sunday remaining one of the most segregated days of the week, but in the movies a community of faith was being established. This righteous propaganda aimed to unite races with an inclusive vision of the American dream, suggesting that God's chosen people were multiracial.

World War II films offered numerous representations of prayer, usually during deaths and burials. In *Back to Bataan* (Edward Dmytryk, 1945), a priest gives the last rites to an intransigent school headmaster who is hanged for refusing to remove the American flag. In a Philippine cathedral, a woman suspected of being a traitor prays in one of the pews—a sign that she is not the enemy. Captain Bonifacio (Anthony Quinn) loves her, but despairs that she has turned traitor. When instructed to go meet the Allies' informant, he goes to a church. He seeks out the priest to tell him he wants to confess; the priest tells him he has just "gotta believe," instructing him to have faith in God and in love. This latter object of faith, love, turns out to be his own beloved, who is actually the key Manila contact. He discovers her praying for the martyrs of the war, that they might "pass this world and sent to the region of peace and light through our Lord and Savior Jesus Christ." All is well, mostly because his woman is true. Indirectly the film reaffirms an ecumenical fellowship of different ethnicities and faiths, uniting Roman Catholics and Protestants in a joint effort against an enemy of the Church.

Some films countered the prevailing hope. *So Proudly We Hail* (Mark Sandrich, 1943) chronicled the war from the woman's perspective, as a squad of nurses is assigned to Bataan in the Philippines just before the

Japanese takeover. At a Christmas party on board ship, fraternizing men and women sing "Silent Night" and enjoy each other's company. The chaplain offers one of the most desultory sermons, wanting to share something sentimental "on his heart."

> Forgive me for being sentimental—we're a sentimental people and I think we're proud of it despite the fact that our enemies deride us. It may be ironic to talk about a spiritual Christmas when war flames throughout the globe, but in tragedy we have faith—not blind faith, but faith in those things in which we believe. We must have such faith, faith in ourselves, faith in mankind, and fight tough to make those tender and sentimental beliefs like Christmas a reality forever. Now God bless us everyone.

As heads bow, he chirps, "And we wish you a merry Christmas!" as a band plays a secular "Jingle Bells." Later, the chaplain prays over a dying young man with rhetorical flourishes that counter the makeshift hospitals in the Philippine jungles. "O sovereign Lord, who desireth not the death of a sinner, we beseech Thee to loose the spirit of this Thy servant, and set him free from all evil that he may rest with all Thy saints in the eternal habitations." The Episcopalian chaplain, with his artificiality and inflated rhetoric, rings as spiritually superficial as "Jingle Bells." Unfortunately, the chaplain is a model of insipid sincerity masked as holiness. Such generic prayers would lead to portrayals of hypocrisy and cant in the coming decade.

But during the war, most prayers were earnest. In Ernie Pyle's *Story of G.I. Joe* (William Wellman, 1945), soldiers pray in foxholes and churches. As they enter a bombed-out church, a soldier calls out an offensive remark against Germans in order to flush out any remaining enemy soldiers. The tactic works and they shoot a German sniper. The sergeant reflects on the irony of causing death in a sacred place: "Funny place to be killing men, isn't it?" he asks, and then kneels and prays. The entrance into the theatres of war ushered in various performances of piety under fire and duress. Yet both sincere and hackneyed prayers would also be uttered by military chaplains.

If ever a film functioned as an apologetic for military chaplains, William Keighley's *Fighting 69th* (1940) rates among the best, offering some of the most honest and genuine prayers in film history.[20] *The Fighting*

69th, "a tale of humor and heroism" written by Frances Marion Bird, tells the story of Father Duffy. Pat O'Brien plays the heroic Father Duffy, with James Cagney as the tough Irish soldier and misfit Jerry Plunkett. Before the all-Irish unit goes on deployment, the battalion commander, "Wild Bill" Donovan, tells Chaplain Duffy, "We'll need your prayers, Father," to which the clergyman retorts wittily, "When did an Irishman need a prayer in a fight?"

The night before shipping off, Father Duffy crosses himself and kneels before a crucifix, hands clasped, eyes open, and in a conversation with God, prays,

> Almighty God, in Thy infinite mercy, grant unto me, Thy servant, the wisdom to guide my young flock through the trials of war. O Father, they're so young. So young and they know so little of life and nothing at all of that terrible and bloody altar towards which they move, carrying so eagerly the bright sacrifice of their youth. Their need will be great, O Lord, and I am weak. Therefore, I beseech Thee through Thy Son, Christ, our Lord, grant me the strength to keep them steadfast in the faith, in decency and courage to the glory of God, their country, and their regiment in the bad times to come. And if in battle You see fit to gather them to Your protecting arms, Thy will be done, but let them die like men, valiant and unafraid.

Duffy lauds the ecumenical nature of the military chaplaincy, recalling how the various denominations share duties, such as Lieutenant Holmes, the Methodist preacher, who has his own pulpit: "How well the various faiths get along over here; it would cause scandal to some pious minds." In contrast to the sectarianism among various Christian traditions in the civilian population, the military promoted significantly more common cause and unity. The film employed the words of shared hymns like "Little Town of Bethlehem" and "O Holy Night" as examples of common faith connections.

In this Irish unit, several characters distinguish themselves. The first, an actual historical person, is the sentimental lyric poet Joyce Kilmer, a sergeant killed at the second Battle of the Marne in 1918, with the 69th. As he translated his Roman Catholic faith into his writing, his poems transformed into prayers. A second significant character is the Jewish soldier Mischa Moscowitz (Sammy Cohen), who chooses to be called

Mike Murphy in order to be identified as one of the Irish guys. When he is dying, he asks Father Duffy for a prayer. The chaplain appropriately intones the Shema Yisrael, from Deuteronomy 6:4, the central prayer of morning and evening Jewish services taught to Jewish children when they go to sleep. It is often the last words of a dying Jew affirming his faith. "Sh'ma Yisrael Adonai Eloheinu Adonai E⊠ad. But if Thou willst my death, Thou art my Redeemer. Hear, O Israel: The Lord our God is One. Elohim Adonai."

The one soldier who isolates and alienates himself from the rest is Plunkett. His bravado camouflages an underlying cowardice, which becomes evident during critical moments of fighting. Duffy invites a reluctant Plunkett to the midnight mass. The congregational singing attracts the lone wolf, but he does not join in the service. "I came over here to soldier," he contends, "not to pray!"

The chaplain preaches the parable that if a man has a hundred sheep and one goes astray, he seeks it out. And if he finds it, he rejoices even more.

Plunkett proves to be cowardly in battle. Duffy tries to teach him the only way to lick being scared, that only faith and prayer can defeat fears. "Open your heart, ask the Lord to help you." Plunkett refuses and becomes culpable for the death of several comrades. Though he is about to be executed in the morning, a bomb explodes near his containment prison cell and he finds himself able to escape. Yet he stops by the makeshift hospital and sees the courage and calm of Father Duffy. Instead of trying to protect himself, Duffy rescues men as shells explode about them, and calls the wounded to say the Lord's Prayer. After each phrase, "Our Father who art in heaven," the men repeat his words. At one point, just before "deliver us from evil," he sees Plunkett kneel and join in the prayers, and Duffy whispers, "Thank you, Father," rejoicing over one sheep that repents. Plunkett comes to Duffy and confides, still swaggering a bit, "I've just been talking to your boss. I am not afraid anymore." He goes out and proves himself a hero, throwing himself on a grenade to save others.

At the end of the movie, Father Duffy appears on the screen, stoic and calm, with superimpositions of marching soldiers who died, with prayers, not for the World War I soldiers, but for those about to endure and suffer in World War II.

O Heavenly Father, hear, I beseech You, the prayer of men who perished
for an ideal that now has perished too. The old enemy has risen again
to set the world aflame: to challenge You and persecute those who worship Your name. Above the shattering din of war, hear the cry of men
who fight for the right to live in peace with all peoples and to serve You.
Comfort them in their agony. Hearten them in battle. Give them victory.
Crush their enemy forever, so that the world may turn to You again in
everlasting peace with faith and thanksgiving. Amen.

The public response was tremendous. One American Legion troop
wrote Warner Bros. extolling the authenticity of the film, and especially
that final scene. "The other night it was my privilege, as well as pleasure,
to listen to the utterance [sic] of as great a prayer as I believe anyone
ever listened to dealing along those particular lines."[21] The London War
Office commended the film as one that was not at all pacifist and "elimi-
nates the American peace angle."[22]

Another film that honored the commitment to help and not retreat
into isolationism was *The Story of Dr. Wassell* (Cecil B. DeMille, 1944).
An actual Arkansas country doctor, Corydon Wassell chose to become
a medical missionary in China in the years before World War II. Joining
the military when the Japanese invaded Java, he stubbornly chooses to
tend the wounded rather than evacuate. Wassell (Gary Cooper) shows
his grit by sticking to his patients and praying for them during the dark
hours of being bombed: "Our Father who art in heaven, please don't
shovel the dirt in yet—not when they're still alive."

Postwar films reiterated the racial and religious diversity of God's
people fighting in the war. Resigning from RKO and coming to MGM,
producer Dore Schary wanted to make a realistic film on the Battle of the
Bulge in 1948, but Louis B. Mayer didn't want it so blunt, with memories
of the war so vivid. Schary chose William Wellman, a former fighter
pilot, as his director for *Battleground* (1949), to deal with a veteran squad
of GIs of the 101st Airborne Division, "thrown into the maelstrom that
was the German offensive in the Ardennes in December of 1944." One
Jansenist character who dies, Roderigues (Ricardo Montalban), displays
courageous piety and prays silently at a crucifix, telling his comrades
that it was a "good time for prayers." Mortally wounded, he lies con-
cealed under a disabled jeep and mounds of snow. When his comrades

return, however, he has frozen to death. The others remember him as a spiritual man, one who believed that a providential God knew our times. One of his squad notes, "He was a religious guy. Whenever anyone got hit, he said it was God's will." Suggesting a Calvinist predestination in this scene, the film differentiates among various Christian traditions, yet includes them as one religiously united fighting force.

In the film, scriptures and prayers not only serve as a reminder that a soldier is in God's providence, but they function as enemy propaganda. Nazis drop sheets of paper on the soldiers reminding them of the sentimental fact that "people back home are praying for you." Appealing to what was dearest and most sacred—home, God, and prayer—the propaganda leaflets try to depress the morale of the soldiers: "Merry Christmas. Back home they're praying for you. Why not just surrender?" However, as one cheeky American shows when he retires to the makeshift latrines, the leaflets have other purposes.

The chaplain (Leon Ames), with bundled-up frozen feet, sets up his altar with cross and Bible in the field at Bastogne for a Christmas service. Both black and white soldiers gather around him. He tells the troops that he is a Lutheran minister and asks, "How many Lutherans?" He makes it a point to tell them that there are other chaplains. "We holy Joes are switch-hitters." At an interfaith service, the chaplain addresses the soldiers:

Now it's nearly Christmas . . . and here we are in beautiful Bastogne enjoying the winter sports. And the sixty-four-dollar question is: "Was this trip necessary?" I'll try to answer that. But my sermons, like everything else in the army, depend on the situation and the terrain. So I assure you this is going to be a quickie. Was this trip necessary? Let's look at the facts. Nobody wanted this war but the Nazis. A great many people tried to deal with them, and a lot of them are dead. Millions have died . . . for no other reason except that the Nazis wanted them dead. So, in the final showdown, there was nothing left to do except fight. There's a great lesson in this. Those of us who've learned it the hard way aren't going to forget it. We must never again let any force dedicated to a super-race . . . or a super-idea, or super-anything . . . become strong enough to impose itself upon a free world. We must be smart enough and tough enough in the beginning . . . to put out the fire before it starts spreading. My answer to the sixty-four-dollar question is yes, this trip was necessary. . . . And now, Jerry permitting, let us pray for this fog to lift.

As he begins to pray for the fog to lift, the artillery drowns him out, so he quickly concludes, "The organist is hitting those bass notes a little too loud for me to be heard. So let each of us pray in his own way, to his own God." Many kneel; all heads bow. What is remarkable about this scene is that the chaplain recognizes that his unit, like America itself, is composed of diverse religious traditions. Secondly, he concedes to this diversity by uttering an acceptably generic prayer.

Formerly a master sergeant in the 35th Division, Robert Pirosh crafted the screenplay that won an Academy Award for writing about the beleaguered 101st. The remarkably literate script still captured the patois and slang of the soldiers, but added a sacred poetry to it all. In particular, he repeated the refrain from Isaiah 40, "They shall mount up with wings as eagles; they shall run and not be weary," as a unifying theme. The scripture's function in the film ranged from cynicism to genuine hope. When the fog finally lifts, and rescue planes arrive with fanfare, parachuting in supplies and reinforcements, an exultation of the verses rings out and the men rise with wings of eagles.

Prayers in war films reflected both the needs and hopes of ordinary fighting troops. They show that there were no atheists in 1940s foxholes and that chaplains were ubiquitous. My own father, Assemblies of God Chaplain John Lindvall, served with the 36th Infantry Division in May 1945. He told stories of prayers and God's providential answers to prayers. The films caught that reality.

Years of war seemed unending in the early to mid-1940s, with prayers seeking to combat evil and bring comfort. But deliverance came. The war ended and America prospered.

By the end of the 1940s, America was ready to teach its baby boom generation how to pray. In a remake of *Little Miss Marker* (1934), Bob Hope stars as the title character in *Sorrowful Jones* (Sidney Lanfield, 1949). A selfish and cheap bookie, "Sorrowful" Jones gets stuck with a five-year-old girl (Mary Jane Saunders) as a marker from a bad racetrack bet. After her father is killed by gangsters, Jones reluctantly adopts the tyke and tries to care for her.

Trying to teach her how to speak "right," Jones suggests that she might not know who is listening. She responds with a question: "Do you mean God?" Jones thinks and says, "Yeah." But she explains that when her "Mommy went away," her Daddy had told her that there was nobody named God. Jones counters that what her Dad said just wasn't right. "I mean there is somebody named God."

"Did you ever see Him?"

"Well, He doesn't hang around horse rooms very much, but if you ever want anything and you can't procure it for yourself, you just ask God. Often as not, He comes through."

"Do you write Him letters like you do Santa Claus?"

"That's where praying comes in; you save three cents."

"Then show me how to pray, please."

Sorrowful tells her to sleep, but she wants to ask for something. "I never knew a dame who didn't. Okay, get outta bed. Don't tell anybody about this. You see, I don't want it to get around. Now kneel down, put your hands together like this [he folds his hands straight up] and shut your eyes."

Asked who made the rules for praying, Jones answers, "While the Race Commission makes the rules at the track, I guess there must be a praying commission someplace." He teaches Mary Jane to repeat his words from the New England Primer, "Now I lay me down to sleep."

She repeats after him, concluding with, "And God bless Sorrowful, Gladys, Regret, and everybody." Then the tyke adds her own prayer, "Please, dear God, buy Mr. Sorrowful a new suit." Jones whispers an addendum: "With two pair of pants, please."

The ironic lesson of teaching a child to pray after her father had been murdered by mobsters seemed to parallel the lives of children left as orphans after the war. Yet it also served as a harbinger of better times and answers to prayers; it augured hope (and prosperity with two pairs of pants). But other questions arose: How would the church explain unanswered prayers after so many of its children had been slaughtered by monsters? The 1950s would raise modern problems regarding faith and prayers. The war decade had seen America move past isolationist barriers to enter into global conflict, not without first invoking America's blessedness and the necessity of struggle against evil. Likewise, Hollywood moved past its reticence on spiritual matters as its characters openly invoked divine help.

The prayers of the movies reflected the gamut of human experience in wartime and the active role of churches in calling men to arms and preparing for loss. Cinematic prayers bolstered courage, recognized the presence of sin in the human collective, called for resistance to evil, ministered to anxious audiences, investigated faith and questioned prayers' efficacy. Through it all, they identified God at work in the shadows, and Divine Providence offered the only hope one could find. Toward the end of the decade, postwar audiences were unsurprised to hear genuine prayers on screen. Invocations from Hollywood's next era would sound altogether different.

4

Postwar Secular Prayers (1946–1963)

After patriotism and piety came lust in the dust. The postwar era brought boys back who had seen death, but now had more on their minds. Even in the era of biblical epics and spectacular historical dramas, sex entered the cinema in both direct and indirect ways. Henry King's *David and Bathsheba* (1951) and Cecil DeMille's *Ten Commandments* (1956) dressed sirens in seductive clothing that would draw voyeurs into the movie houses. Religion and sex would become strange and cozy bedfellows during this period of reentry into a semi-normalcy, if such a state ever existed. Biblical epics and religious movies dominated the cinemascope screens during the decade, from the 3-D *The Robe* to Stevens's "longest story ever told."[1]

As young families settled down and the baby boom got underway, churches experienced exponential growth for the next two decades. The economy flourished and suburbia sprouted. Prosperity and creeping materialism spread into religious enterprises and across the social landscape, except among the poor and racially segregated neighborhoods. Rumblings of future tensions were sowed in the American civic soil. There would be "hard times in Paradise" soon.

The disquiet of this time of reconstructing the world percolated with the crises of the impending Cold War, the superpower United States and its allies face-to-face with the Soviet bloc, and a simmering China on the back burner. As American industries sparked an unprecedented economic and technological growth, old imperial forces would decolonize, and independent states, from India to Israel, would emerge. The hegemony of Christianity would give way to a resurgence of other religious traditions, such as Hinduism and Buddhism. The European church would decline with the rise of existential questions and skepticism about all forms of authority. Only in America did Protestantism reign as a cultural force, with church attendance reaching a new high, followed by a revival of evangelical Christianity, all challenged in the

1960s by the social upheavals of divorce, legalized abortion, recreational drugs, civil rights issues, and plummeting rates of churchgoing. By the end of this era, however, Pope John XXIII and Vatican II would revivify a stagnant church and set an agenda for Roman Catholic worker-priests, laity movements, and even the American presidency.

Various issues regarding the government and religion erupted. Should the government keep prayers out of public schools? In *The Restructuring of American Religion*, sociologist Robert Wuthnow noted how polls measuring the political and cultural climate of the country portended uneasy change. Groups campaigning for a ban on prayer and Bible reading in public schools, such as the National League for Separation of Church and State (1946) and Americans United for Separation of Church and State (1947), emerged with evangelical fervor against evangelicals.

Gallup polls taken since the 1930s asked questions about church attendance, finding that about a third of adults claimed to have attended services in any given week. Fledgling National Opinion Research Center studies began in 1946. Shortly after World War II, a study found that 90 percent of the public engaged in prayer (with 86 percent regarding the Bible as the divinely inspired word of God).[2] Will Herberg's book *Protestant-Catholic-Jew* suggested that the level of commitment was somewhat more complex than poll results indicated, hinting that polls captured what was fashionable more than they did conviction.[3] Weekly prayer meetings and other catechumenal sessions, such as the class meetings of the Methodists, persisted, but then declined at the end of the decade.

During this decade, as Wuthnow emphasizes, everyone, especially those in the Protestant, Roman Catholic, and Jewish traditions, knew how to pray; bedtime prayers, thanksgiving at meals, devotional readings, social function formalities, and church liturgy piled prayer upon prayer. Prayers were a habit of the heart; however, as many prayers, such as the Lord's Prayer, were memorized, they began to take on a formulaic or rote performance. Generic rather than Catholic Christianity would dominate as religion in the public square took on a less distinctive character. All denominations started to look alike, especially to outsiders.

For mainline Protestants in the public square, it was, as scholar Bill Romanowski pointed out convincingly, a time for reform. Concerned that a Roman Catholic mafia unduly influenced Hollywood, many Prot-

POSTWAR SECULAR PRAYERS (1946–1963) | 99

estant leaders sought to dialogue with filmmakers to make a positive impact on the content of movies. Ironically, the "honest" movies that emerged reflected more of an existential crisis than any doctrinal reaffirmation. Movies began to ask questions about the purpose and meaning of life, even the religious life. Graham Greene's 1940 novel *The Power and the Glory*, about a deeply flawed whiskey priest hiding out in Mexico, would be adapted for the 1947 John Ford movie, *The Fugitive*.[4]

Sex and religion were only two concerns as hardened troops returned from the war and the heinous crimes of the Holocaust were uncovered; liberal theology underwent its own reassessment. Human nature did not seem as good as progressives had espoused. The reality of sin had erupted on personal, institutional, and national fronts, and those who struggled to reevaluate their personal identity and meaning sought some stabilizing force. Man was immoral, and society was more immoral.

The quest for understanding justice and hope in the bleak postwar world opened floodgates of provocative films, many from Swedish director Ingmar Bergman and other Continental directors. Some, like the French film *Monsieur Vincent* (Clauche, 1947), a story about the founder of the Congregation of the Priests of the Mission, looked to religion for positive answers. In a bombed-out Europe, the Marshall Plan imitated Vincent's mission to evangelize the poor, saving lives first, and then souls. Even Hollywood tinkered with larger questions about race and anti-Semitism. One way was to shout religion, and the 1950s experienced a flood of biblical epics, both to attract new family audiences and to compete with the emergence of the small screen of television.

American attitudes leaned in several directions. The predominant theme among the masses became materialism, the rise of consumerism paralleling a postwar boom in inventions, products, and the pursuit of *viele Dinge* (many things). Secondly, an uncertainty about the fate of the world and the individual loomed ominously. The Cold War and its paranoia would seep into elementary school classrooms, where "duck and cover" exercises were façades of protection against the bomb. In theological circles, religious doubts would culminate in the Death of God movement. In contrast, the hypnotic integration of religion and pop psychology arose with the publication of Norman Vincent Peale's bestselling *The Power of Positive Thinking* (1952), reiterating the mantra-like prayer "Every day, in every way, I am getting better and better." In this self-affirming philosophy, God became a sort of master psychiatrist, eventually leading to a "gospel of prosperity."

Preceding Peale's affirmation of the self's aseity, *The Razor's Edge* (Edmund Goulding, 1946) charts the journey of wealthy loafer Larry Darrell (Tyrone Power). After experiencing the trauma of death in World War I, he leaves his fiancée, Isabel (Gene Tierney), to search for peace and meaning. What he discovers is something akin to Peale's auto-hypnotism.

His quest is to find whether "there is any sense to life, or is it a stupid blunder?" When Darrell meets a defrocked priest working in a coal mine, he discovers that the priest is running from God, having felt that the Lord hounded him with judgment and was going to place His "terrible hand on my shoulder." He didn't mind facing punishment, but couldn't face God's mercy. The apostate priest directs Darrell, "a very religious man who didn't believe in God," to a mystic in India.

The old guru tells him that peace and happiness come from within oneself.[5]

> The road to self is difficult to pass over—as hard to pass through as the sharp edge of a razor. All religions teach that there is a spark of infinite goodness from the Creator in every man, and that one joins the infinite in death. We Indians believe there are three roads that lead to God: the path of faith and worship; good works performed for love of God; the path that leads through knowledge to wisdom.

Darrell is told that all paths are one. Enlightened from his mountaintop experience and armed with snow-capped platitudes, Darrell returns home and uses hypnotic suggestion to help his friends. It is the power of positive thinking that may save humanity.

In stark contrast, the Southern Baptist evangelist Billy Graham called for millions to repent during his worldwide crusades. Through indoor and outdoor integrated public meetings, utilizing the media of radio, film, and television, his evangelistic preaching called for men and women to "accept Jesus as their personal Savior." Significantly, by 1953 in cities like Chattanooga, Tennessee, he would tear down ropes that segregated his audiences and invite Martin Luther King Jr. to share his pulpit in rallies.

Prayer *Noir*

In the postwar era, gritty war films turned into gritty street dramas. The total depravity of man seemed much more attuned to the postwar realities. A genre that acknowledged the mean streets and shadows of the human heart crept onto the scene as *film noir*.

When the kind Father George Lambert (Wyrley Birch) is killed on a street corner in *Boomerang* (Elia Kazan, 1947), the film's narrator tells us that his everyday work was with ordinary people of his parish, "and especially with those who sought his advice and counsel. Since he was a man of God, his labors sometimes led him into the sinister secret places of men's souls. He was just and forgiving, but he was also a man, and a stern and uncompromising judge of character." One such character he meets is the emotionally sick Jim Crossman (Philip Coolidge). An anguished Crossman debates with the priest in a spiritual struggle.

Father Lambert tells him, "Even if I wanted to forgive you, I . . . I couldn't. It's out of my hands." Crossman cannot be forgiven until he confesses to his mother. After Crossman kills Lambert, prayers are given at the priest's wake:

> Grant that Thy servant priest, George, dwelling in this world with holy gifts, may even rejoice with glory in Thy heavenly mansion. We beseech Thee, grant that we may also be joined with them in perpetual fellowship so Jesus Christ our Lord, who with Thee and the Holy Ghost, lives one God without end. Amen. Have compassion and *forgive this* . . .

The police have been watching those who come to view the body. As the words *"forgive this"* are said, Crossman appears beside the casket. The film raised dilemmas of justice versus mercy for churches that sought to understand how to deal with those who kill and are unrepentant.

Invalid hotel owner James Temple (Lionel Barrymore) calls down judgment upon the notorious gangster Johnny Rocco (Edward G. Robinson) and his sadistic crew in *Key Largo* (John Huston, 1948). Following a model of an imprecatory psalm, Temple invokes the curse of a hurricane on his enemies: "Make the big wave! Send it crashing down on us. Destroy us all, if need be, but *punish* him."

In the bleak *film noir Detective Story* (William Wyler, 1951), a tough, legalistic, and vindictive detective, Jim MacLeod (Kirk Douglas), collars criminals and has a particularly aggressive press on one abortionist, Schneider, whom he wants to fall on like "the sword of God." When he discovers late in the film that his wife, Mary (Eleanor Parker), had an abortion with Schneider before they had met, he comes unglued, even suicidal. MacLeod laments, "I'd give my soul to take out my brain, hold it under the faucet and wash away the dirty pictures you put there tonight."

He sacrifices his life in "the line of duty." As he dies, he forgives a petty embezzler and cries out an act of contrition, especially for his wife to forgive him, "In the name of the Father, Son, and Holy Ghost. O my God, I am heartily sorry for having offended Thee, and I detest all my sins, because I dread the loss of heaven and the pains of hell . . ." He is unable to finish. MacLeod's partner of many years, Detective Lou Brody (William Bendix), finishes the prayer for him: "but most of all for having offended Thee, my Lord, who is all good and deserving of my love. I resolve, with Thy grace, to confess my sins, to do penance and to amend my life. Amen." As in Hitchcock's *Lifeboat*, the act of finishing another's prayer suggests a sharing in the sufferings of others, a human connection beyond death. Again, the issues of contrition and grace haunt the screen.

In Graham Greene's black comedy *Our Man in Havana* (Carol Reed, 1959), Milly Wormold (Jo Morrow), the pampered daughter of a vacuum salesman, Jim Wormold (Alec Guinness), prays for her mother to become a good Catholic again (but not come back to them). Her self-centered prayers concentrate on getting a white horse and being able to join the country club. "Isn't it wonderful how all our prayers are answered?" she asks her father, who acquiesces to becoming an international spy to fund her wishes.

One of the most ironic moments in the film juxtaposes the funeral services of two men. A foreign agent murders Wormold's friend, German doctor Carl Hasselbacher (Burl Ives). This assassin is then shot by Wormold. The two funerals are conducted within earshot of each other. At the first, the priest prays, "Forasmuch as the spirit of the departed has entered the life immortal, we therefore commit the body of this our brother Carl Hasselbacher . . ." Twenty feet away, we hear another priest saying, "Receive into Thy merciful hands, O Lord, the soul of this, Thy servant Hubert Carter [as the chief of police ironically plays with a letter of deportation for the departed]. Grant him an entrance into the land of light and glory."

Back at Hasselbacher's casket, topped by his German helmet, we hear, "Father, into Thy hands I commit his spirit." The murderer and the murdered end up together in paradise. The bells toll for all. Writing about forgiveness in his *Mere Christianity*, C. S. Lewis reflected on his World War I experiences and wondered whether, if some young German Christian and he had simultaneously killed one another, the moment after their death would showcase the irony that neither of them "would have felt resentment or even any embarrassment. I think we might have laughed over it."[6] The fact that God forgives one's enemies, even one's murderer, complicated the easy morality of some church teachings. However, these darker films paralleled the rise of neo-orthodoxy that took sin seriously. Liberalism's naïve faith in the nobility of human nature was a direct casualty of the war.

Sinners in Need of Prayer

Certain truths stuck out as veterans came back from the war. First, things were not the same. Second, challenges arose with shell-shocked vets and independent Rosie-the-Riveter women. Sexual tensions seethed as the period of readjustment confronted the traumatic plight of men, with unemployment and alcoholism appearing in films like William Wyler's 1947 Academy Award–winning *The Best Years of Our Lives*. Suffering from post-traumatic stress disorder and having lost both his hands, Harold Russell won the Oscar for best supporting actor, where he poignantly conveyed the power of prayer in dealing with his disability and with his war experience.[7]

Many postwar films inserted prayers more forcibly into their narratives. The theme of broken men and desires shaped two prayers in King Vidor's sprawling epic *Duel in the Sun* (1946). Preacher Sinkiller (Walter Huston) prays with gusto over the sultry half-breed convert Pearl Chavez (Jennifer Jones) in this cinematic Cain and Abel story. With the friendly Laura Belle McCanles (Lillian Gish) looking on, Sinkiller lays one hand on Pearl's head and lifts his other:

"Yessiree Bob, you gotta sweeten yourself with prayer. Pray in the sweat. You'll save yourself eternal hellfire. Understand that?" "Yessir!" "Then on your knees."

Pearl gets on her knees, clasps her hands, and bows her head. The preacher places his mighty hand on her and booms forth: "I'm going to start to quote salvation. O Lord, look upon this Thy creature. She is a weak vessel as Thou knowest, but she wants to be Thy handmaiden. Give her horse sense not to go wandering off in the doolies with worthless cowpokes. Amen. Amen."

Pearl looks up in wonder. Laura Belle adds, "Amen."

Putting his hand under her chin and looking her sumptuous features up and down in her skimpy outfit, he realizes he hasn't prayed enough. "It won't get you into heaven, but it will comfort you on your way there. That is, if you use it right. Say, La, don't you think we oughta be saying a few words of prayer for them worthless cowpokes? I have a feeling they will be needing consolation." Laura Belle quietly folds her hands.

"On your knees again," he orders Pearl. "O Lord, have mercy on all men, young and old alike, who gaze upon *this*, Thy regained servant. Amen." In its own droll way, the film brought to the forefront an issue confronting the temptations of the flesh. Sin-killing churches would soon have to deal with Hugh Hefner's publication of *Playboy* in 1953, with a nude Marilyn Monroe adorning its cover.

In *Madame Bovary* (Vincente Minnelli, 1949), the provincial eponymous adulteress Bovary (Jennifer Jones) is dying (from suicide), and her husband (Van Heflin) stands by idly, unable to do anything. The priest (Vernon Steele) gives her last unction.

Prosecuted for obscenity, *Bovary* author Gustave Flaubert defended the book as a moral warning. One obvious lesson targeted the bored and foolish bourgeois, Emma Bovary herself. She was always busy reading novels, usually bad books that mocked religion (often borrowing phrases from Voltaire). Yet, in spite of her proclivities to mere amusement, she is warned, "But all that leads you far astray, my poor child. Anyone who has no religion always ends by turning out badly."

Life does turn out tragically for Emma, even as the secular chemist sprinkles disinfectant over her dead body and the priest Bournisien prays and sprinkles holy water in the last rites. As she is dying, the white-frocked priest administers the final sacrament: "Through this holy unction and through His divine mercy, may the Lord pardon all the sins you have committed through the sense of hearing. Amen." He proceeds to ask pardon for sins committed through the senses of sight, taste, speech, and touch, covering just about everything except spiritual sins.

The priest folds her hands over her breast and puts the cross at her lips; she kisses it and expires. Her husband, teary-eyed and cuckolded, hears the last words: "And so it was, a woman had been born into this world and died." Her only good work is that she touched other lives. Flaubert defended her life as "true," however offensive and inconvenient it may have been. The courts acquitted him. Conservative churches were not as lenient.

Rather than the previous liturgy of prayer, an impassioned prayer of repentance reveals more anguish in director Robert Siodmak's 1949 *The Great Sinner*, adapted from Dostoyevsky's short novel *The Gambler*. Fedja's (Gregory Peck) whole story is a prayer confession. A writer on his way to Paris, Fedja is seduced into staying at Wiesbaden, a luxurious health spa and gambling casino, by a card-playing beauty, Pauline Ostrovsky (Ava Gardner). During his stay, he befriends an old compulsive gambler, who eventually commits suicide. At his memorial service, attended only by a few, the priest faces the altar in pre-Vatican II ritual, and speaks Latin prayers.

After becoming addicted himself, Fedja loses all his money, stumbles to a chapel, and prays desperately for divine help, even as he is tempted to rob a church poor box to feed his compulsion. The relationship of prayer to addiction explodes with fierce passions. Lighting a votive candle to mitigate his guilt, a scruffy-bearded Fedja prays, "Glory be to God Almighty, hear me; You know me as I am, a sinner full of hate and darkness. It's myself I hate above all—don't let me listen to them. Give me strength. Help me. Where there is pity, where there is hate, give me love; where there is darkness, give me light. Save me. Save me from the devil within me."

As people put coins into the church poor box, he tries to close his ears in anguish. Hearing the sound of money, he grovels in the shadows and moans, even while eying the church coffers and being tempted to steal the money. Then an un-embodied voice speaks: "And they divided my garments among them and they cast dice for my robe." Realizing the greed of those who crucified Christ, he kneels and resists vigorously, assuming a cruciform position before a giant crucifix. With light shining down on him, he kneels as a true penitent to the crucified Christ.

As the choir ends its singing, he receives grace and cries, "Hallelujah, hallelujah, the song of choir tells me my prayer is answered."

The film ends with Fedja's lover, Pauline, reading his manuscript, *Confessions of a Sinner*, which he hoped would pay his debts on earth, with the addendum that "I only hope that one day she may read this book and forgive, as this isn't the last chapter." In 1946, three years before the release of the film, the Jewish gangster Bugsy Siegel brought in organized crime to build the high-class casino the Flamingo. It would open the floodgates for a new sin for churches to combat.

In Robert Siodmak's *The Killers* (1946), a *film noir* adaptation of Hemingway's short story, the funeral of the "Swede" (Burt Lancaster) initiates an investigation into his murder by professional killers. The story of a good man unfolds through flashbacks involving *femme fatale* Kitty Collins (Ava Gardner), a beautiful double-crossing dame.

At the graveside burying the innocent Ole "Swede" Anderson, the priest (played by the famous pastor of Hollywood, Neal Dodd) stands under an umbrella beside the wreathed grave. "All that the Father giveth me," he prays, "shall come to me, and him that cometh to me will I in no wise cast out. He that raiseth up Jesus from the dead will also quicken our mortal bodies by His Spirit that dwelleth in us."

At this point, Jim Reardon (Edmond O'Brien) whispers to another insurance agent and cop about trying to "find out who killed Ole." They notice a man with a derby, possibly a manager, trainer, or simply an old-time hoodlum, standing by the cross.

The minister commends his soul to God and his body to the ground, reminding all that in God's "right hand are pleasures forever more." For a nice guy who trusted in a faithless, duplicitous woman, only the joys of heaven can offer comfort. Prayers point to the only secure and trustworthy person.

The forgiveness of sin permeates *Bedevilled* (Mitchell Leisen, 1956), in which seminarian candidate Gregory Fitzgerald (Steve Forrest) performs an act of mercy for an American lounge singer, Monica (Anne Baxter), who has murdered a man. Trying to elude his revenge-motivated relatives, they escape into a church, where a Parisian Roman Catholic congregation recites the liturgy. As the killers close in, the seminarian prays

POSTWAR SECULAR PRAYERS (1946–1963) | 107

and finds refuge for the two expatriates. In an exchange that sounds almost like a catechism, Monica asks Fitzgerald what is sin ("the willful breaking of the law of God"), how is one forgiven of sin ("but must do penance"), and other theological questions. Realizing how she has compromised him, she slips into the night, where she is shot.

As she lies mortally wounded, he comes and she cries, "Help me!" He begins, "O my God, I am heartily sorry for having offended Thee." She ekes out a phrase of being sorry. "I detest all my sins, because I dread the loss of heaven and the pains of hell, but most of all because they offend Thee, my God, deserving of all my love." "I detest," she murmurs. He concludes, "I firmly resolve with the help of Thy grace to confess my sins, do penance, and amend my life." "Amend my life," she whimpers, and as he says, "Amen," she dies in his arms.

The film closes with a priest teaching his seminarians, "What does it mean to be a priest?" Part of the answer is to "share all suffering, heal all wounds, teach, pardon and bless always." The film has done just that.

Ernest Hemingway's *Snows of Kilimanjaro* (Henry King, 1952) showcases severely wounded writer Harry Street (Gregory Peck) as he reviews in flashbacks the disappointments, sorrows, and triumphs of his professionally successful but spiritually bankrupt life and loves. Lying in delirium and fearful he is going to die, he rues losing his first beloved wife, Cynthia Green (Ava Gardner), a nurse riding in a medical jeep that is bombed in the midst of a raging battle. Trapped under the ambulance, she prays, "Blessed Mary, Mother of God, Blessed Mary, Mother of God, oh please let Harry find me. In Thy great bleeding heart, please find room for my prayer."

Harry immediately stumbles upon her and calls her name; she weeps. "O God!" "You're hurt," he says, "you're very hurt," and embraces her bleeding body. As he shouts desperately for a stretcher, she laments about their miscarried child, confessing that God would punish her for his death. As she is carried away on the stretcher, he tries to retreat from the battle to be with her. One of his own officers shoots him in the leg and he fails to reach her. Ironically, God had answered her prayer to see Harry one more time, but she dies on the stretcher, out of reach of her wounded husband.

When Harry finds a snow leopard frozen at eighteen thousand feet on Kilimanjaro, he asks what the animal sought at such an altitude.

Here is the parable of his (and perhaps Hemingway's) life, of why his own perverse curiosity for story material has led to his own impending death. His wife, Helen (Susan Hayward), attends to him throughout his feverish rantings. When a "witch doctor" arrives and uses divination to diagnose Harry's ailment, Helen decides to lance the very large swelling on his leg and prays, "God help us!" After a night of watching, a hyena sniffs his blood, but is chased away by Helen's screams. Helen then kneels beside the bed, clasps her hands in prayer, and looks heavenward. By morning, a second prayer is answered, this one for the life of her husband and the unexpected arrival of a heaven-sent plane. The dozens of filthy vultures in the tree awaiting Harry's demise remain hungry. God's answer of Helen's prayers has robbed them of a meal.

Crashing in a South American jungle, jaded pilot Bill Lonagan (Robert Ryan) must choose which five people out of eleven can fit on the limited space on his plane in *Back from Eternity* (John Farrow, 1956). Cannibals, wild animals, and other dangers threaten the group. However, when some sharp shooting lands them a healthy supper around the campfire, little Tommy Malone (Jon Provost) suggests a prayer before eating. All look on wearily, but retired professor Henry Spanger and Tommy lead the others in reciting an emotional rendition of the Lord's Prayer.

Everyone joins in except for a condemned criminal, Vasquel (Rod Steiger), who wanders to the edge of the group but listens intently. He later assumes the role of God, determining who will stay and who will go. He chooses to stay behind with an elderly couple who volunteer, restoring his faith in humanity. He murders them to spare them the horror of approaching headhunters, praying for forgiveness and awaiting his death. At the point of death, sinners need prayers.

For Alfred Hitchcock, all men and women were guilty, even the seemingly innocent ones. In his *The Wrong Man* (1956), Manny Balestrero (Henry Fonda), falsely accused of a crime (and without Miranda rights), kneels, fingers intertwined and eyes closed. His mother asks, "Manny, have you prayed?" "Yes." "What did you pray for?" "I prayed for help." "Pray for strength, Manny!"

Manny's faith wavers: "I don't see how anything can help, if I don't get some luck. Somebody committed those holdups. Where is he? Maybe in jail already for some other crime in some other state. He'll never be suspected for anything he committed in our neighborhood."

His mother persists: "My son, I beg you to pray."

"Gotta go to work," he says resignedly. His mother sobs, as he puts on his shirt; but then as he gazes on a poster showing the Sacred Heart of Jesus, he begins to mouth his prayers. The scene dissolves to show the true criminal superimposed and coming into focus, just as he is about to be caught. Hitchcock's tight editing answers the prayer immediately. Hitchcock confided,

> If there is one thing I'll never be able to do, it's turn my collar back to front and play the part of the preacher. When people ask me what I think of movies that administer philosophic and moral lessons, I say, "don't you think it's up to philosophers to teach philosophy and priests to teach morals?" People don't go to the movies to listen to sermons. If that were the case then instead of buying a ticket they'd put a coin in the collection plate and make the sign of the cross before taking a seat in the stalls. People go to the movies to be amused. And they pay a lot to be amused. Morality, you know is much less expensive than amusement.

Hitchcock did acknowledge that his characters typically became embroiled in conflict with the "Devil" and could only "escape through avowal, through confession . . . and attrition"—that is, death. "[Maybe] there is a search for God [in my films], . . . but it is unconscious."[8] What Hitchcock revealed through his characters' prayers was the universal sense of guilt, with a need for redemption. Such a state of sinfulness would be addressed in the mid-1950s by the emergence of Protestant evangelist Billy Graham, who would call audiences convicted of the presence of sin in their lives to confess a prayer of repentance, a "Sinner's Prayer" for salvation.

In *Lust for Life* (Vincente Minnelli, 1956), Vincent van Gogh (Kirk Douglas) doesn't believe in the god of the clergymen, but cannot escape the mandate of the Gospel to help others. In his early ventures to be a minister, he fails in a mission to coal miners. He prays in his church, but people turn away.

"Father," he asks, "we pray Thee to keep us from evil and despair. Feed us with the bread that does not perish, which is Thy word, O Lord. Amen." But his prayer does not provide bread for the poor families. Seeking simplicity and meekness of heart, he grows discouraged. By the end of his tortured way, he discovers that he can only say "what I'm feeling: I do believe in a God of love," resigned to serve God not through the pulpit or books, but through painting.

Men and women returning from the war had seen horrors that haunted them. Such shock over the human capacity for evil disturbed the psyche of a nation, and cinematic prayers reflected the dismay and despair many had experienced. These prayers reminded the church that sin had not been extinguished by a world war. Hearts of darkness persisted, with sins of cruelty, sexual immorality, and gambling escalating. It was a battle that religious communities were just beginning to fight, a fight against evil in their own hearts.

Global Prayers

With the Marshall Plan enacted and America emerging as a superpower to combat communism, missionaries spread across the globe, making the world their parish. Yet their expansion into new and often exotic territories was accompanied by crises of faith. Attuned to America's increased global interaction with other nations and religions, films reflected the bewilderment that modern Christians experienced when relating to other cultures. In *Black Narcissus* (Michael Powell, E. Pressburger, 1947), Roman Catholic nuns wrestle against vestigial pagan elements in a Buddhist culture. Instead of getting a gaggle of concubines at his "house of women," an old general tells Angu Ayah that the women "are not coming for fun. These are nuns. Do you know what a nun is?" To which Ayah replies disdainfully, "They kneel and pray all day like the monks you invited last year." The repressed sexual memories of one nun lead to madness, regardless of fervent prayers. When Sister Clodagh (Deborah Kerr) confesses that she doesn't know what to do, the agnostic Mr. Dean (who is "objectionable when sober and abominable when drunk") retorts, "What would Christ have done?" It was a question for global missions as well as film narratives.

Roman Catholicism dominated these final decades of the Production Code, due in part to the presence of Roman Catholic censor Joseph Breen. Of course, many directors had been raised in Roman Catholic homes and were, as Flannery O'Connor was to put it, "haunted by

Christ." In Alfred Hitchcock's *I Confess* (1953), the director did seek information on a variety of topics: the attire of priests (do they wear cassocks on the streets of Quebec?), the stations of the cross, the burning of votive candles throughout the night, and the procedures of defrocking and unfrocking a priest.

Moments of authentic melodrama haunt *The Nun's Story* (Fred Zinnemann, 1959), based on Robert Anderson's screenplay about the testing of Belgian nun Sister Luke (Audrey Hepburn), who encounters the sardonic Dr. Fortunati (Peter Finch) in a Belgian Congo medical mission. The film opens declaring the kind of sacrifice each is called to make, that "he that shall lose his life for me shall find it. If thou wilt be perfect, go and sell what thou hast and give it to the poor and come follow me."

Sister Luke's vocation obliges her to attend to the needs of her fellow sisters and practice humility in a life of sacrifice. She must learn strict obedience to the bells, which represent the voice of God, an act pointing to her struggle with obedience itself. Thinking that she would reach a "resting place where obedience would be natural," she finally comes to realize her duty in offering help to the Belgian underground against the Nazis. She kneels in prayer, asking, "Dear Lord, forgive me. I cannot obey anymore. What I do from now on is between You and me alone." Christians on foreign soil sought to do what Christ would have done.

A fraudulent Jim Carmody (Humphrey Bogart) disguises himself as Father O'Shea in *The Left Hand of God* (Edward Dmytryk, 1955). As a Max Beerbohm "happy hypocrite," Carmody is transformed while pretending to be a clergyman, similar to Griffith's silent film *The Converts*. As he arrives at a remote mission in China in 1947, threatened by the warlord Mieh Yang (Lee J. Cobb), an elderly Chinese man is dying, waiting for the new priest.

Nurse Anne "Scotty" Scott (Gene Tierney) suggests that O'Shea pray. Jim mutters the Lord's Prayer and a Hail Mary over the dead man. Scotty kneels in devotion while the doctor and his wife look on suspiciously. When the eldest man in the village comes for a blessing, Jim lays his hand upon his head, but then kneels before him and says, "I too seek a blessing." Called to preach to the villagers, Jim finds a book of sermons. After reading I Peter 2:11–19 to them in English (many falling asleep), he begins just to talk to them in Chinese. They wake and smile. Later, he walks into the dark chapel alone, looks up and talks to God:

> Here I am, Lord. I'm not going to pray. What I'd like to say I'd like to say standing on my feet. These people think I'm a priest. I had nothing to of-fer but faith in a God I didn't believe in or think existed. It doesn't matter now whether I was right or wrong in what I did. . . . There's nothing left to do but square the account a little. Well, that's just about how it stands. I wanted You to know.

"Father" O'Shea ends up playing dice with Mieh Yang for the lives of the villagers versus his servitude, citing the Crucifixion, when the sol-diers parted Jesus's garment and cast die for them. When the warlord throws three sixes, he jokes, "Father, Son, and Holy Ghost." O'Shea throws four threes and quips, "You shouldn't have invoked the Trinity." At the end, even the left-hand instrument of God recognizes that "God's trap is bigger to get out of than Yang's." As poet George Herbert once quipped, there are divine traps everywhere, "Bibles laid open, millions of surprises, fine nets and stratagems," so that even a hypocrite can be redeemed by grace.

Religion permeates Leo Tolstoy's epic *War and Peace*, adapted into a sprawling but plodding film by King Vidor (1956). Count Pierre Be-zukhov (Henry Fonda), an intellectual observer of the war, acknowl-edges that "I have sinned, Lord, but I have several excellent excuses." He paraphrases the Apostle Paul's internal conflict of Roman 7 when he confesses,

> If my headache is bad enough, I say, "Pierre, today you must take steps to become a saint." I want to discover why I know what's right and still do wrong. I want to discover what happiness is and what value there is in suffering. I want to discover why men go to war and what they say deep in their hearts when they pray to God. I want to discover what it is that men and women feel when they say they love.

When Pierre goes into a cathedral, a red-bearded Russian Orthodox priest leads the desperate congregation in a plea for victory as "Moses's victory over Amelecks, Gideon's over Midian, David's over Goliath.

Smite down our enemies and destroy them swiftly beneath the feet of Thy faithful servants. Confound and put to shame those who have devised evil against us. May they be, before the faces of Thy warriors, as dust before the wind."

Pierre's friend Andrei explains that "war is the vilest thing in the world. . . . [Men] come together to kill each other, they slaughter and maim tens of thousands . . . and then they say prayers of thanksgiving for having slaughtered so many people. . . . How does God look down and listen to them?" As religious Americans prayed for the destruction of the Soviets, this adaptation of Russian history offers the irony of boomerang prayers, quietly reprimanding those who have forgotten to love their enemies.

On their way to spend their imprisonment working at a children's leper hospital, three convicts are detoured when their plane stops on another Pacific island. The crusty, hard-drinking, white-haired priest Father Doonan (Spencer Tracy) in *The Devil at Four o'Clock* (Mervyn LeRoy, 1961) tries to persuade them to redeem their lives and rescue the children from an erupting volcano. To make it more enticing, the governor promises to consider commuting their sentences. Doonan looks at one of the hardened convicts, Harry (Frank Sinatra), and quips, "I'll bet you were a sweet little altar boy." To which Harry retorts, "Weren't we all?"

An old proverb suggests that "it's hard for a man to be brave when you know you're going to meet the devil at 4 o'clock." Facing death, the thief Charlie (Bernie Hamilton) tells the priest that his mother used to say "it's never too late" to change. Doonan tells him, "She was right. She kept after me—kept tellin' me—there was another thief once dyin' on the cross, right next to Christ."

"The Good Thief," responds the Father. "He didn't chicken out. He just got smart and at the very last moment, he stole heaven."

"That's pretty good stealin', huh?"

Charlie will sacrifice his life trying to hold up a bridge enabling the children to cross to safety during the evacuation. Father Doonan stays behind with him, hearing Charlie's confession and offering last rites just as the volcano erupts and covers them with lava.

Kneeling before a giant rock, Harry prays, "O my God, we are most heartily sorry for offending Thee, and we detest all of our sins because we dread the loss of living and the pains of hell"—here he heaves, groans deeply, with eyes longingly looking heavenward, and continues—"but most of all, because they offend Thee." The redemptive elements of the film bring the altar boys home to their faith. Even wandering in foreign lands, prodigal sons can find their way home.

In 1961 the International Missionary Council would become the Division of World Mission and Evangelism of the World Council of Churches (WCC). As numerous churches sent their missionaries around the globe, they not only recognized the diversity of the people they were evangelizing and serving, but the need to translate their faith into other cultures. Yet as the saints they sent were also sinners, they conceded the wisdom of John Wesley's confession after his inaugural missionary foray into Georgia: "I went to America to convert the Indians, but, oh, who shall convert me?"

Enduring Piety

Images of the 1950s American heartland endured as traces of Laura Ingalls Wilder's little home on the prairie and Dorothy's Kansas, where people valued land, family, and friends and insisted that there's "no place like home." As Robert Wuthnow noted, "The stuff of movies and television helped Middle Westerners reinvent themselves" as caring, independent people.[9] Yet from the transition from the Dust Bowl era through growing agribusiness and the emigration of their young to colleges and big cities, their identity as plain-speaking, honest religious people would undergo changes.

Piety existed on the plains, translated practically into public service to the community. In such a way, religion contributed to populism, emphasizing cooperation among neighbors. Wuthnow defined the grassroots movements as a quiet conservatism that liked Ike and generally welcomed strangers.[10] Methodists and Catholics would reinforce a moderately conservative civic ethos in states like Kansas, as the building of social capital focused upon good citizenship and care for the needy. It wouldn't be until the next two decades, with divisions in the church and the rise of the religious right seeking to regulate abortion and protest the homosexual rights movement that this hometown religion would feel under attack. But the postwar era celebrated the success of religious sentiment and revived a pathos of nostalgia.

Jane Wyman signs the Lord's Prayer in the poignant *Johnny Belinda* (Jean Negulesco, 1948).

Few films capture the poignancy and power of incorporating the Lord's Prayer in a screenplay as much as *Johnny Belinda* (Jean Negulesco, 1948), with Jane Wyman as the abused mute woman Belinda living in the fishing village of Cape Breton. Locky, the local drunken thug, not only rapes Belinda, but kills her good father, Black McDonald, who is just learning to communicate with his daughter through sign language. The hypocritical Locky and his wife, Stella, themselves childless, win approval to adopt Belinda's baby, Johnny.

Just after the murder of her father, Belinda kneels beside his body in a heart-wrenching scene and begins to sign the Lord's Prayer.

In a scene in a living room in the late foggy afternoon, a reflection on the window glass shows Belinda lighting a candle. Two men, in dripping raincoats, stand with their hats in hand, near the door. Her father's body lies on the sofa, covered by a blanket. Dr. Richardson and Belinda's aunt stand near the sofa. As Belinda lights a second candle, she kneels and begins to sign the Lord's Prayer. In an exquisite depth of focus, all the characters in the room watch as she kneels with folded hands, bathed in luminosity. Richardson speaks the prayer as Belinda signs it, as hard old men and even her grieving Aunt Aggie join in. She gently signs, "Thy will be done" over the moribund body. The prayer almost pauses with a telling shot on the doctor and Belinda as they pray in unison, "Forgive us our debts as we forgive our debtors," as both recognize the wrong done to her.

The scene almost didn't happen. Producers expressed concerns about whether they could show the dead face of Black McDonald during the prayer and how to spell the word "hallowed."[11] Producers also waffled over whether to use the Twenty-Third Psalm or the Lord's Prayer in the climactic scene. Finally, they opted for the Lord's Prayer, as it was the only spot in the picture where they could economically insert it. This particular scene was the movie's highlight, "very moving for the many millions of churchgoers in the country." Congregational minister Gerald Martin from Iowa commended Warner Bros. on a picture that was "not only superb entertainment but a spiritual challenge . . . and moral inspiration."[12]

Such inspiration was echoed in what would become, much later, a Christmas classic, though it was not as successful on its initial release. Frank Capra's dark Christmas parable *It's a Wonderful Life* (1946) gathers the prayers of the people for the film's hero, George Bailey (Jimmy Stewart). While the strains of "O Come, All Ye Faithful" play prophetically in the background, George suffers a crisis of personal meaning and worth. Capturing the small-town simplicity of Bedford Falls, Capra coordinates a series of tender intercessory prayers for the good man, with prayers moving from the general petition of succor to the emotional depths of a child praying for her father:

"I owe everything to George Bailey. Help him, dear Father."

"Joseph, Jesus, and Mary, help my friend Mr. Bailey."

"Help my son George tonight."

"He never thinks about himself, God, that's why he is in trouble."

"George is a good guy. Give him a break, God."

"I love him, dear Lord. Watch over him tonight."

"Please, God, something's the matter with Daddy."

"Please bring Daddy back."

Even as George cries out for help, desperately sobbing on the bridge, a klutzy angel, seeking to get his wings by performing a good deed, appears. "Clarence, Clarence, help me. Clarence, get me back. Get me back. I don't care what happens to me. Get me back to my wife and kids. . . .

George Bailey (Jimmy Stewart) in *It's a Wonderful Life* (Frank Capra, 1946) as the prayers of his family and community support him in his crisis of personal significance.

Please, please. I want to live again. I want to live again. . . . Please, God [weeping], let me live again."

In true Capra-corn style, the community rallies to save George; the angel Clarence gets his wings for doing a good deed; American virtues are reaffirmed; and God answers the dozens of prayers opening the film. The film hails all the heartland virtues of small-town America, where prayers are said with simplicity and hope.[13]

In Arthur Penn's award-winning *The Miracle Worker* (1962), the half-blind Yankee schoolgirl Annie Sullivan (Anne Bancroft) comes to teach the blind and deaf Helen Keller (Patty Duke). After an infamous dinner scene in which teacher and spoiled student fight and wrestle, Helen learns how to fold her napkin, but it is not enough for the family. Helen's half-brother Jimmy tries to offer a pragmatic philosophy for giving up. Sullivan protests that maybe they might, but her idea of original sin is "giving up!"

At a homecoming party for Helen back with her family, Jimmy offers a "very strange grace," with one very quirky but allegorically apt prayer:

And Jacob was left alone and wrestled with an angel until the breaking of the day. And the hollow of Jacob's thigh was out of joint as he wrestled, and the angel said, "Let me go, for the day breaks." And Jacob said, "I will not let thee go except thou bless me." Amen.

It was a fitting prayer from the good book, argues Jimmy. Then, in the company of her family members, who spoil her, Helen throws her napkin down and starts a tantrum, throwing water from a pitcher on her teacher. Annie drags Helen outside to discipline her. Jimmy stands up for Annie's ways against his father. At the pump, Helen finally recognizes the "word" for water, and the miracle of understanding has occurred. The angel has blessed her!

These quiet films reaffirmed the pieties of many American congregations, whose faith in prayers and goodness underlay their daily lives. Such prayers, too, inspired feelings of affection, summoning spectators to put sentiment into practice and to not "give up." Even in the sentimentalized story of the Brontë sisters, *Devotion* (Curtis Bernhardt, 1946), Emily (Ida Lupino) and Charlotte (Olivia de Havilland) express the charity of prayer and ask, "For what we are about to receive, make us truly grateful." Prayers of thanksgiving for both the miracles and small blessings of life permeated the heartland.

Adventures of Prayer

When the war ended, the church felt a need for global missions and restoration, for branching out beyond its borders. Within three years, it would organize the World Council of Churches (WCC) and support the establishment of the state of Israel. America generally was ready for adventures, but more fictional ones. Director Henry King's revisionist history *Captain from Castile* (1947) follows the adventures of a Castilian caballero. Captain Pedro de Vargas (Tyrone Power) chooses to explore the New World with Cortez rather than be imprisoned by the Spanish Inquisition for the alleged killing of inquisitor Diego de Silva, who actually remains alive.

On a seashore of rocks and sand, the captain sits reflecting when a rotund Father Bartolomé (Thomas Gomez as the hallowed saint who opposed slavery in the New World) inquires why he has not been to mass. He confesses that he has killed a man who "caused the death of my sister and the imprisonment of my parents. I place myself in your hands." After hearing his confession, the priest forgives him, tears up an order for his arrest, and calls him to do penance. "Pray for the soul of the man you killed. God's love is a heavy burden. Are you prepared to carry it out? Do you accept the penance?"

"Yes, father." He kneels, receives absolution, and joins the expedition. When the villainous de Silva reappears, he is actually murdered and the captain is condemned to a cell to await being hanged. Father Bartolomé kneels in the captain's cell before an altar and prays for his charge, "Blessed Jesus, in my place of darkness and torture, receive us into Thy paternal bosom. We praise and glorify Thee." While he prays, a Native whispers to him that it was he, not Pedro, who killed the man. "In God's name, speak!" commands the priest. The Indian Coatl, who killed the villain, confesses.

The priest informs the captain that God did not desert him and re-unites him with his wife. He speaks of the great compassion of God, and blesses them and their unborn child: "Blessed, you have been given a second chance. May you walk in that knowledge all the days of your life." Father Bartolomé then preaches a democratic Gospel to the entire company: "Go forward, not as conquerors, but as men of God. Here all men shall be equal, according to God's plan, a haven for the weak and a refuge for the strong." The prayers of American films sought to spread not only the Gospel around the world, but democracy as well.

The same theme occurs in John Huston's classic *The African Queen* (1951), where he drags his boat through swamps, mud, leeches, and exhaustion. The *Queen's* captain, Charlie Allnut (Humphrey Bogart), is saddled with the Methodist missionary Rose Sayer (Katharine Hepburn). Her brother, Reverend Samuel Sayer of First Methodist Church (a splendidly corpulent and sweaty Robert Morley), preaches and leads hymns, vainly, in a war zone.

When Charlie's boat comes to dock at their mission, the congregants leave the church to trade with him. However, encroaching Nazis threaten them all and Charlie helps Rose flee the danger after her brother is killed. At one desperate point, when the boat is mired in a dried-up bog, Charlie confesses his affection: "Even if we had enough strength, we'd never get off this mud. We're finished. I'm not one bit sorry I came. It was worth it."

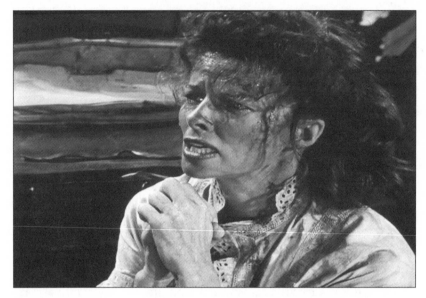

The efficacy of Rose Sayer's (Katharine Hepburn) desperate prayer in *The African Queen* (John Huston, 1951) is immediate as God literally opens the heavens for her.

He suffers terribly from a fever. After wiping his brow, Rose folds her hands and prays, "Dear Lord, we've come to the end of our journey. In a little while, we'll stand before You. I pray for You to be merciful. Judge us not for our weakness but for our love. And open the doors of heaven for Charlie and me." A point of view from the heavens looks down on the weary couple, and quietly raindrops begin to fall on lilies, and the showers come. In answering her prayers, heaven does indeed open its doors, flooding the marsh where the *African Queen* lies stranded and floating it out to the lake. They escape, only to be captured by a Nazi ship, which leads to marriage conveniently combined with an execution ceremony. Prayers are not only immediately efficacious, but propel the narrative into its romantic denouement. The film demonstrated that the lives of two somewhat pious pilgrims can thwart the enemies of democracy and forces of nature through faith, prayer, and love.

Plymouth Adventure (Clarence Brown, 1952) begins with an off-screen chorus singing, "Confess Jehovah thankfully, for He is good; His mercies continueth forever." The passengers joining the *Mayflower* for a journey to the New World are identified as Dissenters who pray differently.

"They pray standing up," rejecting the Church of England because of their new notions of how to say their prayers, with such zeal that they "say their prayers even standing on their heads if they have a mind to." A drunken and lusty Captain Jones (Spencer Tracy) assaults and then seduces Dorothy Bradford (Gene Tierney), mocking her for her "hymns and prayers, that's all you've ever known." Her husband, William (Leo Glenn), author of the Mayflower Compact, rescues and then forgives her.

However, a ponderous voice-over narration rewrites history, throwing in pious bits such as "Cleanliness is next to godliness." When the death of a young passenger from scurvy leads to a formal funeral oration, the Puritans look to "the Resurrection of the body that the sea shall offer up." Conveniently, and much too abruptly, land is sighted, even before the "Amen" is sounded. With its blatant apologetic for religious freedom and a calling to stand together to form a new government, the script resounds more with Cold War rhetoric and broadly nondescript Christianity than the pieties of the Pilgrims. The senior elder, William Brewster, who would become the spiritual leader of the Separatist community, offers an oddly generic prayer: "We are not alone in this room, but God is in this room. For whenever a man goes upward, he takes another step toward the fulfillment of the godhead that lives within us all." One expects Brewster to be turning over in his holy grave. Nevertheless, the American way is prepared by the prayers of the saints.

The 1950s saw a surge of interest in the western mythos. The Protestant imagination blended with the American myth of expansion as expressed in the western through its severe delineation of right and wrong, its depiction of ensuing judgment when a moral code is broken, and its message about the need for repentance and redemption of individuals.

At the height of Roy Rogers and Gene Autry's popularity, the western genre established a cowboy's moral code that fit the ethos of mainline denominations and promoted American democracy.[14] A cowboy never takes unfair advantage, even of an enemy, always tells the truth, is kind to small children, to old folks, and to animals, respects womanhood and the laws of his country, and possesses other civic virtues. These commandments of the West would serve the B-grade films well.

Prayers could civilize the ornery characters in the West. In *Count Three and Pray* (George Sherman, 1955), reformed hell-raiser, brawler, and Union veteran Luke Fargo (Van Heflin) returns to his hometown to rebuild the church and be its pastor. He takes in the backwoods scamp Lissy (Joanne Woodward in her film debut) to civilize her. He explains, "We give thanks before we eat in this house," before he knows they are eating a chicken that she has stolen. Energetically, she gets him back with "One, two, three, pray. You forgot to holler 'Thanks to the Lord' out loud."

In his church service, they awkwardly sing "Abide with Me," with an emphasis upon calling for "help for the helpless." When confronted with a challenge, "Why don't you talk about hell?" he retorts to his parishioner, "You've raised enough around here," causing the congregation to laugh. Yancey Huggins (Raymond Burr), the town's tyrant and banker, threatens him and the churchgoers with cutting off their credit, saying, "Go ahead and pray and then try eating your hymn books."

Fargo's antagonists compete with each other in playing "Little Brown Jug" on their banjos, with the musical duel leading to fighting in the church on Sunday. Fargo keeps his mission clear: "Come to the church, not me." Yet he knows that he is as empty as his church and begins to preach about "things missing in me." When a bishop comes to investigate Fargo's work, he finds that he isn't ordained. As they gather to eat cookies, Lissy tells them all, "You got to say grace first, you know." Asked who taught her to say grace, she responds that Fargo did. She explains that Fargo once mumbled thanks over some chicken, while she waited until he had a full mouth and then confessed that she stole it ("and he choked so hard on that chicken"). The bishop concludes that Fargo's unorthodox methods, while raising a considerable amount of dust, did much good; he ordains him and weds him to Lissy. The celebration of ordinary Christians promulgated an image of normal American life, reaffirming that flawed saints would lead the church.

The playfulness in western religion can also be seen in *The Twinkle in God's Eye* (George Blair, 1955). Prayers and preaching mark the return of an idealistic frontier preacher, Reverend Macklin (Mickey Rooney), to the cow town of Lodestone, where his father had been killed and his church burned down. His calling is to rebuild his father's church on the original spot, inconveniently supplanted by a saloon.

Macklin's strategy for converting the saloon owner, Marty Callahan (Hugh O'Brian), is through humor. When the reverend asks for milk at the bar, he discovers it's as expensive and rare as ice in the desert. He preaches about an arrow shot at his mother, but it sunk into her Bible, to which an incredulous listener responds, with the message of the film: "You mean the Bible saved her?" He banters with Callahan over the property site, with the saloon owner conceding that church has been in business for over two thousand years "longer than I have," which is "an awfully large handicap" for the saloon owner to overcome.

Observing that his potential congregation is not too eager to get to heaven, Macklin rues that "most of them are heading the other direction." The only hymn the prospectors know by heart is "Frankie and Johnnie." He tells them that everything the devil says is a lie, and points to a twinkle in God's eye that promises new beginnings.

When a gang steals money from the saloon, they hide it in the ruins of the church. Macklin thinks they're kneeling and praying (when they are simply burying the money), but they confess that they don't know much about praying. He offers to teach them to pray. As the ladies join the makeshift outdoor chapel, with wooden cross and benches on stone piles, Macklin offers his invocation: "We'll start off our service this morning by saying a prayer: 'For Marty Callahan, Grant to us, Lord, the ability to think and do things as are right.'" Later, when Callahan's estranged girlfriend Laura is hurt in a rodeo, he calls upon the robbers to join him in a prayer for her: "Would you care to join me, gentlemen?"

Macklin prays, "Grant the strength of the weak and the comfort of the sufferers. Mercifully accept our prayers and grant to Thy servant the help of Thy power that her sickness may be turned into health and our sorrow into joy through His name's sake. Amen."

When a mine caves in and endangers some prospectors, the townspeople lose hope. The little reverend inspires them with positive thinking: "You've got to have faith. You've got to believe that what you're doing is right. I've got big beams here [to rescue the mine collapse victims]. The church was made for man, not man for the church. Let the men be reached in time. Let us pray." Within seconds, they rescue them. So Macklin prays in gratitude, "Everybody's saved! Father, we thank Thee." By the end of the film, Macklin officiates at the wedding of a restored Marty and Laura, with a twinkle in his eye. The theme of the first meeting of the WCC in Amsterdam had been "Man's disorder and God's design." Macklin's flexible theology reflected this mission in adapting to the migrants, refugees, and outcasts to create an inclusive body in old Lodestone.

The global vision of peace and forgiveness shaped several western films. On the night before a hanging in *The Bravados* (Henry King, 1958), the preacher teaches a crowd of Protestants, Latino Catholics, and one Jewish family that "at Golgotha, Christ took time to pardon a common thief." He instructs them to pray for those about to die. A stranger, Jim Douglas (Gregory Peck), has come to see the men suffer, believing that the four outlaws had killed his wife and daughter in cold blood.

However, one of the irreverent and brutal killers, Zachary (Stephen Boyd), says mockingly to Primo, the deputy, "Primo, would you pray for us?" When Primo asks what he should pray for, Zachary says, "That we'll go to heaven."

"I can't do that," says Primo, "but I will pray for God to forgive you."

Zachary says sarcastically, "We'll settle for that." However, they escape and Douglas hunts them down, killing them unmercifully, one by one. Just as he is about to kill the fourth, who sits before him with his own wife and child, Douglas discovers that the men are innocent of this one crime. Douglas cries out, "Oh my God, my God!," covering his face in shame and guilt. He walks to the Catholic cathedral and kneels in a pew, telling the priest that he was wrong, that he sought only personal revenge. The priest counsels him, "Some people think prayers will help." As he is walking out of the church, the townspeople applaud his ridding them of the villains, offering to keep him in their hearts. "And," he adds, "in your prayers, *please*."[15]

Vengeance also motivates Civil War veteran Ethan Edwards (John Wayne) in *The Searchers* (John Ford, 1956), out to kill the Comanche who had kidnapped his niece Debbie (Natalie Wood). Just before an Indian attack, the quirky Mose Harper (Hank Worden) prays, "That which we are about to receive, we thank Thee, O Lord." The irony is palpable, but the sentiment is also real.

The Texas Ranger captain, Reverend Clayton (Ward Bond), holds a funeral service for the victims of the attack. After the hymn, he begins to pray, but Ethan yells at him, "Put an Amen to it!"

"I ain't finished yet."

Ethan stomps off to his horse, barking, "There's no more time for praying! *Amen!*"

Yet Clayton demands that even in their dealings with the Comanche they act like Christians, doing what the good book commands. At the end, Ethan shows mercy to Debbie by not killing her for being tainted by foreign foes. Even in a country suspicious of its enemies, mainline churches in the 1950s sought to love their global neighbors, seeking an ecumenical peace among all.

During the Cold War, Americanism was mixed with religion, and the phrase "under God" was added to the Pledge of Allegiance in 1956. Even Davy Crockett (John Wayne) has his born-again experience before dying in *The Alamo* (John Wayne, 1960). A preacher (Hank Warden) traveling with him and noticing his wayward behavior, confronts him: "Davy, don't you ever pray?" to which Crockett answers, "I never had the time." The parson indirectly prophesies the destiny of the men when Smitty (Frankie Avalon) notices that "so many times every day, you stop and give thanks, but mostly I don't catch on what you're thanking the Lord for. I mean, there's nothing special."

He answers, "I give thanks for the time and for the place."

"The time and the place, Parson?"

"The time to live and the place to die. That's all any man gets. No more, no less."

When the pastor dies, Davy looks heavenward and allows that the preacher did not die in vain, but that his faith lives on through the adventurer, a reincarnation of a Puritan pilgrim. By the end, the frontiersman will fight and die for the Republic and for God, as Dimitri Tiomkin's score plays in the background, including the lyrics "and the small band of soldiers lies asleep in the arms of the Lord."

With strains of "Rock of Ages" enveloping the epic saga of Cinerama's *How the West Was Won* (John Ford et al., 1963), four generations of Americans make their way westward. Zebulon Prescott (Karl Malden) prays his gratitude after successfully battling pirates, thanks the Lord for salvation, and prays that the Lord receive their dead, help them tend the wounded, and help them know what to do with some wicked men sent his way. Even when Zebulon and his wife, Eve (Carroll Baker), drown under the rapids, the pioneer spirit itches to get on. At his graveside, their descendants call out, "Help me pray, Pa, help me pray."

The expansionist western faith seeps through even B-grade western movies like Robert Rossen's *They Came to Cordura* (1959). During the

1916 pursuit of Pancho Villa, a guilt-stricken army major, Thomas Thorn (Gary Cooper), must recommend men for the Congressional Medal of Honor. His own cowardice at a battle haunts him as he earnestly strives to find worthy recipients of the military's highest honor for bravery.

The regiment's Colonel Rogers (Robert Keith) plans a daring and foolhardy old-fashioned cavalry attack on a rebel holdout, during which several men display acts of courage. The Roman Catholic colonel prays for success and, after winning, kneels before a statue of the Virgin Mary. He tells Thorn, "I have been praying and thanking God for giving me a victory." However, his actions and words reveal an egocentric officer. He leads this last cavalry charge to garner good press for a promotion to general. His façade of piety reveals narcissism.

One young hero, Private Hetherington (Michael Callan), confides that he jumped into battle as the Lord came upon him, regaining a faith that he had rejected as a child when his father beat the Bible into him. Stricken with typhoid fever, he prays deliriously in the desert, "The Lord thy God bringeth me to a new land, flowing with brooks of water." Others meet his feverish confession of faith with cynicism and hostility. But he survives.

Both Rogers's and Hetherington's prayers are answered, but the gloomy mood, with the fallen humanity of every "hero" exposed for its selfishness and savagery, diminishes the worth of the nugatory prayers, no matter how effective they seem to be. The film raises questions about the motives of religious leaders, stirring up ethical concerns within the Body of Christ.

Biblical views of brotherhood challenge racism in several films. An Apache wedding prayer in *Broken Arrow* (Delmer Daves, 1950) reads like Saint Paul's discussion of marriage in his Letter to the Ephesians, in which the two will be shelter and warmth to each other.

The "Christian general" Oliver Howard (Basil Ruysdael) tells Tom Jeffords (Jimmy Stewart), who is trying to broker a peace (and break the arrow) between Cochise's Apaches and white settlers, "The Bible I read preaches brotherhood for all of God's children."

"Suppose," says Jeffords, "their skins weren't white. Are they still God's children?"

"The Bible says nothing about the pigmentation of their skin," responds the general. While some Southern Baptist churches were held captive to southern culture, many of their northern brothers were rais-ing the issues of racism and equality. The church in the 1950s was under-going a slow conversion of cultural awareness, debating the purpose of the Gospel in the public square.

In futile attempts to draw television viewers back to the theatres, Hollywood went epic with modern westerns. George Stevens's sprawl-ing *Giant* (1956) dealt with pressing themes of racism in Texas as well as the oil boom and the passing of the old guard, with the historical sweep of Edna Ferber's novel. This painting of a slightly askew Norman Rockwell family still contained a prayer at dinner. With father, cattle rancher Jordan "Bick" Benedict Jr. (Rock Hudson), away, mother Leslie Benedict (Elizabeth Taylor) tries to jolly her three children at a larger family Thanksgiving meal, as they each wear bright Indian headdresses.

She prays, "Most merciful Father, we bow our heads in gratitude on this our Thanksgiving Day. We give Thee humble and hearty thanks for this, Thy bounty, beseeching Thee to continue Thy loving-kindness to us that our land may still yield her increase to Thy glory and our comfort. Amen." However, as the children have learned that their turkey dinner is the old pet Pedro, they cry unceasingly. The film exposes the American dream of abundance, baptized with sanctimonious prayers, as some-thing disturbing.

An upsurge of critical commentary on optimistic national visions also occurs in Sam Peckinpah's *Major Dundee* (1965). After playing Moses and Ben Hur, Charlton Heston mounts the saddle as Dundee to round up Confederates and blacks. Reverend Dahlstrom (R. G. Armstrong) joins him in his quest to capture Apache renegades in Texas. (At one point, their leader, Sierra Charriba, mocks Dundee, suggesting he make "his peace with your Christian God because you're going to join him.") When the preacher joins up, he has his Bible with him as he declares, "Any man who has a just cause should travel with the word of the God."

Dundee replies, "With all due respect, God has nothing to do with it. I intend to smite the wicked, not save the heathen." Dahlstrom warns that "those who destroyeth my flock, shall so be destroyed." Dundee smiles, murmurs, "Reverend," and welcomes him into the company. When Dahl-strom gets in a fight, he is commended for "kicking up a lot of dust" with his sermon. His words are actions. When he disarms a French soldier dur-ing a raid, he proclaims, "Mighty is the arm of the Lord!"

Later, after a major bloody defeat, they bury soldiers in a circular grave. The surviving soldiers take off their caps and bow reverently. Holding his Bible, the minister prays, "We ask Thee, Lord, to take these soldiers who have fallen in Thy service." The remaining black and white troops sing "Shall We Gather at the River?" After Dundee's wild bunch liberates a Mexican village from the French army, peasants kneel before an outdoor altar to pray for thanks and then put on a festival with fireworks and roasted mules to celebrate their freedom. The American belief that religious democracy would save the poor around the world remained an enduring hope. While the era began with a mutual effort of God and country to save the world, showing how prayer could defeat Nazis and other enemies, by the end the country was growing skeptical of such unlikely bedfellows as religion and politics. However, some fantasy films sought to replace such political concerns with an emphasis upon spirituality.

Spiritual Prayers

The genre of *film blanc* wafted out of the heavens of Hollywood after the war, bringing fantasy, comedy, and whimsy into sentimental films. Angels descended with ease into the lives of ordinary citizens of earth.

Cary Grant plays the debonair rascal angel Dudley in Henry Koster's *The Bishop's Wife* (1947), the seeming answer to Episcopal Bishop Henry Brougham's (David Niven) prayer for help in building a cathedral. Dudley is a character (tweaking Alexander Pope: "Sometimes angels rush in where fools fear to tread") and appears to be redirecting the affections of Brougham's wife, Julie (Loretta Young). When she protests that she never knows when Dudley is joking, he quips, "Ah, I am at my most serious when I'm joking." Hollywood sought to be more serious about spiritual matters in its own comedies, preaching that personal relations were more important than building programs.

When the bishop tells Dudley that he was praying for a cathedral, the angel responds, "No, Henry, you were praying for guidance." What he receives is a Christmas revelation that they should never "forget the birthday of the child born in a manger and find what *He* would want in His stocking," which turns out to be "loving-kindness, warm hearts, and the stretched-out hand of tolerance, all the shining gifts that make peace on earth." *New York Times* critic Bosley Crowther dismissed the film: "Most of us have some dark misgivings about the tact of the makers of films when they barge into the private area of a man's communication with his God."[16] Religion, for many in the 1950s, was private and relegated to Sundays. Virtues, however, were public.

An angel (James Whitmore) representing the Archangel Gabriel thunders from the heavens at foul-mouthed manager Aloysius "Guffy" McGovern (Paul Douglas) of the Pittsburgh Pirates (in last place) in *Angels in the Outfield* (Clarence Brown, 1951). A bit perturbed, he would not have intervened except it "seems someone down there is sending up a lot of prayers."

"Someone praying for me? Gee," says Guffy, who then wonders, by the way, are there "ball players in heaven?" "Plenty of ball players," responds the angel, "but very few managers."

However, continues the angel, before "I answer those prayers I have to clean you up." He sets down certain rules for Guffy to follow. First, cut out the blasphemy. Second, start treating your fellow man with more respect and understanding. Third, "love and stop slugging thy neighbor, hear me?" When Guffy asks for a sign, the angel says, "Look for a miracle in the third inning."

Fresh, naïve reporter Jennifer Paige (Janet Leigh) follows the Pirates and discovers a moppet from Saint Gabriel's Home of Orphan Girls, Bridget White, who espies angels. When questioned, she allows that she prays every morning and night, and sometimes during arithmetic.

Both Guffy and Paige informally adopt Bridget, taking her to ball games and to Guffy's home to celebrate his birthday. When Paige unfortunately cooks veal with leather rather than olive oil, she serves it. When Bridget protests, Paige asks her what the matter is.

"Grace," answers the orphan. "Grace who?" mutters Guffy. "Oh dear, grace, I almost forgot." Bridget prays, "O Lord, make us truly thankful for these Thy gifts, which we are about to receive. Amen." Her prayer indicates a special relationship with the divine. As the media investigate Guffy, he allows that he does in fact hear from angels and that they have helped his Pirates toward winning the pennant. However, he still has a problem with his temper. About to get into a fight, he asks a nun, "Is it always right to turn the other cheek, Sister?" He does, and gets walloped. The nun explains, "Well, the meek shall inherit the earth."

Kneeling at second base talking to the angels, he learns that one of his old friends whose pitching skills have declined is about to be signed up "in the spring for the Heavenly Choir team." Guffy has learned that human relations are more important than winning and puts his friend in as his starting pitcher for the game that will decide whether they win the pennant.

At a hearing with the baseball commissioner on Guffy's sanity, a psychiatrist opines that all religions are merely attempts to explain mysteries.[17] However, the defense calls three clergymen, a minister from Trinity Church, a rabbi, and an Irish priest. When asked about the existence of angels, they quote Exodus: "Behold, I send an angel before them," and the testimony that the Angel of the Lord encamps about His people.

Guffy's nemesis, Fred Bayles (Keenan Wynn), challenges them: "Why would an angel ever watch over such a profane and foul guy as Guffy?"

The priest answers with the parable from Matthew 18:12: "If a man have a hundred sheep and one of them goes astray . . ." Both poignancy and humor mark the rescue of Guffy and eventually of his Pirates. In the remake of *Angels in the Outfield* (William Dear, 1994), the orphaned kid Roger (Joseph Gordon-Levitt) offers a politically correct, gender-neutral prayer: "God, if there is a God, if You're a man or a woman . . . I would really like a family. My dad says that will only happen if the Angels win the pennant, so maybe You could help them out a little. Amen, or a-woman." The tagline for this Los Angeles Angels team to win the pennant is "Ya gotta believe!"

Defending Roger, foster parent Maggie Nelson (Brenda Fricker) argues,

One of these boys is the child who can see angels. He could stand up right now and tell you what's going on and I know you'd just laugh at him. But when a professional football player drops to one knee to thank God for making a touchdown, nobody laughs at that. Or when a pitcher crosses himself before going to the mound, no one laughs at that either. It's like you're saying it's okay to believe in God, but it's not okay to believe in angels. Now, I thought that they were on the same team.

The arrival of angels in this postwar period would often supplant the need for God. Heavenly intermediaries could stand in for the divine, or a competent manager.

Prayers occur in other fantastic worlds as well, but with earthbound characters entering marvelous worlds, rather than celestial beings visiting theirs. In the quaintly enchanted *Brigadoon* (Vincente Minnelli, 1954), two lost American hunters, Tommy Albright (Gene Kelly) and a cynical Jeff Douglas (Van Johnson), find themselves emerging from a mist into a magical world in Scotland that appears only once every hundred years. Tommy meets and falls in love with Fiona Campbell (Cyd Charisse) in this utopian hideaway.

One of the inhabitants, Mr. Lundie (Barry Johns), tells the pair about Reverend Forsythe, the old minister of the kirk whose prayers protected the blessed place from evil. "Two hundred years ago, the highlands of Scotland were plagued with witches, wicked sorcerers that were taking the Scottish people away from the teachings of God and putting the devil into their souls. They were indeed horrible destructive women. I dinna suppose you have such women in your country?" Tommy responds incredulously, "Witches?" with Jeff muttering sarcastically, "Oh, we have 'em. We pronounce it differently."

Going out to a hill beyond Brigadoon, Forsythe asked God for a miracle to protect his parish. He asked that God make Brigadoon a vanished nation that returns "for one day every hundred years with no changes in the lives of people." Thus, as the scriptures suggest regarding eternity, every day is like a hundred years. But no one ever saw the minister again; some say a sacrifice had to be made in this covenant with God. The enchantment is broken if someone leaves.

Two problems exist in this Eden, however. First, Lundie informs them that while Forsythe's miracle happened two hundred years ago in the highlands, most folks don't believe in miracles, as miracles require faith and faith seems to be dead at present. Second, when they ask whether a stranger could stay, Lundin replies that Forsythe provided for that. The interlopers learn that one can stay in Brigadoon only if one loves someone deeply enough to lose everything else. Finding a pearl of great price, one must sacrifice everything. Tommy realizes that there must be a lot of people out there searching for a Brigadoon, but concludes that if you love someone enough, anything is possible, even miracles. The film promises a Brigadoon on earth, a sort of spiritual Shangri-La for romantics.

Episcopal priest Robert Ellwood pointed out that in a decade rife with Catholic-Protestant tensions, conflicts between theology and popular faith, and burgeoning forms of spirituality, such as Zen Buddhism, Merton's monasticism, and Joseph Campbell's revival of mythology, many were looking for a Brigadoon.[18] Old forms of traditional faith would wane, as angelic fantasies and spiritual presences would wax in the next decade.

Militant Church

In a clever adaptation of George Bernard Shaw's switched roles, *The Devil's Disciple* (Guy Hamilton, 1959), the stolid and sober Presbyterian minister, upright Puritan Reverend Anderson (Burt Lancaster), is transformed into a patriot, while the scalawag Dick Dudgeon (Kirk Douglas) allows himself to be captured as the pastor. While a Tory Anglican vicar tries to curry favor by ingratiating himself with General Burgoyne (Laurence Olivier), praying ostentatiously for King George and his military men, the ne'er-do-well Dick turns into a man of conscience during the War of Independence.

After seeing the horrors of a public hanging, Anderson enters his church late one night, kneels, and prays. His prayers are interrupted by laughter outside the chapel and he discovers the "devil's disciple," Dudgeon, who scoffs at the world cringing in fear before an "Almighty." Taunting that he prays secretly to the devil, the witty and irreverent Dick is nevertheless asked to supper, where he spouts such lines as "You know, I've never met a minister that doesn't ask you to dinner and treat you to a sermon."

At a reading of a will for the Dudgeon family, Dick presents himself as the prodigal son, looking for the fatted calf. The will is read: "Finally, bequeathing my soul to my Maker's hands, I humbly ask forgiveness for all my sins, hoping I have not done wrong in the perplexity of my last hour in this strange place. Amen." While Anderson performs customary prayers, at the funeral of the hanged man ("And now we devote his body to the ground") and as a blessing at the table ("For what we are about to receive, make us truly grateful"), he will turn into a heroic man of action, militantly defending faith and American freedom. American civil religion unites both minister and skeptic against an external enemy.

Censors told Raoul Walsh, notorious for his coarse gruffness, to eliminate the uttering of oaths in his war film *Battle Cry* (1955), following troops from boot camp to battleground combat. More importantly, they demanded that he change the frequent use of the words "God" and "Lord," when not appearing as part of prayers. According to the Breen Code, such terms should only be used reverently. Instead of saying "Hidy, tidy, Lord Almighty," they recommended a substitute for Lord Almighty, such as "back to Blighty."[19] Walsh learned how to appear reverent, but keep his films gritty. In his adaptation of Norman Mailer's *The Naked and the Dead* (Raoul Walsh, 1958), a Baptist minister grunt prays for people in the hospital and then at the climax of the film, he and a fellow "wandering Jew" carry a stretcher with a dying Lieutenant Hearn (Cliff Robertson) to the shore. With no help in sight, the minister kneels beside the casualty and takes off his hat, looking heavenward and praying, "Lord, I've never asked much for myself, but I'm asking You help us get this man back alive." A boat immediately appears with medics on board and transports them back to their lines. Answered prayers in films paralleled the teachings of evangelist Billy Graham, calling people to converse with God and expect the miraculous.

Remembering divine faithfulness in war, several films revisited faith under fire. *Battle Hymn* (Douglas Sirk, 1957) features the true-life chronicle of clergyman Dean Hess (Rock Hudson), who rescued orphans in Korea. Guilt-ridden from being "Killer Hess," a World War II pilot who accidentally bombed an orphanage associated with his grandmother, Hess leaves his civilian post as a minister to train Korean nationalists for the Air Force.

In the mess hall, the troops are singing "Little Brown Jug" when one soldier stands up and says, "Dad always said grace at Thanksgiving. Not that we were extra religious. It's just that with a table piled high with food, we should give thanks. Fellows, I'm not good at this sort of thing, so if somebody here feels more qualified . . ." When no one responds, he continues, "Seems like I'm stuck."

Hess says nothing; the soldier prays, "Dear Lord, first off, we want to thank You for all of us being well. And I want to say You sure did put

Yourself out setting this table. Seems a person never could be hungry and if we ever get to complaining about anything, You just put a stop to it." As the soldier says, "Amen," a Korean orphan, like a hungry mouse under the table, steals some bread.

When a black friend strafes some refugees and wrestles with the horror of his act, Hess responds with true empathy from his own agonizing misdeed. Hess reminds his friend of the Gospel text that God watches over every sparrow. A wise Buddhist had instructed Hess that such "good deeds are your purest prayers." He practices these living prayers.

When a frightened friend is dying, Hess comforts him that there is nothing to fear. The friend confesses, "I thought I knew how to live, but I didn't. I don't know how to die. Say a prayer for me." Hess tells him, "It's already said. Don't be afraid. Life is a shadowy place. Think of a door just beyond. When that door opens, we pass through from darkness into light." Comforted, the soldier quietly says, "Thank you, Reverend. If you say so. A wind came from the wilderness and carried me where men can never reach alone." "The Battle Hymn of the Republic" plays in background.

A crusty marine corporal, Allison (Robert Mitchum), has to cooperate with a nun, Sister Angela (Deborah Kerr), in John Huston's *Heaven Knows, Mr. Allison* (1957) as they find themselves castaways on a South Pacific island about to be overrun with Japanese. Similar in many ways to *The African Queen* with a crude male and a religious female hiding from World War II enemies, the literate exchanges and bickering between the two make for a compelling story. When Sister Angela first begins to pray, "Hail Mary, full of grace" before lit candles, Allison snuffs them out, lest Japanese ships see the glow. When she informs him that only God knows what'll happen to them, he banters back with "And He won't tell, huh, ma'am?" She smiles and says, "He might."

She prays that Mary intercede for the two of them, even in the aptly phrased "hour of our death." When he thinks she was talking to him, she counters, "I was saying my prayers, Mr. Allison. Do you ever say yours?"

"No, ma'am."

"But did you never pray?"

"No, ma'am."

"But you do believe in God the Father?"

"Oh sure, ma'am. Anybody that has any sense believes in God."

When a makeshift church on the island is bombed and destroyed, the crucifix burnt, she thanks God that no one was there to be killed.

As Allison falls in love with her and proposes marriage, she affirms that she had already given her heart to "Jesus Christ our Lord." Later, drunk with sake, he mumbles about the island being like Eden with just one Adam and Eve and complains about his bad luck: "If ya gotta be a nun, why ain't ya old and ugly? Why do ya gotta have big blue eyes . . . and a beautiful smile . . . and freckles?"

Sister Angela prays for her companion and entreats God not to judge him too severely, as he's "only a Marine, but he's a good man, brave and very, very honest. I humbly implore You that when his time comes, be merciful and receive him into Thy holy presence."

Burning tall grass and bamboo shoots, the Japanese try to smoke them out. Just before they discover them in their cave in the climactic scene, they are rescued not coincidentally, but providentially. Sister Angela prays just before their rescue, suggesting that Someone up there is listening. Suddenly the Allies begin their bombing. Allison acknowledges that when God "tells what's going to happen," it is "big and loud, not from within. He just told me." Then Sister Angela assures him, "He'll protect you." As he dismantles the guns and so saves many marine lives, he ends up only wounded, safe and secure from all alarms. America's films, as much as its ministers, preach of God's sovereignty over past crises. These postwar films reassured those returning from combat and those agonizing over survivor guilt that God did indeed hear their prayers and that His providence kept them alive that they might continue to serve others. Prayers supplied the balm needed for healing.

Praying Men of God

Clergy and religious characters continued to populate the screen in significant ways, becoming much more visible as members of the community.[20] Films depicted these primary dispensers of prayer both positively and negatively, but moved toward more ambivalent portrayals throughout this postwar period.

Early in Jacques Tourneur's *Stars in My Crown* (1950), the hardy parson Josiah Grey (Joel McCrea) arrives in Walesburg and goes to the saloon to give his first sermon. The rowdies laugh until he brings out his six-gun pistols; they duck. Then he starts preaching, "In the beginning was the Word and the Word was with God and the Word was God."

Indirectly responsible for the spread of typhoid by his visitations, Parson Grey ultimately saves the town from an epidemic by discovering the source of a poisoned school well. When a widow is on her deathbed, attended to by the modern agnostic doctor, Grey kneels by her bedside, praying silently, until the doctor tells him it's over. "No," says the parson, "it's just beginning." Later the parson visits Faith, the doctor's schoolteacher fiancée, who is also dying. As he prays, the wind blows the curtains, her hand touches his folded hands, and she looks up. Faith recovers and the man of science and the man of faith unite in friendship.

At the climax of the film, Parson Grey confronts a KKK lynch mob stirred up to hang Uncle Famous, an innocent black man they have known since childhood. Grey says he wants to read the last will of the condemned man, giving generously to each of the hooded men standing there, and recalling how he taught one to fish and how he helped each of them in a time of need. Ashamed, the mob breaks up. After they have dispersed, his son looks at the supposed will to find a blank piece of paper. "This ain't no will!" he says, and Grey responds, "Yes, it is, son. It is the will of God." With more Methodists engaged in social action, particularly at the forefront of racial justice, the "will" of God was more than just a legal piece of paper. It was a religious calling.

John Ford's excursion back to Ireland introduced friendly Roman Catholics and Anglicans in *The Quiet Man* (1952) with two mutually affectionate clerics, Irish Father Lonergan (Ward Bond) and Anglican Reverend Playfair. The two faith traditions are teasingly blended, with even Father Peter at one point commanding his Roman Catholic flock to "cheer like Protestants." Arriving from Pittsburgh (where the "steel's so hard and hot you lose your fear of hell"), Sean Thornton (John Wayne) returns to his old family farm in Innisfree (another word for heaven), where one local can boast that "the last trout I got was so big I expected Jonah to jump out of its mouth." Thornton meets up with Father Lonergan, who tells him to come to early morning mass. After kneeling before the stained glass and genuflecting, he comes outside and sees Mary Kate (Maureen O'Hara), who looks "like the sight of a girl coming through the fields with the sun on her hair [and] kneeling in church with a face like a saint." Nature and grace conspire to make this Irish beauty.

After conniving with the father to liberate Mary Kate from her brother's control, Michaleen Oge Flynn (Barry Fitzgerald) looks at his fellow conspirator, confesses his sin of chicanery, and assigns himself his own penance: saying "three Our Fathers and three Hail Marys." The friendship between Lonergan and Flynn, rival clergymen, hinted at the harbinger of an ecumenical brotherhood, one that would not happen until Vatican II.

In stark contrast, several shadowy clerical figures appear in the *film noir* narratives. One such "man of the cloth" was the sinister preacher in *Night of the Hunter* (Charles Laughton, 1955). Laughton's direction of Robert Mitchum as the sinister religious fanatic Harry Powell made James Agee's screenplay eerier.

As Powell tells his little story of good and evil, he sits behind the bars of his cell, his knuckles tattooed with LOVE and HATE, holding a knife between the palms of his praying hands. He insinuates that God works in mysterious ways, and not without violence. He looks heavenward and drawls, "Lord, You sure knowed what You was doin' when You put me in this very cell at *this* very time. A man with $10,000 hid somewhere, and a widder in the makin.'" Powell is "plotting skullduggery" as his prison mate reveals a secret cache kept by his wife. Released soon after his prison mate's execution, Powell heads out to meet and marry Willa Harper (Shelley Winters), who possesses the money and two children.

Prayers and hymn singing stretch from the beginning of the film to its climax. Driving to his destination/destiny, the villainous hymn-singing, scripture-spouting Preacher Powell chats with God, itemizing things that the Lord hates: "Perfume-smellin' things, lacy things, things with curly hair. Not that You mind the killings! There's plenty of killings in Your book, Lord." When asked what religion he professed, Powell allows, "The religion of the Almighty and me worked out betwixt us." Powell embodies all the corruption of religion characterized by a love for money and an aversion to the sexual body.

He arrives at Willa's home, where he woos and soon weds her. But on their wedding night, Willa interrupts his prayers and he growls back at her. He waxes eloquent on the evils of carnal lust, bullying her into abject subservience. She apologizes and then receives a sermon on the body of a woman, "the temple of creation and motherhood. You see the flesh of Eve that man since Adam has profaned. That body was meant for begettin' children. It was not meant for the lust of men!" She cowers into bed, and whimpers her prayer: "Help me to be clean, so I can be what Harry wants me to be."

After he has killed Willa, the preacher is asked where she is. "Uh," he says, "she run off with a drummer . . . durin' prayer meetin'." However, he wasn't able to retrieve the money, as her two children have desperately run away with it. They meet the elderly, sturdy Rachel Cooper (Lillian Gish), who prays for the children. "My soul is humble when I see the way little ones accept their lot. Lord, save little children. The wind blows and the rain's a-cold. Yet they abide. . . . They abide and they endure." When the menacing preacher comes to her porch, threatening to abduct the children, he starts singing "Leaning on the Everlasting Arms." Rachel sits in the dark, watching him with her shotgun in her lap, and sings, "leaning on Jesus." Her stress on the personal name of Jesus rather than just "everlasting arms" constitutes a sharp contrast to his loveless religion. Her intimate faith reflected the growing evangelical movement and its wariness for liberal wolves in sheep's clothing.

In the early 1960s, the National Council of Churches (NCC) expressed "grave concerns" regarding two films being released: *Sins of Rachel Cade* and *Elmer Gantry*.[21] *Sins of Rachel Cade* (Gordon Douglas, 1961) attempted to mitigate the controversy by emphasizing that the wayward woman (Angie Dickinson) it features is a medical missionary in the Belgian Congo, not a religious missionary, a nurse rather than a godly woman. Censors demanded minor corrections like altering the script from "The Book says man is not to lie with a woman outside the marriage vows" to "The Book says so." In particular, the line "I have seen your people come and go—I've seen you treat the syphilis the men who support your churches brought here two generations ago" was viewed as a "vicious attack on the Protestant church." Letters to the president of the MPAA, Eric Johnston, protested that no Christian missionary would make such remarks. In the Cold War era, one letter argued, "probably the greatest bulwark against Communism has been the unselfish work of countless missionaries of all religious faiths. Particularly is this true in Africa, where this picture takes place. This screenplay is grist for the Communist mill, as it casts aspersions on those who have dedicated their lives to the service of God in the mission fields."[22]

More exuberant was Burt Lancaster's portrayal of the protagonist of Sinclair Lewis's earlier work *Elmer Gantry* (Richard Brooks, 1960). A caveat that was scrolled before the opening credits asserted,

> We believe that certain aspects of Revivalism can bear examination—that the conduct of some revivalists makes a mockery of the traditional beliefs and practices of organized Christianity! We believe that everyone has a right to worship according to his conscience, but—Freedom of Religion is not license to abuse the faith of the people! However, due to the highly controversial nature of the film, we strongly urge you to prevent impressionable children from seeing it!

In an early remarkably positive scene, Gantry comes strolling into a black church, with Rex Ingram playing the good preacher. The congregation sings "Marching to Zion" with genuine enthusiasm. Gantry lustily joins in, shouting that he is "on the road!"

When he comes to meet up with evangelist Sister Sharon Falconer (Jean Simmons), he meets his match. He joins her roadshow and provides fast-talking, emotional tirades, even preaching against the writer Sinclair Lewis, the very author of the bestselling book from which the film is adapted. He also takes a swipe at satirist H. L. Mencken, caricatured as journalist Jim Lefferts (Arthur Kennedy).

The charismatic scoundrel preaches how every sinner is doomed to perdition. One of his earlier converts, now a prostitute, Lulu Bains (Shirley Jones), gives her testimony: "Oh, he gave me special instructions back of the pulpit Christmas Eve. He got to howlin', 'Repent! Repent!,' and I got to moanin', 'Save me! Save me!,' and the first thing I know he rammed the fear of God into me so fast I never heard my old man's footsteps."

One "clean-up man" for the revival testified, "Mister, I've been converted five times. Billy Sunday, Reverend Biederwolf, Gypsy Smith, and twice by Sister Falconer. I get terrible drunk, and then I get good and saved. Both of them done me a powerful lot of good—gettin' drunk and gettin' saved."

Yet Sister Falconer's appeals seem shockingly authentic, as she calls for her congregation to pray: "If I am lost in the wilderness, then God will show me the way back. Will you pray with me for guidance? Will you? God won't mind a little dirt on your knees."

One man with crutches speaks up: "I believe in you, Sister." The worship band starts playing "What a Friend We Have in Jesus," but Sister Falcon protests, "No, no music, please. No singing, no music. Let us just pray." Almost everyone gets on their knees, next to old wooden benches and on sawdust floors. A banner proclaims her theme: "Thou shalt love thy neighbor as thyself."

As she starts her prayer, "Dearest God," Lefferts, the journalist, doesn't move. She turns and gazes directly at him. "Are you too proud to kneel? You may not believe in God, but God believes in you." Young and old kneel throughout the tent. Holding her Bible at her breast, she continues to stare and he relents. She goes on with her prayer:

> Dear God, I am set upon by enemies and I know not why. . . . Now is my soul troubled. But what shall I say? Shall I say, "Father, save me?" But it is for this cause that I came into this hour. Dearly beloved [the congregation echoes the remainder], avenge not yourself, for it is written, "If thine enemy hunger, feed him; if he thirsts, give him drink. Be not overcome with evil, but overcome evil with good." Amen.

The sister's prayer paralleled the fervor and revival spirit of the developing evangelical movement. The film also conveyed mainline liberals' suspicion of this fresh enthusiasm.

A more modern portrayal of 1920s fundamentalists examined hypocrisy and evolution's specious victory over faith in director Stanley Kramer's reconstructed story of the Scopes Monkey Trial. The opening hymn of *Inherit the Wind* (1960) rings out one side of the religious battle: "Give Me That Old-Time Religion." Religion takes a beating as the Reverend Jeremiah Brown (Claude Akins) prays to God instead of listening to his daughter Rachel (Donna Anderson), who is dating the young science teacher Bertram Cates (Dick York), accused of teaching evolution. Brown orders his daughter to get down on her knees and pray, "for you have betrayed me, betrayed your faith. Your mother is looking down from heaven." For Brown, prayer is a means to hammer others, both enemies and loved ones.

The reverend rants with large clasped hands and quivering voice,

Forgive her, Mommy; forgive her, dear Lord. Tell me what to do, dear Lord God. I love my daughter. How can I save her? Tell me what to do. I will sprinkle clean water and you shall be clean from all your filthiness and from your idols will I cleanse you. A new spirit put within you and I will tear out the stony hearts of flesh and I will give you a heart of flesh.

Lit from the diabolical flame of his cigarette, the cynical journalist Hornbeck smirks as he watches the reverend incite the crowd with his diatribe, and asks, "Whatever happened to silent prayer?"

Brown violently lashes out at Cates. "O Lord, of the tempest and the thunder, strike down this sinner, as Thou did Thine enemies of old in the days of the pharaohs! Let him know the terror of Thy sword! Let his soul, for all eternity, writhe in anguish and damnation!"

His daughter screams out, "No! No, Pa! Don't pray to destroy Bert!"

The unmoved father escalates his rant: "Lord! We ask this same curse for those who ask grace for this sinner! Though they be blood of my blood and flesh of my *flesh!*"

Even in the midst of the carnival atmosphere of the *Scopes*-like trial, defense attorney Henry Drummond (Spencer Tracy) quotes a biblical proverb to the overzealous Brown, that "he that troubleth his own house shall inherit the wind." When asked what he considers holy, Drummond answers, "The individual human mind. In a child's power to master the multiplication table, there is more sanctity than in all your shouted 'amens' and 'holy holies' and 'hosannas.' An idea is a greater monument than a cathedral. And the advance of man's knowledge is a greater miracle than all the sticks turned to snakes, or the parting of the waters."

The film shaped a religious debate between liberals and conservatives, paralleling the political chasm between progressives and traditionalists that Mary Brennan discusses in *Turning Right in the Sixties*. While the Protestant liberal establishment seemed to be thriving in the 1950s, the mainline churches would be in disarray within the decade, marking the beginning of a long decline.

The Music of Prayer

Less controversial films covered religion and prayer more gently and traditionally. Taking place during the Civil War, *Friendly Persuasion*

(William Wyler, 1956) posits an eager Professor Waldo Quigley trying to sell organs, "instruments of the devil," to Quakers. He argues that a "church without an organ is like a tree without a bird." Realizing his futility, he asks, "Where's the Methodist church?" When Quaker Jess Birdwell (Gary Cooper) loses a horse buggy race to church with his Methodist neighbor, a friend says he might do better "if you talked more to the Almighty as you do to this horse."

The Quaker's great temptation is his desire for music, as he secretly covets an organ. After he purchases one, his daughter and her beau are upstairs playing it. Quaker elders visit to check on Birdwell's spiritual temperature, and he must cover the sound of the new organ: "Shall we seek wisdom in prayer? Let us pray. Let us lift our hearts in prayer." "Amen to that," they say. As the Friends pray for peace and guidance in the Civil War, Birdwell prays more fervently and incoherently to drown out the music. When the prayers cease, one fellow Quaker tells him, "Thy prayer carried me so near to heaven's gates, I thought I heard the choiring of angel voices."

After the elders leave, the parents don't hear the organ melodies. When they suspect a bit of spooning by the young couple, Birdwell interprets the quiet as the practice of silent prayer.

Juxtaposed to the plain meetinghouse of the Friends is the enthusiastic singing of the Methodists, with their bells and integrated men and women. The Quakers follow Proverbs 33:1 to be quiet from a fear of evil, and wait patiently upon the Lord for direction. When plundering Confederates endanger the community, Birdwell confesses, "If I defend, I hope and pray I can be an instrument of the Lord. Let us pray that we follow His will, when we learn war no more." Struggling with the encroaching war, Birdwell prays, "Dear God, make me an instrument of peace on earth." As music invites one to raise one's heart to God, it functions like a prayer, for both Methodists and Quakers. As Shakespeare wrote, "There is nothing in the world so much like prayer as music is," a quotation that fits both worship and romance.

Six scruffy-bearded backwoods men, frontier brothers who act like hogs and eat like hogs, need taming in the toe-tapping and rollicking musical *Seven Brides for Seven Brothers* (Stanley Donen, 1954). Their new sister-in-law Milly (Jane Powell) clasps her hands to pray in desperation over the loutish boys in her care. She grabs her Bible and reads,

"Cast not your pearls before swine lest they trample them under their feet and turn again and rend you." It is a good and timely word.

Trying to civilize them, she denies them a breakfast of eggs, pancakes, biscuits, bacon, ham, and hot fresh coffee until they are well-shaven and cleaned up. "Wanna eat?" she taunts. When they finally wash up, she leads them in prayer: "O Lord, Thou hast brought us through desert, mountain, and wilderness to a good land, a land of wheat and grain where we need never hunger. We thank Thee, O Lord, for Thy loving care and Thy bounty. Amen." The boys all say, "Amen."

Each also learns to say "after you" as they pass around the food. Later their eldest brother, Adam (Howard Keel), teaches them about the Romans abducting Sabine women. His parable directs them to go out and find good wives and bring them back, but he reminds them to capture a parson as well to officiate the weddings. They kidnap Reverend Elcott, whose own daughter has been captured. When the girls' fathers come to rescue them and hear a baby, they panic. Even the preacher sighs to the Lord and laments, "Oh no, not that!" Not knowing that the baby is Milly's, they all happily agree to six shotgun weddings, dancing and praying with thanksgiving.

Tennessee Williams's soap opera *Sweet Bird of Youth* (Richard Brooks, 1962) incorporates music as a call to prayer. Returning home after an attempt to make it in Hollywood, gigolo Chance Wayne (Paul Newman) pursues Heavenly (Shirley Knight), the daughter of Boss Finley (Ed Begley). Forbidden to see Heavenly, Chance invades the church as the congregation at the Easter service ironically sings "Abide with Me," derived from Johann Bach's "Sleepers Awake" cantata, based on the parable of the ten virgins in Matthew 25. Chance wants the opportunity to be at a wedding feast.

Hollywood situates religion easily in historical dramas, such as *Song without End* (Charles Vidor, George Cukor, 1960), the biopic of musician Franz Liszt (Dirk Bogarde). The womanizing composer is out drinking after midnight with his friends George Sand, Frédéric Chopin, and his manager, when a priest ringing a bell awakens his conscience. Living in adultery with a nonbelieving countess (who complains that his music is "too religious"), he escapes into a chapel to pray. He proceeds to the church organ, and while his manager works the bellows, he plays lustily.

His mother senses his temptations, warning that he is wasting his life in "mocking God," but he confesses to being "part gypsy/part priest," at war with himself. He asks her to pray. "What shall I pray for, Franz?" she asks. "Pray for your son." He asserts that he will not play in a cathedral for pay, only for charity. A bishop calls Liszt a libertine and forbids him to marry in the Roman Catholic Church. His princess appeals to the Vatican, but when her deception in trying to get an annulment is exposed, the wedding is canceled. She ruefully realizes that she was God's instrument to bring Liszt back into the fold of the Church, as he enters a Franciscan monastery. These musical films not only hint at the rise of young men and women in the church, the new demographic of teenagers, but also nod to the emergence of *their* music. Music drew the seven brides and seven brothers together, suggesting that its evocative power would have more of an impact than parents realized.

The Emergent Baby Boom Family

Surprisingly, a family film erupted as one of the more controversial films of the postwar era, Michael Curtiz's 1947 *Life with Father*. Censors warned Jack Warner to make "certain that the finished picture contains nothing offensive to religious minded people" and suggested he seek advice from ministers regarding church scenes, particularly scenes with the minister, Dr. Lloyd. The Breen Code demanded that Lloyd not be portrayed as the comic butt for "Father" Clarence Day (William Powell). "The laughs should be on Father Day and not on the minister."[23] Memos also insisted that producers omit the words "damn and damnation" and change an offensive reference to "psalm-singing monkeys."

Some comic bits were retained. When little Jimmy's mother, Vinnie (Irene Dunne), wants to know why her son didn't kneel in church, he says directly, "I just couldn't." She asks, "Has it anything to do with Mary [their attractive houseguest]? I know she's a Methodist." "Oh no, Mother, Methodists kneel. Mary told me. They don't get up and down so much, but they stay down longer."

Joseph Breen expressed concerns about the derogatory depiction of the Protestant minister. Bishop Stevens, the Episcopal bishop of Los Angeles, had itemized certain concerns, particularly in holding an Anglican clergyman up to ridicule, protesting that people need to know that the Episcopal

Church has not given its approval to this "unfortunate representation of the Anglican minister."[24] Warner Bros responded to such pertinent matters raised by the Reverend Herbert Smith of Beverly Hills regarding the character of the minister: "As you know, I would like to see the minister be a little more of a human being and a little less stiff and stuffy."

As you know, many Protestant groups have been complaining because of the over-emphasis of Catholic themes in pictures. They have even gone so far as to set up the Protestant Film Foundation to protect the interest of Protestants in motion pictures. One of their principal complaints is that whenever a Catholic priest is shown on the screen he is always pictured as a warm, likeable, human character, while Protestant clergymen are almost always pictured as stiff and unpleasant.[25]

In one scene, Vinnie becomes ill. Jack Warner was not terribly concerned about Bishop Stevens's problems with Lloyd praying for Vinnie's healing. He was more concerned with what he thought was the tactless use of the phrase "miserable sinner" (not being aware that such a phrase was a mainstay in the Book of Common Prayer), which Warner felt made Lloyd look like a fool. But Warner sensed that "there has been a growing feeling of resentment in Protestant circles over what they consider unsympathetic portrayals of Protestant clergymen on the screen. Rightly or wrongly, they feel that Catholic Priests are always portrayed as 'regular fellows' while the portrayals of Protestant Ministers have been somewhat less complimentary." A different pressure was emerging with the organization of the Protestant Film Commission.

Producers remade Dr. Lloyd as a character who would "compliment members of the Protestant faith rather than to make them feel a little ashamed and resentful" but also resisted altering "the comedy situation or our story goes out the window." Eric Johnston, president of the Motion Picture Association of America, consulted with Breen on the crucial penultimate scene of the film. Father Day steps out of his triumphal chariot carriage, and a policeman tips his cap and says, "Morning, Mr. Day, going to the office?" To which Father replies, "No, I'm going to be baptized, damn it!" Johnston actually authorized the use of the words.[26]

Breen acquiesced to the inclusion of "damn" in Day's "I'm going to be baptized, damn it!,"[27] but did not approve the use of "damn" spoken by the Father when he finds the minister in his house or when referring to himself as a "damn good Christian."[28]

The filmmakers also modified the uses of "Amen." First, they altered "two Amens at the end of the church sequence" into "low, deep, and reverent" utterances. Second, when the congregation said "Amen," it came across as a "roar," and for Episcopalians, not noted for enthusiasm, "this must definitely be subdued so that it is in a reverent, subdued tone."[29]

When the film was released, several letters called the comedy "blasphemous." One letter writer asserted that "the sacrament of Holy Baptism is a sacred, God-ordained act, intimately connected with our soul's salvation." The writer complained that "no film company has the right to drag into the field of farce, to ridicule, to offend, to misrepresent something so precious to the spiritual feelings of humble and sincere Christians."[30] The British Board of Film Censors went so far as to cut a scene of the minister's prayer. In particular, when the baptismal office affirms, "Except a man be born of water and of the spirit, he cannot enter into the kingdom of God. He that believeth and is baptized shall be saved, but he that believeth not shall be damned," Father Day mutters, "Until you stirred Him up, I had no trouble with God. Oh, tarnation. Hallelujah! Amen." The producers ended up feeling like their poor eponymous hero.

The family film augured the emphasis on family prayers. However, political issues about prayer in schools festered. Plaintiffs called for the government to clamp down on school prayers, culminating in the *Engel v. Vitale* case, which outlawed prayer in schools in 1962. Even so, films portrayed children talking to God. *The Wonderful World of the Brothers Grimm* (Henry Levin, Georg Pal, 1962) taps into the family mealtime grace of the elder Grimm brother's family. His two children, looking like an archetypal Hansel and Gretel, argue over who gets to give thanks: "It's my turn." "No, it's my turn." "It was your turn yesterday." Finally, both pray, "Bless us, O Lord, and these Thy gifts, which we area about to receive from Thy bounty."

In *My Six Loves* (Gower Champion, 1963), the solid Reverend Jim Larkin (Cliff Robertson) brings six abandoned children to stay at the home of exhausted Broadway star Janice Courtney (Debbie Reynolds). As they gather for dinner, hollering, wearing paper bags and tin pans as hats, he pops a paper bag to get their attention. Holding out his hand, he instructs the youngster on his right, "Come on." They hold hands (except for the defiant elder son) and give thanks for the fruit of God's goodness.

Prayer simultaneously functions as a weapon and as an encouragement in Michael Curtiz's adaptation of the Mark Twain novel *The Adventures of Huckleberry Finn* (1960). Huck (Eddie Hodges) sits captive at the dinner table between the kindly Widow Douglas and the judgmental Sarah Watson. The latter snidely remarks that Huck's mom lies dead in the churchyard and his dad lies drunk with the hogs by the riverside. His guardian defends him.

Miss Watson initiates the prayer: "Dear Lord, we thank Thee for this food and all Thy blessing. And we beg Thee to share Thy light before this sinner and make him stop running around town barefoot, eating like a pig, and not going to school." Huck looks askance at her. Then the widow interrupts with her grace, praying that Huck might discover "the wisdom of education" and that he'll "become a good and honorable man," to which the condemnatory Watson concludes, "So when the knell of doom sounds, he won't have to run forever in the eternal fires of hell! Amen!" Huck coughs out an "amen."

In contrast to the fraudulent Percy, an impious clergyman who shouts "hallelujah," runaway slave Jim (Archie Moore) prays with sincerity, seeking forgiveness for his sins. He points out to Huck that God's heaven has so many stars. Huck tells Jim that he has never seen "nobody pray like you, Jim." Jim responds gently, "Can't pray too much, not when you know you're a sinner and the Lord knows." The prayers of family and children were modeled on the work of American illustrator Norman Rockwell, who in 1951 painted the *Saturday Evening Post*'s Thanksgiving issue cover. *Saying Grace* depicted a mother and son quietly bowing to pray in a crowded diner. In the illustration, two puzzled observers look on, even as film spectators might have looked at children praying in the movies.[31]

The End of the Age

Many prayers attended to the dark clouds looming on the horizon—the pressing concerns of the age, the Red scare, existential crises—and sought hope in what British author J. R. R. Tolkien termed a "eucatastrophe."

With overt images of faith, such as crosses and people praying, Edmund North, screenwriter of *The Day the Earth Stood Still* (Robert Wise, 1951), acknowledged the inclusion of religious elements in the film: "It was my private little joke. I never discussed this angle with [producer] Blaustein or [director Robert] Wise because I didn't want it expressed. I had originally hoped that the Christ comparison would be subliminal. I didn't honestly expect audiences to pick up the allusion. . . . I never wanted it to be a conscious thing, but I thought it had value being there."[32] Klaatu, known as Mr. Carpenter, seeks to bring peace and goodwill, but dies and comes back to life. Yet he warns of an impending judgment if earth does not put down its swords.

The Breen Office rejected the version of Edmund North's screenplay in which Klaatu is resurrected because, as it stipulated, "only God can do that." Wise and North worked out a compromise in which he mentions that the power of life and death doesn't derive from Klaatu's humanoid robot, Gort, but with the "Almighty Spirit."

Destruction of the entire world loomed as the ominous theme of George Pal's revisionist production of H. G. Wells's novel *War of the Worlds* (Byron Haskins, 1953). The thought that one could rely on the goodwill and piety of religion to counter the alien evil during the Cold War was quickly dismissed as the clerical-collared Pastor Matthew Collins walks toward the invading force quoting the Twenty-Third Psalm. He politely takes off his hat and says, "Though I walk through the valley of the shadow of death, I will fear no evil." Just as he proclaims, "I will dwell in the house of the Lord forever," alien rays incinerate him. The good liberal Protestant, holding up a Bible emblazoned with a cross, as if warding off vampires and believing in world peace, requires a wake-up call. He gets vaporized by a Martian death ray.

Scholar Doug Cowan keenly points out the "fatal naïveté of priests who try to reason with monsters," quoting Joe Dante's jest that it was polite of the Martian to let him finish his prayer.[33] The film subverts liberal notions that one can make peace with aliens (that is, communists). As the aliens wreak havoc on civilization, Dr. Clayton Forrester (Gene Barry) seeks his girlfriend, Sylvia (Ann Robinson), in and out of various churches.

In the first church a minister in the pulpit prays, "We humbly beseech Thy divine guidance, O Lord. Deliver us from the fear which has

Unfortunately, the minister discovers that the Twenty-Third Psalm is no weapon to match aliens in *War of the Worlds* (Byron Haskins, 1953).

come upon us, from the evil that grows ever nearer, from the terror that soon will knock upon the door of this Thy house. O Lord, we pray Thee, grant us the miracle of Thy divine intervention." In the second church, a Spanish Roman Catholic priest recites rosaries. The priest tells Forrester, "Don't go, son. Stay with us." He continues to a third congregation, in which a Baptist minister in a white shirt, black tie, and gray suit leads his people bowed in their pews. "In our peril, we plea, succor and comfort us in this hour, please God." Forrester acknowledges, "We are all praying for a miracle." The entire denouement offers a stark reversal of Wells's atheist perspective.

Suddenly, in a miracle of divine intervention, Forrester not only finds his woman, but looks up and hears church bells. As the aliens come crashing down, the narrator explains it all:

The Martians had no resistance to bacteria in our atmosphere, to which we have long since become immune. Once they have breathed our air, germs which no longer affect us began to affect them, and the end came swiftly. All over the world the machines began to stop and fall. After all that men could do had failed, Martians were destroyed and humanity was saved by the littlest thing which God in His wisdom had put upon this earth.

The film concludes with people streaming out of the churches praying and singing "Now Thank We All Our God," ending in the line "in this world *and* the next." Owing more to Von Balthasar's idea that "faith [is] a window to reality rather than a buffer against it" than Wells's dystopian vision, where religion would not be around for much longer, the film was its own bulwark against the red menace and UFOs.

In Don Siegel's *Invasion of the Body Snatchers* (1957), Dr. Miles Bennell (Kevin McCarthy) of the small town Santa Mira, California, notices that people are acting strangely. Fleeing the pods that turn humans into robotic doppelgängers, Miles and his girlfriend, Becky, hide in a cave. When he goes to investigate some heavenly romantic music, he orders Becky to "stay here and pray that they are as human as they sound." After finding out that the music is recorded, he returns to find that Becky has fallen asleep, and quips the greatest line in the movie: "I never knew fear until I kissed Becky." It seems she hadn't prayed enough. In this film, prayers were insufficient to ward off potential invaders.

Fear of the bomb, of communists, of an apocalypse, evoked the prayers of fundamentalist churches and impassioned sermons. Yet fears concerned not only atomic bombs, but existential struggles as well. Confronting the crisis of personal meaning, *The Incredible Shrinking Man* (Jack Arnold, 1957) features Scott Carey (Grant Williams) encountering a strange radioactive and chemical mist that causes him to decrease in size and significance. As he disappears, his final prayer confesses in the face of both his existential confusion and marital disintegration that while he is "smaller than the smallest, I meant something, too. To God, there is no zero. I still exist."

While science fiction films fed off of paranoia about an uncertain future, religion offered some comfort. In contrast to modernity's denial of the supernatural, it persisted both in alien monsters and in conversations with the Almighty.

Postwar Traumas

Alcoholism, depression, racism, religious crises, and a host of other ills percolated under the gloss of the age of prosperity and the man in the gray suit. In *Come Back, Little Sheba* (Daniel Mann, 1952), Doc Delaney (Burt Lancaster) wrestles with his alcoholism and recites the famous Alcoholics Anonymous Serenity Prayer (composed by Reinhold Niebuhr) for his dowdy wife, Lola (Shirley Booth).

She asks, "And did you ask God to be with you all day, and keep you strong?" When he answers in the affirmative, she responds, "Then God will be with you, Doc." Sitting at the kitchen table as he is drinking his orange juice, she requests, "Say your prayer for me, Daddy. I love to hear it." He speaks with clarity and directness.

"God, grant me the serenity to accept the things I cannot change, courage to change the things I can, and wisdom always to know the difference."

"Oh that's so nice, so pretty."

However, they take in a young, pretty boarder, Marie (Terry Moore), who is visited by a boyfriend. A busybody, Lola confesses to spying on

In *Come Back, Little Sheba* (Daniel Mann, 1952), alcoholic Doc Delaney (Burt Lancaster) tries to live by the Serenity Prayer written by theologian Reinhold Niebuhr.

them wooing, and she asks her husband, "Is there anything wrong? They always behave so nice, Doc, I know. I watch them." When he asks what she means that she watches them, she answers, "Well, nights when you haven't been home, I let them use the parlor."

Stunned that she would be such a voyeur, he repeats, "You watch them?" She answers logically enough, "Well, you watch young people making love in the movies, Doc, there's nothing wrong with that. I thought it's the sweetest time in life. Makes me feel young again!" When Doc sees Marie take the boy into her bedroom, he assumes the worst, and what he imagines of young lust disturbs him so much he goes back to the bottle, summoning the need for another AA prayer. Churches sought to help alcoholics find that "greater power" and supported the Twelve Step Program, frequently offering their basements as meeting places. Many churches saw their social mission of helping those addicted or destitute and made room on the margins for their succor.

Lust provides the energy of the quintessential soap drama of the 1950s, *Peyton Place* (Mark Robson, 1957). Nestled in New Hampshire, the town of Peyton Place offers citizens a smorgasbord of churches: Chestnut St. Baptist Church (its marquee quotes Martin Buber: "The Man who loves God loves also him whom God loves"); Saint Bernard's Church, Our Lady of Good Hope Church, and Saint Thomas Episcopal Church. The plethora of churches reflected the fact that on a typical Sunday morning during this era, almost half of all Americans attended church, the highest percentage in U.S. history.

Tucked away in this placid model community, many scandals and ugly prejudices simmer in the summer months. Raised in the town since the start of World War II, Allison MacKensie (Diane Varsi) reflects on her adolescence. After the attack on Pearl Harbor, she writes, "I prayed for them." Her uptight mother, Constance (Lana Turner), wrestles with her own problems, desperately calling out, "God, help me!"

Allison's best friend, Selena Cross (Hope Lange), lives across the tracks in a shantytown with an abusive stepfather. Nevertheless, in spite of her struggles, she goes to church with her younger brother, joining in singing the doxology, "Praise God from whom all blessings flow." However, she will be tried for the stepfather's murder, bringing to light numerous crises in the community.

The film emphasizes escalating problems with teenagers, what sociologists were viewing as a growing yet undefined generation gap. *Peyton Place* dealt with scandalous books on sex in plain wrappers, repressive parents, illegitimacy, abortion, miscarriages, adultery, rape, incest, suicide, and rebellion against the hypocrisy of town leaders. Ministers intone funeral rites, praying that the deceased may "know His love and peace" and then lead congregations in reciting the Our Father. Allison finds her heaven in a bucolic place of solace called Road's End overlooking the Atlantic Ocean in New Hampshire: "Nobody knew this place but me and God."

Attracted to the new young high school principal, Constance visits his house on Christmas, wearing a red dress symbolizing reconciliation. "O Come All Ye Faithful" and "Joy to the World" play in the background, representing certain values lacking in the town. With all the churches in town, authentic faith plays like notes in the Christmas carols, unnoticed and a mere part of the scenery. Contrasting the idyllic pastoral setting are the tumultuous domestic scandals. Churches and secular life seem clearly delineated from each other.

In *East of Eden* (Elia Kazan, 1955), John Steinbeck's gritty novel set in 1917 is informed by the biblical story of Cain and Abel, with Raymond Massey playing Adam Trask, the father of good son Aron (Richard Davalos) and bad son Cal (James Dean). Even the sheriff quotes the story of Cain slaying his brother in the land of Nod (Genesis 4:9, 16), expressing how every son needs the love of a father. Cal has essentially chased his brother off to the war by revealing that their mother is a prostitute running a brothel. As he denies knowing about Aron, he asks, "Am I my brother's keeper? And Cain went out from the presence of the Lord, and dwelt in the land of Nod, on the east of Eden."

At the dinner table, after a rebellious Cal has trashed the ice used to preserve his father's lettuce crop, the father reads from Psalm 32, "Blessed is he whose transgression is forgiven, whose sin is covered." In the darkened house, the patriarch forces Cal to read, starting with the fifth verse: "Five. I acknowledge my sin unto Thee, and mine iniquity have I not hid. I said, I will confess my transgressions unto the Lord and Thou forgavest the iniquity of my sin. Selah." His father asks him to slow down and not read the verse numbers. Cal continues, "For this shall every one that is godly pray unto Thee. And surely in the floods of great waters they shall not come nigh unto him. Selah."

The exchanges expose the hardness of both father and son, with Adam denouncing Cal: "You have no repentance! You're bad! Through and through, bad!" In a paradoxical moment, Cal actually confesses the truth of the psalm, even in his disobedience: "I am bad—I've known that for a long time. Aron is the good one." Director Kazan angled shots to suggest that man has a choice, even though his mother is a madam in a brothel. (Censor Joseph Breen expressed concern over the scenes in the brothel and demanded changes regarding imprudent references to Mary, the Mother of Christ.[34]) Overall, the film foreshadowed the crack between generations that many ignored. The film also portended the emerging eruption of a hard-line fundamentalism that would argue vehemently for a literal interpretation of the inerrant Bible. Prayers and scriptures would become weapons, arrows to shoot at secular enemies.

Stanley Kubrick's mischief was on display in his 1962 version of Vladimir Nabokov's novel *Lolita*, about a middle-aged man's obsession with a nubile teenager. Marrying the lonely and desperate Charlotte Haze (Shelley Winters), French literature professor Humbert Humbert (James Mason) aims at getting closer to her nymphet daughter, Lolita (Sue Lyons).

When Charlotte discovers Humbert's nasty opinion of her ("the cow, the obnoxious mama, the brainless *baba*"), she fumes and despairs, writing him a letter of "confession." "I love you, and last Sunday in church I asked the Lord what I should do and what I am doing now. If you stay, you will want me like I want you. . . . Pray for me . . . if you ever pray." Watched over closely by the Production Code Office and the Catholic Legion of Decency, Kubrick still managed to sneak in a bit of subversive eroticism and religious skepticism. As she sits before a triptych of saints on her bureau, alongside her former husband's ashes, Charlotte asks her new husband, Humbert, "Do you believe in God?"

His answer captures the cynical despair of Humbert and the era: "The question is, Does God believe in me?" This naughty satire captured the caustic wit of sophisticated intellectuals, who were losing faith in all religion.

The crisis of faith takes a comic turn in *God's Little Acre* (Anthony Mann, 1958), where Robert Ryan plays Farmer Walden incessantly looking for his grandfather's buried gold. In a hurry to find quick money, he neglects the rich farmland and digs everywhere he can. He has promised God the treasure if it is found buried on the small plot of land he has tithed to God.

Whenever he plants a cross on his land, he acknowledges that if there is a treasure under it, it will be given to the holiness church. Of course, when he suspects that the treasure might just be on "God's little acre," he moves the acre just in case, replanting it by the house, where he prays. Kneeling, biting his nails, and rubbing his chin amidst comic music, he takes off his hat and speaks to heaven:

> God, please forgive me. I had to move Your little acre. Just had to put myself out of temptation. If I'd found gold way up there, I'd been sorely tempted not to turn it over to You. You wouldn't want me into temptation. I know that. I don't mean to cheat You none, oh no, I don't. You can have anything that grows on this piece of ground. Flowers, honey, or anything else.

Interrupted by his sexy daughter-in-law, Griselda (Tina Louise), always in a low-cut, revealing dress, he asks whether she has brought out the ripe watermelon (her own bountiful breasts inviting the viewer's gaze), as he is "ready for *it.*"

After he digs a large hole under his house, he stands bowed and bloodied, with his family falling apart. Walden entreats God again: "Dear Lord, give me strength to spread out my arms to the ends of my fields. Let me fill up those holes and make the land smooth. I'll never dig another hole again except to plant seeds for things to grow." His earnest repentance continues as he is plowing at the end of the film; however, when he hits metal, his grandfather's shovel, he thinks it may be a sign from the Lord, and he greedily goes back to digging one more time. The faith and self-confidence of Americans, summarized in the positive thinking of Norman Vincent Peale, suggested that anyone could surmount any obstacle in life. What it did, ironically, was not increase faith, but supplant it with materialism and a prosperity gospel.

In Michael Curtiz's comedy *Trouble along the Way* (1953), the coaching career of divorced Steve Aloysius Williams (former USC football player John Wayne) has hit a snag. He fights his ex-wife for custody of

their daughter, while Child Welfare Agency social worker Alice Singleton (Debbie Reynolds) changes sides during the trial. At one point, she
declares that "he hasn't got a prayer for keeping his daughter."

Meanwhile, the financially struggling Saint Anthony's Academy (patron saint of the lost) seeks a miracle to stay open. Father Burke (Charles
Coburn) hires Coach Williams, believing that the way to save the school
is by recruiting a football team. He kneels before a crucifix. Before he
gets up and looks out the window, the coach and his daughter are arriving, with church bells chiming. It is a movie of last resorts, where the
assembled team "couldn't beat a high school debating team." Coach Williams's own sullied coaching image needs cleansing as well.

The coach decides to find inspiration in the Holy Bible. Father Burke
instructs him to consult Deuteronomy 32:15. Other priests, trying unsuc-
cessfully to locate a Bible, look helplessly at one another. Burke mocks
their inability to find one: "Well, well? Is there a Bible in the house, or do
you have to go to a hotel?" When the coach finds the passage, it advises
getting "fat and kick." Thus the message is to train some tough athletes.

Father Malone, suggesting that the team had become lazy and pliant,
concedes an ineffective biblical model: "'Do unto others as you would
have others do unto you.' But, usually, the others do it to us first." When
the coach schedules games with powerhouse teams like Villanova and
Notre Dame in the first year, a priest wonders whether he couldn't have
booked one Protestant school for a breather.

His prayers center on his daughter. He asks Singleton, "What do you
know about love? [It is] sitting beside a sick kid's bed waiting for the
doctor, praying it isn't polio." Love, as a failed human being understands,
is praying through suffering, hoping in spite of trouble. What the film
also contributed to the national conversation was that Roman Catholicism wasn't that much different from mainstream Protestantism. What
emerged, as Will Herberg observed in 1955, was that it was important to
have "some" religion rather than any particular religion. Even President
Eisenhower modeled a generic Presbyterian and articulated that government should be based on a deeply felt religious faith; although he added,
"I don't care what it is."[35]

While the 1950s offered the façade of a prosperous religious community, cancerous growths were beginning to show. Faith slowly eroded
as affluence flourished, and the prayers in movies exposed the under-

belly of skepticism about mainline churches and prophesied a coming secularism.

During the postwar boom, everything on the big screen seemed bigger, from historical dramas to biblical epics to sex. While tensions simmered worldwide, from the Cold War to racism and economic disparity, Americans knew how to pray, as Roman Catholic and Protestant Christianity held sway in the culture. Yet in this material-driven age, movies openly provoked questions about the meaning of life and religion. Cinematic explorations of human nature ranged from examinations of depravity (in the emerging and enduring genre *film noir*) to reaffirmations of traditional truths via Main Street stories and biblical epics. Nothing propelled these tributaries more than the after-effects of war, giving voice to the personal trials of returning veterans and to the now more guarded notion of home and small-town values. These values informed the cowboy code in westerns, which broke down morals into black and white and where helping one's neighbor was dramatized literally. Prayers, though of varying sorts, were staples of adventure films and of *film blanc*'s celestial stories. They took on a more fearful tone in films of large-scale catastrophe, and provided a penetrating light in darker examinations of postwar prosperity and domesticity. And with the emergent baby boom family, children's prayers were featured more. Yet by the next decade, the kids will not even confess to being sinners. After the relatively inoffensive 1950s, they would besiege all authority on earth and in heaven.

5

Cynical Prayers (1964–1976)

At midcentury, institutional religion stood as a bulwark against communism and secularism, but cracks had already appeared. In the 1960s social upheaval would rock this serene landscape, with racial tensions, the sexual revolution and its pill, the civil rights movement, women's liberation, the generation gap, and the divisive conflict in Vietnam raising questions about traditional teachings. Moreover, Eastern spirituality offered alternative religious trends. Implicated as part of the establishment, the church joined big government and big business as suspect institutions. But counterculture movements among the poor and outcast would witness the Jesus movement of the late 1960s, seeking to revive biblical Christianity.[1]

Sociologist Robert Wuthnow marked key changes in the restructuring of institutional denominations and the evolution of a spirituality movement.[2] Spirituality (experiences of the transcendent) supplanted religion (the ties of doctrine and dogma that bind a community). Spiritual seekers, eschewing the materialism of the 1950s, began to experiment with new forms of expressing their faith. Beliefs and lifestyles changed. Out of the 1950s spirituality of dwelling (houses of worship, denominations, and so forth) emerged the 1960s spirituality of seeking.

Alexander Solzhenitsyn described the 1950s as one of the most spiritually impoverished eras of the imagination, one erupting into a more cynical era. Secular society sought to squeeze religion out of the public square, as "man had come of age." Theologically, the Death of God movement paralleled the existential crises in Ingmar Bergman's profoundly provocative films, which found a ready audience with a doubting liberal clergy. While films may have started out with the simple harmony and piety of *Lilies of the Field* (1963), by the end of this period the range of films, from James Collier's *The Hiding Place* (1972) to Sarah Kernochan and Howard Smith's documentary exposé, *Marjoe* (1972), about a boy Pentecostal evangelist turning charlatan, would show a bifurcation in American culture.

Neo-orthodoxy and evangelicalism marked two other growing trends of the postwar period, but much of the optimism that accompanied the election of the first Roman Catholic president evaporated with his assassination on November 22, 1963, coincidentally the same day that authors C. S. Lewis and Aldous Huxley died. The presidential ascent of Lyndon Johnson, a vulgar Texan, did not pump much enthusiasm into a decade that saw an American military-industrial escalation in Southeast Asia. Anti-war protests against Vietnam and demonstrations for civil rights were fueled in part by diverse clergy marching for justice.

In August 1970, the cover of *Esquire* magazine featured a doctored image of Riverside Cathedral flashing a movie marquee; the special issue was titled "The New Movies: Faith of Our Children." The article essentially argued that movies shaped the moral and spiritual condition of American youth more than did schools and churches. A decade later, in 1982, filmmaker George Lucas opined that "films and television tell us the way we conduct our lives, what is right and wrong. . . . For better or worse, the influence of the church, which used to be all-powerful, has been usurped by film."[3] The films of this turbulent era, from the 1960s to the mid-1970s, would direct people to live their lives in more radical ways, and mark a transition from tradition-based morality to a modern relativism.

Historical

Rather than hark back to a nostalgic era, historical films of the 1960s and early 1970s tended to investigate times of upheaval when men and women of character would take a stand. These films offered lessons in character and integrity, and many included substantial prayers. The two wilding friends of *Becket* (Peter Glenville, 1964), Thomas Becket (Richard Burton) and King Henry II (Peter O'Toole), wench and drink their way through the British kingdom—at least until the king appoints his thoughtful friend to the pivotal position of archbishop of Canterbury. However, Becket comes to realize that the office confers deeper obligations upon him than does the crown.

A contrite, stripped king kneels penitently before the mausoleum statuary shrine, less concerned about the honor of God than ameliorating tensions with his fellow Saxons who might protest against the Norman king. His careless words, "Will no one rid me of this meddlesome priest?," have led to the death of his friend and nemesis.

The prayers of Becket himself reveal a saint in the making. He asks, "O Lord, how heavy Thy honor to bear," and looking reverently at a crucifix, he says, "I wonder, Lord, are You laughing at me?" He chants his Latin prayers, "Deus, in adjutorium meum intende" (O God, come to my assistance), both in obedience to the integrity of his sacred office and in search of help as he stands up to the king. Religious courage would make him a martyr, one who through his prayers and actions stood as a witness against corrupt authority.

Like *Becket, A Man for All Seasons* (Fred Zinnemann, 1966) documented the tension between the British crown and the integrity of a Roman Catholic saint, offering clerical models for those who would reject arbitrary authority during the Vietnam era. Thomas More (Paul Scofield) stood up to King Henry VIII (Robert Shaw), in particular on religious grounds regarding his divorce from Catherine. The politically expedient Cardinal Wolsey (Orson Welles) tries to persuade him to consent to the divorce, as Catherine is as "barren as a brick. Are you going to pray for a miracle?" Sir Thomas More replies, "There are precedents." When Cromwell accuses More of being malicious, the chancellor quietly answers, "Not so. I am the king's true subject, and I pray for him and all the realm." The filmmakers displayed, intentionally or not, More as a man for the season of resistance, a man who would stand and suffer for his conscience.

Sitting alone in her chair, Queen Mary of Scotland (Vanessa Redgrave) utters the first prayer of *Mary, Queen of Scots* (Charles Jarrott, 1971): "Almighty God, if You love Francois more than I do, then take him from me . . . but take me, for I have no wish to live without him." Immediately interrupted by a messenger, she is taken away. Her second groom, Lord Darnley (Timothy Dalton), the lustiest and best-proportioned man that the queen had seen, will sire James VI of Scotland. However, Darnley murders the queen's private secretary and proves unfaithful to his wife. He ends up weeping alone, entreating God, "Forgive me, forgive me." In contrast, prayers of thanksgiving are given for the ambition of Puritan Robert Dudley, for he "has provoked the queen [Elizabeth] to wise policy against her will," but to God's glory.

Elizabeth (Glenda Jackson) eventually sentences Mary to die. Knowing that she faces death, Mary prays alone. "O Lord, I have put my trust in You. Do not let me be confounded." As she walks to her death, she confesses a psalm of faith, putting her hope only in the Lord:

In You, my Lord God, are the thing I long for. You are my hope. . . . Protect me from evil things. My sure trust shall always be in You. Let my mouth be filled with Your praise that I may sing of Your glory and honor all the day. Forsake me not when my strength fails me; go not far from me. God, my God, hasten to help me. I will go forth in the strength of the Lord God.

Her last lines address a sympathetic executioner just before her beheading: "I forgive you with all my heart. I thank you even. I hope this death shall put an end to all my troubles. For in my end is my beginning. Lord, into Your hands I commend my spirit." Such a tragic romantic figure evocatively drew sympathy from those who felt estranged from power structures. In all these British episodes, the character with integrity and faith prays and suffers.

In the lavish, even operatic, romantic aesthetic of director Franco Zeffirelli, the inspirational biopic of Saint Francis of Assisi springs forth in *Brother Sun, Sister Moon* (1972), spinning the sacred stories of the troubadour of God. It has all the marks of the 1960s counterculture, with the mellow-yellow minstrel music of Donovan ringing out as prayers of praise and thanksgiving for all of creation.

In these films, the religious integrity and courage of historical saints spoke to growing secular audiences. Prayers were the verbal marks of holiness in these men and women, and demonstrated noble (and somewhat idealistic) models of faith for a generation seeking to separate itself from hypocritical authority and assert its conscience above the dominant cultural values. As these men and women stood for righteousness, so could others strive for goodness and uprightness.

Corrupt Religion

But not all religious ritual was benign. Films also depicted the precipitous decline of orthodox belief and the fallibility of clergy. Fascination with corrupt clergy can be seen in films like *They Call Me Mister Tibbs!* (Gordon Douglas, 1970), where Inspector Tibbs (Sidney Poitier) uncovers a crime committed by the Reverend Logan Sharpe (Martin Landau), a reform-minded, liberal crusading minister, who has killed a prostitute. The political preacher pushing for reform attracts devoted crowds. Calling followers to change the city, he shouts, "If we don't do it for ourselves, no one will do it. Anger will not do it. Votes will!" His leads his congregation in praying, "Lord, teach us to love ourselves so we can love. Teach us to respect ourselves so that others will respect us." Opening his eyes wide and holding his head high, he continues, "And dear Lord, give us this, our first victory! Amen." Politics and religion begin to make strange bedfellows, as each would corrupt the other's realm.

Fallible clergy were not limited to evangelistic preachers, but included defrocked mainline characters. The Reverend Dr. Edward Hewist (Richard Burton) sits in the chapel of his Episcopal boys' prep school after having committed adultery with free-spirited Big Sur artist Laura Reynolds (Elizabeth Taylor), when his wife, Claire (Eva Marie Saint), comes looking for him in *The Sandpiper* (Vincente Minnelli, 1965). "Are you praying?" she inquires. "No, just thinking," he says. "That's a kind of prayer," she replies, oblivious that his thoughts of Laura and his prayers to God are not quite the same thing. For the liberal Hewist, thinking and praying are interchangeable. Faith has been supplanted by vain imaginings, which ultimately condone his adulterous behavior.

In his last feature film, John Ford released *Seven Women* (1966), based on Norah Lofts's short story centering on a Christian mission in China in 1935. Marauding hordes of Chinese bandits lawlessly roam the countryside massacring civilians. One of the most notorious, Tunga Khan, invades the remote mission and instigates a reign of terror. However, the religious element is oddly secular, with Doctor Cartwright (Anne Bancroft), a liberated, cigarette-smoking, irreligious medical worker, challenging the tyrannical authority of the mission head, Miss Agatha Andrews (Margaret Leighton). Several women are excessively whiny, peevish, hysterical, mercurial, and annoying.

The film diametrically contrasts a stern religious attitude with altruistic motives of self-sacrifice. A novice who works with Chinese girls teaches them to sing, "Jesus loves me, this I know / for the Bible tells me so. / We are weak, but He is strong." The words ironically foreshadow the arbitrary killing of weak children. When a plague strikes, the doctor orders the novice to take the children into the fields, where she sings "Shall We Gather at the River?," another mocking moment, as the hymn frequently serves as a funeral dirge in Ford's films. Portents of death suffuse the chosen hymns.

Various moments of table grace appear. The devout missionaries stand behind their chairs while the matron commands, "Now let us say grace," without any sense of what her prayers concern. "Dear God, from whom all blessings spring, we render thanks for what we are about to receive. Give what Thou wilt, as much as Thou wilt, and when Thou wilt. Only Thou knowst what is good for us. Amen." The spinster Andrews demonstrates the form of religion without its power or love.

Eddie Albert, playing the henpecked and badgered husband of a middle-aged pregnant woman, must bury children killed by the plague. He leans on his shovel, falls to the ground, clasps his hands desperately, and prays, "O God," surrendering to the horrors of the situation. He will, however, finally rouse his courage and stand against the bandits. Back at the dinner table where the women wait, the repressed leader prays yet again: "We offer thanks, O God, for Your having delivered us from the perils of the plague, and we pray for those poor souls who have departed and we give thanks for what Thou are about to offer us." At that moment the doctor, drunk and exhausted, barges in and shouts, "What the hell are you all so gloomy about?," breaking the piety of the moment. When one accuses her of sin, she quips, "Well, then, pray for me." Cartwright's bold transgressing contrasts vividly with the cowardly emptiness of the austere missionaries. The film also prophetically raises political questions of why Americans would be in such an unwelcoming Asian country anyway.

Peter Glenville's adaptation of Graham Greene's *The Comedians* (1967) also raises the relevant issue of why Americans would become embroiled in foreign affairs. Graffiti on a wall of a cell suggests that one political prisoner in Papa Doc Duvalier's Haiti prayed to the God of war. The pusillanimous British arms-dealing mercenary Major Jones (Alec Guinness) caustically observes that the prayer wasn't answered in time, as the incarcerated is now buried. The cynical hotel owner Brown (Richard Burton), who has "no faith in faith," meets up with the voluptuous Martha Pineda (Elizabeth Taylor). Pineda declares fidelity to her lover by refusing to make love with her cuckolded husband (Peter Ustinov).

She stays faithful to adultery as she and her husband "slept like two bodies in a morgue." When Brown quotes the Song of Solomon to Pineda, she responds, "I think you're a defrocked priest."

As Brown tries to sell his hotel and escape from the political turmoil, he finds himself constrained by friendships and the island's politics. When offered two thousand dollars to betray Jones to the authorities, Brown quips, "Inflation everywhere; used to be only thirty pieces of silver." At the end, however, Jones admits to Brown, "I understand why people went to confession. Death is such a bloody affair." Needing to own up to his sins, Jones falls on his knees in a cemetery crowded with crosses, and confesses that he is a con man; he has stolen the identity of another man. As Jones dies, Brown, the sinful adulterer, offers absolution, saying, "Sleep well." The film sardonically preaches that all men and women are fools, comedians playing a part on *terra firma*, but that redemption comes in being true to oneself. The models for a counterculture are not religious people, but depictions of authentic sinners, the antiheroes of the 1960s.

Filmmakers showed a vitriolic antagonism toward the seeming hypocrisy of mainline denominations. In the era of Watergate and Vietnam, prayers seemed irrelevant. Director George Roy Hill's version of James Michener's novel *Hawaii* (1966) (by blacklisted screenwriter Dalton Trumbo) jabbed at the Reformed Church of John Calvin. Excoriating the zealous and self-righteous missionary, as well as the effects of colonialism on native cultures, the film makes angry Christians of all Calvinists. After reading a letter from a potential wife, the Reverend Abner Hale (Max von Sydow) is asked whether he thinks she will accept him. His reply, expressing his belief in predestination, is "If God wishes it." The determinism of extreme Calvinism offered no alternatives.

As the family of rigid saints gather around the table before Abner is to set out for his mission in Hawaii, the stern patriarch prays,

> Almighty God, look down with pity on this miserable company of sinners, conceived in lust, delivered in evil, and slaves to every loathsome appetite the flesh is heir to. We have held fast against atheism, Romanism, Unitarianism, and a score of lesser evils, and we thank Thee that Thou hast chosen one of us to carry Thy holy word and the precious light of John Calvin to the wicked and benighted heathen of Hawaii.

On board ship to Hawaii, Abner reads on deck, praying for the heathen, until seasickness overcomes him and he must go below to vomit. The loveless religion of Michener's missionaries contrasts with the vitality of the heathens and of Abner's wife, Jerusha (Julie Andrews), who shows compassion to the local Queen Malama (Jocelyne LaGarde). Malama issues a proclamation that captures the sanctimonious spirit of the interloping missionaries: "Next law: everyone will love Jesus." When a native clergyman, Keoki, who had been a student at Yale Divinity School with Abner, dies during an outbreak of measles, his wife rejects Abner's invitation to pray, as she sees him as a man serving a hateful and cruel God. Jerusha relentlessly appeals to Abner to show grace to the natives of God's exotic islands, but he remains adamantly judgmental. As critic Vincent Canby expressed it in his *New York Times* review, "Not since the Rev. Mr. Davidson went after Sadie Thompson [in *Rain*] has Protestant Christian proselytism come off so poorly on screen."[4] The distrust of global evangelism as an outbreak of neocolonialism reached its zenith in such films.

Sociologist Robert Putnam also chronicled the shift in American religion and civic engagement, with church and synagogue membership at an all-time high in the 1950s, and dropping off in the late 1960s and early 1970s as disaffected baby boomers sought personal fulfillment outside institutional frameworks. Their quest for the ideal self would eventually lead to what became known as the "me decade" of self-serving, narcissistic habits. Robert Bellah discerned similar habits of the heart shifting from a communitarian spirit to a more privatized individualism. His classic example was the almost caricatured model of Sheila Larson's religion of "Sheilaism": "I believe in God. I'm not a religious fanatic. I can't remember the last time I went to church. My faith has carried me a long way. It's Sheilaism. Just my own little voice."[5]

In *Pulp* (Michael Hodges, 1972), a sarcastic writer of sleazy detective fiction, Mickey King (Michael Caine), is drafted to ghostwrite the biography of a pompous Hollywood legend, Preston Gilbert (Mickey Rooney), who not only has played gangsters, but has notorious ties to the Mafia.

Arriving at his publisher's office, King flirts with the secretary in the restroom while the publisher, suffering from a weak bladder, frantically waits for the lavatory to be available. With effusive hand gestures toward the heavens, he first yells, "Son of a bitch," but then quickly repents: "O Jesus, I've blasphemed. O God, I beseech You one favor. Open this door. Why have You deserted me? What have I done wrong? Show me a sign." The toilet flushes and King comes out, quipping, "Knock and it shall be opened unto you," flippantly citing his source, "King of Kings, or was it Matthew?" The clever jesting reveals a profane attitude throughout the film. For example, sitting on a bus with a man and a rooster, the cock crows, and King mutters that it "made me uneasy; it was too near Easter." The subtle allusion to Peter and his denial of Christ requires a biblically literate audience. King attends a funeral service and mutters to himself, "Remember thou art pulp, and to pulp thou shalt return."

Outdoors at his Mediterranean mountaintop villa, Gilbert sits with King at a sumptuous banquet and intones, "Dear Lord, bless this meal we're about to receive in Christ's name." "Surprised?" he asks King. "I'm a good Catholic boy." His deaf mother, wearing black, joins them at table and he mutters, "Mama must have heard me say grace." When he learns that the man contracted to assassinate him has been murdered, he says, "I don't have to say my prayers anymore." However, such hubris leads to his inevitable death. The flippancy of the film ironically showed the consequences and wages of its characters' sins. The selfishness of "Sheilaism" results in death.

In Somerset Maugham's *Of Human Bondage* (Ken Hughes, Henry Hathaway, 1964), clubfooted medical student Philip Carey (Lawrence Harvey) carries on an affair with roving waitress Mildred Rogers (Kim Novak). Mildred's funeral, interrupted with train blasts and church bells, follows the formal rite for burials, with perfunctory words about the dearly departed being committed to the ground, "earth to earth, ashes to ashes, dust to dust." For an untethered life, the hope of the resurrection of the dead sounds like mere words. Carey leaves his old flame, now extinguished, to join his new fiancée. Funeral prayers in *Darling* (John Schlesinger, 1965) also highlight that flesh is like grass, passing away. Although vivacious model Diana Scott (Julie Christie) appears to be a happy "Honeyglow Girl" in the swinging sixties, she lives in a world of narcissism and feckless self-indulgence. While Diana pauses to pray with an old Italian woman with her head covered, the addiction to the permissive lifestyle proves too strong. The individualized religion is insufficient to ground her.

"Sheilaism" is also expressed by the irrepressible and amoral title character (Michael Caine) in *Alfie* (Lewis Gilbert, 1966), another care-free rogue, vain and self-centered. After his irresponsible dallying re-sults in a child with a woman, his lack of commitment leads the mother to marry a kindly bus conductor. The mother and stepfather take their boy for infant baptism, amid church bells, while Alfie watches from a distance. The familiar ritual of "I baptize you in the name of the Father, and of the Son, and of the Holy Ghost" is followed by a recitation of the Our Father, with the repeated mentions of the Father emphasizing the loving-kindness of the new "father."

When an affair with a middle-aged woman ends with an abortion, Alfie is warned not to go behind a curtain, but he does and sees the aborted baby. His weepy prayer rambles:

> Perfectly formed being, don't know what I expected, half expected it to cry out, musta had some life, of course, quite touched me. I started to pray, saying things like "God help me" and things like that. I started to cry, prayed for me bleeding self. Helpless little thing like that, he'd been quite perfect, you know. What you've done?—You murdered him. What's it all about? What's the answer?

In Alfie's recognition of his selfishness, he acknowledges what "he's done for all the birds." Lyricist Burt Bacharach's song asks the question again: "What's it all about, Alfie?" with damning implications. God may watch the sparrows, but Alfie has killed an innocent, unborn child. In the remake (Charles Shyer, 2004), Alfie (Jude Law) reflects at a funeral that he used to think there was nothing worse than death, but the death of the aborted child points to consequences of immoral behavior, a haunting emptiness. Crying for the little one (and for himself), he confesses that he "never meant to hurt anybody," but is told, "But you do, Alfie. Next time, think before unzipping." His amorality has consequences. Roman Catholics and evangelicals viewed abortion as cultural selfishness stem-ming from an indulgent lifestyle. The 1973 Supreme Court decision legalizing abortion in *Roe v. Wade* galvanized the pro-life movement, with the tragedy of *Alfie* providing a too-painful parable.

The ultimate in self-absorption and cruelty can be seen in the home of history professor George and his wife, Martha (Richard Burton and

Elizabeth Taylor), in *Who's Afraid of Virginia Woolf?* (Mike Nichols, 1966). George's sarcastic asides to his wife, who is wearing an embarrassingly revealing outfit ("Why Martha! Your Sunday chapel dress!"), parallel his specious prayer chant, a sort of Latin requiem for the dead or dying. As he chants, he marks the passing of his and Martha's bogus son. (When they found they couldn't have children, they conceived an imaginary child, which became the only glue to their sadomasochistic relationship.) As the couple peel away layers of selfishness and illusions, George offers a prayer that mocks the phoniness of their marriage and the emptiness of a speciously sophisticated society. The ugly depths of the dysfunctional pair reflected what many church counselors experienced. Divorce rates spiked, rising from 24 percent in the mid-1950s to 48 percent by 1985. The argument that "the family that prays together stays together" would be sorely tested in the coming years.

War Prayers

The threat of unleashing a Doomsday apocalypse occurs in the canny satire *Dr. Strangelove* (Stanley Kubrick, 1964). However, when it appears that the bombers accidently sent to pulverize the Soviet Union are retreating from the targets, cheering erupts among all the dignitaries in the War Room. General Turgidson (George C. Scott) whistles loudly, calling the room to attention: "Ah, gentlemen, gentlemen."

The War Room falls silent, with Dr. Strangelove (Peter Sellers) veiled in the shadows. The gum-chewing general begins, "Mr. President, I'm not a sentimentalist at all, by nature, but I think I know what's in every heart in this room. I think we ought to all just bow our heads and give a short prayer of thanks for our deliverance. Lord, we have heard the wings of the angel of death fluttering over our heads from the valley of fear. You have seen fit to deliver us from the forces of evil—"

A phone call interrupts the convoluted prayer: "Excuse me sir, Premier Kissov's calling again and he's hopping mad." As the one renegade plane has broken through all the fail-safe mechanisms, the crisis escalates. The angel of death begins flapping his wings wildly. The prayer was only a superficial covering of a militaristic mindset. The comically outrageous mix of religion, politics, jingoism, and the apocalypse ac-

General Turgidson (George C. Scott) offers a fleeting prayer of gratitude from nuclear annihilation just before he discovers its futility in *Dr. Strangelove* (Stanley Kubrick, 1964).

centuates the insanity of war, just as President Johnson was committing more troops to Vietnam.

The futility of praying in wartime seeps through Dalton Trumbo's *Johnny Got His Gun* (1971), in which a World War I quadruple-amputee, Joe (Timothy Bottoms), cut off from human contact, dreams and fantasizes. When he fears that a rat is attacking him, he questions what's real, the rat or a nurse: "Oh, Jesus Christ, how will I be able to tell the difference?" Jesus (Donald Sutherland) appears and tells him to yell, open his eyes, or tell himself that he's going to sleep and not going to have any nightmares. However, all recommendations are useless, so Jesus tells him he needs a miracle. When Joe finally discovers how to communicate via Morse code, the military hospital officials are concerned, as all he says is "Kill me, kill me, kill me!" One doctor asks the padre whether he doesn't have some message for him. The priest shakes his head and looks to the floor.

The doctor barks, "You could at least tell him to put his faith in God, couldn't you?"

The priest says, "I'll pray for him for the rest of my days. But I will not risk testing his faith against your stupidity."

The military doctor retorts, "Well, you're a hell of a priest, aren't you?" To which the priest responds, "He's the product of your profession, not mine." Jesuit priest Daniel Berrigan and other radical religious activists echoed the accusation, even to the point of pouring blood on draft records, confronting not only American military imperialism, but the deafening silence of their own church hierarchy as well. The film, however, raised the moral quandary of a just war, sparking debates in seminaries and churches across the land.

In the opening scene of the family supper in *Shenandoah* (Andrew McLaglen, 1965), Charlie Anderson (Jimmy Stewart) sits down with eight children and stutters through his bold prayer, smacking of self-sufficiency. Starting with "Lord, *we*," he pauses as his youngest comes in late and forgets to take his hat off. He informs them, "Now your mother wanted you all raised as good Christians." He continues,

> Lord, we cleared this land. We plowed it, sowed it, and harvested it. We cooked the harvest. It wouldn't be here and we wouldn't be eating it if we hadn't done it all ourselves. We worked dog-bone hard for every crumb and morsel, but we thank You, Lord, just the same, for the food we're about to eat. Amen.

By the end, the Civil War has not only ravaged much of their land, but decimated their family. Charlie sits with half his family left and the film is bracketed by the same prayer, but this time wearily and painfully. "Lord, we cleared this land. We plowed it, sowed it, and harvested it. We cook the harvest. It wouldn't be here and we wouldn't be eating it if we hadn't done it all ourselves."

Anderson leaves off the prayer at that point, full of the tragic sense of loss, not able to "thank the Lord, just the same." The idea to "praise God from whom all blessings flow" lingers in the background like the bittersweet aroma of late honeysuckle.

Vietnam brought the issue of an unjust war to the forefront of American political and religious debate. In *Patton* (Franklin Schaffner, 1969), the morality of praying is addressed, camouflaging the issue under a desire for victory over "evil." Reminiscent of earlier debates on God siding with one people or another, *Patton* set forth a brazen apologetic from a hard-driving, swashbuckling military leader. When a chaplain sees a Bible beside General George Patton Jr.'s (George C. Scott) bed, he asks the disciplined commander whether he actually finds time to read it. Patton, the devout Episcopalian, responds, "I sure do. Every goddamn day!" Later, when Patton has been reprimanded for slapping a soldier, he bows before an altar and finds comfort in Psalm 63:

> O God, Thou art my God, early will I seek Thou. My soul thirsteth for Thee. . . . But those that seek my soul, to destroy it, shall go into the lower parts of the earth. They shall fall by the sword, they shall be a portion for foxes. . . . Everyone that sweareth by Him shall glory. But the mouth of them that speak lies shall be stopped.

Humble, yet defiant, he apologizes to his troops.

Later, when the 101st Airborne is surrounded in Bastogne and the weather so inclement that rescue is nigh impossible, Patton calls for his Third Army chaplain (Lionel Murton). He arrives and asks, "You wanted to see me, General?"

Patton barks out, "Oh yeah, Chaplain, I'm sick and tired of having to fight the Germans, the supermen, command, and no gasoline, and now this ungodly weather. I want a weather prayer. See if you can't get God working with us."

The chaplain responds tentatively, "It'll take a pretty thick rug to do that kind of praying." The audacious commander retorts, "I don't know or care if it takes a flying carpet." The chaplain responds, "I don't know how this is going to be received, General, praying for better weather so we can kill our fellow man?" Patton concludes, "Because of my intimate relations with the Almighty, if you write a good prayer, we'll have good weather. I expect the prayer within an hour."

Amid scenes of warfare, destruction, and death of individual soldiers, Patton puts on his glasses and unfolds the requisitioned prayer:

> Almighty and most merciful Father, we humbly beseech Thee of Thy great goodness to restrain this immoderate weather with which we have had to contend. Grant us fair weather for battle. Graciously hearken to us as soldiers who call upon Thee, that armed with Thy power, we may advance

from victory to victory and crush the oppression and wickedness of our enemy and establish Thy justice among men and nations. Amen.

As skies clear, Patton tells his adjutant, "Just got the weather report for tomorrow. Weather's perfect. Get me that chaplain. He stands in good with the Lord, and I want to decorate him."

The war is more chaotic and desperate in *Slaughterhouse Five* (1972), George Roy Hill's adaptation of Kurt Vonnegut's time-warping novel. Billy Pilgrim (Michael Sacks), an optometrist and writer, relates a jumbled tale of how he became "unstuck in time," with jumps of time from the World War to being kidnapped by aliens. During the war, Pilgrim, a chaplain's assistant (whom one character mocks as being less substantial than a man carved out of a banana), is under fire by the Germans and kneels in the middle of the snow. As other soldiers fight among themselves, he suggests, "Let's start praying."

His fellow soldiers are more concerned with bickering. "Where the hell are we?" "Belgium, stupid." Shivering, Billy calls out, "Our Father who art in heaven, hallowed be Thy name. Thy kingdom come. Thy will be done, on earth as it is in heaven. Give us this day our daily bread . . ." At this point he stops and looks up. He realizes that he has randomly been transported to another time and another place. What seems like an arbitrary transfer in time may have well been providential care—God answering his prayer.

A similar parody of this "military mentality" occurs in Mike Nichols's *Catch-22* (1970), a favorite of the anti-war movement. When Captain Yossarian (Alan Arkin) wants to plead insanity to get out of the war, the doctor tells him that "anyone who wants to get out of combat isn't really crazy," so he can't be released. Adapted from Joseph Heller's novel, the narrative satirically introduces an Anabaptist chaplain, Captain Tappman (Anthony Perkins), who holds a "lifelong trust . . . in the wisdom and justice of an immortal, omnipotent, omniscient, humane, universal, anthropomorphic, English-speaking, Anglo-Saxon, pro-American God." The only help the chaplain offers confused soldiers is books or cigarettes. When the chaplain suggests allowing enlisted men to join the officers in a prayer meeting, the colonel is astounded, thinking that they should have a God and chaplain of their own. He is amazed that enlisted men pray to the same God as officers and that God listens.

The colonel tells his chaplain that his business is not to help the soldiers, but to work up some "nice snappy prayers" so that the *Saturday Evening Post* will publish a full-page picture of him.[6]

These wartime prayers reflect the conundrums and contradictions within the religious community regarding war. When Fuller Theological Seminary invited anti-war Republican senator Mark Hatfield to speak on its campus in the early 1970s, it sparked a controversy with other evangelicals. Churches and films wrestled over what God was doing in such tragic settings, and prayers were a weapon in the arsenal of both sides.

Sound of Prayers

In *My Fair Lady* (George Cukor, 1964), adapted from Shaw's play *Pygmalion*, Professor Henry Higgins (Rex Harrison) takes on the challenge of transforming a deliciously low street urchin, Eliza Doolittle (Audrey Hepburn), into a proper English Lady. He first changes her focus from God to self-improvement. Modernity has arrived with education. He orders Eliza, "Now every night before you get into bed, where you used to say your prayers, I want you to say, 'The rain in Spain stays mainly in the plain' fifty times. You'll get much further with the Lord if you learn not to offend His ears." The comic line points more to Anglican decorum than to honest expressions of prayer.

In *The Sound of Music* (Robert Wise, 1965), the hills are alive with music. The film echoes the Psalms, with mountains called to sing and rivers clap their hands with joy. The ever sanguine and ebullient Maria (Julie Andrews) sings her prayers. Her faith holds to a trust that whenever the Lord closes a door, somewhere He opens a window. His lines of communication and providence are always open, even in Nazi-controlled Austria.

Fresh from the convent, Maria becomes the governess for strictly disciplined children, praying for each of them with an authentic conversational style. The eldest girl, Liesl, on the verge of womanhood, is sneaking in late and catches Maria at her bedside, where she overhears Maria's prayer:

Dear Father, now I know why You sent me here. To help these children prepare for a new mother. And I pray this will become a happy family in

Thy sight. God bless the captain. God bless Liesl and Friedrich. God bless Louisa, Brigitta, Marta, and little Gretl. And I forgot the other boy. What's his name? Oh, well, God bless what's-his-name. God bless the Reverend Mother and Sister Margaretta and everybody at the abbey. And now, dear God, about Liesl. Help her know that I'm her friend and help her tell me what she's been up to.

Liesl worriedly asks whether Maria is going to tell the captain on her, but Maria playfully continues, "Help me to be understanding so I may guide her footsteps. In the name of the Father, the Son, and the Holy Ghost. Amen." Maria is a trusted confessor and models both personal prayer and moral instruction.

Later, when Captain von Trapp's (Christopher Plummer) family has just sung its reprise at the Salzburg Music Festival, he articulates his heartfelt prayer. Where the Nazi regime has curtailed liberty in Austria, Maria has brought freedom into his household. Rather than serving in the Third Reich, the captain chooses to leave his beloved homeland. He addresses his fellow Austrians: "I shall not be seeing you again, perhaps for a very long time. I would like to sing for you now . . . a love song. I know you share this love. I pray that you will never let it die." Singing "Edelweiss" and "So Long, Farewell," the family escapes to climb every mountain into Switzerland. Their songs and prayers are interchangeable.

In *West Side Story* (Robert Wise, 1961), the most beautiful sound that Tony (Richard Beymer) has ever heard is "Maria" (Natalie Wood), a name that can sound like music playing, or when said softly, "it's almost like praying." The star-crossed Romeo and Juliet romance of New York City weds the Anglo and Roman Catholic Puerto Rican gangs in its tragic tale. After dancing on the roof because she believes her lover, Tony, is stopping a rumble, news arrives that Tony has killed Maria's brother. Running to her bedroom, she kneels before the Holy Family and prays in Spanish. When Tony arrives, her rage melts to pain and they sing hopefully that there is a place for them "Somewhere." Their prayers voice the groaning of their heart for a utopian refuge.

Musical prayers in this period not only expressed sentimental notions, but provided satirical commentary on the suspect institution of the church. In the Who's rock-opera *Tommy* (Ken Russell, 1975), prayers lose all efficacy. After the trauma of seeing his father murdered, Tommy becomes desperately catatonic. As his stepfather Frank Hobbs (Oliver Reed) sings, "Tommy doesn't know what day it is / He doesn't know who Jesus was or what praying is / How can he be saved / from the eternal grave?"

Not even the preacher (Eric Clapton) or the specialist can help. The prayer of the deaf, blind, mute boy remains a plea for someone to "see me, feel me, touch me, heal me." When he comes into his own, Tommy baptizes his mother by stripping her of her jewelry and symbolically baptizing his followers. Director Russell once said that his films are an "intense affirmation of faith,"[7] and composer/writer Pete Townshend indicated that the film was an attack "on the hypocrisy of organized religion."[8]

Robert Altman's satiric *Nashville* (1975) intersects stories of various characters around the country-western political rally, offering another critique of organized religion. Snapshots of various characters reveal a sardonic view of religion. Short and sanctimonious, Haven Hamilton (Henry Gibson) may pray at his church, but he is as superficially religious as the rest of the cast of musical fools who wander around Nashville trying to make sense of their lives. When British broadcaster Opal (Geraldine Chaplin) observes a black gospel choir (which she describes as "Masais" from Kenya), she asks whether they carry on with such rhythms in church.

Critic Adam Cohen explains that, while the "characters are church-goers," the movie argues that "religion cannot save them. One brilliant montage cuts from one Sunday service to another, showing how families are divided, not brought together. Linnea sings in her African-American church while her family worships in a white one; Haven prays at a Protestant church, while his wife genuflects in a Catholic one."[9]

The convergence of protest folk, rock and roll, Broadway musicals, soul music, and Nashville and Bakersfield country music pushed aside traditional hymns as America opted for cultural change. Yet diverse religious music, such as the Edwin Hawkins Singers' "Oh Happy Day," Barry McGuire's "Eve of Destruction," and George Harrison's "My Sweet Lord," in praise of the Hindu god Krishna, was consigned to the margins until the grassroots explosion of Christian praise and worship in the late 1960s. Music, from all sources, evolved into melodic prayers, prayers that could set the hills to singing or ridicule those who performed them, often more for a public than for God.

Suffering Freedom

Cool Hand Luke (Stuart Rosenberg, 1967) offers a Christological parable of antihero Luke (Paul Newman), whose prison number 37 alludes to the Gospel verse Luke 1:37, "For with God nothing shall be impossible." Sentenced to hard labor on a chain gang for destroying municipal property (parking meters), Luke meets Dragline (George Kennedy), who names him "Cool Hand Luke" for winning at cards with nothing but bluff. As they dig ditches in the hot sun, they are delighted one day to view an overendowed woman washing her car. Dragline spouts a playful, facetious prayer: "O Lord, whatever I done, don't strike me blind for another couple minutes." The prayer functions as a light prologue to more grave conversations with the Almighty.

Music saturates the hot sweltering world of the southern prison, where inmates sing "Just a Closer Walk with Thee." The lyrics ask the question, "Who but Thee my burdens share?" The religious atmosphere permeates the prison as a guard expresses sympathy when he hears of Luke's dying mother, promising, "I wanna say a prayer for your Ma, Luke."

After his mother dies, Luke plays his only inheritance, a banjo, and sings, "I don't care if it rains or freezes, long as I've got my plastic Jesus glued to the dashboard of my car. You can buy them, phosphorescent glows in the dark. He's pink and pleasant; take him with you when you're travelin' far." He concludes, "Virgin Mary, I want to go to hell," preparing for his own death and descent into darkness. Having lost a reason for his release, Luke feels liberated from obeying the prison rules. Thus the prison captain (Strother Martin) pronounces that Luke should be kept off the road lest he try to break out.

Luke does try, but is captured and forced to dig and undig and redig a grave. As he does, Babalugats (Dennis Hopper) drones the symbolic ballad "Ain't No Grave Going to Hold My Body Down."

Seeing Luke's fatigue, the captain snarls at him. Feigning submission, Luke cries out in obsequious tones, "O God, O God, I pray that you don't hit me anymore." He finally escapes to an abandoned chapel. Here, he will deliver heartfelt, conversational prayers, trying to connect with God in what approximates his Garden of Gethsemane crisis, a dialogue of questions and confessions:

Paul Newman plays the title character in *Cool Hand Luke* (Stuart Rosenberg, 1967), who in his own Garden of Gethsemane, doubts and debates with the Almighty.

Anybody here? Hey, old Man, You home tonight? Can You spare a minute? About time we had a little talk. I know I'm a pretty evil fellow, killed people in the war, and I got drunk and chewed up municipal property. I got no cause to ask for much, but You gotta admit You ain't dealt me no cards in a long time. Looks like You got things fixed so I can never win out. Inside/outside all them rules and regulations and bosses. You made me like I am. Just where am I supposed to fit in? Old man, I gotta tell You, I started out pretty strong and fast, but it began to get to me. When does it end? What ya got in mind for me? What do I do now? All right, all right.

He assumes a pious prayer position, kneeling with folded hands and closed eyes. "On my knees asking," he says, as he peeks up at the rafters with one eye. Then, resignedly, he yields to the deafening silence, even as God the Father answered Jesus with silence. "Yeah, that's what I thought. I guess I'm pretty tough to deal with, huh? A hard case, yeah. I guess I have to find my own way." Essentially he concedes, "If that's the way You want it," a paraphrasing of "Not my will, but Thine be done."

The answer that God sends is the authorities coming to arrest him. "That Your answer, old Man? I guess You're a hard case too." Dragline comes in and begs him to just give up, play it cool. However, Luke goes to the open door and mocks his pursuers, parodying what the captain has yapped earlier in the film: "What we got here is a failure to communicate." The sunglass-wearing boss with no eyes shoots him. When Dragline retells Luke's story, he asserts that Luke died smiling. They "weren't ever going to beat him. [He was] a natural-born world-shaker." The analogy to Christ's sufferings and victory may be only metaphorical, but the story of the miraculous Luke lives on.

Easy Rider (Dennis Hopper, 1969) erupts as a surprise in the study of prayer for this turbulent time period, yet it captures both the American quest for freedom and a religious revival, where hippies and outcasts worship Jesus. As Wyatt "Captain America" (Peter Fonda) and Billy "the Kid" Mendoza (Dennis Hopper) set out to cover America, they not only dismantle the American dream, but they stumble upon the budding impact of the late 1960s Jesus movement that started at Calvary Chapel in Costa Mesa, California. Remarkably, the film celebrates sincere prayers in both Hispanic and hippie communities. Yet the film darkly implies that someone will have to suffer and die for America.

Captain America and Billy the Kid are invited to eat at a boys' home, and Mendoza watches a mother teach her child how to pray. Mendoza awkwardly folds his hands, as the child's father quietly prays, "We thank Thee, O Lord, for these Thy gifts, received from Thy bounty in the name of Thy only begotten son, our Lord Jesus Christ."

At their next stop, they join a seemingly free-spirited hippie commune. A disheveled leader, a short man with a reddish beard, leads a group of attractive young men and women in an earnest, leisurely petition: "We have planted our seeds. We ask that our efforts be worthy to produce simple food for our simple tastes. [A rooster crows.] We ask that our efforts be rewarded. We thank You for the food we eat from other hands [a baby gurgles] that we may share it with our fellow man and be even more generous when it is from our own. Thank You for a place to make a stand." He sighs deeply and concludes, "Amen, amen," followed by a chorus of "Amens." Then he invites all, "Let's eat." In this passing scene, the film celebrates the simplicity and innocence of the early hippie Jesus movement, praying and having all things in common.

However, religious themes become more ambiguous as the duo heads to New Orleans to celebrate Mardi Gras. In a trippy graveyard scene, the pilgrims and two prostitutes (one called Mary) partake of LSD and pray the rosary along with a recitation of the Lord's Prayer. The cemetery serves as a harbinger of their imminent death. In their final meal, Wyatt confesses, "We blew it." The day of their death occurs on Ash Wednesday, when repentance should enable them to reflect on *memento mori*, the theological reminder of death of all sinners.

The suffering of sinners provides a sort of purgatory for their imprisoned souls. Hollywood constructed appealing antiheroes who would seek freedom, even through death. The American quest to find personal identity and purpose could not shake off the lingering religious conscience, the habits of praying that helped make sense of suffering. Dialogue was necessary, even if God didn't seem to be present. More and more, praying seemed to assume more of a function of therapy and working out one's confusion. And if there were no answers, and no one there, films opted for more cynical and sacrilegious responses.

Toward Blasphemous Prayers

The rush to produce cheap independent films in the mid-1960s resulted in numerous Roger Corman movies. When *The Wild Angels* (1966) hit the screen, the terror of Hell's Angels motorcycle gangs allegedly ravaging the country incited fear in the American imagination. An apocalypse seemed imminent. In the film, a funeral service in the Sequoia Grove Community Church turns into a drunken orgy. The minister, drafted to conduct a service for Joe "Loser" Kearns (Bruce Dern), finds the coffin draped in a swastika flag. He begins with the religious phrase of an Episcopal wedding ceremony, "Dearly beloved, we are gathered here," and then switches to the incongruous line "to pay last respects to Joseph Kearns." However, as he tries to affirm that the deceased was one of God's children, citing John Donne's "No man is an island and every man is a piece of the continent," he dribbles into other random clichés: "Naked he came out and naked he shall return . . . The Lord gives and the Lord taketh away." The gang of "angels" erupts in heckles and giggles: "You're so full of bull." They see themselves not as "children of God," but heading toward hell, right after they party and get loaded.

In malicious mischief, they put the preacher in the coffin and prop up the corpse of Kearns smoking. Their church funeral bash degenerates into a gang rape, with bongos pounding, drinking, and drugs. In a curious comic act of rebellion, they demolish pews and smash up the church. The Babel-like atmosphere releases a torrent of assertions: "We are Lucifer, Isaiah. Thus says Isaiah: 'We don't want anybody telling us what to do.' Wanna be free." One stoned girl hums a prayer: "Just a closer walk with Thee. Let it be, dear Lord, let it be. I am lost. Jesus, keep me from all wrong." Her plaintive voice mumbles in the background of a lost generation.

Wilma McClatchie (Angie Dickinson) takes her two daughters on the road to rob banks in Steven Carver's cheesy, trashy drive-in *Big Bad Mama* (1974). They are surrounded by religion as much as hounded by the law. Mama ushers her younger daughter to church to get married to a local yokel, but ends up sabotaging the wedding herself. The congregation sings Charles Wesley's hymn "Love Divine, All Love Excelling," whose lyrics entreat God to enter every trembling heart. However, the petition is not realized, mainly because there are few contrite hearts. When the preacher asks the good country folk to bow their "heads in gratitude for the blessings He has bred among us," Mama mutters, "Bullshit" just before his amen.

Even with a poster proclaiming, "Jesus Christ, thank you for everything" displayed prominently in the background, the McClatchie ladies say no thank you and skedaddle out into a life of crime and bootlegging. Along the way they meet Reverend Johnson (Royal Dano), a profanity-spewing preacher ("That's goddamn blasphemy!") who spits out prayers for the dead, a "God rest his soul" being sufficient to mark the passing of the high-spirited uncle when he is shot. Fleeing Keystone-type cops, they serendipitously stumble across a white-suited, healing evangelist driving his Holy California Crusade bus. Singing "Onward Christian Soldiers," they find the meeting providential, as they can hide in the bus of the bogus minister. As the con man minister wants to discuss baptism with them, Mama says, "Reverend, I've had all the dunking I need."

His sermon carries a jumbled, Depression-era message of hope: if you're on the bread line, give thanks, as the Lord moves in mysterious ways. Instead of receiving bread, the script suggests that the suckers (who give their offerings to the healing preacher) get only pipe dreams.

Mama ridicules religious rituals, testifying that her "prodigal daughter is returned to her mother," spouting, "The Lord is my Shepherd, He restoreth my soul. Heal, sweet Jesus." Prayers are opportunities for flippancy.

Blatant blasphemy marks Ring Lardner Jr.'s brilliantly scripted *M*A*S*H** (Robert Altman, 1970), with its open ridicule of belief in God. The bumbling and clueless chaplain, Father John Patrick Mulcahy (Rene Auberjonois), is given the nickname "Dago Red" as a reference to the sacramental wine frequently stolen from him.

Father Mulcahy tries to find a prayer in his little book for Major Frank Burns (Robert Duvall) when the latter goes crazy. We first meet the hypocritical caricature of Burns teaching a young Korean mess-hall boy how to read the Twenty-Third Psalm. "Walk through the val-lee of sha-dow of death for Thou are with me. My cup runneth over." Burns's new tent mates, Hawkeye and Duke Forrest (Tom Skerritt), give the boy a pornographic magazine as an alternative way to learn how to read. When Burns kneels to pray the Lord's Prayer beside his bunk, his tent mates drink their martinis in the background. "Our Father who art in heaven, hallowed be Thy name . . ." When he finally gets to "Amen," they both echo, "Amen" and toast their glasses. Hawkeye asks whether he'd ever seen this syndrome before, to which Duke answers, "Not after the age of eight."

Burns continues praying, "And dear God, protect our young men on the field of battle, that they may return home to their dear ones. And dear God, protect our supreme commander on the field and our commander in chief in Washington, D.C." Astounded at such a public display of sanctimony, Hawkeye inquires, "Frank, were you always religious, or did you crack up over here?" Duke asks, "How long does this show go on?" Burns retorts, "Longer, because now I have your soul to pray for and Captain Pearce's." Burns's inflexible fundamentalism provided an easy target for director Altman. Reflecting that the film, like war itself, didn't end, "it just tailed off," Altman scalds religious cant with a penultimate prayer from the prayer book of Mulcahy:

O Lord God, listen favorably to our prayers. With Your right hand bless this jeep. Send Your holy angels so that all who ride in it may be delivered and guarded from every danger, and as You granted faith and grace by Your deacon Philip to the man from Ethiopia who was sitting in his chariot and reading holy scriptures, show the way of salvation to Your servants.

The prayer has a patina of genuine piety to it, with the sincerity of the priest, but Altman points out a strange irony that the army hymnal actually contained a prayer about blessing an army vehicle. He concluded, "I thought it was quite bizarre." Thus, even the indirect blessing upon the soldiers is viewed through a distorted lens, with the last line, appropriately enough, "God damn war!" The cynicism of the 1970s scapegoated organized religion. With the vacillation of mainline denominations, an awkward reconfiguration of the Roman Catholic Church after Vatican II, the birth of the Jesus movement, and the eruption of evangelical engagement in culture, the church was in flux.

Delivered from Evil

In the 1960s and 1970s the devil made a remarkable reappearance in popular culture, taking on various manifestations. During the English Civil War, the unscrupulous Witchfinder General seeks to root out and burn witches in *Witchfinder General/The Conqueror Worm* (Michael Reeves, 1968). The Witchfinder, Matthew Hopkins (Vincent Price), incurs the wrath of a military Roundhead who has vowed revenge upon Hopkins after Hopkins killed his fiancée Sara's uncle, the village priest, John Lowes (Rupert Davies).

Sara and her fiancé, Marshall, hide from the Witchfinder in a desecrated church, where Sara confesses to having been raped by Hopkins's assistant. Evil appears in the guise of the bogus religion of Hopkins and his minion. Marshall takes Sara's hand, wearily pulls out his sword at the altar, and prays, "We kneel before Thee, O Lord, in humility, to ask for Thy blessing on our union. We ask for the forgiveness of our sins and strength to live righteous lives as man and wife. We pray also for the soul of Thy servant John Lowes. May he know eternal peace." Releasing her hand and lifting the sword, he continues, "And 'tis in Thy sight, O Lord, that I hereby swear that I shall not rest from the pursuit of his murderers till they stand before Thee ready to answer to Thee for their sins." Censored extensively by the British Board of Censors for its sadistic brutality, the film connected religious fanaticism with cruelty and genuine prayers with vengeance.

In *The Fall of the House of Usher* (Roger Corman, 1960), a demonic Roderick Usher (Vincent Price) prepares to bury Madeline Usher (Myrna Fahey) prematurely, to stop the cursed bloodline of his family. He mouths sanctimonious platitudes such as "one candle before the darkness" as her breathing body is entombed. Madeline's fiancé, Philip Winthrop (Mark Damon), kneels before her coffin, hands clasped and tears streaming down his face. A butler stands obediently in the background, between images of Jesus being nailed to the cross and Veronica's veil (a cloth relic of the face of Jesus). Winthrop hopes and prays that Madeline has finally found peace, only to hear that she is merely cataleptic. When a crazed and vengeful Madeline comes back to life, judgment falls and destroys the Ushers.

The films of Vincent Price collect prayers as much as blood. In *Theatre of Blood* (Douglas Hickox, 1973), spurned actor Edward Lionheart (Vincent Price) commits a series of gruesome murders, aptly connected to Shakespeare's plays. He schemes to dispose of a slew of theatre critics who did not celebrate his genius. One ironic scene features a victim, the effeminate dramatic critic Meredith Merridew (Robert Morley), wearing gaudy chartreuse and pink saying a sweet prayer of grace before gobbling down a delicious pot pie. He was "chosen" as the special celebrity guest of a supposed television program, *This Is Your Dish*.

Merridew prays, "For what we're about to receive, may the Lord make us truly thankful." Immediately after saying grace, Merridew wonders where his two pampered and precious poodles, Georgie and Georgina, have gone. Lionheart responds, quoting from Shakespeare's *Titus Andronicus*: "Why, there they are both, baked in that pie. Whereof their mother daintily hath fed, eating the flesh that she herself hath bred." The serial killer force-feeds the critic, making him devour his own "babies." Perfunctory prayers could not protect the critic from his own sins, and the poetic justice of Shakespeare inflicts the wages of sin upon his characters.

One breakout independent film of the period was George Romero's zombie debut, *Night of the Living Dead* (1968). The female protagonist, Barbra (Judith O'Dea), bows at the graveside to honor the dead. Her brother, Johnny, soon to be dinner, razzes her, "Hey, come on, Barb, church was this morning." As timely thunder rumbles, a slow-moving zombie heads their way.

Johnny puts on his gloves. "Hey, I mean praying is for church, eh? Come on!"

She responds, "I haven't seen you in church lately."

"Ah," Johnny scoffs, "well, not much sense in my going to church. Remember when we were little, I jumped out from behind a stone and Grandpa said, 'Boy, you gonna be condemned to hell.'" Romero slyly insinuates that his time has come as the dead overwhelm him.

More frightening was Brian De Palma's story of religious fanaticism in *Carrie* (1976). The telekinetic Carrie (Sissy Spacek) is domineered by an obsessed fundamentalist mother, Margaret White (Piper Laurie). When Carrie gets her first period, her mother chastises her for her carnality. When Carrie has accepted a date to the prom with a nice boy, her mother tells her to go to her closet and pray: "Ask to be forgiven!" "Everything isn't a sin," Carrie remonstrates, to no avail. Towering over her browbeaten daughter, who has just experienced an issue of blood, Margaret rants, "For the Lord sent you an evil, a curse, a curse of blood."

Unaware of what is happening in her adolescent body, Carrie shouts, "You should have told me, Mama. You should have told me." Margaret strikes her on the head with the "Woman's Bible." "And God made Eve from the rib of Adam. And Eve was weak and loosed the raven on the world. And the raven was called sin. Say it, the raven was called sin." She strikes Carrie in the face.

Her mother continues, "And the first sin was intercourse. The first sin was intercourse." Carrie protests that she didn't sin, even as her mother maniacally repeats the phrase "And Eve was weak." "Say it!" she orders. Resisting as long as she can, Carrie finally relents and says, "Eve was weak. Eve was weak."

Margaret speaks without listening. "And the Lord visited Eve with the curse, and the curse was the curse of blood." Kneeling down and grabbing Carrie's hand, she screams and goes berserk. "O Lord, help this sinning woman to see the sin of days and ways. Show her that if she had remained sinless, the curse of blood would never have come upon her. The temptation of the Anti-Christ would never have come upon her."

Carrie cries out, "Oh Mama, you should have told me."

Telling her that she discerns lustful thoughts inside her, Margaret dictates, "We'll pray. We'll pray, woman." She throws Carrie into the closet. Her daughter shrieks and beats the door, calling, "Please let me out. Mama, please let me out."

When Carrie kneels before a crucifix, she sees a distorted image of Christ in a broken mirror, reflecting dark eyes. Yet it is at the penultimate climax that Margaret exposes her own demons. Speaking of her wedding night, she screeches,

> Ralph promised never again. He promised, and I believed him. But sin never dies. We slept in the same bed, but we never did it. And then, that night, I saw him looking down at me that way. We got down on our knees to pray for strength. I smelled the whiskey on his breath. Then he took me, with the stink of filthy roadhouse whiskey on his breath, and I liked it. I liked it! With all that dirty touching of his hands all over me. I should've given you to God when you were born, but I was weak and backsliding, and now the devil has come home. We'll pray.

The appeal to prayer is met with willingness by Carrie, but her mother becomes fixated. "We'll pray. We'll pray. We'll pray for the last time. We'll pray." She holds Carrie to her, strokes her red hair, and picks up a large kitchen knife. As she says, "Our Father who art in heaven, hallowed be Thy name, Thy will be done," she brutally stabs her daughter in the back. In Stephen King's novella, prayer functions as a prologue to death. Evil also appears in religious garb, as the devil not only appears as an angel of light, but as a fundamentalist mother.

On April 8, 1966, *Time* magazine had emblazoned a black cover with the question "Is God Dead?" in bold red letters. The magazine would have a cameo two years later in Roman Polanski's *Rosemary's Baby* (1968). The film advertised itself in white-on-black billboards that proclaimed, "Pray for Rosemary's Baby." Mia Farrow would meet the devil, even as Polanski's real girlfriend, Sharon Tate, would meet the Manson cult. Living in their Gothic Manhattan apartment, Rosemary Woodhouse's (Mia Farrow) husband, Guy (John Cassavetes), barters with Satan for success in an acting career (beyond playing in Osborne's *Luther*) as a Faustian bargain, offering up his wife's body and soul. Offended by demeaning references to the pope, Rosemary mentions that she was raised Catholic, but now "she didn't know" what she believed. As a lapsed Catholic, she is more vulnerable to be a tool of Satan. She is drugged by a coven of witches and then, while unconscious, impregnated by the devil. Rosemary's hallucinatory dreams are replete with religious imagery, from Michelangelo's *Creation of Adam* to the pope, all seemingly irrelevant to her plight and ineffectual for her salvation.

Rosemary unknowingly gives birth to the devil's child in June 1966, alluding to the symbolic 666. The coven cheers, "Hail Rosemary," an obviously twisted reference to the Hail Mary and the rosary. Her prayers are simply "O God" uttered in fear and horror, especially when the Satanists declare, "God is dead. Satan lives." Praying desperately, "O God! O God," she is ordered, "Oh, shut up with your 'O Gods' or we'll kill you, milk or no milk!"

Following the fictional birth of the Anti-Christ, a whole legion of demonic and apocalyptic films exploded on the scene. *The Exorcist* (William Friedkin, 1973) traced the demonic possession of Regan MacNeil (Linda Blair) and her agnostic mother, Chris's (Ellen Burstyn) futile attempts to deal with it through secular means. When the priests arrive, and the psychiatrists and physicians depart, prayers roll. Father Damien Karras (Jason Miller), undergoing a crisis of faith, assists the elderly Roman Catholic priest Lankester Merrin (Max von Sydow) in the exorcism. They repeat, "The power of Christ compels you!" to the demon.

Merrin warns Karras to avoid conversations with the demon, as he is a liar. "He will lie to confuse us, but he will also mix lies with the truth to attack us. . . . So don't listen to him." As prayer is as much listening as expressing oneself, the admonition to not pray with Satan is fundamental.

In contrast to the high horror of *The Exorcist*, a more lighthearted series of prayers spring up in *Bedazzled* (Stanley Donen, 1967), a fresh adaptation of the Faustian legend with Peter Cook as the devil (also known as the Horned One), George Spiggott. George is the proprietor of a nightclub "licensed to buy and sell *spirits*." He tempts a short-order cook, Stanley Moon (Dudley Moore), to gain the world in exchange for his soul. Arguing that Stanley should sell his soul, the unholy one explains that his soul is "rather like your appendix: totally expendable." Stanley asks what God is like: "He is English, isn't He?" Spiggott replies, "Oh yes, very upper-class."

Stanley reads the contract he is about to sign in return for seven wishes, including a romp with Lillian Lust (Raquel Welch): "I, Stanley Moon, hereinafter and in the hereafter to be known as 'The Damned'— The damned?" He sells his soul.

The devil complains about God's omnipresence and shouts for Him to leave, only to realize that shouting won't work. So he feigns humility in his talk with God: "Excuse me, Your Ineffable Hugeness, I wonder if You would be gracious enough to step outside for a moment while we miserable worms get our drawers on." But after finding each deadly sin a disaster, and it appears that Moon will have to remain damned forever, he anxiously says, "*I need to talk to God. It's urgent!*"

Grace prevails, and the stupid Stanley Moon is redeemed. The devil talks to God again: "I've done a good deed. I gave that little twit his soul back. Wasn't that generous?" By the end, the devil tries to blackmail God: "All right, you great git, You've asked for it. I'll cover the world in Tastee-Freez and Wimpy Burgers. I'll fill it with concrete runways, motorways, aircraft, television, automobiles, advertising, plastic flowers, frozen food, and supersonic bangs. I'll make it so noisy and disgusting that even You'll be ashamed of Yourself! No wonder You've so few friends; You're unbelievable!" God laughs loudly. As Martin Luther quipped, "The best way to drive out the devil, if he will not yield to texts of scripture, is to jeer and flout him, for he cannot bear scorn." For his part, Saint Thomas More wrote, "The devil, . . . that proud spirit, . . . cannot endure to be mocked." In comic films about the devil, the laughter of prayer functions as the exorcism.

The fascination with the devil stemmed in part from *Time's* cover asking, "Is God Dead?" Charting a rise in atheism, the question echoed Nietzsche's assertions that "God remains dead. And we have killed him. Yet his shadow still looms." The theological debate of the Death of God movement had raised an adjunct question of whether the devil was real. The possibility of God's absence thus haunted prayers that could not shake the felt presence of the devil. Ingmar Bergman's existential knight in *The Seventh Seal* (1957) interviewed a witch to see whether she had seen the devil. For if Satan exists, so must God. Thus cinema kept the devil alive.

Last Frontier Prayers

Tuco (Eli Wallach), the Ugly in *The Good, the Bad and the Ugly* (Sergio Leone, 1966), prays in his brother's monastery for the Good, Blondie (Clint Eastwood), who is close to death, but who holds a secret as to the whereabouts of a treasure. Switching sides in the Civil War, Tuco cheers for the Confederacy, claiming that God is with us "because he hates the Yanks too," only to have Blondie spit and growl, "God is not on our side, because he hates idiots also." As a prophetic parable on violence, the western warned against hubris and greed. Prayers in *Hang 'Em High* (Ted Post, 1968) exposed how religious authorities legitimated the hanging of innocent young men. When the government began drafting trusting patriots for Vietnam, the church supplied prayers more for their funerals than their safekeeping.

During the late 1960s, questions of violence and peace loomed large in the American consciousness and conscience. Glenn Ford plays tough and determined Pastor Jim Killian in *Heaven with a Gun* (Lee Katzin, 1969), a former gunslinger/convict turned minister. Killian sets up his Mission of the Good Shepherd in a barn, seeking to reconcile cattle ranchers and sheep men. His delivers his first sermon to a packed congregation:

> Now let us think about something from the book of James. There is fighting among you, even lusts among you in your members. Ye have not because ye ask not. The point is the good Lord made the earth very large for every man, woman, and child under the sun. It is God's command that we live together in peace. Now how can we live in peace with so much violence, two sides violently opposed to each other, sheep men and cattle men?

Pastor Jim then takes his congregation outside to demonstrate a parable about how sheep and cattle will drink from the same water, showing them living peaceably and sharing, an exemplary model for the two sides.

Saloon owner Madame McCloud (Carolyn Jones) knows the pastor's checkered past. She finally confronts him with his own tendency to use violence to solve problems, admonishing him that he must choose one vocation or the other. He puts his guns away and walks by faith, with the townspeople behind him, a lesson lost on American international policy. The conflicts between following the Man of Peace and taking up a sword were debated throughout Christendom.

Director Ralph Nelson's *Wrath of God* (1972) is surprisingly unpredictable. Renegade and prodigal priest Father Horne (Robert Mitchum), a weary, machine gun–toting man of the cloth, rejects the institutional church, where merchants pay off bishops who neglect the poor. As a priest, he still provides last rites to poor men about to be executed, giving some modicum of mercy.

When Mexican Colonel Santilla (John Colicos) spares him and two other gunrunners from a firing squad, they are given a dinner instead of a coffin. The colonel drafts them as an unholy trinity to assassinate an atheist tyrant, Thomas de la Plata (Frank Langella). One of the trio, the mercenary Jennings, quotes scripture in a happy distorted way, hoping "the Lord leads him beside the still of waters"—that is, liquor. But when the caustic Horne is asked to say grace, he barks, "Rub-a-dub-dub, thanks for the grub."

Horne recognizes that he has landed in quite a desolate place. As his Irish companion observes, "If God had wanted to give the world an enema, he'd have stuck the nozzle in here." As a priest, Horne is "not exactly what the Lord had in mind," but he fulfills his calling in unorthodox ways. Coming upon the village of Saint Raphael, populated with poor and oppressed people, Horne seems like a sacrilegious parody of a priest. When he says that he will turn the other cheek, he rolls over to show his behind. Saint Raphael is a place where they murder priests and where La Plata has forbidden the practice of Christian faith, but Horne is unfazed. He gets on his knees to clean the floor of a desecrated church, with leaky roofs and trespassing goats.

Father Horne blesses an ore mine: "Compassionate God, look kindly upon these who toil here and by the grace of Thy Son, lead them to everlasting life through the same Christ our Lord." When the mine caves in, he affirms that those who die go on to everlasting life. As the priest stays with an injured man, he prepares to hold an illegal mass of thanksgiving for those who did not die.

Just before confronting La Plata, Horne cautions the citizens, "I don't wish any of you to risk your lives. Instead, I ask each of you to go to your homes and pray for me, that I may be brave and resolute in bringing to La Plata the wrath of God." La Plata threatens him that if he administers one sacrament, he will die. Horne chooses to hear confessions all night and listen to hymns and communal prayers. When an altar boy is murdered, he chooses to trade himself for men about to be martyred. He approaches his enemy, preaching that one should never underestimate the power of scripture. He holds a gun hidden in a hollow Bible, but is found out. As La Plata hangs the priest on a cross, the villain's devout mother shoots her own son. With his enemy vanquished, Father Horne marvels that "God works in mysterious ways."

The mysterious workings of God are also portrayed in *Appaloosa* (Sidney Furie, 1967), in which buffalo hunter Matt Fletcher (Marlon Brando) returns home, where his beloved Appaloosa horse is stolen. Humiliated and tortured throughout the film, Fletcher seeks to get his horse back from bandit leader Chuy (John Saxon).

What makes this film particularly relevant to the open and honest era of the 1960s is the candid vernacular of Fletcher's confession in a church. He mumbles, "I'm having a little trouble getting started, Father."

The priest says, "You are in the house of God now, my son. Speak from your heart."

"Well," he confesses, "I've done a lot of killin'. I've killed a lot of men and sinned with a lot of women. But the men I killed needed killin' and the women wanted sinnin', and well, I never was one much to argue." The admission of his trespasses and a search for penance paralleled the spiritual journeys of many seeking to make sense of their lives. Yet his brooding declaration of guilt lacked the moxie of the rascally eponymous hero of *The Ballad of Cable Hogue* (Sam Peckinpah, 1970). Double-crossed and left to die in the arid desert, Hogue (Jason Robards) not only lives by his wits, but keeps up a running conversation with the Lord:

> Ain't had no water since yesterday, Lord. Gettin' a little thirsty. Just thought I'd mention it. . . . Yesterday, I told You I was thirsty and I thought You might turn up some water. Now about sinnin', You just send me a drop or two and I won't do it no more . . . whatever in hell it was that I did. Four days without water . . . if You don't think I've put in my sufferin' time, You oughta try goin' dry for a spell. Listen to me! If I don't get

some soon, I ain't gonna have no chance to repent. . . . [He collapses from thirst.] Lord, You call it. I'm just plain done in.

At that point, he glances at his boot and realizes that it's covered with "mud." Scraping around, he locates a small water spring. According to historian Paul Seydor, this living water seems to be a gift from God when Hogue finally shows some humility before Him.[10] He later capitalizes on turning the site of the spring into a thriving stagecoach stop, Jackass Flats.

The questionably Reverend Joshua Sloan (David Warner), a veritable snake-in-the-tumbleweed, announces that Hogue has made an "oasis out of a wilderness," but Hogue demurs, indicating that he only stumbled upon that mud hole. Sloan is the kind of minister who decides to raise hell as he cannot rouse heaven in any congregation. As a specimen of the genus of hypocritical clergy, he is more fit to sin than to preach. Sloan points out to Hogue "how wise and bountiful God was to put breasts on a woman. Just the right number in just the right place. Did you ever notice that, Cable?" Hogue sardonically answers, "Well, where in the hell would he put 'em? On their backside?" When Sloan reminds Hogue that vengeance is the Lord's, Hogue retorts, "Well, that's fair enough with me . . . just as long as He don't take too long and I can watch."

One passenger on a stagecoach that stops at his spring refuses to fraternize with Hogue and cites Ephesians 5:6 ("Let no man deceive you with vain words; for because of these things the wrath of God cometh upon the children of disobedience"—with "these things" referring to coarse jesting, fornication, and uncleanness—the very vices that Hogue indulges in). As the stagecoach driver, a friend of Hogue's, whips his horses on, the passenger's goods fall off. The driver excuses himself by noting, "The Lord giveth and the Lord taketh away." The verse from Job not only marks the theme of Hogue's life and death, but provides a comic rejoinder against a religious bigot.

Sloan speaks a final prayer over the cantankerous bastard Hogue's coffin. "Lord, as the day draws towards evening, this life grows to the end of us all, we say 'Adieu' to our friend. Take him, Lord, but knowing Cable, I suggest You do not take him lightly. Amen."[11] The film offers a casual and individualistic relationship with the Almighty, essentially suggesting that one doesn't need a church to be a denizen of heaven.

According to John Wayne, Peckinpah's *The Wild Bunch* (1969) destroyed the myth of the Old West, with its senseless and bloody violence. The film starts, however, with Reverend Wainscoat (Dub Taylor) admonishing his flock about the strong drink that "biteth like a serpent." The moral posturing of the temperance crowd will lead to one of the bloodiest openings of a western, with innocents killed alongside gunslingers. Responding to the crimson finale of this opening, Peckinpah asserted that "killing a man isn't clean and quick and simple. It's bloody and awful. Maybe if enough people come to realize that shooting somebody isn't just fun and games, maybe we'll get somewhere."

When the Wild Bunch need to bury a dead outlaw gang member, its leader, Pike Bishop (William Holden), pauses. But Dutch Engstrom (Ernest Borgnine) removes his hat and mockingly says, "I think the boys are right. I'd like to say a few words for the dear, dead departed. And maybe a few hymns would be in order. Followed by a church supper. With a choir!" The mocking of organized religion plays out with unleashed abandon. The untethered spirituality of an aging, morally conflicted leader, Pike Bishop, curiously corresponds with the controversial 1960s California Episcopal bishop James Pike, who would attack the political views of his own church and deny some of their basic doctrines. Bishop Pike would die like Pike Bishop, exploring his own wilderness of temptation, even as he espoused séances with the dead. The *New York Times* described him as an "anti-hero in a Lost Generation novel, looking for God in the wrong places."[12] In these ways, Bishop Pike looked a lot like Pike Bishop.

Clint Eastwood's cowboys pray earnestly. In *The Outlaw Josey Wales* (Clint Eastwood, 1976), Civil War veteran Josey stands over the graves of his wife and child and prays the plaintive lamentation of Job, "The Lord giveth; the Lord taketh; blessed be the name of the Lord." *High Plains Drifter* (Clint Eastwood, 1973) embeds the text of Isaiah 53:3–4 on the church board, referring to a man despised and beaten, cut off from the land of the living because of the transgressions of the people of the alleged "God-fearing" city of Lago. "He had done no violence; nor was there any deceit in his mouth." The men of the city hid their faces from him and despised him, not helping when he called for help while being whipped. Yet by the stripes of Marshall Jim Duncan, the guilty and complicit citizens are not healed; rather, they are punished with the vengeance of innocent blood and even forced to paint their town red, becoming the locale of "Hell." Even the church is painted red, indicating the hypocrisy of the preacher, whose conscience is bothered only when it doesn't cost him anything. The identification of American youth with outlaws and outsiders made characters like the drifter and Josey Wales irresistible.

The continuing image of religious corruption also emerges out of *Fools' Parade* (Andrew McLaglen, 1971), with a sadistic Doc (George Kennedy) bullying three convicts just released from prison. Underlying the oafish Doc's religious haranguing of the men is the hymn "Shall We Gather at the River?" (where the ex-convicts later hide under a railroad trestle). Doc moralizes that there are rules in the good book and that there are consequences if one doesn't follow them. He tells the three boys, "Me and Jesus could have saved ya, if you were in my Sunday school class."

The brutal Doc takes money, impervious to any moral compunction, as he claims it will come in handy for the mission fund and the vacation Bible school. Leaving the prison in the town of Glory, Mattie Appleyard (Jimmy Stewart) retorts sarcastically that it wasn't his grace that sent them to prison, it was "his honor."

Doc hires two thugs to kill the three ex-convicts early the next morning, conspiring to hijack them at a railroad depot. One young gunslinger, Junior Kilfong, brags that he will kill only atheists, so he is told they are infidels. When Kilfong finds them trapped in the train car, he orders, "You wanna pray 'fore we get into the depot? You'se just atheists. Never shoot anybody but atheists. Love it when they repent, just before I do it to them."

Mattie, who has one glass eye, starts to pray, "Oooo God, Ooooo Lord. Is that You?" He gazes upward. "Is it really You, Lord? I know, Lord, I know You tried to show me the way, but I just couldn't see it. . . . Whatja say, Lord?" Turning his gaze on Kilfong, he says, "Didja hear that, son? He said, 'If thine eye offend thee, pluck it out.'"

"Then, Lord," Mattie says, redirecting his prayer heavenward, "reach down and draw from this sinner's face the eye that hath offendeth righteousness." Mattie takes his glass eye from the socket and moves it toward the kid. "You say what? You won't take it, Lord?" To the killer he says, "Boy, He wants you to have it." Kilfong goes berserk over the eye touching him, which allows the three fugitives to escape. As they flee, Mattie looks heavenward, exclaiming, "Much obliged, Lord." It is Mattie's folk-spun wisdom that tells the others, "God uses the good ones; the bad ones use God." In contrast to singular models of corrupt religion, *Fools' Parade* reveals that there are some fools that God loves.

In *Butch Cassidy and the Sundance Kid* (George Roy Hill, 1969), Sundance (Robert Redford) has cleaned out everybody in a card game and hasn't lost a hand since he got to deal. An adversary asks Sundance, "What's the secret of your success?"

Sundance laconically responds, "I pray."

Later, the outlaws parrot the voice of a woman they are pretending to harm to get the detective locked in the train's vault car to open the door. Butch (Paul Newman) prays the Lord's Prayer in a woman's falsetto voice to fool the guard: "Our Father who art in heaven . . ." The guard opens the door to save the lady, only to find the merry bandits grinning. The charismatic thieves know how to use the word of God to find their treasure.

In *Chisum* (Andrew McLaglen, 1970), cattle baron John Chisum (John Wayne) fights crooked land developers. When a cowhand (Ben Johnson) says that there's "no law west of Dodge and no God west of the Pecos," Chisum disagrees. "Wrong, Mr. Pepper. Because no matter where people go, sooner or later, there's the law. And, sooner or later, they find God's already been there." At a funeral for a friend, the minister speaks sections of the Sermon on the Mount over the grave, and adds prayers that the Lord might "have mercy on his soul." Pepper persists, however, in arguing that "speechifying, store keeping, prayer meeting don't amount to spit in a river." What is needed, he asserts, is action, a fight. But it is a higher justice that Chisum seeks, based on a biblical God.

In *Rooster Cogburn* (Stuart Millar, 1975), old Sheriff Rooster (John Wayne) picks up Episcopal spinster Miss Eula Goodnight (Katharine Hepburn) after an attack on his Indian mission killed her father. She reminds Rooster that "those who live by the sword must die by the sword." When he says, "Huh?," she explains Matthew 26:53. "Oh," he mutters.

In an early scene, an outlaw attempts to scare Goodnight by shooting at her feet, and she boldly recites Psalm 23, from "The Lord is my shepherd" through its conclusion of "Deliver me from evil." In her recitation, Goodnight is duly protected and delivered from evil. Later she asks Rooster whether his name is written in "the Lamb's Book of Life," a reference to those whom the Lord will save at the last judgment. When she confesses that she is more aggressive than a woman should be, Rooster mutters, "Amen, Amen," to which she gladly retorts, "You're praying, the first step on the road to conversion."

When they successfully conclude a gun battle, the bodies of their attackers lie about. "Marshall, I'd like to say a few words over the dead. Good or bad, they're God's own," Goodnight informs him. He relents. "Looks like they're past caring, but go ahead." She begins her prayer book litany:

> Lord, have mercy on us for what we did. I am the Resurrection and the Life; he that believeth in me, though he were dead, yet shall he live. . . . The Lord gave and the Lord taketh away. Blessed be the name of the Lord. We brought nothing into this world and it is certain that we can take nothing out of it. [She takes a pocket watch from the corpse.] Unto almighty God I commend the souls of these men, dust to dust.

"Hurry up, sister, or we'll be joining them," growls Rooster. She continues unperturbed, but more quickly: "For Thine is the kingdom and the power and the glory, forever and ever. Amen. Earth to earth, dust to dust." They both recite, "Ashes to ashes." She follows the Prayer Book for burial services, believing that all men are made in the image of God, and that all will meet their maker soon enough.

Prayers in western films dealt not only with death and corruption, but also with humor. In *The Wild Rovers* (Blake Edwards, 1971), brooding Ross Bodine (William Holden) works for the patriarch Walter Buckman (Karl Malden). With his family around the table, Buckman prays, "Dear Lord, we thank You for this food we're about to receive and we pray that You take our recently departed friend Barney into Your loving care and keep him safe. Amen." Then he yells, "Soup!" and his Chinese cook appears immediately, providing the food.

When the parson hears that some travelers have just been rescued from hunger and cold in *Paint Your Wagon* (Joshua Logan, 1969), he announces to California prospector Ben Rumson (Lee Marvin) that he's entering his "house to pray for the unfortunate victims" who are recovering. "Not tonight, Parson," quips Rumson. "These folks have suffered enough. Now why don't you do that outside where He can hear you better, 'cause I'll be talking in here?"[13]

The vulgar spaghetti western *Trinity Is Still My Name* (Enzo Barboni, 1972) places three grubby cowboys sitting around a table with a turkey and a bottle of booze. They start grabbing the grub. But their boozy mother stops them. "You ain't gonna feed your faces without praying first."

"Arrgh," says the eldest, "there she goes again with that religion of hers. Always trying to break a guy." Ignoring her crude brood, she prays,

> Dear Lady up in heaven, you were a mother just like me and from what I hear tell, you had a son who gave you quite a few worries too. So you can understand when I'm asking you to look after my young 'uns too.

When she finishes, she yells at them, "I said 'amen,' you varmints." "Amen," they grunt and then start chewing away. This exchange is not only humorous but also hints of an imminent theological trend of employing feminine language about God. The feminist movement was gaining influence in many mainline denominations, opening doors to female priests and altering the ways many believers spoke to God.

A "traveling man spreading the Lord's Gospel in these troubled times" named Moses Pray (Ryan O'Neal) meets up with a canny orphan, Addie Loggins (Tatum O'Neal), and they team up to sell Bibles during the Depression in *Paper Moon* (Peter Bogdanovich, 1973). At a funeral for Addie's mother, a minister inappropriately prays, "Judge me, O Lord, for I have lost mine integrity. I have trusted also in the Lord; therefore, I shall not slide. Examine me, O Lord, and prove me. Try my reins and my heart, for Thy loving-kindness is before mine eyes, and I have walked in Thy truth." The narcissistic confessional suggests that the clergy during this era were focusing upon their own spiritual struggles. They would soon make their personal religion more public, as Bogdanovich's film previews a coming era of selling the Gospel, though not door-to-door, but through the slicker and more pervasive mode of television evangelism.

Westerns do reflect a bygone past, but the films of the 1970s also raised contemporary issues about war, violence, faith, law, justice, and death.

Addressing bogus ministers and a blemished church, they mirrored how prayers could be self-serving. Yet they also reflected the growing personal expressiveness of praying. Even though *Rooster Cogburn* may still reference Anglican liturgy, most of these films feature spontaneous prayers.

Playful and Irreverent Laughter

Ida Lupino's merry comedy *The Trouble with Angels* (1966) delighted in various pranks played at Saint Francis Academy for Girls. Mother Superior (Rosalind Russell) says grace before dinner, as Rachel, a redheaded prankster (Hayley Mills), sits with her friend. Both wear white-monogrammed shirts, and dishes of cantaloupes sit before them. "Bless us, O Lord, and these Thy gifts we are about to receive from Thy bounty." Rachel squeezes lemon on her cantaloupe and squirts Mother Superior in the eye, stopping the prayer.

Mother Superior finds the girls making bubbles and admonishes them to pray hard for the math test tomorrow. Her prayers are instructive and exemplary. In fact, when she prays weeping over the coffin of a sister who died in her sleep, Rachel watches and ultimately decides to become a nun herself. The prayers of a saint are passed on to a novice.

The western parody reached its apotheosis in Mel Brooks's zany *Blazing Saddles* (1974). In a church meeting, the effete old minister Reverend Johnson (Liam Dunn) (everyone is named Johnson, even Howard Johnson, who has an ice cream stand with one flavor) addresses the congregation from the pulpit: "Then let us pray for the deliverance of our new sheriff. Will the congregation please rise? I shall now read from the books of Matthew, Mark, Luke"—suddenly a stick of dynamite is pitched through the church window—"and *duck!*" The church congregation sings its anthem, "Now is a time of great decision / Are we to stay or up and quit? / There's no avoiding this conclusion / Our town is turning into shit."

When the townspeople are introduced to Bart (Cleavon Little), the newly arrived black sheriff, Reverend Johnson holds up his Bible, imploring them as their spiritual leader "to pay heed to this good book and what it has to say!" The townspeople blast the Bible and blow it up. Looking at the new sheriff, the reverend whispers, "Son, you're on your own."

Later, as the town struggles against the land grubbers of Hedley La-
marr (Harvey Korman), the minister perks up with "O Lord, do we have
the strength to carry on this mighty task in one night or are we just
jerking off? . . . Amen." Finally, while gunfighter Jim (Gene Wilder) is
trying to concentrate on his shooting, Johnson interrupts, "O Lord, keep
this man's eye keen and may God bless—" and the townfolk whack the
preacher.

Earlier Mel Brooks directed his Soviet comedy, *The Twelve Chairs*
(1970), in which the mother of a disenfranchised aristocrat reveals to
him that she hid the family jewels in one of twelve chairs. Characters try
to locate the valuable chair. However, Father Fyodor (Dom DeLuise), a
Russian Orthodox priest, has heard the mother's confession during last
rites and decides to claim the diamonds for himself. He begins to shave
his grand beard and then kneels and looks up, "O Thou who knowest
all. . . . You know!"

Fyodor's eagerness to garner earthly treasures propels him to call
upon God in times of trouble. When he doesn't find the chairs easily, he
complains, "O Lord, You're so strict." Without a clue as to their whereabouts, he finds himself at a carnival, and Fyodor pleads, "O Lord, O
Lord, Your lamb is lost. Please help me. Oh please, help me, Lord." When
he immediately sees a chair, he cries out, "Thank You!"

Cornered by his competitors against the foot of a rock cliff, he yells,
"Come on, God!" and finds himself on the pinnacle of the precipice.
When they leave him stuck on top, he prays, "O Lord, if this is Your
pun—ish—ment—how did I get here?" He is left behind. His desperate
prayers are utilitarian means for his own self-serving advantages.

Brooks directed some of the best movie parodies ever, inserting
prayer scenes with panache. In *Young Frankenstein* (1974), Frankenstein's
monster (Peter Boyle) roams the countryside. A blind hermit (Gene
Hackman) holds on to his praying beads beside his bed, and with the
kitchen fire blazing and violin music playing, he imitates the prayer of
Whale's classic 1931 horror film: "A visitor is all I ask, a temporary companion to help me pass a few short hours in my lonely life." The door
slams open and the monster growls. "Thank You Lord, thank You!" the
hermit exclaims.

Reviving the dead tissue and discovering he has created a monster,
Dr. Frankenstein exclaims, "O God in heaven, what have I done?" His

incredulity pales in comparison to the song/prayer of Elizabeth, his former fiancée (Madeline Kahn). Elizabeth weds the monster instead of the good doctor, and as he approaches her on their nuptial night, she squeals with a hymn of thanksgiving, "Mine eyes have seen the glory . . . glory, glory, hallelujah!"

Brooks mocks the capitalist god of America in *Silent Movie* (1976). In the boardroom of Engulf and Devour (Harold Gould and Ron Carey), chairman Engulf looks at his watch. An intertitle announces, "Gentlemen, it's time for our morning prayer." All the board members rise in unison, with organ music, and pray to a giant dollar sign: "O Mighty Dollar, we pray to thee, for without thee, we are in the crapper." If any prayer could expose the greed of the contemporary church, it was this scathing petition by the inimitable Mel Brooks.

The years 1964 through 1975 mostly saw America and its religious institutions in "the crapper." Social unrest and civil disobedience erupted, in part, because of the apparent hypocrisy of the institutions of authority. Yet this decade shows, more than most, how shifts in culture shape the contours of cinematic prayers. The distrust of authority, the decline of the mainline churches, and a more flippant and agnostic attitude toward religion shaped prayers that ridiculed and devalued their significance and valence. The Death of God movement killed the positive thinking of the 1950s, but it also made way for the fresh hope of the Jesus movement, with a revival of Christianity occurring mostly outside the mainline establishment. With the bicentennial approaching, cynicism would decline, and fresh, heartfelt streams of prayer would flow back onto screens.

6

Revival of Prayer (1976–1988)

With the 1976 bicentennial celebration, Hollywood rediscovered the classic American myths of heroic behavior and virtues of community, faith, and courage. After a decade of corruption at home and defeat in Vietnam abroad, America sought to rediscover its roots in worship. *Newsweek* magazine declared 1976 "the year of the evangelical." Jimmy Carter, a Georgia peanut farmer, confessed to being a born-again Baptist and won the presidency, followed after one term by a secular savior from California, Ronald Reagan, directly out of Hollywood casting.

An ethnic lower-class bum emerged to show himself capable of winning in John Avildsen's crowd-cheering *Rocky*, enacting virtues of fortitude and perseverance. This boxing bonanza was prefaced by the gracious face of Jesus painted over the Redemption Gym, with Bill Conti's inspired and inspirational "Rocky's Theme" pumping faith and adrenaline into God's humble warrior. Just before the fight begins, Apollo Creed sits high on his bench while Rocky kneels in prayer before an ordinary sink.

Spielberg's *Close Encounters of the Third Kind* (1977) previewed scientific personnel awaiting what Doug Cowan called "one of the few truly transcendental moments" as human pilgrims courageously board the spaceship (which landed at the base of the Devil's Tower).[1] Praying for their safety, a priest proclaims, "God has given His angels charge over you" and prays that the pilgrims have a "happy journey and peaceful days, so that with Your holy angel as a guide, they may safely reach their destination." Accompanied by the spectacular score of John Williams, the humble prayer intimates that we should not fear the alien.

Vietnam lingered in the national consciousness, with prayers quietly reentering the entertainment media, as Americans tried to make sense of the recent morass. At the wedding of Sal and Angela in *The Deer Hunter* (Michael Cimino, 1978), a Pennsylvania community sings Russian Orthodox hymns and Psalm 174. The priest intones, "Blessed is the

Rocky (John Avildsen, 1976) celebrated America's bicentennial with its ordinary small-time boxer Rocky (Sylvester Stallone) achieving the American dream.

kingdom of the Father and of the Son and of the Holy Spirit, now and ever and unto ages of ages," to which the congregation responds, "Amen." These steel mill workers, hunters, and friends love their mountains and each other. Serving in the war, several are imprisoned in a Viet Cong "pit." An exasperated Nick (Christopher Walken) wonders whether any bombing missions might rescue them. Michael/Merle (Robert De Niro) asks, "What, are you hoping?" "What else?" he responds. "I thought you might be praying." Nick concedes, "I'm doing that too." At Nick's graveside funeral, the priest reads the Twenty-Third Psalm and the mourners join in the Lord's Prayer. A final remnant sings Irving Berlin's "God Bless America." Even a film about Vietnam tragedies ends with a reaffirmation of the American dream.

The following year, plunging deeper into the heart of darkness, Francis Ford Coppola's *Apocalypse Now* (1979) chronicled Captain Benjamin Willard (Martin Sheen) on a secret assignment to assassinate a renegade Green Beret, Colonel Kurtz (Marlon Brando). Early on, an Army chaplain leads a prayer for a bunch of GIs, blessing them before going into battle. From his makeshift altar, with bombs blasting all about, he leads them in the Lord's Prayer. It is part of the spectacle of war. Meanwhile, in the background, helicopters fly back and forth and tanks shoot flame-throwers, dramatically contrasting heavenly prayers and earthly destruction.

Just before one battle, "Chef" Hicks (Frederic Forrest) silently whispers a prayer in the helicopter, praying for survival. It is granted temporarily, as he is not killed in this scene. Later, however, Kurtz will decapitate him. Even in tragic war pictures, traditional prayers made a comeback, suggesting a longing for absolution. Exposing the national anguish and the moral lies of American involvement in Vietnam, the film functioned as a religious confession. As Coppola put it, "People are being brutalized, tortured, maimed, and killed" in warfare, and this was being presented as moral.

The Twenty-Third Psalm forms the confessional liturgy for the deeply moving prayer of Megan (Sydney Penny) in *Pale Rider* (Clint Eastwood, 1985). Near the start of the film, a gang roughs up a gold mining camp and shoots Megan's dog. Over her dog's grave, she provides personal commentary on the psalm:

> The Lord is my shepherd. I shall not want, . . . but I do want. He leadeth me beside still waters, He restoreth my soul. But they killed my dog. Yea though I walk through the valley of the shadow of death, I shall fear no evil, . . . but I am afraid.

Storm clouds gather and thunder in the distance as she continues her lamentations.

> Thou art with me; Thy rod and Thy staff they comfort me. We need a miracle. Thy loving-kindness and mercy shall follow me all the days of my life, if You exist. And I shall dwell in the house of the Lord forever. I'd like to get more of this life first. If You don't help us, we're all going to die. Please. Just one miracle. Amen.

While she wrestles with God, a man on a white horse, the Pale Rider from Revelation (Eastwood), makes his apocalyptic descent. The mysterious preacher riding down from the mountain is her miracle. The film offered the tagline "And hell followed with him." The apocalyptic films ushers in its day of judgment for the immoral killings, seeking to establish a land of justice and peace. The film paralleled the rise in the late 1970s of the religious right, who turned to politics to fight what they saw as moral and spiritual decline. For many conservatives, their pale rider and redeemer would be the conservative presidential candidate from California.

Country Prayers

John Sayles's *Matewan* (1987) offers a dramatic rendition of a 1920 West Virginia coal miners' strike. Both sympathizers of the union and anti-union workers attend the missionary church. The Freewill Baptist Church offers two preachers, Hardshell, the Primitive Baptist preacher (Sayles), and the fifteen-year-old miner/preacher Danny (Will Oldham). When Danny's friend is senselessly murdered, he says, "I think all God plans is that we get born. Then we got to take up from there. So you rest in peace, Hillard. You rest easy, 'cause we gonna take up where you left off."

In contrast, Hardshell preaches that the union and the devil are interconnected. Under suspicion for supporting the union, with its mix of natives and immigrants, blacks and whites, Danny is under surveillance by anti-union agents. Not able to communicate explicitly to his fellow workers about the injustices going on, Danny retells the biblical story about Joseph and the false testimony that put him in prison. Unlike a direct mode of preaching like Hardshell's, Danny's ingenious method circumvents his enemies by telling indirect stories, like Jesus's parables. Their meaning is grasped and a life is saved. As Flannery O'Connor recommended, when you tell a story, tell it slant. Danny's sermons and prayers do just that. His listeners have ears that hear and understand his warnings.

With the emergence of the environmental movement, many churches took up the cause of ecology and Christian stewardship. Prayers for the earth joined with prayers for peace. *The River* (Mark Rydell, 1984) contrasts family life on a farm with financial troubles versus the twin challenges of capitalism and nature. The film mixes Bible Belt practices with New Age devotions. When Tom Garvey's (Mel Gibson) tractor hose breaks, he finds the equipment dealer at the local bar on Sunday, swigging his beer. He says, laughingly, "I'm a Christian. I ain't open on

Sundays." Mae Garvey (Sissy Spacek) leads her children in the obligatory grace before meals, but in gratitude to Gaia: "Earth that gave us
all this food. Sun that made it ripe and good. Dearest Earth, dearest
Sun. We will not forget what you have done. Amen." Ironically enough,
Mother Nature almost wipes them out as she unleashes a flood of biblical proportions.

Critic Pauline Kael called *Cross Creek* (Martin Ritt, 1983) an account
of a "woman's struggle to become a writer, given a supernal glow. Everything is lighted to look holy."[2] A voice-over monologue reinforces the
earth religion: "Consciousness of land and water must lie deeper in us
than any knowledge of our fellow beings. We were bred of the earth before we were born of the earth and we cannot live apart from the earth.
Something shrivels in man's heart when he turns away from it and concerns himself only with the affairs of men." *Christian Century* magazine
felt the oppressive Everglade humidity sticking to the treacly film.[3]

In contrast, in Alice Walker's Pulitzer Prize–winning epistolary novel
adapted for the screen *The Color Purple* (Steven Spielberg, 1985), Celie
(Whoopi Goldberg) begins her letter with "Dear God." But God, at first,
is an old white man, a controlling, powerful patriarch. Her sister Nettie
(Akosua Busia) writes of God in personal terms, "Celie, God sent me
to love your children. It's a miracle." God moves from being a religious
construct to a spiritual experience. Shug (Margaret Avery) brings love
into Celie's life, but also wrestles with her own relationship with God,
paralleling her broken relationship with her estranged preacher father.

"God is vain. It pisses God off if you walk by the color purple and
don't notice it." Yet Shug most deeply desires reconciliation with her father. In a remarkably creative juxtaposition of a juke joint blues and a
church choir, two musical themes compete to finally reconcile with the
lyrics "God's trying to tell me something . . . speak to me, Lord, speak to
me." As one who disavows the traditional religion of the church, particularly her father's church, Shug still comes back, claiming to her father
that even "sinners have soul." While the narrative tends to invert the idea
that "God is love" into "Love is God," the prayers of hearing provide a
significant aspect of the ritual. That God speaks and that one listens are
fundamental aspects of praying.

The apotheosis of country prayers and faith appears in *Places in the
Heart* (Robert Benton, 1984). More melodramatic, but nonetheless quite

moving, Robert Benton's populist film, situated in Waxahachie, Texas, opens with Moses (Danny Glover) receiving a handout of food from a back porch, bowing his head, and giving thanks. The hymn "Blessed Assurance," with its line "This is my story, this is my song," underlies the Depression-era tale, as misfits join together to help Edna Spalding (Sally Field) run her cotton farm and pay her mortgage. The montage of images of people praying sets the landscape. Sheriff Royce Spalding (Ray Baker) sits with his family at Sunday dinner and prays,

> Our heavenly Father, bless this meal and all those who are about to receive it. Make us thankful for Your generous bounty, and Your unceasing love. [A gunshot is heard in the distance.] Please remind us, in these hard times, to be grateful for what we have been given, and not to ask for what we cannot have. And make us mindful of those less fortunate among us, as we sit at this table with all of Thy bounty. Amen.

Investigating the gunshot, the sheriff is accidently shot and killed by a young black man, Wylie (De'voreaux White), one of the less fortunate, who is also killed. At Spalding's funeral, the congregation sings "Blessed Assurance." Widow Edna and her two children are joined by Moses and Mr. Will (John Malkovich), a blind World War I veteran, to create a broken and fragile community of outcasts. Yet the haunting line "This is my story, this is my song" reverberates throughout the film, pointing to the presence of grace and hope in the stories of these good country people.

In a reenactment of the stolen candlesticks from Victor Hugo's *Les Miserables*, Moses steals some silver spoons, but is redeemed by Edna. Moses has his superstitions entangled with his faith, as he takes seven steps back with his rabbit's foot: "Thank You, Lord Jesus. Amen. Give You my rabbit's foot."

The final scene was puzzling to many viewers, taking place in the community church, where the pastor reads Paul's I Corinthians 13 on love. The congregation partakes of communion, sharing the blood and body of Christ. The preacher reads, "On the night before His Crucifixion, our Lord gathered with His disciples. He broke the bread, and blessed it, saying, 'Take, eat; this is my body.' And He took the cup and said, 'Drink; this is my blood, which I shed for thee.'"

As the congregants pass the elements to one another, we begin to see anomalies, in which Moses sits among white southerners receiving the same wine and bread. Finally, we discover that sitting next to his wife is the dead Royce Spalding, who takes the small cup and says, "Peace of God," as he passes it on to Wylie, the young man who killed him and had been murdered himself, who responds, "Peace of God." All those who sinned, all who were rejected, join in the Supper of the Lamb, who brings peace to all. The film celebrates the living and the dead, all forgiven saints in a communion of life.

In many ways *Places in the Heart* parallels the rural film *Country* (Richard Pearce, 1984), which also offers prayers before dinner and hymn singing in the small clapboard church. The stalwart mother, Jewell Ivy (Jessica Lange), begs her family to join in solidarity and prays the standard grace: "Bless us, O Lord, and these Thy gifts, which we are about to receive, from Thy bounty, through Jesus Christ. Amen." Both stories threaten the ravages of nature in tornadoes. Both celebrate the American virtues of perseverance, community, and endurance through suffering. *Cineaste* critic Alice Cross opines that the latter film, however, posits union solidarity as the hope of the community, while the former offers a "populist view that rugged individualism can triumph."[4] However, Cross misses the centrality of the sacrament in the film. *Places* is grounded more in its hope in the Gospel, in a God who intervenes and creates community through His Spirit.

New Yorker film critic Pauline Kael expressed an "aversion to movies in which people say grace at the dinner table in establishing the moral strength of a household. The opening montage of Sunday-night supper in one home after another in 1935 Waxahachie—a whole community saying grace—made me expect the worst." Yet she goes on to say,

The movie's major accomplishment is that it never goes over the brink into utter corny shamelessness—that's where the pristine, courteous style of the writer-director Robert Benton comes in. This is another movie, like *Tender Mercies*, that has a positive human message. (God knows it's got heart, but it doesn't need that slopes-of-Parnassus title. What places? . . . It turns out that the places are where we lived as children—where our roots are. But those places may not be in our hearts. And more than that it's about America, and about Christian love, and about forgiveness of those who fail to live up to it. It's about decency.[5]

So, too, in *Witness* (Peter Weir, 1985), Kael again complains of a "compendium of scenes I had hoped never to see again." "*Witness* also takes first prize in the saying-grace department: a whole community of people bow their heads over vittles. It's like watching the Rockettes kick. We can't have prayers in the public schools, but movies are making up for it." She finds in Weir's violent drama about the Amish a little paradox, as the film "exalts people who aren't allowed to see movies—it says that they're morally superior to moviegoers. It's so virtuous; it's condemning itself."[6]

She is a bit unfair, as one should expect to see prayer among religious communities just as one would expect to see vanity in movies about Hollywood. In fact, the film opens with a funeral service, a place and time for prayer. Following the archetypal journey format of home/away/home, Amish widow Rachel (Kelly McGillis) and her son Samuel (Lukas Haas) go to Philadelphia, where she promises him, "You'll see so many things." He does see things that propel the narrative: he sees a murder committed by corrupt policemen.

One comic scene uses prayer to distinguish the difference between Philadelphia cop John Book (Harrison Ford) and Rachel and Samuel. At a deli restaurant, Book buys hot dogs and coffee. He and the two sit at a window table, and while he squeezes mustard on his dog and chomps down with relish, the two Amish stop to give quiet thanks. A bit flummoxed, Book awkwardly smiles and gulps, realizing his gauche goof, as they finish their silent prayer.

When asked whether they have to stay in Philadelphia, Rachel responds to her son, "Just tonight. Say your prayers." He folds his hands in bed and silently obeys. Samuel shares the ethic and the ritual of his community. When the Amish raise a barn in a day, they gather to eat and pray. They have all things in common and continue in prayer and fellowship. Later, when Rachel and John begin to feel a mutual attraction, she is asked, "Can you see John at a prayer meeting?" She laughs heartily. Can this man of violence be incorporated into a family of peace? The contrast of country faith with urban sophistication became symbolic of a spiritual divide within the country.

The Comic Impulse

In his study on how one can laugh with God, Robert Lamm poses the question of what happens when laughter enters the presence of God.[7] The Reagan era erupted with the risible in the sanctuary; comedy is inserted more frequently into religious rituals than in any previous time. President Reagan not only seized upon any opportunity, from the National Prayer Breakfasts to presidential debates with Mondale, to extol the power of prayer, but did so with humor. Greeted with applause at he opened a Convention of the National Association of Evangelicals, Reagan quipped, "A speaker devoutly prays that that's what will greet him when he finishes speaking."

Comic prayers appeared as profane and devout. Even in *Spaceballs* (1987), Mel Brooks's amazingly silly parody of George Lucas's *Star Wars*, the religious element pops up. Princess Vespa (Daphne Zuniga) presents herself as "daughter of Roland, King of the Druids." Lone Star (Bill Pullman) mutters, "Oh great. That's all we needed, a Druish princess." To which Barf (John Candy in a *Star Wars* Chewbacca role as a Mog or man/dog—he's his own "best friend") observes, "Funny, she doesn't look Druish." Barf panics as their intergalactic RV has run of gas. In desperation, he starts reciting the Lord's Prayer for their space Winnebago, satirizing those who use prayer for frivolous needs.

Using prayers as bargaining chips increases the comic incongruity of the scenes. The title characters in *The Out of Towners* (Arthur Hiller, 1970) are George and Gwen Kellerman (Jack Lemmon and Sandy Dennis), who have found their cultural immersion from Ohio into New York City to be a total disaster. When they flee into a Central Park church to pray, a television crew tells them that they can't pray there: "I got my orders from the network. This is a closed TV rehearsal. There is no one allowed in the church until two o'clock."

In other words, protests Kellerman, "You're denying my divine rights to worship the God of my choice in the house of the Lord of my desired faith?!" "Yeah," agrees the crewman, "until two o'clock, when you'll get your divine rights back." After being thrown out of the church, Kellerman vindictively barks, "Mr. Moyers, don't know if you're a religious man, but if I were you, at two o'clock, I'd start praying for my job."

Wendell Sonny Lawson (Burt Reynolds) haggles with God while trying to survive in *The End* (Burt Reynolds, 1978).

Wendell Sonny Lawson (Burt Reynolds) tries to recall all Ten Commandments in *The End* (Burt Reynolds, 1978). Thinking that his death is imminent, Sonny decides to commit suicide by drowning himself in the Pacific Ocean wearing his jogging suit. He bursts out of the water, miles from shore, gasps, "I wanna live! I wanna live!" Grunting, he starts swimming toward land and prays, "I can never make it. Help me, Lord, please. I promise not to try and kill myself anymore. Save me and I swear I'll be a better father. I'll be a better man. I'll be a better everything. . . . All I ask is make me a better swimmer."

He suddenly turns into Jacob, whose prayer with God in Genesis 28:20–22 was a form of haggling. Jacob had vowed that "if God will be with me and will keep me on this journey that I take, and will give me food to eat and garments to wear, and I return to my father's house in safety, then the Lord will be my God."

So now, floundering in the ocean, Sonny calls out, "O God! Let me live, and I promise to obey every one of the Ten Commandments. I shall not kill . . . I shall not commit adultery . . . I shall not . . . I . . . uh . . . I'll *learn* the Ten Commandments, and *then* I'll obey every fucking one of them!" He continues bartering.

> Just get me back to the beach. I'll be honest in business. I promise not to sell lakeside lots, unless there is a lake around. I want to see another sunrise. I want to see another sunset. It was a mistake, God, I never really wanted to kill myself, I just wanted to get Your attention. Help me make it. I'll give You 50 percent of everything that I make, God, 50 percent. I want to point out that nobody gives 50 percent. I'm talking gross, God.

The recognizable humor emerges as he approaches safety. Out of the foxhole, the atheist returns to his insouciance. "I think I'm going to make it. You won't regret this, Lord. I'll obey every commandment. I'll see my parents more often. No more cheating in business, once I get rid of those nine acres in the desert. I'm going to start donating that 10 percent right away. I know I said 50 percent, Lord, but 10 percent to start, but if You don't want Your 10 percent, don't take it."

Like Jacob, the final gag hangs on the tithe, on the money. Then, out of the crisis, Sonny even throws back his salvation: "I know that it was You who saved me, but it was also You who made me sick."

The dark comedy carried a tagline that proposed, "Think of death as a pie in the face from God." Debates with God do reveal personal relationships. In trying to make sense of what God is doing, Sonny goes to a young minister, Father Dave Benson (Robby Benson), and asks whether he had a personal calling from God, to which the embarrassed cleric confessed that it was "more of a whisper."

The spiritual ignorance of those who call upon God is exemplified by the middle-class American family of the Griswolds in *National Lampoon's Vacation* (Harold Ramis, 1983). As Clark Griswold (Chevy Chase) tries to get to Wally World for his kids, Aunt Edna (Imogene Coca) dies along the way. They stop in the rain to deliver a eulogy. Ellen Griswold (Beverly D'Angelo) tells her husband that they *have* to say something about her.

"Okay, bow your heads," he orders. "O God, ease our suffering in this our moment of great despair. Yea, admit this good and decent woman into the arms of Thine flock in the heavenly area, up there. And Moab, he lay us upon the band of the Canaanites, and yea, though the Hindus speak of karma, I implore You: give her a break."

The saying of grace at Thanksgiving mixes with the Pledge of Allegiance in *National Lampoon's Christmas Vacation* (Jeremiah Chechik, 1989), a comic expression of civil religion.

His wife reprimands him. "Clark." He continues in a downward descent into his own glossolalia, blending Jewish blessing, Hindu worship, and Pentecostal praise: "Baraka tau alleluia."

Exasperated, Ellen interrupts. "Clark, this is a serious matter. I'll do it myself."

He tries to excuse himself by acknowledging that he is not an ordained minister and is trying to do his best. However, Ellen doesn't get too much farther: "Lord, we loved this woman with all our hearts." Her daughter Audrey (Dana Barron) now interrupts her mother: "Let's not overdo it, Mom."

"Shut up," snaps Ellen. "We know she deserved better than this, but my husband wants his beloved family to get to Wally World to have our vacation. I hope You understand. Have mercy on his soul."

In *National Lampoon's Christmas Vacation* (Jeremiah Chechik, 1989), when the Griswolds are headed out to a frigid forest to chop down a Christmas tree, Clark somehow gets stuck under a large truck, at which Ellen prays, "Our Father who art in heaven, hallowed be Thy name, forgive Clark for being stupid." Gathering for Christmas dinner with odd relatives, Clark announces, "Since this is Aunt Bethany's eightieth Christmas, I think she should lead us in the saying of grace." Everyone agrees with ooohs and ahhs.

However, Aunt Bethany (Mae Questel, the erstwhile voice of Betty Boop) is deaf and doesn't know what has been asked. Her husband slowly says, "The *blessing!*"

Now comprehending, Aunt Bethany begins, "I pledge allegiance to the flag [Clark opens eyes in amazement, but no one else does] of the United States of America and to the republic for which it stands, one nation, under God, indivisible, with liberty and justice for all." Cousin-in-law Eddie (Randy Quaid) stands and puts his hand over his heart, and all join in reciting the pledge, an American prayer of sorts.[8] In spite of his hopes for an "old-fashioned family Christmas" being smashed, Clark offers his resigned "Amen."

The slapstick comedy *Home Alone* (Chris Columbus, 1990) offers one of the most religious comedies ever made. The simple inclusion of a prayer at dinner, sitting at a formal table setting all by himself, features Kevin McCallister (Macaulay Culkin), who crosses himself and says his short grace: "Lord, bless this highly nutritious microwaved macaroni dinner and the people who sold it on sale. Amen."

Accidentally left home by himself, Kevin must thwart bungling burglars, but also find succor and support from a mysterious, frightful neighbor who reveals himself in a church during the rehearsal of "O Holy Night." Director Chris Columbus subtly inserts several images of the stigmata onto the powerful next-door neighbor who incites fear. First, in the drugstore, Columbus shows a close-up of the wounds in the old man's hand. In the church we see it again, healing, and then at the end, restored.

The providential meeting of Kevin and his neighbor, Old Man Marley (Roberts Blossom), seals the religious subtext in the slapstick comedy, where two meaningful Christmas hymns are included in the score. "O Holy Night" seemingly runs counter to the imminent danger of an abandoned and deserted kid, Kevin, to a couple of incompetent burglars, who will fall on their knees, faces, bums. After hiding in a crèche, Kevin enters the church and sits alone in his pew, while a children's choir practices for the Christmas Eve service. The man next door, whom every-

Beneath the façade of mere slapstick comedy, *Home Alone* (Chris Columbus, 1990) smuggles in a theology of providence and grace.

one fears, enters and acknowledges that everyone is welcome in church. He sits with the forgotten child and assures him of his neighborliness. He tells Kevin that he doesn't need to be afraid of him, even though there are lots of rumors going around. Instead, he brings words of good cheer, even as the "Carol of the Bells" rings ominously. He is the gospel to a dark and lonely world, one in which the world does lie in sin and error pining. It is in the church that a thrill of hope brings rejoicing, and when the new and glorious morning breaks, all is well. Old Man Marley will rescue the endangered boy with his strong right arm, and a mighty shovel.

Reflecting the buoyancy of the Reagan era and the affability of the Convergence Movement, with its creative blend of charismatic, evangelical, and liturgical churches defining fresh approaches to worship, film prayers invited laughter into the sanctuary.[9] One is called, as the Westminster Catechism mandates, not only to glorify God, but to "*enjoy* Him forever." Such comic prayers spurred this enjoyment, this liberating pleasure of being in the presence of God.

Adventure Comedy Prayers

Within the subgenre of adventure comedies, in which danger, thrills, and action dominate, prayers took on the casual informality of the Reagan and Clinton presidencies. Both presidents practiced a likeable and gregarious style, living out their faith traditions with a jovial demeanor. One might not ignore their flaws as men, but their easygoing flair delighted their followers. Even in their high calling as America's leader, each brought a sense of humor to his term.

In one sense, gags in prayers reflected the easy quips and asides of the two genial American presidents, enjoying the twin processes of governing and jesting. Like potholes on a road of adventure (or as scholar Donald Crafton calls them, pies in a chase), religious gags pop up in film narratives to distract, detour, and delight the journey. For example, in *Ghost* (Jerry Zucker, 1990), Oda Mae Brown (Whoopi Goldberg), a bogus psychic medium, encounters the ghost of Sam Wheat (Patrick Swayze), panics, and prays for divine protection.

Trying to make sense of it all, she speculates that Sam is stuck between worlds. "You know it happens sometimes that the spirit gets yanked out so fast that the essence still feels it has work to do here." When Sam asks her to stop rambling, she accuses him of having an attitude problem. He cusses and she scolds him, "Don't you 'God dammit' me. Don't you take the Lord's name in vain with me! I don't take that!"

An irreverent mealtime grace in *Hook* (Steven Spielberg, 1991) captures the adolescent prayers of boys who never grow up, an expression of a "Let's just get to the food" mentality. When the adult Peter Pan tells the lost boys that it is time to say grace, he starts praying, and they all yell the word "Grace," and pig out, without restraint or decorum, just like boys who never grow up.

Hudson Hawk (Michael Lehmann, 1991) follows an ordinary cat burglar (Bruce Willis) leaving prison only to reenter a world of crime, blackmailed into stealing works of da Vinci. In a running gag, he is often foiled in trying to drink a cup of cappuccino. Sitting at a bar right after his release, he holds the cup, looks up, and says, "Thank You, Jesus, thank You." He meets a Vatican antiquities expert (and nun), Sister Anna (Andie MacDowell), who goes into confession and prays, "Bless me, Father, for I have sinned. It's been 1,200 hours since my last confession." A weary priest yawns. "Hit me with your best shot." She continues, "I betrayed a man. A good man. An innocent man. A thief." When she confides that she loves Hudson, the cleric replies that she has to: "It's your job." She has a "thing for sinners" even as he has a "thing for sinning." Though it turned out to be a box-office bomb, the film still managed to convey the human comedy of religious characters.

In *Monty Python and the Holy Grail* (Terry Gilliam, Terry Jones, 1975), the one thing God (usually in a cloud and a bit grumpy) can't stand is people groveling. When God commands that King Arthur (Graham Chapman) pursue a sacred quest to seek and find the Holy Grail, Arthur responds, "Good idea, O Lord," to which God storms, "Course it's a good idea!"

Coming up against a killer rabbit, the knights pray over their holy hand grenade. The first cleric (Michael Palin) begins,

> Saint Attila raised the hand grenade up on high, saying, "O Lord, bless this Thy hand grenade, that with it Thou mayest blow Thine enemies to tiny bits, in Thy mercy." And the Lord did grin. And the people did feast upon the lambs and sloths, and carp and anchovies, and orangutans and breakfast cereals, and fruit-bats and large chu—

Brother Maynard (Eric Idle) interrupts him, "Skip a bit, Brother." The cleric continues,

> And the Lord spake, saying, "First shalt thou take out the Holy Pin. Then shalt thou count to three, no more, no less. Three shall be the number thou shalt count, and the number of the counting shall be three. Four shalt thou not count, neither count thou two, excepting that thou then proceed to three. Five is right out. Once the number three, being the third number, be reached, then lobbest thou thy Holy Hand Grenade of Antioch towards thy foe, who, being naughty in my sight, shall snuff it."

To which the company says, "Amen."[10] The Pythons jest about the bloated religious language and obscure practices of medieval rituals, reducing liturgy to comic material.

Following one of the taglines of *Monty Python and the Meaning of Life* (Terry Jones, Terry Gilliam, 1983), "God took six days to create the world and Monty Python just 90 minutes to screw it up," the film tackles the idea of the groveling worshipper as Chaplain Humphrey (Michael Palin) leads his congregation in prayer.

> Let us praise God. O Lord, oooh You are so big. So absolutely huge. Gosh, we're all really impressed down here, I can tell You. Forgive us, O Lord, for this dreadful toadying. But You are so strong and, well, just so super. Amen.

The excessive verbiage continues regarding how big the Lord is as the congregation repeats the minister's extravagent compliments: "So big." "Ooh, You are so big." "So absolutely huge." "So absolutely huge." Yet the chaplain and congregation must repent of their dreadful toadying and barefaced flattery, which never cease. There is a profound silliness in the British comedy troupe's films, but one that caught the imagination of a religious community that saw its own humor magazines (for example, *Wittenberg Door*) and websites (for example, Ship of Fools) proliferate. The fin de siècle would also see a lively emphasis on humor in preaching. And with the proliferation of television evangelists and their public gaffes, humor and satire in all forms of religious activity would flourish.

Mischievous Prayers

The presence of comedy in prayers stemmed in part from the media heyday in lampooning hypocritical television evangelists. By the early 1980s, television provided an effective medium for a legion of preachers evangelizing spectators and hawking their wares. From Robert Schuller to Robert Tilton and Pat Robertson, television became a platform for preaching, praying, politicking, and pandering. Comedy could be naughty in ridiculing some of these bogus religious productions, such as the programs of Jim and Tammy Faye Bakker and Jimmy Swaggart, whose careers would end in scandal in the late 1980s. The quite coarse Martin Luther once quipped in his *Table Talk* that "where God built a church, there the devil would also build a chapel. . . . In such sort is the devil always God's ape."

Cinematic prayers found easy targets to satirize. Public piety was mischievously parodied. In *The Three Musketeers* (Stephen Herek, 1993), the trio of heroes tries to thwart the evil designs of Cardinal Richelieu (Tim Curry). Aramis (Charlie Sheen) calls upon the Lord with an anachronistic serenity prayer to "grant us the serenity to accept the things we cannot change, the courage to change the things we can, and the wisdom to know the difference." Porthos (Oliver Platt) demands that he stop praying and join the revelry, for "I need my spirits lifted. I'm old, I'm weak. My strength is gone."

Aramis protests, "Porthos! I'm praying." His friend counters, shouting, "I just said you're praying. Are you deaf, too? I know you're blind, because if you'd seen the tits that just walked out of here, you'd have tears in your eyes." Aramis's attraction to women over his prayers results in one crisis. Entering a woman's bedroom, Aramis is overwhelmed with her kisses. "Madam," he confesses, "I'm flattered, but I am here to tutor you in theology."

"Forgive me, monsieur, but when you started talking about original sin, I lost control and became impassioned by it. It won't happen again. Please go on." Aramis demurs. "There is nothing unholy about expressing one's emotion. On the contrary, religion should be experienced in an all-encompassing way. We should feel free to express our spirituality."

"Yes, darling," she sighs. Suddenly there is a loud commotion at the door, and she exclaims, "My husband!" "You're married? We must pray for our sins." As he starts his prayer, the husband bursts in shooting. As he jumps out the window, Aramis concludes, "On second thought, God's awfully busy."

The selfishness of prayer, with its tendency to be egocentric, is brilliantly portrayed in the dark comedy *Election* (Alexander Payne, 1999). On the eve of a disputed high school election, three separate prayers are made simultaneously.

The overachieving Tracy Flick (Reese Witherspoon), wearing her designer pajamas, insists that the Lord help her

win the election tomorrow because I deserve it and Paul Metzler doesn't, as You well know. I realize that it was Your divine hand that disqualified Tammy Metzler and now I'm asking that You go that one last mile and make sure to put me in office where I belong so that I may carry out Your will on earth as it is in heaven. Amen.

Outcast Tammy Metzler (Jessica Campbell), who doesn't believe in God, assumes the posture of prayer and speaks caustically:

> Dear God, let's see, what do I want? I want Lisa to realize what a bitch she is and feel really bad. . . . I still want Paul to win the election tomorrow, not that cunt Tracy. Oh, and I also want a really expensive pair of leather pants, and someday I wanna be really good friends with Madonna. Love, Tammy.

Finally, popular star football player Paul Metzler (Chris Klein) expresses his simple heart and superficial mind:

> Dear God, thank You for all Your blessings. You've given me so many things, like good health, nice parents, a nice truck, and what I'm told is a large penis, and I'm very grateful. Please help [Tammy] be a happier person because she's so smart and sensitive and I love her so much. Also, I'm nervous about the election tomorrow and I guess I want to win and all, but I know that's totally up to You. You'll decide who the best person is and I'll accept it. And forgive me for my sins, whatever they may be. Amen.

The competing prayers echo the selfishness of passengers who prayed for good winds in Mark Twain's *Innocents Abroad*. Each traveler prays for his or her own convenient weather. So, too, in *Election*, the juxtaposition of each student's petitions exposes their narcissism.

In *Happy, Texas* (Mark Illsley, 1999), Wayne (Steve Zahn) is asked to pray before the children's dance performance. Wayne swallows uncomfortably and then says, "All right. Bow your heads." One little girl asks, "What about holding hands?" "All right," he replies, "hold hands."

> Okay God, just want You to look down on these girls here. They're like little flowers and the rain You send 'em gotta be gentle and sweet. We come to You today and we ask You just help 'em help us grab them by the balls and rip 'em off. I mean if those judges don't like us, then screw 'em. These girls here, they're talented, they're pretty, and if those judges say anything different, then I hope that on Judgment Day, You put their asses through a meat grinder. Amen.

"*Amen!*" shouts one little girl.

In an even darker black comedy, *Heathers* (Michael Lehmann, 1988), prayers are offered at the coffin of a Heather, one of the unlikeable popular "in-crowd" girls of Westerberg High School. Veronica Sawyer (Winona Ryder) stands outside the malicious clique of girls all called Heather. She meets a transfer student, sociopathic Jason Dean/JD (Christian Slater), and her life spirals into a downward descent of accidental murders of her detestable friends.

The selfish prayers of various students at the funeral are both funny and mean-spirited. Ram asks, "Jesus, God in heaven, why'd You have to kill such hot snatch?" When someone objects, he smiles and says, "It's a joke, man. Geez, people are so serious." He alters his prayer with a serious face: "Holy Mary who art in heaven, pray for us sinners . . . so we don't get caught," then grins and explains, "Another joke."

Several others follow suit. Peter begs, "Dear Lord, please make sure this never happens to me," and adds that he wants "early acceptance into an Ivy League school and please let it be Harvard. Amen." Heather Duke (Shannen Doherty) confesses, "I prayed for the death of Heather Chandler many times and I felt bad every time I did it, but I kept doing it anyway. Now I know You understood everything. Praise Jesus, Hallelujah." When Veronica Sawyer pauses over the casket, she says spitefully but candidly, "Hi, I'm sorry. Technically, I did not kill Heather Chandler, but hey, who am I trying to kid, right? I just want my high school to be a nicer place. Amen. Did that sound bitchy?"

Yet the superficial religion of the high schoolers and mean girls reflects the faux hipness of Father Ripper, who tells them all at the funeral, "We must pray that other teenagers of Sherwood, Ohio, know the name of that righteous dude who can solve their problems: it's Jesus Christ, and he's in the Book."

At a funeral in the blaxploitation parody *I'm Gonna Git You Sucka* (Keenen Ivory Wayans, 1988), the deceased black man has been stripped of his gold to pay for the service. The reverend (John Witherspoon), a collared preacher, prays, "Lord, we ask You to look down upon this young soul known as June Bug Spade." Everyone except his mother and widow get up because they discover they are at the wrong funeral. The minister still calls out, "Don't I get an 'amen'?" The satire of undeterred preachers points to mercenary leaders like Reverend Ike of Los Angeles, an infamous prosperity gospel preacher.

Car Wash (Michael Schultz, 1976) offers a motley collection of characters, not the least of whom is greedy Daddy Rich (Richard Pryor), the top television evangelist of the Church of Divine Economic Spirituality. Allegedly based on the Reverend Ike, Daddy Rich arrives at the car wash with his bevy of beautiful, sexy women in his chauffeured Cadillac. "Praise the Lord! Praise the Lord!" To which the crowd shouts, "Hallelujah" and one transvestite says, "Praise this car, honey."

Asked what his secret is, Daddy Rich announces that there is no secret, just "believe in the Lord, but most of all, believe in that federal green, because money walks and bullshit talks." Strutting with his white suit and cane, the carnal cleric has hoodwinked everyone, except for one Muslim character, Duane (Bill Duke). Sitting in front of photos of Kennedy and Martin Luther King Jr., Duane challenges Daddy Rich on how he got so rich. Daddy responds, "My God's doing all right by me. Why don't you come on board, brother, and believe in me, and for a small fee I'll take you nearer to God to thee. I'll show you everything it takes to make it with money. 'Cause it's better to have money than not having it. There is a good place in this world for money and I know where it is. It's right here in my pocket!" Such financial exploitation echoed the cant of many televangelists.

Two businessmen bet over whether heredity or environment shapes a man's ability in *Trading Places* (John Landis, 1983). Scam artist Billy Ray Valentine (Eddie Murphy) feigns being a blind amputee veteran when the police come upon him. When they pick him up out of his cart, he exclaims, "I can see! I can see! I have legs! Oh shit, look at this. I can walk!" He looks up to heaven. "Oh, Jesus, praise Jesus, I appreciate this! Thank You! Oh, beautiful, I don't know what to do! Praise God. Thank You, Jesus." Then he moves away as fast as he can. Later, the wily trickster Valentine teams up with the pompous commodities broker Louis Winthorpe III (Dan Aykroyd) to deliver a comeuppance to corporate tyrants.

In *Coming to America* (John Landis, 1988), the minister (Eddie Murphy playing multiple roles) addresses Prince Akeem (Eddie Murphy), "I want to pray for you, just as the Lord helped Samson, and helped Daniel out of the lions' den, and helped Gilligan get off the island."

Reverend Brown (Arsenio Hall) surveys the comely ladies at a beauty pageant and sings praises that there's a God somewhere, one "who sits on high and looks down low. Man cannot make it like this. . . . Only God above, the Hugh Hefner on high, can make it for ya!" In an era of the corrupt ministry scandals of Bakker, Swaggart, and Benny Hinn, the comic appeal of bogus clergy reached an apex. Prayers of hypocritical televangelists appeared in many films, but the reality of Swaggart's coupling with a prostitute and Bakker's tryst with Playboy playmate Jessica Hahn proved more ridiculous than film comedies.

Reporter Fletch (Chevy Chase), also known as Elmer Fudd Gantry, investigates a shady television evangelist in *Fletch Lives* (Michael Ritchie, 1989). "Are you religious?" asks Calculus Entropy (Cleavon Little). Fletch responds in a dig at televangelists, "I believe in a God that doesn't need heavy financing." Televangelists' prayers were exposed as hypocritical and mercenary. Disguised as a Pentecostal minister, Fletch meets Louisiana cable broadcaster and ex–used car salesman Jimmy Lee Farnsworth (Lee Ermey), raising money for a Bible Land amusement park, featuring a Noah's Ark where it floods every ten minutes. Parodying fraudulent evangelist Peter Popoff, Farnsworth picks out audience members' ailments by way of an ear microphone. When he tells one sick man to expose his problems, he displays hemorrhoids.

When Fletch comes on stage at his revival, Farnsworth orders him to "admit you are a sinner." He responds, "Uh, well, I've sinned. I didn't take any Polaroids or anything, but yeah, I've sinned." Farnsworth announces, "The Lord forgives ya!" Fletch responds, "Thank you. Thank you very much."

Corrupt television evangelists are depicted as slavering hypocrites in several forgettable films, including *Dragnet* (Tom Mankiewicz, 1987), *Rented Lips* (Robert Downey Sr., 1988), and *Pray TV* (Rick Friedberg, 1980), where a sleazy evangelist transforms a failing TV station, KRUD, into the successful cable channel KGOD. He schedules religious programming around the clock, from the early morning exercise show *Jump for Jesus* (hosted by a young Paul Reubens) to a religious soap, *One Life to Lose*. To get into heaven, viewers must do the hardest thing in the world, which is "give everything you have to God." A chorus then chimes in about how someone who didn't give them money was hit by a bus.

In *Stardust Memories* (Woody Allen, 1980), Woody Allen tells his studio executive that the whole point of his Fellini-esque film is that "nobody is saved." "This is an Easter film," the producer objects. "We don't need a movie by an atheist." Woody retorts, "To you—to you, I'm an atheist. To God, I'm the loyal opposition." The misanthropic artist Frederick (Max von Sydow) attacks fundamentalist television evangelists in *Hannah and Her Sisters* (Woody Allen, 1986), ranting that "third-grade con men telling the poor suckers that watch them that they speak with Jesus, and to please send in money. Money, money, money! If Jesus came back and saw what's going on in His name, He'd never stop throwing up."

Thinking he has a malignant tumor, hypochondriac Mickey (Allen) tries to make a deal with God: "I'm going to make a deal with You, God. No brain operation and I'll do whatever You want." In his search for God, a desperate Woody considers the Roman Catholic Church. His father quacks at him, "And you're gonna believe in Jesus Christ?" "I know—sounds funny," says Mickey, "but I'm gonna give it a try." Asking his father about the existence of God, his father responds, "How the hell do I know? I don't even know how the new can opener works." Desperate and suicidal, Woody enters a movie theatre, seeking the solace of the Marx Brothers to "put things back into rational perspective."

With the sexual antics of Bakker and Swaggart, along with the excesses of the prosperity gospel, religious practices were ripe for satire. In 1986 *Saturday Night Live* sketch comedian Dana Carvey created Enid Strict, the smug Church Lady who mocked those who begged for donations and showed their "naughty parts." Even church members picked up her catchphrases ("Could it be . . . *Satan*?") to distance themselves from the more unsavory representatives of the Gospel.

A decade later, *Leap of Faith* (Richard Pearce, 1992) offered another exposé of revival evangelists. The high-tech Elmer Gantry, Jonas Nightengale (Steve Martin), dances across the platform with his happy feet, bringing hope and snake oil to country rubes. He shouts and hollers with enthusiasm, "I believe we are going to see some serious miracles tonight. He's coming through me. Special delivery." He lays hands on a large black woman who is slain in the Spirit. Little difference can be discerned between his ministry and showmanship. "Oh, oh, the fever is on me! The fever is on me! [In the] power of Jesus Christ, prepare to receive your miracle. I'm feeling the power tonight! I cure rheumatism with this fresh anointing."

However, Jonas's own chicanery convicts the fraudulent faith healer. "Hey, Boss," he converses in a soliloquy prayer in the deserted tent after the crowds have gone. He throws a funeral fan.

> Remember me? Jack Newton. I got a question for You. Why did You make so many suckers? [He poses in a cruciform position in front of a crucifix.] You say love never endeth. While I say love never starteth. You say the only thing the meek shall inherit is the earth, and I say the only thing the meek can get is the short end of the stick. You say is there one among you who is pure of heart, and I say not one.

When an inexplicable miracle occurs in the crippled body of Boyd (Lukas Haas) through the praying of the agnostic evangelist, it is enough to shake his doubts. Ironically, Hollywood's construction of the hypocritical prayers of televangelists could not measure up to the sheer pomposity and outrageousness of the actual performances. Reality trumped fiction.

Liberation Theology

In the 1970s, mission work included an evangelical concern for salvation *and* a social and political emphasis upon helping the oppressed. As articulated by theologian Gustavo Gutiérrez in *A Theology of Liberation*, the faithful are called to walk in the footsteps of Jesus and denounce poverty. Liberation theology sought to uproot the social manifestations of sin, namely, poverty and social injustice.

Most films dealing with missions fell into a melodramatic category, investigating how neocolonialists disrupted indigenous cultures. A vicious critique of missions is presented in *At Play in the Fields of the Lord* (Hector Babenco, 1991). Fundamentalist missionaries Martin and Hazel Quarrier (Aidan Quinn and Kathy Bates) come to the Amazon to convert the natives. The narrow-minded and hysterical Hazel even tries to teach them how to sing "Jesus Wants Me for His Sunbeam."

When Martin arrives, he gives gifts and food, baptizing the natives. They see his overtures as a negotiation rather than a call to faith. Martin worries about his techniques: "I feel we're bribing the Indians to love Jesus." In contrast, their young son, Billy, demonstrates a freedom in going native and sparks laughter that communicates with them.

However, when Billy is dying of blackwater fever, in spite of the prayers of his parents, he asks whether God hates him. When told that God doesn't, he asks, then "why did He make the mosquito?" Both the Lord's Prayer and the Twenty-Third Psalm are recited during this poignant scene of grief, but they bring neither healing nor hope. In discussing his purpose, director Babenco averred, "I'm not Gandhi, I'm not waving the sword of democracy. All I want is to make people feel something about what's going on around them."[11] What one encounters, however, are mostly intolerant missionaries, ignorant about their impact on other cultures, offering futile prayers as the fruit of a fundamentalist faith.

Similarly, in *The Mosquito Coast* (Peter Weir, 1986), the main nemesis to headstrong inventor Allie Fox (Harrison Ford) appears in the deceptive, self-serving missionary character, Reverend Spellgood (Andre Gregory). Trying to re-create a new Garden of Eden in the rainforests of Belize with his family, Fox expresses disgust with modernity, consumerism, and missionaries; yet he becomes the creator of Fat Boy, his giant ice-making machine. Traveling up a river, he comes upon natives who worship a facsimile of his machine as an idol. As he is asked to lead prayers to it, a clever trope for the atheist's worship of modernity, the film equates him with the missionary arrogance that he detests. Liberation theology critiqued the colonial invasion of religion, as it was mixed with capitalism, and championed a more equitable distribution of goods for the poor.

Two additional films set up a juxtaposition of two forms of liberation, prayerful versus action-oriented missionaries. In David Putnam's production of *The Mission* (Roland Joffe, 1986), eighteenth-century Jesuits seek to establish a mission among the South American Guaraní Indians. They create a democratic utopian Jesuit Republic, which lasts for over a century before the "imperialist monarchies of Spain and Portugal, abetted by the central Roman Catholic hierarchy," destroy it.[12]

When Father Gabriel (Jeremy Irons) arrives, he plays his flute, soothing the "savages" and gaining their curiosity and trust. But slave traders capture several converts. One of the worst mercenaries, Rodrigo de

Mendoza (Robert De Niro), agonizes over killing his brother. When Gabriel invites him out to join the Jesuits, Mendoza begins a journey of repentance. Gabriel tells him that at the mission in San Carlos, he can pray, away from all the distractions of the city. "There your prayers might meet with better fortune. I think, there, God would tell you what it would be good to do. And he'd give you the strength and grace to do it, whatever it costs you."

On the onerous climb to the mission, Mendoza tortures himself by dragging baggage of weapons and armor as penance. At one point, an Indian whom he had mistreated comes at him with a knife. It appears he will slit Mendoza's throat, but he cuts off the ropes entangling Mendoza, releasing his burden of "sin." The burden is washed away by a river and Mendoza is duly baptized, rising with joy in his heart. In thanksgiving, he later quotes I Corinthians 13, celebrating the love of God.

As Portuguese and Spanish invade, the two different missionaries attempt alternative strategies: one with the sword, one with prayer. Both die trying to save the mission. The struggle suggests that neither traditional missionary work nor liberation theology can triumph in this fallen world of greed and sin. Yet, at the end, a small cadre of children return and salvage some religious artifacts before disappearing into the dark jungle. The film then proclaims that many priests continue the battle for the rights of indigenous people, citing the Gospel of John that "the Light shineth in the darkness, and the darkness hath not overcome it."

Agnostic director Joffe invited Father Daniel Berrigan, a Jesuit priest and anti-war protestor, to advise him throughout the filmmaking. Berrigan documented his story in a diary, as a testament to the fight against social and economic injustice among oppressed people.[13]

The strange relationship between those called by God to speak good news and their audience is depicted in Bruce Beresford's epic *Black Robe* (1991). The film raises a question about the efficacy of missionary work among Third World peoples. A seventeenth-century Jesuit priest, Father Laforgue (Lothaire Bluteau), sets out for a distant mission through Quebec to proselytize Algonquin Indians. From the clash of European and a particularly resistant Native American culture, Laforgue learns to adapt. He discovers that it is not his white skin but his black robe—symbol of celibacy—and his pronouncements about paradise beyond death that separate him from others. When he writes, Natives regard him as a demon, one communicating supernaturally. As he travels across the rugged terrain, he prays, "Lord, if it be Thy wish that I suffer greater privations in the days ahead, I welcome it. Thou hast given me this cross for Thy honor and for the salvation of these poor barbarians. I thank Thee."

He prays fervently for those God has brought into his care, "Lord, I beg You, show Your mercy to these savage people, who will never look upon Your face in Paradise." His compatriot, Father Jerome, wants to baptize them before they understand the faith, which puzzles Laforgue, but after his friend dies, he asks God, "Lord, why is Father Jerome with You in heaven, while Chomina lies forever in utter darkness? Help me."

Others, like the shaman Ougebmat, distrust the Black Robe. As Laforgue administers last rites to a dying child, praying, "O God of mercy, please bless this innocent child," the chief Chomina explains that the priest is talking to his God. But when Laforgue makes the sign of the cross and recites, "In nomine patris et filii et spiritus sancti," Ougebmat panics: "See that sign? That's how they steal our spirit."

After abandonment and rejection, Laforgue makes it to a village of Hurons, baptizing and Christianizing the whole village. The narrative, however, concludes with a historical epilogue, stating that all the peace-loving Huron Christians were conquered and killed and the mission destroyed by the Iroquois fifteen years later. These films offer indirect critiques of both evangelistic and political missions of the church, suggesting, from a secular point of view, the futility of interfering with Rousseau's "noble savages." While acknowledging the pacifism of Berrigan and others, the films raised exposure to the problems addressed by liberation theology, wondering when was the time to act and when was the time to pray.

Horrible Prayers

The contemporary crisis of the war evoked a sense of guilt over past injustices. One appropriate vehicle for dealing with generational curses was the horror genre. In John Carpenter's low-budget ghost story *The Fog* (1980), phantoms come to wreak revenge upon descendants whose founding fathers massacred them in a burning ship, the *Elizabeth Dane*. The sins of the fathers are visited upon the sons. Father Malone (Hal Holbrook) retrieves a gold cross, which glows with an eerie light, along with his Bible, from the chapel; neither protects him from a curse on his family. The fear of judgment presses in on the community so much that when one mother, Stevie Wayne (Adrienne Barbeau), finds her lost child, she thanks God for his life. Gratitude in horror films reflected that many felt that they deserved judgment.

The ranting preacher-boy Isaac leads a cult of perverse revivalism in Fritz Kiersch's *Children of the Corn* (1984), as children with machetes and scythes repeatedly chant, "Praise God! Praise the Lord!" Concerns about the cultic behaviors of Scientology, the Unification Church, and Peoples Temple, with its mass suicide-murder at Jonestown, provoked fear in ordinary citizens, seemingly showcasing religion gone mad. Mixing piety, charismatic leadership, and demands for blind obedience, their actions shocked traditional churches. Ominously, the prayers of a cult sounded no different from those of a Methodist.

Wes Craven graduated from Wheaton College, an evangelical school whose teachings he discarded; nevertheless, traces remain even in his *Nightmare on Elm Street* (1984), about a razor-gloved soul-killer, Freddy Krueger (Robert Englund), slicing and mangling teenagers in their sleep. "If they don't wake up screaming, they won't wake up at all." Nancy Thompson (Heather Langenkamp), the only character who survives this film, prepares for bed, pulling her covers down and sitting up. Protection seems to come for her through her recitation of the eighteenth-century bedtime prayer appearing in the New England Primer: "And now I lay me down to sleep, I pray the Lord my soul to keep. If I die before I wake, I pray the Lord my soul to take." The clock ticks ominously and the lights go out in one of the eeriest and most appropriate settings for such a childhood prayer. (A little girl recites the same prayer for safety in Tom McLoughlin's 1986 slasher movie *Friday the 13th VI*.)

When Freddy returns (in what seems sequels *ad infinitum*) to terrorize the teens in *A Nightmare on Elm Street 4: The Dream Master* (Renny Harlin, 1988), a title card quotes a warning from Job 4:13–14: "When deep sleep falleth on men, fear came upon me, and trembling, which made all my bones to shake." A chorus of children sing the bedside prayer.

At a graveside funeral for a high school boy garroted by Freddy's razor-sharp hand, the minister speaks generic words about a boy in his prime: "We grieve but take comfort in knowing such a man rests in the kingdom of God. Let our faith supersede our knowledge, for the Lord

Characters find little protection against supernatural violence other than a child's prayer and a crucifix in *A Nightmare on Elm Street* (Wes Craven, 1984).

works in mysterious ways." Then Freddy reappears with "Hello, babee!" Evil cannot be destroyed by human means.

However, in spite of what seems to be the killer's supernal power, his defeat occurs in a decrepit dream church. Alice Johnson (Lisa Wilcox) arrives through a stained glass window. She pummels Freddy, who mocks that she may have the power of lost souls, but he has their souls. Standing before a golden cross and surrounded by broken but holy stained glass imagery, Alice pronounces that when evil sees itself, it will die. The souls of his victims embedded in his own flesh revolt, tearing him apart from the inside. In a perverse Inferno, the heads of his victims devour him and liberated souls soar heavenward as Freddy descends to hell. Harlin gives oppressed viewers a moment of relief, at least until the next *Nightmare* sequel.

In the B-grade *The Howling II* (Philippe Mora, 1985), Christopher Lee goes slumming as Stefan Crosscoe in this bloody folk tale. Its setting in the Eastern European country of Transylvania offers a strange locale with superstitious customs. Some old tales remain (a puppet play shows the ghastly end of Red Riding Hood). Crosscoe goes into a candlelit church to pray. "Hear my prayer, O Lord, and let my cry come unto Thee in the name of the Father, and of the Son, and of the Holy Ghost. Let my cry come unto Thee. Protect us, almighty God, from the evil of man and the malevolence of the beast." As he stands over the open coffin of a young woman, Crosscoe prays, "Let this woman be sanctified and purified from all evil." Even though werewolves invade the church, divine protection against the onslaught of lycanthropes and their Wiccan queen arrives.

Werewolves also lurk in the Stephen King adapted novel *Silver Bullet* (Daniel Attias, 1985). When a cop finds a young man torn to pieces outside at night, he utters a Hail Mary to himself: "Hail Mary, full of grace, the Lord is with thee. Blessed art thou among women, and blessed is the fruit of thy womb . . . pray for us sinners now and at the hour of our death." Reverend Lowe (Everett McGill), an evil-looking yet serene man, gives advice to the boy's paralytic friend Marty (Corey Haim): "The face of the beast always becomes known, and the time of the beast always passes." Marty and his sister suspect the minister as the villain and hope that he "gargles with broken glass or eats a rat-poison omelet."

The reverend does turn out to be the killer werewolf, but dreams that a congregation of wolves will destroy him. He wakes abruptly in a sweat and moans, "Let it end, dear God, let it end." God answers his prayer with a silver bullet.

When aliens control his father in *Invaders from Mars* (Tobe Hooper, 1986), David turns to religion, praying to God for his parent's safety. The symbolic function of prayers in horror films stems from the fact that people believe that prayers help in dire situations. The use of prayer may suggest innocence, purity, or goodness, such as children praying for protection from monsters, but prayers are also included as acts of desperation, as frantic efforts to escape evil. What is remarkable is that against seemingly indestructible monsters and demons, cinematic prayers remain one effective means of warding off evil. Yet in this era, horror films reminded ordinary churchgoers that something sinister lay deep in the hearts of all people, even children. Even in a time of economic and religious prosperity, evil lurked on the edges of imagination and in the hearts of men and women.

The Drama of Prayer

The 1980s recognized the need for spiritual renewal. Dramatic prayers in films reflected the personal wrestling that many undertook to make sense of their lives and to find the right way to live. In the Academy Award–winning *Chariots of Fire* (Hugh Hudson, 1981), Olympic runner Eric Liddell (Ian Charleson) sees his speed as a gift from God and gives thanks for this special talent: "I believe God made me for a purpose, but He also made me fast. And when I run I feel His pleasure." Liddell must struggle with his selection to run for Britain in the 1924 Olympics or to honor the Lord's Sabbath. The inspirational film opened the decade with a challenge to viewers to find their personal calling and discover their spiritual calling.

In *The Year of Living Dangerously* (Peter Weir, 1982), foreign correspondent Guy Hamilton (Mel Gibson) witnesses the 1965 uprising in Indonesia against President Sukarno. Much of the dialogue spoken is Filipino (not Javanese), as in a crucial scene when Billy Kwan (Linda Hunt) comes to the slum home of a dead child. The mother cries and spoons flower blossoms on the dead boy's naked body, gently preparing him for death. A davening old man speaks the Lord's Prayer in Tagalog.

Billy loves whomever God puts in his path, helping a starving mother and child and ministering in the poorest slums of Jakarta. He constantly asks the scriptural questions that Tolstoy struggled with at the end of his life, found in Luke 3:10: "What shall we do then?" His deep empathy and compassion for others lead to his Christ-like sacrifice when he displays the provocative banner "Sukarno, feed your people" out of a hotel window and is thrown to his death. While Billy's sacrifice ultimately converts Hamilton, the story-hungry writer is the one who inadvertently betrayed Billy. Billy tells him, "I gave you my trust. I gave you your eyes. I gave you stories."

When Hamilton says, "I would have given up the world for Billy," his paramour (Sigourney Weaver) counters, "You wouldn't even give up one story."

The grossly disfigured John Merrick (John Hurt), suffering from Proteus syndrome, memorizes the Twenty-Third Psalm in David Lynch's *The Elephant Man* (1980). In nineteenth-century Victorian society, surgeon Frederick Treves (Anthony Hopkins) rescues Merrick from an abusive carnival freak show. Merrick has bellowed out, "I am not an animal. I am a human being. I am a man."

Treves seeks to demonstrate Merrick's humanity and secure him medical care. He exhibits Merrick to Carr Gomm (John Gielgud) to get him admitted to the modern hospital. But Merrick's performance falls short, even as he stands in his room praying, "The Lord is my shepherd. I shall not want." Gomm commends the brave attempt to show Merrick's intelligence, but believes that Merrick merely mouthed the words. However, Merrick continues with words he wasn't taught. "Thou art with me. . . . Thy rod and Thy staff shall comfort me. Goodness and mercy shall follow me all the days of my life, and I will dwell in the house of the Lord forever." His prayer of assurance of God's care compels the doctors to recognize that he *was* made in the image of God.

On the holy day of Easter, Greek Orthodox believers greet one another with the prayerful confession, "Christ is risen." "He is risen indeed." *Eleni* (Peter Yates, 1985) celebrates this communal prayer of hope in the historical account of the heroic mother, Eleni (Kate Nelligan), who dies protecting her son, Nicholas Gage (John Malkovich), during the 1948 Greek Civil War. Years later, as a *New York Times* journalist, Gage wants to investigate how his mother died, and why. Discovering her executor, he seeks revenge, until grace interrupts him.

The black church congregation had been singing "When We All Get to Heaven" when they came out of a worship service in *Mississippi Burning* (Alan Parker, 1988) and are brutally attacked by the KKK. A young teenage boy kneels outside the church in a posture of prayer as others are beaten or flee. One KKK member comes up to him and assaults him as he prays, kicking and screaming at him. Like an early church martyr, the boy witnesses the cruelty of hatred, resisting with gentle courage.

Scriptwriter Paul Schrader (a graduate of Calvin College) directed a personal film in *The Light of Day* (1987). In a dysfunctional family, matriarch Jeanette Rasnick (Gena Rowlands) coddles her good son Joe (Michael J. Fox), and spiritually abuses her rock band daughter, Patti (Joan Jett). She browbeats her with a legalistic view of scripture and condemns her for giving birth to an illegitimate child. At a dinner with her children and the minister, the sanctimonious Reverend Ansley (Tom Irwin), who had impregnated Patti, the matriarch demands that they say grace.

Our Father who art in heaven, we thank Thee for bringing us together. [Patti glares at her mother.] We ask Thee to watch over Patti, Joe, and Little Benjamin. Grant them health. Help them through their trials and tribulations. We in particular ask Thy help for Patti. We ask Thee to show her a special measure of grace. Help her to understand her life. [She holds a fork and taps it against the table angrily.] Guide her ways. Forgive the sins of her youth.

Patti, in a rage, stomps out.

Schrader's own conservative mother in Michigan frowned on drinking, smoking, and the performing arts. She once smashed a clock radio when Pat Boone was singing "A Wonderful Time Up There." Schrader acknowledged that "when you're writing original material you try to combine some personal expression with some social metaphor, [such as] the ascent of loneliness of the cab driver. . . . In this case, it was a sense of family relationships and how to forge an individual personality *vis-à-vis* your parents, and the context seemed to be perfect for rock and roll."[14] For Schrader, as for Patti, the prayers meant nothing, with a mother closing a door to love.

Having stirred up trouble in a Cuernavaca bar during the Mexican Day of the Dead, a self-destructive British diplomat, Geoffrey Firmin (Albert Finney), adjourns to a chapel with his friend Vigil (Ignacio López Tarso) in *Under the Volcano* (John Huston, 1984). Even while claiming that hell is his natural habitat, he accompanies Vigil into a cavernous cathedral. When Vigil walks up to an elaborate statue of the Virgin, Firmin sits drinking in a pew, reflecting on how his wife had left him. Vigil tells his friend to pray to the Virgin and ask her for his lost spouse, explaining that the Virgin is for those who have no hope. "Ask her!" Firmin mutters, "I can't. It's like asking my fairy godmother for three wishes," as he swigs his bottle.

Vigil speaks directly to the Virgin Mary about his wretched friend: "You must forgive my compadre, and he ask for your help. Please!"

"Pray to the Virgin!" he tells Firmin. The luminous face looks kindly down on Firmin, who speaks to the woman he loves: "I'm dying without you. Come back to me, Yvonne." It is a prayer directed both to the Mother of God and his estranged wife.

REVIVAL OF PRAYER (1976–1988) | 233

With *Tender Mercies* (1982), director Bruce Beresford found his story on the doorstep, as film theorist Siegfried Kracauer described realist cinema. Picking up Horton Foote's screenplay, he quietly unfolded the drama of country singer Mac Sledge's (Robert Duvall) life of drunkenness and divorce. At a low point in his life, Mac meets the widowed Rosa Lee (Tess Harper), who comforts him with gentle care. His daughter visits him and tries to remember a song that he once sang to her, a holy prayer of peace, "On the Wings of a Dove." He denies remembering it. However, when she leaves, he begins to sing about God sending "His pure, sweet love, signs from above, on the wings of a dove."

His daughter dies in a car accident, leaving him with more questions and doubts.

Laying her head on her pillows, Rosa prays with eyes open while a car pulls up on the gravel outside. "Show me Thy way, O Lord, and teach me Thy path. Lead me in Thy truth and teach me, for Thou are the God of my salvation and on Thee do I wait all the day." As his footsteps pause upon entering the house, she asks, "Mac? You okay?" It is she whom God will use to help him become okay.

The dedicated faith of Rosa Lee climaxes in the astounding double immersion of her son, Sonny (Allan Hubbard), and Mac, in church, but on a glassed-in stage with a red theatrical curtain. While criticizing the baptismal scene as "potentially ludicrous," critic John Simon thought that "religion is treated with fine restraint." What elevated the film for Simon was "Rosa Lee's transcendent smile and the quiet gravity of the others," which "precludes if not amusement then certainly all disrespect."[15] On the way home after the Baptist immersion, Sonny says, "So, we've done it, Mac. We were baptized. Everybody said I'd feel like a changed person. Guess I do feel a little different, but not a whole lot. Do you?"

"Not yet," says Mac.

Sonny continues, "You don't look any different. Do I look different?"

"Not yet."

New Yorker critic Pauline Kael was more cynical: "Once I got it straight, I knew how I was supposed to react to her faint smile of gratification as she watches Mac, now her husband, getting himself dunked— along with her nine-year-old son. Mac is born again."[16]

At the end of the film, Mac stands in a small garden, hoeing. He confesses to Rosa, "I was almost killed once in a car accident. I was drunk and I ran off the side of the road and turned over four times. They took me out of that car for dead, but I lived. And I prayed last night to know why I lived and she died and I got no answers to my prayers." He continues,

> I still don't know why she died and I lived. I don't know the answer to nothing, not a blessed thing. I don't know why I wandered out to this part of Texas drunk and you took me in and pitied me and helped me to straighten me out and marry me. Why? Why did that happen? Is there a reason that happened?

The wind blows, the Holy Spirit whispers. The quiet and humble gravity of grace pervades the entire story.

The Reverend Shaw Moore (John Lithgow) practices his sermons in *Footloose* (Herbert Ross, 1984). His legalism and the small midwestern town's antiquated ordinances against dancing and rock music suppress the vitality of its young people, as he is afraid of its slippery slope to greater sins. He practices his sermon:

> He is testing us. Every, every day our Lord is testing us. If He wasn't testing us, how would you account for the sorry state of our society, for the crimes that plague the big cities in this country, when He could sweep this pestilence from the face of the earth with one mighty gesture of His hand? If our Lord wasn't testing us, how would you account for the proliferation these days of this obscene rock and roll music with its gospel of easy sexuality and relaxed morality?

The preacher's kid Ariel (Lori Singer), a free spirit like her Shakespearean namesake, rebels against her father's rejection of loud music and dancing. When she confronts her father practicing a sermon, she lambastes him for performing "show business." When she confesses that she's no saint, not even a virgin, he replies, "Don't talk like that in here!" She responds, "Why not? Isn't this where I'm supposed to confess my sins to my preacher? Here in church? I ask to be forgiven. Am I forgiven?" She tells her father, "I just don't know that I believe in everything you believe in, but I believe in you." Reverend Moore begins to change.

The new kid in town, Ren McCormack (Kevin Bacon), knows his Bible as well as the city council. Of course, he is the handsome, cool kid who would like to "fold *Playboy* centerfolds inside every one of Reverend Moore's hymn books," but he shows his truly decent character when he reasons from the Bible.

> From the oldest of times, people danced for a number of reasons. They danced in prayer. . . . And they danced to celebrate. That is the dancing we're talking about. Aren't we told in Psalm 149, "Praise ye the Lord. Sing unto the Lord a new song. Let them praise His name in the dance"? And it was King David—King David, who we read about in Samuel—and what did David do? What did David do? What *did* David do?

As the audience laughs, Ren answers his own question: "David danced before the Lord with all his might . . . leaping and dancing before the Lord." He smacks the table in front of Reverend Moore and repeats: "Leaping and dancing." He continues,

> Ecclesiastes assures us . . . that there is a time for every purpose under heaven. A time to laugh . . . and a time to weep. A time to mourn . . . and there is a time to dance. And there was a time for this law, but not anymore. See, this is our time to dance.

The subtle contradictions and challenges of faith simmer and boil over in *Amadeus* (Milos Forman, 1984), a film about envy and the unfathomable mysteries of God in giving gifts to less-righteous sinners. The great musician Salieri (F. Murray Abraham) looks back over his life and, as a bald, wizened old man, he confesses to a priest. When he was a child sitting in church, his prayers formed a conversation with God, or more accurately, a deal.

> While my father prayed earnestly to God to protect commerce, I would offer up, secretly, the proudest prayer a boy could think of: Lord [while gazing on a crucifix], make me a great composer! Let me celebrate Your glory through music and be celebrated myself! Make me famous through the world, dear God. Make me immortal! After I die, let people speak my name forever with love for what I wrote. [The prayer concludes with

Salieri as the old man remembering it all.] In return, I will give You my chastity, my industry, my deepest humility, every hour of my life. Amen, and amen.

At lunch, he exclaims, "You know what happened? A miracle!" His father, who opposed his music, chokes on a chicken bone and ends in a coffin. "My life changed forever. Of course, I knew God had arranged it all."

The problem is that while God blesses Salieri as a great composer, He pours more genius and talent upon a giggling, dirty-minded, and very vulgar Amadeus Mozart (Tom Hulce). Salieri continues to bargain with God, moving from petitions to threats:

Dear God, enter me now. Fill me with one piece of true music. One piece with Your breath in it, so I know that you love me. Please. Just one. Show me one sign of Your favor, and I will show mine to Mozart and his wife. I will get him the royal position, and if she comes, I'll receive her with all respect and send her home in joy. Enter me! Enter me! Please! *Te imploro.*

Old Salieri's voice-over fumes as he realizes the favor given to Mozart, that such a worm would be God's instrument:

From now on, we are enemies, You and I! . . . Because You will not enter me, with all my need for You; because You scorn my attempts at virtue; because You choose for Your instrument a boastful, lustful, smutty, infantile boy and give me for reward only the ability to recognize the Incarnation; because You are unjust, unfair, unkind, I will block You! I swear it! I will hinder and harm Your creature on earth as far as I am able. I will ruin Your Incarnation.

The issues of making sense of one's faith and understanding the significance of comedy at the heart of that faith emerged in Jean-Jacques Annaud's adaptation of Umberto Eco's *The Name of the Rose* (1986). Apocalyptic-like murders ruin the serenity of a medieval monastery. One monk believes that Franciscan monk William of Baskerville (Sean Connery) is the "answer to my prayers": "We pray almighty God no grounds for expecting an evil spirit among us. . . . We also thank God for sending us William of Baskerville." He soon discovers that William isn't the answer he wanted, but is the answer God gave.

When William's novice lies with a local girl accused of being a witch, the boy runs to a statue of the Virgin Mary and confesses his sin, but also pleads for the girl's safety, begging the Mother of God not to let her suffer for his wrongdoing. The girl is rescued. However, the Venerable Jorge, who hates laughter as it might allow men to laugh at God, dies horribly. William yet prays that God receive "his soul and forgive his little vanities." Both this film and *Amadeus* reveal the quests for spiritual renewal that often go astray, as they unmask overlooked spiritual sins like pride and envy in those who inhabited the church pews. They offered a timely rebuke for the rising Moral Majority, which focused primarily on carnal sins, ignoring the need for repentance of spiritual sins for one's sanctification.

Dramatic prayers reflected the honest grappling of many for spiritual renewal. They revealed that even in times of prosperity, suffering continues, and conversations with God remain as necessary as ever. Whether dealing with personal death, family estrangement, or injustice, people needed to express their anguish and pain. The prayers of cinema provided the words for such crises.

Muscular Christianity

In the 1980s Robert Bly articulated a need for men to step up and take responsibility for their lives and their families. He promoted a reinvigorated muscular Christianity in his men's movement. It was fulfilled by the emergence of the Promise Keepers, especially through the leadership of the University of Colorado football coach Bill McCartney, who inspired thousands of evangelical Christians to gather in football stadiums to reclaim their calling as husbands, fathers, and leaders. Sports films reaffirmed many of its principles.

Hoosiers (David Anspaugh, 1986) is nostalgically centered in small-town America in 1954 with all its virtues and inspirations. Basketball coach Norman Dale (Gene Hackman) takes a ragtag group of players to a state championship amid the petty squabbles and personal crises of the citizens of the fictional Hickory, Indiana (where songs such as "Do Lord" are common staples of worship). Preacher Purl and Reverend Doty stand as backboned and quiet supporters of Coach.

Muscular Christianity takes ordinary young men and makes them heroes in *Hoosiers* (David Anspaugh, 1986).

When one of his key players fouls out in a crucial game leading to the championship, Coach substitutes Strap Purl, the preacher's son, an average player at best. Coach orders him, "Strap, you're going to play for Everett. Don't shoot the ball unless you're under the basket all by yourself. Understand? We have two minutes and fifteen seconds. All right! Be patient, work for the good shot. Got it?" Putting their hands together, they shout, "Team!" "Let's go, guys!"

At this point, with everyone else on the floor ready to play, Strap has knelt to pray. Coach urges him, "Let's go, Strap. . . . Strap, God wants you on the floor."

Strap raises his head with a victorious grin. The rousing music of Harold Leckrone's high school fight song follows him through an impressive series of moves, fakes, and made shots. At a time-out, Coach asks Strap, "What's gotten into you?"

The kid answers, "The Lord. I can feel His strength." Not knowing what to say, Coach jests, "Well, keep His strength in the dribble, all right?"

At halftime of the state finals against a much superior team, Reverend Purl enters the locker room. Strap kneels as his father speaks to the underdog team. "With God of heaven, it is all one, to deliver with a great multitude or a small company. For the victory standeth not in the multitude of hosts, but strength cometh from heaven. And David put his hand in a bag and took out a stone and slung it and struck the Philistine in the head and he fell to the ground. Amen." The team members gather to put their hands in a circle as Coach concludes, "I love you guys." They, of course, win, just like David.

Anspaugh continued with his sports movie *Rudy* (1993). The dependable, old-fashioned priest Father Cavanaugh (Robert Prosky) appears at the University of Notre Dame, counseling a Fightin' Irish football wannabe without the size or talent needed, Daniel "Rudy" Ruettiger (Sean Astin), who dreams of playing football. Seeing him praying in the chapel for admission to the prestigious university, the priest asks, "Taking your appeal to a higher authority?"

Rudy answers, "I'm desperate. If I don't get in next semester, it's over. Notre Dame doesn't accept senior transfers. . . . Maybe I haven't prayed enough." To which the wise old priest says, "I don't think that's the problem. Praying is something we do in our time; the answers come in God's time." Acknowledging that he has done everything he possibly could, he asks the priest if he could help.

Father Cavanaugh answers whimsically, "Son, in thirty-five years of religious study, I have only come up with two hard incontrovertible facts: there is a God, and I'm not Him." Miraculously, Rudy is admitted and gets on the football team, albeit as the tackling dummy.

As Coach Dan Devine (Chelcie Ross) prepares his team, he leads them in prayer: "You already know this, but this is the most important game of your lives. No excuses. Do the work. Our Lady of victory—" and they all shout, "*pray for us!*"

Rudy thanks Coach Ara Parseghian (Jason Miller) for letting him be a part of the football team. Parseghian replies, "Rudy, I never thought I'd be saying this, but it's been an honor." Rudy confesses, "But I've come to realize that God made some people out to be football players, and that I'm not one of them." The coach answers, "I wish God would put your heart in some of my players' bodies." Rudy's perseverance, passion, and spunk so impress the coach and the team that he plays in the last game. He makes a tackle and is hoisted off the field on the shoulders of his teammates. The underdog story of the 1980s carries the day, with prayers entering the sports arenas, culminating in the phenomenon of outspoken celebrity Christians in the next century.

And so the 1976 bicentennial celebration arrived in time to close the door on a dark decade culminated by reverberations of the Watergate scandal and the fading morass of Vietnam. Hollywood responded by relaunching America's classic myths of heroism and virtue, returning to its roots in worship, which were reflected in its prayers. A proliferation of country-pastoral films offered what moviegoers hadn't seen in decades: dinner-table prayers denoting a community's strength. Filmmakers also found religious subjects in liberation theology, reflecting America's heightened involvement in Central American politics, and in mission work of a social kind. Meanwhile, prayer rituals were marked by comedy more than ever, including parody, easily achieved at the peak of the televangelist scandals. And the times were ripe for the flourishing horror genre, in which prayers, remarkably, were an effective weapon against evil.

However, even in film comedies, a sense of the supernatural could appear. In one of the rare moments of the numinous, awe before the Almighty humbles Joe (Tom Hanks), drifting hopelessly in the middle of the Pacific Ocean, in *Joe versus the Volcano* (John Patrick Shanley, 1990). The hypochondriac Joe had been given six months to live, but eccentric millionaire Greynamore (Lloyd Bridges) offers him a month of unlimited spending and living it up, if he will just help the natives of a Pacific island appease their fire god by jumping into an active volcano. Set adrift in the middle of nowhere at night, Joe looks up at an incredibly large and beautiful moon. Falling on his knees, he lifts his hands in praise: "Dear God, whose name I do not know. Thank You for my life. I forgot *how big!* Thank You." Prayers in the 1980s revealed how big God was in American culture.

While the cinematic prayers of the 1980s Reagan era celebrated old-fashioned values in films like *Rudy*, demonstrating the efficacy of prayers in ordinary life, they also hinted at a loss of faith in the traditional God of Judaism and Christianity. Biblical illiteracy increased. More Eastern religious thought seeped into the culture. Even the Methodist-raised George Lucas adopted a Zen-like spirituality; yet when he dreamed of facing God at the end of his life, God looked down at him and said, "Get out!"[17] The years leading up to the Millennium would ignore such signs and frolic in the end of the century. The Generation X era would be, in the words of writer Douglas Coupland, "the good decade."

7

Postmodern Prayers (1989–2000)

With the Berlin Wall falling in 1989, the Cold War thawed around 1991. Other struggles took center stage. Societal racism concerned many religious leaders, even as Billy Graham preached reconciliation in Atlanta, Georgia, and, after twenty-five years of imprisonment, Nelson Mandela was elected president of South Africa in 1994. The World Wide Web and cable television opened up unparalleled modes of technological communication. Many became aware of a multicultural globe, of different peoples, styles, music, and ideas.

With significant decline in mainline denominations, the rise of seeker-friendly churches for millennials, and the ascent of contemporary Christian music to appeal to the young, the Hollywood prayers of the 1990s waned in significance compared to other decades. The Supreme Court had ruled against public prayers at sporting events, but several high-profile religious athletes did pray in public. New Age spirituality with exotic practices built upon a multifaceted "harmonic convergence," while cults like the Branch Davidians offered messianic hopes. A dominant focus of prayer concerned the impending end of the millennium. It seemed that Hollywood thought we were overdue for an apocalypse.

War Revisited

However, the 1990s were marked by revivals among men, beginning in 1991 with the first Promise Keepers gathering of 4,200 fathers and husbands at the University of Colorado, who were challenged to stand firm for their faith and for their marriages, families, and communities. By the end of the decade, over a million men would stand together at the National Mall in Washington, D.C. Cinematic tropes of battles, echoing the world war in which their fathers fought, would provide models for them to demonstrate their commitment to a higher calling.

Over fifty years after the Greatest Generation vanquished Nazi Germany, Steven Spielberg remembered the events in his epic *Saving Private Ryan* (1998), evoking a renewed sense of patriotism and integrity. Surrounded by suffering and violence on the beaches of Normandy, July 6, 1944, a chaplain administers last rites to dying soldiers. With the Allied forces pinned down, wounded soldiers confess sins and pray. Captain John Miller (Tom Hanks) calls his sniper, Private Jackson (Barry Pepper), to take out Nazi guns, but just before he does, he prays psalms of vengeance, praying with "all my strength, Lord help me," and "Let me not be ashamed. Let not my enemies triumph over me—God grant me strength." Jackson's aim is piercingly accurate.

The sniper, a preacher from Tennessee, tells his captain that God gave him a "special gift, made me a fine instrument of warfare." As he lines up his sniper shots, he breathes scriptures into his prayers.

> Be not that far from me, for trouble is near; haste Thee to help me. . . .
> Blessed be the Lord my strength, which teacheth my hands to war and
> my fingers to fight. . . . I trust in Thee. Let me not be ashamed. Let not
> mine enemies triumph over me. . . . My fortress, my high tower, and my
> deliverer, my shield, and He in whom I trust, who subdueth my people
> under me. . . . Here you go, baby.

Miller, Jackson, and the band of brothers give up their own lives for Ryan. The task of the company was to bring Private Ryan (Matt Damon) home alive as his three brothers had died in action. Just before their final battle, Captain Miller tells Ryan about all those who sacrificed their lives that he might live and challenges Ryan to "earn this. Earn this." The call is to complete the duty of another's sacrifice. In theological terms, how does one respond to the sacrifice of Christ dying for you? What is required as a proper response? Such a mission would underlie the Promise Keepers' task to live out a life of courage and integrity.

As Private Ryan travels home, General George Marshall sends a letter to his mother, commending her on her son's courage and steadfast dedication. He shares some words that had "sustained him through long, dark nights of peril, loss, and heartache":

"I pray that our Heavenly Father may assuage the anguish of your be-
reavement, and leave you only the cherished memory of the loved and
lost, and the solemn pride that must be yours to have laid so costly a
sacrifice upon the altar of freedom."—Abraham Lincoln.

However, the final prayer offered is a question, one that the old Ryan's
presence before thousands of crosses in the Normandy cemetery raises.
He kneels before the cross of Miller and whispers that he tried to live his
life the best he could and hoped that was enough. Emotionally drained
and humbled, he asks his wife whether he is a good man. She answers,
"You are." The question of whether one is worth the sacrifice by another
is poignantly addressed.

Facing their first battle during the Civil War, black Union soldiers
reaffirm their trust in God in *Glory* (Edward Zwick, 1989), saying silent grace before eating or preparing an assault on the Confederate Fort
Wagner. Trying to relax, the all-black 54th Massachusetts Regiment sits
around a campfire singing an old southern hymn about Noah leading
the animals onto the ark. While singing, they always come back to the
chorus, "Lord, Lord, Lord," as they clap and sing together. Interspersed
with their worship, three soldiers pray to God.

First, an enlisted soldier, Private Jupiter Sharts (Jihmi Kennedy),
prays aloud, emboldened by being able to fight for emancipation. "Tomorrow we go into battle, so Lordy, let me fight with the rifle in one
hand, and the good book in the other. So that if I may die at the muzzle
of the rifle . . . die on water, or on land, I may know that You, blessed
Jesus Almighty, are with me . . . and I have no fear."

Second, Sergeant Major John Rawlins (Morgan Freeman) faces their
daunting challenge with courage.

Lord, we stand before You this evening, to say thank You! And we thank
You, Father, for Your grace, and Your many blessings! Now I run off, leaving all my young 'uns and my kinfolk in bondage. So I'm standing here
this evening, heavenly Father, to ask Your blessings on all of us. So that if
tomorrow is the great getting-up morning, if that tomorrow we have to
meet the Judgment Day, O heavenly Father, we want You to let our folks
know that we died facing the enemy! We want 'em to know that we went

down standing up amongst those that are fighting against our oppression. We want 'em to know, heavenly Father, that we died for freedom! We ask these blessings in Jesus's name. Amen!

Finally, after another round of "Lord, Lord, Lord," the independent and caustic Private Trip from Tennessee (Denzel Washington) initially doesn't know what to say, muttering, "I ain't much about no prayer now." He goes on to reflect, "I ain't never had no family, just my momma," and he "feels funny praying." But moved by the sense of unity, he declares, "Y'alls is the only family I got and I love the 54th. Ain't much a matter of what happens tomorrow, but we men, ain't we? *We* men! Shiieeeet!" Trip joins the community of faith, men committed to each other and to a higher purpose.

In the gallant story of Confederate General "Stonewall" Jackson (Stephen Lang), *Gods and Generals* (Ronald Maxwell, 2003), both sides of the Civil War read scriptures and appeal to God. About to lead the Confederate army, Jackson reads 2 Corinthians 5:1 with his wife. "For we know that if the earthly tent we live in is destroyed, we have a building from God, an eternal house in heaven, not built by human hands." After reading the verse, he prays for his safety during the war, a request that, ultimately, is not granted.

The Confederate artillery names its four cannons Matthew, Mark, Luke, and John. Humorously, Jackson tells their leader, "Spread the Gospel wherever you encounter the enemy." His own prayers before battle suggest a submission to the will of God, indicating that if God's will is for him to die, he gives himself up willingly. Asked how he manages to remain so calm throughout the tumult, Jackson explains that "my religious faith teaches me that God has already fixed the time of my death; therefore, I think not of it. I am as calm in battle as I would be in my own parlor. God will come for me in His own time." He spends time praying with his black cook, Jim Lewis (Frankie Faison), for God to watch over both their families. Jim asks in his prayer how good Christian men can tolerate slavery. Jackson's reply, "Show us the way, Lord, and we will follow," suggests that he is not certain.

Courage under Fire (Edward Zwick, 1996) provides a more cynical perspective in the post-Vietnam era, reflecting dissatisfaction with the past as Colonel Sterling's prayer sets up the film. After leading his troops in a prayer, he orders, "Now let's kill 'em all!" In contrast, Eli Mariachi (Antonio Banderas) is the title character in *Desperado* (Robert Rodriguez, 1995), whom we first see crossing himself in a church and lighting a candle. As he walks out of the confessional booth, a priest asks whether he wants confession. "Heh? Well, maybe later, Father, 'cause where I am going, I'd just have to come right back." Carolina (Salma Hayek) later asks where he is going. He responds that he is returning to the church. When she asks, "Why?" he answers, "To confess my sins. I am a sinner." Yet, just before the final climax of his fight against evil, he prays, "Give me the strength to be what I was and forgive me for what I am." Similar confessions and quests for transformation marked not only the Promise Keeper movement, but numerous revivals of the decade from Toronto to Brownsville.

After fighting in Muslim countries, Robin Hood (Kevin Costner) returns to England in *Robin Hood: Prince of Thieves* (Kevin Reynolds, 1991). Gathering a tribe of merry men, he is joined by Friar Tuck, a plump priest who dispenses prayers. Robin asks a pretentious cleric of the corrupt court whether the church is still giving alms to the poor. Posturing for his earthly benefactors in the large medieval cathedral, the priest pontificates,

> We beseech Thy blessing, Lord, on all Thy people, but most especially on our noble Sheriff of Nottingham. Grant him the strength to bring to justice the lawless mob who would threaten its safety and prosperity and the judgment to punish them.

Lady Marion goes to light a candle and genuflects. She prays silently while Robin sneaks up, whispering, "Alms for a blind man who can see your beauty." "What are you doing here?" she asks. "Searching for my soul," Robin answers. Actually, he searches for his soul mate.

Later the gluttonous and besotted Tuck, who comes begrudgingly to join the merry men of Sherwood Forest, is upended and reprimanded, but prays, "Thank You, Lord, for teaching me humility." He joins the meek of the earth and ministers to them. "Ah," he says, "the Lord reveals Himself in mysterious ways." As he teaches his fellow peasants to make ale, he invites them to give thanks to God: "Let us give praise to His person!" In a final battle with the corrupt sheriff's men, Friar Tuck sends the hypocritical cleric to the afterlife, first giving him thirty pieces of silver.

Simultaneous to the national men's movement, Rick Warren of Saddleback Church in southern California reified the divine calling for men and women of the churches, writing the bestseller *The Purpose Driven Church*, which celebrated how this generation would commend God's works to one another. Prayers for such spiritual ventures and battles were echoed on the screens.

Praying to Win

The ubiquitous presence of religion in sports, with its ritualized aspect of praying before games, pointed to a muscular Christianity during the years leading up to the millennium. An article in *Sports Illustrated*, "In the Fields of the Lord," probed such religious practices. One finds both earnest piety and glaring hypocrisy amidst the public displays of huddled prayers, pointing to the heavens. Comedian Jeff Stilson cast a jaundiced eye upon the unholy alliance, where "winning players always give credit to God and the losers blame themselves. You know, just once, I'd like to hear a player say, 'Yeah, we were in the game, until Jesus made me fumble. He hates our team.'"

The irony of a team praying for success ignores that when God helps one team to victory, He must necessarily deny the prayers of opponents. Few athletes would claim a higher degree of holiness or goodness over their adversaries, except of course, Notre Dame with its Football Jesus. How could USC pray, unless God likes the former semi-Methodist university over the Irish Roman Catholics? Such prayers were presumptuous in several ways.

Varsity Blues (Brian Robbins, 1999) portrays the obsession with football as a communal religion, where star players and coaches are deified, and "church" services are scheduled for every Friday night. Second-string quarterback Jonathan "Mox" Moxon (James van der Beek) is elevated to the top position when an injury sidelines the first-string leader. Mox's younger brother, Kyle, prays throughout the film; his father jokes that he prays for more playing time. The humor pointed to a fresh informality in praying by men. Among seeker-friendly faith practices, humor in petitions to God appeared more frequently.

Major League (David Ward, 1989) offers a campy comic take on the misfits of a Cleveland Indians baseball team. Religious traditions overlap when the pushy Christian Eddie Harris (Chelcie Ross) approaches Pedro Cerrano (Dennis Haysbert) praying to the image of his deity, Jobu, in the locker room before a game. Cerrano believes that his bat is sick and afraid and cannot hit a curveball. He asks Jobu to take the fear from the bats, offering him a cigar or rum (or even sacrificing a live chicken). At an inappropriate time, Harris mockingly says, "You know, you might think about taking Jesus Christ as your savior instead of fooling around with all this stuff." Cerrano responds, "Jesus, I like Him very much, but He no help with curveball."

Later, Cerrano is ready to throw out Jobu because he doesn't help him hit a curveball. Harris calls on the manager and asks, "Are we gonna have a prayer? You know, we're not all savages, like Cerrano over there." He begins, "Dear Lord, may we have . . ." and Cerrano ignites his ritual smoke. Harris shouts, "Jesus Christ, Cerrano," which denies his own piety. Cerrano is unaffected. "I gotta wake up my bat." Such behaviors are also exaggerated for comic effect in *Johnny Be Good* (Bud Smith, 1998). The small, skinny Johnny Walker (Anthony Michael Hall) is actually a desirable football recruiting prospect. Wayne Hisler (Paul Gleason) offers the customary pre-game prayer, sounding more like a pep talk:

> Dear Lord, we pray that we may win this game today. We ask that You give us the strength and the courage to win our second straight state championship. We ask, Lord, that nobody on our side is seriously injured. We know that we are the best team. We ask that You allow us to win this game. The Lord wants you to put your foot on their balls and believe in it, because that's what wins football games. Not jumping off-sides like a bunch of wimps and faggots. All right, lift your heads, boys, prayer's over. I talked to God. I'm through talking to God. Now I'm talking to you. . . . I'm a winner. I'm an American. Who wants to be John Wayne? . . . Let's go!

In addition to such comic portrayals, ironic depictions of prayer occurred in sports films. In *Friday Night Lights* (Peter Berg, 2004), Coach Gaines (Billy Bob Thornton) spurs his Permian High Panther team in his halftime locker room speech. Their star player tailback had torn his ACL in the season's first game. The football-crazy town of Odessa waits hopefully for them to win again. The coach reminds them of their brotherhood and challenges them to not let each other down. At the end of his speech, Coach Gaines calls on Ivory, the Preacher Man, who catches his cue and begins, "Our Father who art in heaven, hallowed be Thy name."

The following image shows their huddled opponents praying the same words. "Thy kingdom come. Thy will be done." Quick editing intercuts back and forth between the two teams: "Give us this day our daily bread," team members pray with their arms around each other. "And lead us not into temptation, but deliver us from evil. For Thine is the kingdom, the power, and the glory [as it all crescendos in both locker rooms] forever and ever." "Forever!" shout the teams as they retake the field. With various athletic teams appealing to God for victory, the question of God's favoritism arises. Just who are God's chosen people? Only the team that wins?

In one of the worst disasters in the history of college sports, a plane crash in November 1970 robbed Marshall University of many varsity football players. The school persevered, as portrayed in *We Are Marshall* (McG, 2006). New coach Jack Lengyel (Matthew McConaughey) preaches to his team from the graves of former players. While not on the field, these men will "still be watching. You can bet your ass that they'll be gritting their teeth with every snap of the football. You understand? How you play today, from this moment on, is how you will be remembered. This is your opportunity to rise from these ashes, and grab glory. The funerals end today. We are *Marshall*! We are *Marshall*! We are *Marshall*!"

Only in a photograph in the final credits do we get a hint of a religious presence amid all this tragedy, where ironically, on a theatre marquee, the words of Job 1:21 ("The Lord giveth; the Lord taketh away") are displayed. Other than that, only the mantra of "We are Marshall" comes close to anything smacking of prayer. However, online comments about this film were concerned about praying for those who had lost loved ones. It was a film that elicited prayers rather than showing them. Seeing frequent demonstrations of prayer during competitions, Christian groups like Athletes in Action would set forth guidelines of how, when, and what to pray.[1]

The remake of *Angels in the Outfield* (William Dear, 1994) doesn't resonate as much as the original, but an orphaned boy, Roger (Joseph Gordon-Levitt), prays that the Los Angeles Angels might win the championship and he would find a family. "God . . . if there is a God . . . if You're a man or a woman . . . if you're listening, I'd really, really like a family. My dad says that will only happen if the Angels win the pennant. The baseball team, I mean. So, maybe You can help them win a little. Amen." Angels do show up and, while no one else can see them, they answer his prayers.

Finally, in *A League of Their Own* (Penny Marshall, 1992), Coach Jimmy Dugan (Tom Hanks) doesn't quite know how to handle his all-girl baseball team ("Are you crying? There's no crying in baseball!"). But when called upon, the alcoholic, washed-up Dugan prays in the locker room for his Rockford Peaches to win the final championship game. Players look heavenward with their eyes open and hands folded. Coach takes a knee and the ladies follow his lead. "Uh, Lord, hallowed be Thy name. May our feet be swift; may our bats be mighty; may our balls . . . be plentiful. Lord, I'd just like to thank You for that waitress in South Bend. You know who she is—she kept calling Your name. And God, these are good girls; they work hard. Just help them see it all the way through. Okay, that's it." The girls all conclude it with their "Amen." Nineteenth-century satirist Ambrose Bierce defined "pray" in his *Devil's Dictionary* as a verb meaning "to ask that the laws of the universe be annulled in behalf of a single petitioner confessedly unworthy." Contemporary sports movies aptly demonstrate Bierce's definition.

Athletic competitions invited supplications for protection and expressions of gratitude. Fostered by such groups as the Fellowship of Christian Athletes and Athletes in Action, sports films underscored the call for men to pray. Cinematic prayers paralleled habits of both professional and university sports teams, enduring as models of masculine humility in the face of a challenge.

Lying Down to Sleep

Prayers often try to make sense of suffering during death. In remarkable works, *Pain* and *The Gift of Pain*, physician Paul Brand and author Philip Yancey explored why God allows suffering in human lives. Thus many prayers are offered during times of suffering, death, and funerals. In *High Fidelity* (Stephen Frears, 2000), Rob Gordon (John Cusack) is addicted to compiling lists, counting the top five of everything. Instead of reciting the Lord's Prayer during the funeral of a former girlfriend's father, he lists five songs about death. Yet, when death and suffering do appear in films, prayers play a pivotal role in comfort and succor.

In *Steel Magnolias* (Herbert Ross, 1989), in which Truvy Jones's (Dolly Parton) beauty parlor serves as the center of conversations among women about friendship, health, death, weddings, prayer, and, of course, hair, Bible thumper Annelle Dupuy DeSoto (Daryl Hannah) joins the close-knit cluster of witty women. She prays unceasingly, but exhibits a legalistic fundamentalism when she dumps her husband, Sammy's (Kevin O'Connor) beer out of her refrigerator. He expresses his displeasure with "Oh Annelle, for Christ's sake!" and a marital tiff ensues. They fight over saying the name of the Lord in vain. Annelle recommends praying. Sammy opts to "eat dirt."

In the shop, Annelle stands up after praying, with an unflinching "Amen." M'Lynn Eatenton (Sally Fields) looks at her friend Truvy, a bit confused: "Was she just praying?" Truvy rolls her eyes and assents. "Why?" M'Lynn asks. Truvy, the heart and soul of her beauty parlor, suggests, "Maybe she's praying for us because we're gossiping. Maybe she's praying because the elastic is shot in her pantyhose! Who knows! She prays at the drop of a hat these days."

M'Lynn's daughter Shelby (Julia Roberts) will both marry and die in the story. Her wedding is all wrapped up and decorated in pink. Alluding to the Apostle Paul's metaphor of the body being a temple of the Holy Spirit, M'Lynn quips that Shelby's "sanctuary looks like it's been hosed down with Pepto-Bismol."

Annelle's primary nemesis is the caustic Ouiser Boudreaux (Shirley MacLaine), who did one religious thing in her life when she dressed up as a nun and went bar hopping. Ouiser snaps at Annelle's religious habits and orders her to "take your Bible and shove it where the sun doesn't shine." Finally, when Ouiser acknowledges that she will be praying for Shelby, Annelle is shocked. "Yes, Annelle, I pray! Well, I do! There, I said it, I hope you're satisfied." When Annelle says that she suspected this all along, Ouiser adds, "Oh! Well, don't expect me to come to one of your churches or one of those tent revivals with all those Bible-beaters doin' God-only-knows-what! They'd probably make me eat a live chicken!"

Loosening up, Annelle retorts, "Not on your first visit!," to which Clairee Belcher (Olympia Dukakis) adds, "Very good, Annelle! Spoken like a true smartass!" While *Steel Magnolias* demonstrated the ubiquity of prayers during difficult times of death and mourning, it also revealed a hearty and humorous trust in providence.

In *Titanic* (James Cameron, 1997), devout congregants huddle around a priest who leads them in prayer on the sinking vessel. In the face of imminent death, he prays steadily even as he slips with the turning of the ship, "Holy Mary, Mother of God, pray for us sinners now and at the hour of our death, amen. Hail Mary, full of grace, the Lord is with thee."

Jack Dawson (Leonardo DiCaprio) leads his beloved Rose Dewitt Bukater (Kate Winslet) past the praying communion and gasps, "This way. Come on, come on." It will not matter which way anyone goes. As the *Titanic* sinks, women scream and people panic. The unsinkable ship that even "God could not sink" is upended. However, even in the jaws of inevitable death, the priest continues with the blessed hope: "I saw a new heaven and a new earth. When the first heaven and the first earth had passed away—and there was no more sea . . ." Such scenes in the romantic tragedy concede the art of dying well with prayers.

The anguish of guilt overwhelms young Will in *Shakespeare in Love* (John Madden, 1998). Tom Stoppard's witty screenplay pauses for a dramatic moment when Will Shakespeare (Joseph Fiennes) tries to atone for whatever part he had in the death of Marlowe, stabbed in a tavern. Beating his chest, Will calls out, "God forgive me!" He runs to church. "It was I who killed him. God forgive me. God forgive me, most merciful Father." The grieving artist struggles in his own private purgatory, but as soon as his confession is over, church bells sound and the story cuts to the object of his affections, Viola de Lesseps (Gwyneth Paltrow), riding in the countryside. Rarely is such remorse answered so cheerfully, but this is a Shakespearean comedy.

In an apologetic call for forgiveness in *Dead Man Walking* (Tim Robbins, 1995), Sister Helen Prejean (Susan Sarandon) goes to death row to pray with convicted killer Matthew Poncelet (Sean Penn), who is awaiting his execution in three days. A prison guard challenges the nun for helping such a despicable character: "You know what the Bible says, 'An eye for an eye.'" She responds, "You know what else the Bible asks for death as a punishment? For adultery, prostitution, homosexuality, trespass upon sacred grounds, profaning the Sabbath, and contempt to parents." He quickly wises up and says, "I ain't gonna get in no Bible quote contest from no nun 'cause I'm gonna lose." Sister Helen prays with Poncelet in his hour of need. At one point, he quips that he has his Bible and is, like W. C. Fields, looking for a loophole. When the good sister calls him a son of God, he rejoices, having been called a son of many other things. In his final walk, Poncelet confesses with a raw, honest, and contrite heart, begging forgiveness of all.

The place of prayer among the dying awakened a calling for hospice and prison work, with churches following the earlier model of Dr. Cicely Saunders, who offered palliative care for the terminally ill and condemned. In the Book of Common Prayer, the ministration at the time of death emphasizes the confession of sins, forgiveness of sins, and the hope of the Resurrection. These films sought to follow such a litany to alleviate pain and bring hope to those who were suffering.

Seeker-Friendly Prayers

While mainline denominations declined significantly during the 1990s, independent, charismatic, and Pentecostal churches prospered. The seeker-friendly megachurches of Rick Warren and Bill Hybels and the independent charismatic Vineyard churches appealed to a postmodern Gen X generation raised on *Star Wars* spirituality. Even the Christian satire magazine, the *Wittenberg Door*, appealed to those who sought new ways of experiencing their faith. In this societal context, prayers in films came to be expressed in more casual and comic ways.

"Please, God, oh please!" cries Chris (Chevy Chase) desperately in *Nothing but Trouble* (Dan Aykroyd, 1991), as he is catapulted into a jagged ironworks about to crush and dissect him. He repeatedly pleads, "Oh please, God" until he is thrown safely into a pile of bones, looks at his intact body, and mutters, surprised, "Thank You, Lord."

A hip, cool, and celibate Roman Catholic Father Brian Finn (Edward Norton) futilely competes with his friend Rabbi Jacob "Jake" Shram (Ben Stiller) for the love of an old girlfriend in *Keeping the Faith* (Edward Norton, 2000). Beginning the film, Father Finn sits confessing to his bartender, a Muslim who is reading *Dianetics*. (Later, a woman in the confessional asks him, "Is it me or is the confession getting a little touchy-feely these days?"—an indication that traditions are adapting.)

Jake's informal prayers about being matched up ("O God, please let this be painless") pale in comparison to his attempt to make the well-known Jewish hymn "Ein Keloheinu" come alive to his synagogue. Jake argues, "It's a joyous song, a prayer about praising the Lord, telling the Lord how much we love him, or her, but no matter what I do, I can't seem to be able to get you folks to sing it with any feeling. I mean, I brought in the band. I brought in my bongos last week. I think we can all agree that was a backwards step. So this morning, I've brought in a little outside help." He had already earned the displeasure of others by offering guided meditations and stand-up improvised comedy sermons (that "people actually enjoyed"), but is criticized when he has his congregation "serenaded by the Harlem freaking gospel choir." He responds, "At least they were praying!"

Prayers in this era not only shaped more casual ways of interacting with God, but showed clergy in a fresh light. *Raising Helen* (Garry Marshall, 2004) shows that even a Lutheran pastor can connect with seekers. Pastor Dan Parker (John Corbett), a handsome, "sexy man of God," functions as the key romantic interest. Walking into a church where the choir is singing "This Little Light of Mine," Helen (Kate Hudson), legal guardian to her deceased sister's children, meets the pastor. She ad-libs, "I know God told us to move here to attend your fine school." He humorously tells her they need blood tests to see if they are really Lutheran. She doesn't get the joke.

Pastor Parker offers the blessing of the animals (and newborn babies) as he prays with outstretched hands: "Dear Lord, we humbly ask that You bless these animals and all of Your creatures throughout the world. Blessed are You, Lord. Amen." The kids applaud.

Millennials marked their faith with straight-talking prayers, seeking authenticity and connection. In *Barcelona* (Whit Stillman, 1994), a stuffy, buttoned-down Ted Boynton (Taylor Nichols) reads Proverbs and Ecclesiastes while listening to "Pennsylvania 6–5000" in an effort to overcome romantic entanglements. His prayers echo those of Saint Augustine: "Dear God, I can do nothing but stammer to You. I can do nothing but hold out my heart to You. You created us in Your likeness. Our hearts are uneasy until they find peace in You." Traveling to Barcelona, he experiences its cultural differences with his cousin Fred (Chris

Eigeman). However, when Fred falls into a coma, Ted confesses in a voice-over,

> I prayed all the time, but with the constant doubt I was kidding myself. I suspected my religious faith was largely bogus. I resolved to stay all the time and do whatever I could . . . to improve Fred's chances for recovery.

He kneels by his bedside and begins to pray, "Our Father who art in heaven, please forgive us our sins. Please bring Fred back to full consciousness . . . with his mental capabilities and everything reasonably intact." Fred opens one eye, perplexed. Ted continues, "Please forgive my doubting, vainglory, and . . . unworthiness." Just then, Fred comes out of the coma, hearing Ted, and mutters, "Give me a break."

A group of Manhattan yuppie friends in the age of disco looks for meaning in director Whit Stillman's "doomed bourgeois in love" series in *Last Days of Disco* (1998). Hymns like "Dear Lord and Father of Mankind" become a mantra as characters sing/pray, "forgive our foolish ways." "Amazing Grace" functions as a prayer of gratitude after Charlotte Pingress (Kate Beckinsale), worried about being pregnant, gets her period. In Stillman's final chapter, *Damsels in Distress* (2011), a moronic frat boy named Thor (Billy Magnussen) had skipped kindergarten and didn't learn his colors. By the end of the film, he spies a rainbow, runs to the roof, names the colors, and thanks God profusely for being able to learn. Prayers are inherently part of human nature, even for yuppies and millennials.

In *Sister Act* (Emile Ardolino, 1992), lounge singer Deloris Van Cartier (Whoopi Goldberg) has seen her mobster boyfriend, Vince LaRocca (Harvey Keitel), kill his chauffeur and then order her execution as well. She flees from Reno into a witness protection program in San Francisco, at Saint Katherine's Roman Catholic Church, disguised as Sister Mary Clarence.

Deloris's early experience with nuns occurred back in 1968 as an impudent, cheeky student. Asked to name all the apostles, Delores answers, "John, Paul, George, and Ringo!" The nun chastises her as "the most unruly, disobedient girl in the school. Now I want you to march right up to that blackboard and write the names of all the apostles alphabetically." Still going for the laughs, she writes John, Paul, Peter, and Elvis, underlining the last in big letters. Her classmates laugh.

"That is enough!" snaps the sister. "You are hopeless, and I wash my hands of you. Mark my words, Deloris, if you continue on this disruptive track, it will lead straight to the devil. Have you any idea what girls like you become?" Little Deloris smiles. However, now she is on the run with gangsters seeking her life. Trying to blend in to the all-white fellowship of nuns ("becoming a penguin"), Sister Mary Clarence feels like Quasimodo in the belfry. She asks what she is going to do among these nuns: "I'm gonna go crazy! There's nothing but a lot of white women dressed as nuns. What am I gonna do here?"

Police Captain Eddie (Bill Nunn), who relocated her to the church, says, "Pray."

"Pray?!" she gulps.

When she is asked to pray for the food, Deloris mutters, "Bless us, O Lord, for these Thy gifts, which we are about to receive. And yea, though I walk through the valley of the shadow of no food, I will fear no hunger. We want You to give us this day, our daily bread. And to the republic for which it stands, and by the power invested in me, I pronounce us ready to eat. Amen."

Sneaking off to a bar, she is caught and reprimanded by the Reverend Mother Superior (Maggie Smith). But Sister Clarence asks, "What about forgiveness? Isn't that what you preach? There's gotta be something around here I can do that's not gonna chip my nails or annoy anybody."

The Reverend Mother responds, "You're right, Mary Clarence. To err is human, to forgive divine. You may stay, but I shall restrict your activities to a single task . . . singing. You will join the choir." To her protests, the Reverend Mother continues, "You will sleep and you will sing. That will be your task until you leave." As she makes friends with the meek, mousy Sister Mary Robert (Wendy Makkena), the droll, deadpan Sister Mary Lazarus (Mary Wickes), and the irrepressibly jolly Sister Mary Patrick (Kathy Najimy), Mary Clarence leads this sour-toned, off-key choir into spirited contemporary worship. When Sister Mary Robert confesses to being nervous and wondering what would happen if she forgets the words, Sister Mary Clarence tells her flatly, "You're gonna go straight to hell."

When the mobsters finally chase her down and take her back to Reno, the sisters come to rescue her. Two of the thugs come upon her with her head bowed. "What is she doing?" asks one. "Oh my God," says the other, "she's praying."

We hear her utter, "Lord I want You to forgive Willy and Joey, because they know not what they do. They're only doin' what Vince told 'em to do, because Vince is too chicken to do it himself! So he's called upon these two men to take care of his business! So I want You to forgive them, Lord. Expectum, Espertum, Cacomb, Toutu, Eplubium, Amen."

When the boys both say, "Amen," she whacks them in their crotches and darts off. The film inserts slapstick into praying, depicting those who pray as wonderfully flawed human beings.

Prodigal Roman Catholic director Kevin Smith tapped into Rabelaisian hilarious vulgarity in *Dogma* (1990). An apostate abortion clinic worker, Bethany (Linda Fiorentino), is called upon to prevent two fallen angels, Loki (Matt Damon) and Bartleby (Ben Affleck), from sneaking back into heaven via a loophole. She gets help from Rufus (Chris Rock), the thirteenth and black apostle, along with two incompetent prophets, Jay and Silent Bob.

Cardinal Glick (George Carlin) introduces Catholicism WOW, with his thumbs-up Jesus and a church redesigned from a passé, archaic institution to a very seeker-friendly church. In its view, Christ came to earth as a booster, a Buddy Christ. Parroting intermediaries in the Roman Catholic tradition, God's representative Megatron (Alan Rickman) explains that prayers with God are not too easy. "Human beings have neither the aural nor the psychological capacity to withstand the awesome power of God's true voice. Were you to hear it, your mind would cave in and your heart would explode within your chest. We went through five Adams before we figured that one out."

Rufus counters that perspective by sharing that God "digs humanity," but "it bothers Him to see the shit that gets carried out in His name—wars, bigotry, televangelism." Rufus also explains that God "likes to listen to people talk. Says it sounds like music to Him. Christ loved to sit around the fire and listen to me and the other guys. Whenever we were going on about unimportant shit, He always had a smile on His face."

Seeker-friendly churches put smiles on the faces of their congregations. In becoming all things to all people, they adopted friendlier and more familiar ways to evangelize. Hollywood noticed the presence of "Buddy Christs" throughout many denominations. Saddleback's Rick Warren's casual appearance (for example, wearing a Hawaiian shirt while preaching) and the emergence of a circuit of Christian stand-up comedians contributed to a laid-back and spontaneous piety.

Family Prayers

In conjunction with new modes of individualized entertainment and communication devices and an increase in divorce rates, the traditional family in the 1990s was in decline. Hollywood looked to the past to represent families wrestling with problems; yet the families also prayed, and their prayers expressed authentic protests against God, and often challenged the church. The opening line summarizes the theme of *A River Runs through It* (Robert Redford, 1992): "In our family, there was no clear line separating religion and fly fishing." Reverend Maclean (Tom Skerritt), a Presbyterian minister and fly fisherman who categorizes Methodists as "Baptists who could read," leads his sons to believe that all Christ's disciples were fly fishermen. And when the good reverend catches the largest rainbow trout, he can thank God: "The Lord has blessed us all today. . . . It's just that He has been particularly good to me." But he knew that all good things—"trout as well as eternal salvation—came by grace."

Eight-year-old Paul challenges his father's authority and refuses to eat a bowl of oats; his father sternly pronounces that "grace will not be said until that bowl is clean." After a long period, the family returns and the father says grace as they kneel beside the table. Nothing is eaten, however, and the father prays, "O God, rich in forgiveness, grant that we may hold fast the good things we receive from Thee. And as often as we fall into sin, be lifted by repentance through Thy grace. Amen." Even as Paul (Brad Pitt) grows up, he proves the daring adventurer, "borrowing a boat" to shoot the rapids. Caught, he is ordered to go to church and pray for forgiveness (as his mother was sick with worry). The boys had learned to cast for fish Presbyterian-style, with the regularity of a metronome, but Paul breaks free to improvise his own rhythms, one of grace over the law.

The Irish prayers of greeting "God be with you" and "God bless you" dot the landscape of *Far and Away* (Ron Howard, 1992). Joseph Donnelly (Tom Cruise) runs away with his landlord's daughter, Shannon Christie (Nicole Kidman). He has already prayed that "God bless this house for drinking the dead" (a toast to the memory of his own father, Joe, in the tavern). When Danty Duff mutters a "God bless your soul . . . poor Joe Donnelly," Duff turns around and Joe comes back to life. His son exclaims, "All saints preserve us! We thought you died, Da!"

"I did, son. I passed away. . . . I've come back to tell you something. You're an especially odd boy." "You came back from the dead to tell me that I'm odd?" Comically, the prayer revives a family tradition of the playful mockery of father to son.

In the autobiographical *Angela's Ashes* (Alan Parker, 1999), Frank Mc-Court (Joe Breen/Michael Legge) prays after two siblings die. Growing up hungry and miserable in his Irish Catholic neighborhood, he holds the church in disdain. "Forgive me, Father, for I have sinned. It's been a minute since my last confession" and then flippantly concludes with "in the name of the Father, the Son, and the holy toast." In the context of endemic poverty and suffering, one understands his biting wit. When Angela McCourt (Emily Watson) shows her children a painting of the baby Jesus, she says, "That's the baby Jesus. And if you ever need anything, you should pray to Him."

Young Malachy whispers to his brother, "Could you tell Jesus that we're hungry?" Frank retorts that Malachy's fatter than the baby Jesus. After being sick for a period, Frank returns to school, where he has been held back. Embarrassed to be assigned to the same grade as his younger brother, Frank prays for a miracle to help advance him. Writing an essay on how Jesus might have fared growing up in Limerick, he projects his own dire circumstances on the Lord. There would be no crucifixion and no Roman Catholic Church, as Jesus would have died of consumption much younger in the cold, damp climate of Ireland. And then, of course, he notes, no one would have had to write papers about Him. Harsh times for his family result in his creative chutzpah.

In stark contrast, the candid but pious prayers of the young deformed Simon Birch (Ian Michael Smith) in *Simon Birch* (Mark Steven Johnson, 1998) portray a saint in the making. He believes that God gave him his stunted height for a reason, and that he is predestined to do good works. The pastor, Reverend Russell (David Strathairn), and a Sunday school teacher disparage his sense of calling. Yet he not only is the reason his best friend, Joe Wenteworth (Joseph Mazzello/Jim Carrey), believes in God, but he also saves a busload of children from drowning. As an adult,

Joe expresses his gratitude for his diminutive friend. "Not a day that goes by that I don't thank God for bringing him into my life."

Simon challenges his mainline church's priorities. He debates with the minister and insists that "if God's made the church bake sale a priority, we're in a lot of trouble." He doesn't understand what "coffee and donuts have to do with God." Reverend Russell explains, "They're merely refreshments so people can socialize and talk about upcoming events." Simon responds, "Who ever said church needs a continental breakfast?" The pint-sized prophet protests the luxury of his church and reaffirms a divine calling for a marginalized saint.

In ironic ways, the prayers of families challenged the authority of institutional religion, underscoring what sociologist Thomas Luckmann had predicted thirty years before in his book *The Invisible Religion*.[2] Luckmann anticipated that individuals would retreat into "private spheres" to find their sacred spaces. People sought to develop a direct intimacy with God that enabled them to recognize hypocrisy in others and to speak forth with what they saw as their own authenticity. Unfortunately, they didn't have mirrors.

Righteous Indignation

In *Lee vs. Weisman* (1992), the Supreme Court ruled that a nondenominational prayer at a graduation violated the constitutional prohibition against the establishment of religion. Coincidentally, a rise in violent youth crime led to frustration over what was viewed as the government's general incompetence. Would it not be better if citizens took justice into their own hands? The late 1980s and early 1990s saw aggressive forms of prayer develop among some evangelicals. According to Elizabeth McAlister, a rise in military spending and neoliberal economic policies provoked some evangelicals to engage in spiritual warfare, using militarized discourse.[3] Such bellicose language would be expressed in anger toward a system that was not protecting its people, especially its youth. Religious citizens would take up arms against evil themselves.

At the funeral of a young black man in *Lethal Weapon 3* (Richard Donner, 1992), the minister prays that the deceased escape judgment and experience a peace in heaven that eluded him on earth. He also preaches against the "scourge of violence that takes the lives of our children." The grieving, weeping mother looks at Detective Roger Murtaugh (Danny Glover) and slaps him in the face, demanding that he find "the man who put the gun in my son's hands."

Predating the major scandals in the Roman Catholic Church regarding child abuse, *Sleepers* (Barry Levinson, 1996) raises issues of guilt and revenge in the murder of a detention center guard who tortured young boys. Four childhood friends go to mass (a priest calls them "defenders of the faith" and "soldiers of Christ") and are devoted to Father Bobby (Robert De Niro), who preaches as much during pickup games as he does in the pulpit. Raised in Hell's Kitchen, the fun-loving boys pull pranks (Father Bobby notes that "nuns are such easy targets") until one goes wrong and they end up at the juvenile center, where they are brutalized and humiliated. About to go to trial for killing one of their persecutors at the center, Shakes (Joseph Perrino/Jason Patric) enters the church to pray at the altar, but experiences horrendous flashbacks of the sexual abuse. His prayers mix with dreadful memories.

The theme of humans assuming the role of God's judges to exact retribution was featured in several films of this period. The most notable was *Boondock Saints* (Troy Duffy, 1999), in which two Irish lads receive a mission from God to become vigilantes for good in their hometown of Boston. The young priest Macklepenny (Robert Pemberton) opens the film by reciting the Lord's Prayer, crescendoing with "For Thine is the kingdom, and the *power*, and the *glory*, now and forever. Amen." But in this film, it is the Boondocks' prayer that has the power, the glory, and the bloody efficacy.

When their priest warns his congregation against indifference and inactivity in the face of evil, citing the infamous Kitty Genovese case, in which a young woman was murdered while people allegedly listened without intervening, the fraternal twin brothers Murphy (Norman Reedus) and Connor MacManus (Sean Patrick Flanery) experience an epiphany, a vocation to rid their town of corruption and violence. Kissing the feet of the crucifix, they take up the destruction of evil mentioned more in the Old Testament than the New. Later in a jail cell, they receive their divine calling to execute evil men. The priest confirms their "calling" to actively resist evil and enact justice as God's messengers.

Their prayer becomes familiar as the brothers engage in a spectacular war on evil. Saying family prayers for a friend, they are joined by a contract killer, Il Duce (Billy Connolly), who upon hearing their prayers, realizes that these are his own sons and allies himself as part of a violent trinity. Together they recite,

> And shepherds we shall be for Thee, my Lord, for Thee. Power hath descended forth from Thy hand that our feet may carry out Thy command. We will flow a river forth unto Thee and teeming with souls shall it ever be. In nomine patris, et filii, et spiritus sancti.

Rather than being the shepherds who guide and tend the sheep, they become the butchers who slay the wolves and other beasts, such as Russian mafia thugs. When an Italian mob boss, Yakavetta (Carlo Rota), spits a "Vaffanculo!" (fuck you!) at them, they join voices to repeat, "That our feet may swiftly carry out Thy command, so we shall flow a river forth to Thee, and teeming with souls shall it ever be." One by one, the three iterate "In nomine patris," "et filii," and "spiritus sancti" before executing Yakavetta.

Il Duce ends their prayer with "When I raise my flashing sword, and my hand takes hold on judgment, I will take vengeance upon mine enemies, and I will repay those who hate me. O Lord, raise me to Thy right hand and count me among Thy saints." The saints have done their spiritual battle, and won.

Fulfilling a call to exact God's judgment, as both jury and executioner, Meiks (Bill Paxton) in *Frailty* (Bill Paxton, 2001) drafts his two young sons in his "demon-slaying." They will be a family of avenging angels against the undetected vice of people. Meiks distinguishes between killing people, which is wrong, and destroying demons, which is good. He has his own list to fulfill God's will.

At first, the boys are oblivious of their father's "vocation," singing children's songs like "I've got the joy, joy, joy, joy, down in my heart, and if the devil don't like it he can sit on a tack." ("Ouch!" says one brother.) Yet, as they follow their father as "God's Hand Killer" accomplices, young Fenton (Matt O'Leary) protests. When assigned to dig a grave, he mutters, "He can make me dig this stupid hole, but he can't make me pray, you hear?" Later, when Fenton (Matthew McConaughey) has grown up, he goes to confess to the investigator of the original series of murders, with a diabolical twist that suggests that the sins of the father are visited upon the son.

In *The Minus Man* (Hampton Fancher, 1999), Vann Siegert (Owen Wilson), a serial killer, wanders across the American landscape, taking the lives of those who complain and who he feels deserve to die. His victims come to him like moths, as he shines like an angel of light. At a church service of hope, the minister prays for one young man who has disappeared, "Dear Lord, take Gene into Your protection. Cherish him. Listen to his grief; let him empty it on You." At this point, Siegert sits in a pew, reflecting upon his role in the murder, and thinks to himself, "I could get up and speak one single sentence, and all this would come to a stop." The minster continues, "In Thy name we pray for his swift return. Let us pray." The avenging angel sits in an ordinary pew. Those who sought to do spiritual battle against injustice and personal demons in the 1990s sat beside other congregants, and no one knew what their prayers were.

Miles in Their Shoes

Research in key concepts rooted in Christian faith, forgiveness and empathy, spiraled during the 1990s, with psychological findings demonstrating that "religious involvement is positively related to the disposition to forgive others."[4] Prayers in film reflected this fundamental aspect of the Christian tradition, frequently by showing how sinful people experienced the love of God and then sought to communicate it to others.

Director and actor Robert Duvall's pet project found no support from Hollywood, so he financed his own script of *The Apostle* (Robert Duvall, 1997). In it, he plays Pentecostal preacher Eulis "Sonny" Dewey, who kills the youth minister with a baseball bat when he discovers he's having an affair with his wife, Jessie (Farah Fawcett). He flees Texas for Louisiana and assumes a new identity as the "Apostle E.F." Befriended by Reverend Blackwell, they revive his church, bringing in both black and white congregants. His employer, Elmo, runs a local radio station and lets him preach, attracting quite an audience. All that Elmo asks is "no speaking in tongues on the air."

Sonny's Momma describes her charismatic son's praying style: "Ever since he was an itty-bitty boy, sometimes he talks to the Lord and sometimes he yells at the Lord. Tonight, he just happens to be yellin' at Him."

The sinner-made-saint displays all the ambiguity of a flawed but holy character. Every utterance of "Praise the Lord," "Thank You, Jesus!" or "Hallelujah" comes straight from the heart. One of the curious side effects of the film was that it challenged the idea that Sunday morning at 11:00 a.m. is one of the most segregated hours of the week. As independent, especially charismatic, churches grew in the next decade, nondenominational communities of faith showed more integration. Duvall's intent was to demonstrate the fruit of grace and forgiveness in the prayers and actions of a Pentecostal group that had been marginalized and disparaged by Hollywood.

Frank Darabont adapted Stephen King's short story for *The Green Mile* (1999). Falsely accused of murdering two young girls, John Coffey (Michael Clarke Duncan), a strong, lumbering black man, is sent to death row in the Louisiana state penitentiary in 1935. When head guard Paul Edgecomb (Tom Hanks) has a urinary tract infection, Coffey prays over him, taking the disease into himself and releasing it as a swarm of flies. Beelzebub is conquered. Coffey heals Edgecomb, who goes home to his wife, Jan (Bonnie Hunt), and has one of the most delightful marital encounters suggested by film, as his parts now work. The scene suggests one of the most efficacious powers of prayer. The remarkable prisoner acknowledges God as his Father and is blessed with unique spiritual powers to heal, release, and forgive.

When the warden's wife suffers excruciatingly, Edgecomb suggests bringing Coffey to help her. The warden asks, "Are you talking about a real praise Jesus healing service?" "Yes," says Edgecomb. "He put his hands on me; he took the bladder infection away." His wife chimes in, "He came home that day; he was all better," and she smiles slyly at her husband. "Ah, now, wait, you talking about an authentic healing, a praise Jesus miracle?" "Oh yeah!" she says, grinning.

The prisoner comes to see the sick woman in bed and mounts her like Elijah. She asks, "What's your name?" He answers, "Johnny *Coffey*, like the drink but not spelt the same, . . . ma'am."

When Coffey asks whether she is ready, she replies tersely, "Yes, go with it." "I see it," he says. "What's happening?" "Shh. You be still, so quiet and so still." He lowers himself onto her; her eyes are wide in terror and uncertainty. He places his mouth on hers. The lights shine as he draws out the sickness and sin. The clock stops; its glass cracks; an earthquake trembles. Her countenance is pure and clean. By his own stripes of suffering, he heals her. Coffey coughs to hold in the flies.

Magnolia (Paul Thomas Anderson, 1999) follows nine lives during twenty-four hours in San Fernando Valley, lives that parallel and interconnect. Cop Jim Kurring (John Reilly) loses his gun and prays desperately for its recovery, with a prayer as old as Job's. "O Lord, why is this happening to me? God, please help me figure this out. I'm lost out here! I don't understand why it's happening. God, please, God! Whatever it is I did, I'm going to fix it. I'm going to do the right thing." Sirens blare in the background as he hunts in the darkness and rain with his flickering flashlight. His prayer is simply for his daily needs.

Among a mosaic of scoundrels and failures, Kurring is a good cop in love with a junkie. Yet amidst the mundane, the miraculous appears, prophesied by various references to Exodus 8:2. A judgment of God comes in the midst of adultery, abuse, venality, cupidity, cruelty, all the vices. A plague of frogs falls in southern California. Yet amidst these calamities, God hears and answers the prayer of this simple man.

Tom Hanks, the title character in *Forrest Gump* (Robert Zemeckis, 1994), reflects about Jenny's father, "He was some kind of a farmer. He was a very loving man, always kissing and touching her and her sisters." It turns out that Jenny's father had been molesting Jenny as a child, which would result in Jenny's path to self-destruction. During the scene when Jenny's father comes looking for Jenny, she and Forrest run into the cornfield. Young Jenny drops to her knees and says, "Pray with me, Forrest." She prays, "Lord, make me a bird so I can fly far, far away from here."

When the prayer is over, white doves fly out of the cornfield, signifying that God has answered her prayer. Forrest states that God works in mysterious ways. God didn't make Jenny a bird, but God had the police let Jenny move in with her grandmother instead. Forrest affirms that if you pray to God, He listens. The miraculous help that God would send came packaged in the ordinary friend, Forrest.

In their fishing excursions, Forrest and his first mate and former Army squad leader, Lieutenant Dan, catch nothing but garbage. Sarcastically, Lieutenant Dan says to Forrest, "Why don't you pray for shrimp?" Dan joins Forrest at church even as he still doubts God's existence, angry at the loss of his legs during the Vietnam War. When they still catch nothing, Dan pesters Forrest, "Where is your God now?" An unexpected, violent hurricane hits the shrimping coast and destroys all the shrimp boats in the area except for Forrest's boat, the *Jenny*, which makes them millionaires. Amazed, Dan thanks the holy fool Forrest for saving his life in Vietnam and jumps off the boat for a swim, looking to the sky and making his own peace with God.

Bess McNeill (Emily Watson) has many a vigorous conversation with God in *Breaking the Waves* (Lars von Trier, 1996). First, she prays that her husband, Jan Nyman (Stellan Skarsgård), return early from working on an oil rig. Her prayers are both memorable and disturbing, frantically inquiring into God's will, pleading, bartering, and struggling with Him. Director von Trier's decision to have Bess change her voice slightly to speak God's responses to her offers unsettling insights into prayer. For example, "God" speaks to her in the cold, stark church: "For many years you've prayed for love. Shall I take it away from you again? Is that what you want?" Bess responds, "Oh, no, I'm still grateful for love." When she impatiently prays for her husband to come home, divine irony sends him home paralyzed in an accident. Like the stubborn prayers of Phaethon to ride his father's celestial chariot or Semele's request of Jove to come to her in all his glory, the answered prayer turns out mocking and disastrous. Her guilt is compounded when her husband asks her to have sex with another man. She feels that God has given her special grace to help her husband heal. Her fervent love for him makes her into a pathetic prostitute, a grim parody of her affection.

Both following and subverting the manifesto of the Dogme 95 movement, von Trier claimed he wrote a story that was "so far-fetched and so full of clichés that no one could take it seriously, but of course the audience liked it. All you have to do is come up with something really stupid, and it will become a great success." One realizes that the final ringing of the church bells punctuates his motive.

When young English novelist Maurice Bendrix (Ralph Fiennes) reconnects with his ex-mistress Sarah Miles (Julianne Moore), he is jealous (over her husband and her stockings—which kiss her legs) and rants at God for "ending the affair" in *The End of the Affair* (Neil Jordan, 1999). In Graham Greene's moving religious novel, Bendrix wants to find out who her "current lover" is, and his warped obsession leads him to discover that it is God Himself. His conversation with God as an atheist—"I hate you, God. I hate you as though you existed"—conveys the irony of director Luis Buñuel's "Thank God, I am an atheist."

But the termination of the illicit love affair occurs during an afternoon liaison. As Bendrix goes downstairs, a bomb explodes. Frantic and fearful, Sarah calls out to God to spare her lover's life: "Dear God, please don't take him. . . . I'll give him up, only please let him be alive. . . . I promise, I'll never see him again." Her compact with God is made as the prayer becomes the most salient moment in the film's narrative.

She weakly struggles to keep this pact, confessing her infidelity and her lack of faith to a priest: "Tell him I'm sorry. I'm too human. Too weak. Tell him I can't keep my promises." Yet it is in her weakness that she rises over sin.

In *Shadowlands* (Richard Attenborough, 1993), the biopic of British author C. S. Lewis (Anthony Hopkins), the scriptwriters invented an apocryphal but compelling quotation by the Christian apologist on the purpose of prayer. In the film, Lewis argues that prayer is not meant to change God, but to change us. He explains to a friend, "I pray because I can't help myself. The need flows out of me. It doesn't change God; it changes me."

Hollywood's recognition of authentic Christian piety was evident in these films, which noted that prayers did not change God's mind so much as transform those who prayed. The films tapped into genuine and often anguished wrestling with God, resonating with sinners seeking understanding and with prayers that sought and gave grace and forgiveness.

Fairy Tale Prayers

Fairy tales, British author C. S. Lewis once observed, are the best ways to smuggle theology past the dragons and watchdogs of culture. That prayers would appear in fantasy tales is remarkable, but they do they find a significant place in dangerous adventures and strange lands. In *Dragonheart* (Rob Cohen, 1996), Monk Gilbert of Glockenspiel (Pete Postlethwaite), who wants to write the chronicles of the last dragon slayer, Bowen (Dennis Quaid), shoots a man in the rear end and yells, "Turn the other cheek, brother." Flying with the dragon Draco (Sean Connery), Gilbert shouts a fearful prayer: "We're going to die. O God, help us!" However, when they reach Avalon, the burial place of King Arthur's Knights of the Round Table, he offers prayers of thanksgiving.

Some prayers are simple. In director Roberto Benigni's *Pinocchio* (2002), God answers Geppetto's (Carlo Giuffrè) prayer that his wooden puppet become a real boy. However, ominous moments haunt the script of *Snow White: A Tale of Terror* (Michael Cohn, 1997), even in the prayers. Priests pray a wedding blessing over Snow White's stepmother and widowed father as they rest in bed, invoking the name of the Trinity. When a young Snow White enters, she throws the Eucharistic cup of wine onto her stepmother, revealing animosity, but also signifying the red blood of death. Later as the king prays, "Father in heaven, in Thy mercy, I pray, grant me a son," he has a son, but he is stillborn. The wicked queen in *Snow White and the Huntsman* (Rupert Sanders, 2012) kills Snow White's father and puts her in prison. Snow White starts a fire with kindling and prays the Lord's Prayer, holding two stick straw figures, as memories of her own parents.

In a version of Little Red Riding Hood, Old Granny (Angela Lansbury) tells her granddaughter, "Never stray from the path, never eat a windfall apple, and never trust a man whose eyebrows meet in the middle." In what seems to be Neil Jordan's multilayered tribute to Bruno Bettelheim's sexual interpretation of lurid and violent fairy tales, *The Company of Wolves* (1984), a priest (Graham Crowden) says a prayer for one young victim, using a prayer book.

> Man is born of a woman, has but a short time to live, and is full of misery. He cometh up and is cut down like a flower. He fleeth as if he were a shadow and never continues; it won't stay. In the midst of life we are in death. Forasmuch as it has pleased almighty God of His great mercy to take unto Himself the soul of our dear sister here departed, we therefore commit her body to the ground. Earth to earth, ashes to ashes, dust to dust.

He reads Isaiah 11:6–8 from the pulpit, conveniently noting that the wolf and the lamb shall also lie down together. However, when Granny falls asleep, spiders fall on the Bible.

The priest comes out of his church and finds a wounded wolf-girl on holy ground reaching out to him. "Are you God's work, or the devil's?

Oh, what do I care whose work you are? You poor, silent creature." As he binds her wound, he says, "It will heal. In time."

Matthew Bright's twisted black comedy update of Little Red Riding Hood, *Freeway* (1996), follows the missteps of violent trailer-park spitfire Vanessa Lutz (Reese Witherspoon) as she thwarts the perverse advances of a freeway serial killer, the aptly named Bob Wolverton (Kiefer Sutherland). Threatened by the would-be rapist, she holds a gun to his head and asks, "This is a crucial question, Bob. Do you believe in the Lord Jesus Christ and take Him for your personal Savior?" As he attacks her, she shoots him multiple times, then kneels in the dust, coughs and spits, and prays, "O God, dear God, that was so fucking bad, but I was at a loss, so I left it up to You. I love You with all my heart and hope You don't hate me more than You already do. Please bless Naomi [Grandma], Larry, and Chopper. Amen." At which point, she observes a shooting star.

In one of the darker fantasy tales, *Cronos* (Guillermo del Toro, 1993), vampirism threatens the church through the weakness of the flesh via a strange device that promises immortality. An alchemist, Uberto Fulcanelli (Mario Ivan Martinez), flees the Inquisition in Spain in 1536, coming to Mexico, where he seeks to invent a mysterious device, the Cronos device, which would give its owner eternal life. However, when used, it possesses the person with a craving for blood. Centuries later, it is stored in a statue of an angel, from whose eyes cockroaches crawl out. Antiques dealer Jesus Gris (Federico Luppi) becomes its final self-sacrificial victim, allowing the device's claws to pierce his skin while he calls out his own name and recites the Lord's Prayer.

Both light and dark fantasy attracted religious audiences as Anglican J. K. Rowling's Harry Potter series burst upon the scene in 1997. Inspired by Lewis and Tolkien, Rowling inserted numerous Christian elements in her fiction; however, reception split between fundamentalists who attacked its witchcraft and more moderate church people who found the books illuminating and fun. Fans of the British literary group the Inklings merrily joined in enjoying her works of fantasy, which smuggled Christian theology past watchful dragons.

Apocalyptic Prayers

The impending turn of the millennium conjured up apocalyptic fears, from Y2K (a bug that was to play havoc on the world's computer systems when the date rolled to 2000) to the church's growing awareness of global warming, persecution of the church worldwide, and for many dispensationalists, the fulfillment of a prophecy of a satanic Common Market based in Brussels from which the Anti-Christ would come. It looked like the imminent destruction of the world, and no prayers would help.

Rapture-obsessed crowds flocked to *Left Behind: The Movie* (Vic Sarin, 2000), in which Buck Williams (Kirk Cameron), a television journalist, investigates why so many "believers" disappeared in a twinkling of an eye, like all the kids in the Pied Piper story. He explores the battle of Armageddon and the rise of an Anti-Christ. The nineteenth-century dispensational idea of a "rapture" works to scare the hell out of spectators and to judge the modernization of the liberal mainline denominations. In one scene, Bruce Barnes (Clarence Gilyard), a black minister left behind, confesses and prays,

> Oh boy. Ha. What a fraud I am. Everybody bought it. Ha. Except me. I knew Your message, I knew Your word, I stood right here and preached it, and I was done. I was living a lie, living a lie. O God, I am kneeling before You now, asking You, God, forgive me for my sins. And I'm asking You, give me one more chance.

Barnes prays, "Use me, O Lord, please just use me." As Buck comes to "see the light" and understand the rapture, he discovers that even one left behind can be used by God. However, the film itself would not usher in the last days, only a plague of sequels.

In *The Prophecy* (Gregory Widen, 1995), cop Thomas Daggett (Elias Koteas) reminisces about studying the Gospels in seminary. While mistaken about its source, he cites what he viewed as the strangest passage in the Bible, the nonexistent verse by Saint Paul that "even now in heaven there are angels carrying savage weapons." God doesn't talk to His angel Gabriel anymore, possibly because he is played by the wonderfully quirky Christopher Walken.

Lucifer (Viggo Mortensen) taunts "Little Tommy" Daggett: "How I loved listening to your sweet prayers every night. And then you'd jump in your bed, so afraid I was under there. And I was!" And then, with some rare orthodox theology in the film, he quizzes him: "Do you know what hell really is, Thomas? It's not lakes of burning oil or chains of ice. It's being removed from God's sight, having His word taken from you. It's hard to believe. So hard. I know that better than anyone."

Daggett concludes that the key is faith, and if "faith is a choice, then it can be lost—for a man, an angel, or the devil himself. And if faith means never completely understanding God's plan, then maybe understanding just a part of it—our part—is what it is to have a soul. And maybe in the end, that's what being human is, after all." His prayers keep communication with God open, even in the midst of the cosmic battle.

In the third installment of the Alien franchise, *Alien 3* (David Fincher, 1992), Ripley (Sigourney Weaver) finds herself on a remote planet at a maximum-security prison of lead ore manufacturing. The all-male inmates are despicable criminals who have become a religious cult.

The jailer Andrews (Brian Glover) takes out his little prayer book for two dead inmates as the twenty-five thieves, rapists, and murderers take off their hats: "Lord, we commit this child and this man to Your keeping, O Lord. Their bodies have been taken from the shadow of our light. They have been released from all darkness and pain. The child and the man have gone beyond our world. They are forever eternal and everlasting. Ashes to ashes, dust to dust." (Juxtaposed to the funeral rites, a Rottweiler dies as it gives new life to an alien stowaway, as the words "been released" are spoken.)

The murderer and de facto spiritual leader Dillon (Charles Dutton) looks at Ripley and asks whether she has any faith. "Not much," she answers. "Well," responds Dillon, "we've got a lot of faith here. Enough even for you."

Andrews informs Ripley, "Just because they have taken on religion doesn't make them any less dangerous. I try not to offend their convictions. I don't want to upset the order." When she asks what kind of religion, she is told, "Some sort of apocalyptic, millenarian, Christian fundamentalist, uh . . ." Dillon assures Ripley that "God will take care of you now, sister!" Dillon resumes his prayer, addressing the problem of theodicy:

Why? Why are the innocent punished? Why the sacrifice? Why the pain? There aren't any promises. Nothing certain. Only that some get called; some get saved. She [Ripley] won't ever know the hardship and grief for those of us left behind. We commit these bodies to the void with a glad heart. For within each seed, there is a promise of a flower, and within each death, no matter how small, there's always a new life. A new beginning. Amen.

Throughout this quasi-religious passion play in space, one foresees an impending violent end with sacrificial human acts. Dillon's prayers try to articulate the hope of a new world order, but fall quite short.

In *End of Days* (Peter Hyams, 1999), Arnold Schwarzenegger plays Jericho Cane (another J.C.), a retired cop called to stop Satan on the eve of the new millennium, December 28, 1999. The opening shot focuses upon a scroll held by a cardinal showing a moon with a white blurred line that reads, *Finis Dierum*, Latin for "end of days."

Disguised as the Man (Gabriel Byrne), Satan seeks a young woman to bear his child. He explains what he sees as the contradiction of God's workings: "Something good happens, 'It's His will.' Something bad happens, 'He moves in mysterious ways.'"

When Father Kovak (Rod Steiger) asks Cane whether he believes in God, he answers, "Maybe once, not anymore." Asked what happened, Cane explains that they had a "difference of opinion. I thought my wife and daughter should live. He felt otherwise." Quoting French poet Charles Baudelaire, Kovak tells Cane, "Satan's greatest trick was convincing the world he doesn't exist."

Cane reads an apocryphal passage from Revelations: "I have seen the earth laid to waste. I have seen the horror to come. Is it a sin to wish you were never born? The thousand years have ended. 20:7." His friend quips, "It ends in a football score? That's nice." The silly humor tries to leaven the apocalypse, but the destruction has already taken place.

In one of the best rejoinders in an apocalyptic film, Julius Levinson (Judd Hirsch) invites Albert Nimzicki (James Rebhorn) to pray in *Independence Day* (Roland Emmerich, 1996), and the latter protests, "I'm not Jewish." Julius responds: "Nobody's perfect."[5]

In the 1990s, nobody was perfect. The Pew Research Center's study "Trends in Attitudes toward Religion and Social Issues: 1987–2007" reported that the "percentage completely agreeing that 'Prayer is an important part of my life' rose from 41% in 1987 to a high of 55% in 1999."[6] However, just saying that prayer is important to one does not mean that one practices it during difficult times. Hollywood prayers of the era waned for the most part, except for those related to an imminent apocalypse. Biblical illiteracy rose with the growth of a "millennial generation," supplying filmmakers with comic material when it came to the use of prayer amidst a lack of religious education. Some classic treatments of prayer returned during the period, such as those voiced by hypocrites, prayers over family, prayers for sports victory, and prayers of vengeance. Meanwhile, other prayers took on new resonance in the new era, such as those seeking to address suffering and theodicy. The period, one of relative quiet militarily and domestically, invited the revisiting of war and racism as religious issues.

Significantly, the generation whose lens for viewing spirituality was *Star Wars* began to demand new, less formal ways of understanding faith. Finally, the approach of Y2K led to Hollywood prayers on opposite ends of the spectrum, informing fairy tales and addressing the end of the world. Even though Y2K petered out into nothing, a temporal apocalypse would come at the beginning of the next era, as Islamic fundamentalists attacked the Twin Towers in New York City.

8

Millennial Prayers (2000–2017)

After a century of prayers in film, *plus ça change*. Prayers returned to popular culture formats during the first decade of the new millennium with a mixture of odd, bad, and bland theology. Country-western singer Garth Brooks's song "Unanswered Prayer" featured a prayer that was blessedly ignored. The song's narrator had prayed for a certain girl to be his girlfriend—even promising to "never pray again," and now many years later, he and his present wife meet the woman he prayed about. He was markedly grateful that that prayer wasn't answered the way he had wished. His prayer, however, took the form of a magical request rather than seeking any significant relationship with God. On the other hand, *American Idol* winner Carrie Underwood sang "Jesus, Take the Wheel," a contemporary hymn, however corny, of submission to the providence and care of God.

Prayers, like much of religion, were sentimentalized and subverted into the post-millennial, hipster era. Prayers in churches were often given musical accompaniment. Innovative trends in worship and liturgy reshaped how many prayed. The proliferation of contemporary music (for example, Hillsong), the experimentation of the emergent church, the liberalization (and decline) of mainline denominations, and the revival of therapeutic television evangelism suggested that either tradition was being scuttled or churchgoers were learning to worship in fresh ways. Yet, even after a century of technological and aesthetic innovation, we discover that films adhered to predictable patterns.

As the twentieth century drew to a close, churches were in crisis, according to sociologist Robert Wuthnow, with financial shortfalls, overworked clergy, declining involvement, and spiritual malaise.[1] Religious prayers in films, however, seemed to prosper, mainly because of a lingering sense of spiritual warfare. When terrorists attacked the Twin Towers in New York City on September 11, 2001, spectators watched in horror. Suddenly, a country awoke to the stark reality of spiritual warfare and death, not only between religions, but in one's very soul.

The Prayers of History

In the early 2000s Hollywood embedded prayers into historical reconstructions. Prayers were specimens of the past, padding for reenactments of special moments. Prayers functioned as nostalgic reminders that God responded in the past, that He heard prayers and responded to His people. The events of 9/11 directly inspired two films, *United 93* (Paul Greengrass, 2006) and *World Trade Center* (Oliver Stone, 2006), both of which situated characters as actual people facing death and praying the Lord's Prayer. United passengers prayed, "Thy will be done," and they died; Port Authority police officer William Jimeno (Michael Peña) and his sergeant John McLoughlin (Nicholas Cage) were trapped under the rubble and prayed, "On earth as it is in heaven," and were rescued.

The placement of prayers in historical narratives says more about the filmmakers than either history or the church. These depictions indicate that writers and directors see prayers as particularly salient to our understanding of pivotal events. They add a touch of authenticity to both the narrative and the characters. In *Frost/Nixon* (Ron Howard, 2008), in an effort to purify his image, Richard Nixon (Frank Langella) tells television interviewer David Frost (Michael Sheen), a Methodist, how he and Kissinger would get down on their knees and pray. In *Argo* (Ben Affleck, 2012), which dramatized the rescue of six Americans stranded in Iran through the use of a bogus film production unit, a church marquee proclaims, "God help our hostages." As Martin Luther King Jr. (David Oyelowo) leads his church congregation and others on a march for equal rights in *Selma* (Ava DuVernay, 2014), they kneel in prayer on a bridge. King discerns that this is not the day to walk in protest, but to seek God's guidance. Whether such moments ever happened was incidental; the key point was that prayers have been part of the fabric of the nation's story, and filmmakers of the early 2000s embraced the belief that they rightly belonged in the retelling.

In *Notorious Bettie Page* (Mary Harron, 2005), the screenwriter researched revival sermons to script prayers that offered a glimpse into the tensions of faith and flesh. A Miami preacher (Victor Slezak) offers an altar call prayer for the iconic 1950s pinup Bettie Page (Gretchen Mol):

O my God, tonight I know that first things come first, and the most important thing of all is that men and women and young people surrender their lives to Christ. God, don't let a mother's boy who heard me preach here tonight go to hell. God, don't let a mother's girl who heard me tonight go to hell. Save them. Save them tonight . . . from all their sins. May they be born again, washed in the blood, saved through and through, I pray. Amen.

When Page is asked what Jesus would think about her wearing slinky lingerie, she answers that she isn't sure, but "I think God has given us some kind of talent and He wants us to use it. That's why He gives it to us. I'm not ashamed. Adam and Eve were naked in the Garden of Eden, weren't they? When they sinned, they put on clothes."

In certain historically based films, prayers play a crucial role in defining the characters. They provide windows into the self-righteous or yearning souls of those who pray. As a salient example, the historical fiction of *Gangs of New York* (Martin Scorsese, 2002) juxtaposes three sets of prayer.

In 1863, Amsterdam Vallon (Leonardo DiCaprio) returns to the Five Points area of New York City, seeking revenge against Bill the Butcher (Daniel Day-Lewis), his father's killer. The bloody draft riots of 1863 set the stage for the personal battles between the Bowery and the slum landfill of Five Points, where the Irish immigrants suffered discrimination and violence. The tensions between the "greatly to be feared" Dead Rabbits and Bill's Know Nothing native-born Americans erupt into militant gangs. When Boss Tweed tries to mollify Bill's tough stance, the brutal nativist spits back with quotes from the book of Revelation: "I know your works. You are neither cold nor hot. So because you are lukewarm, I will spew you out of my mouth," a vivid allusion from the Lord to a lukewarm church of Laodicea.

The prayer of Isaiah 1:15 would underlie all their petitions: "You may multiply your prayers; I shall not listen. Your hands are covered with blood; wash, make yourself clean." Just before the massive bloodbath, the two leaders and one rich merchant go to prayer.

Irish Roman Catholic Vallon opens the prayer vigil wearing a cestus on each hand: "Lord, place the steel of the Holy Spirit in my spine and the love of the Virgin Mary in my heart." The battle preparations get underway as Vallon sets about his "father's business," sharpening knives. His father, Priest Vallon, had taught him about Saint Michael, and repeatedly quizzed his son about Michael's accomplishments. "He cast Satan out of Paradise," the son would dutifully answer.

The Protestant Bill the Butcher kneels over a bench covered with an American flag and prays, "Almighty Lord, You are the dagger in my hand. Guide my hand on this day of vengeance."

Meanwhile, in a luxurious upper-class home, with his family gathered around a table set with china and crystal, a patrician offers a platitudinous thanksgiving: "We give thanks to the Lord, for He is good."

Vallon echoes the words of the Hebrew prophets: "To You, the swift cannot flee nor the strong escape."

So, too, Bill intones, "Let my sword devour until its thirst is quenched with blood and my enemies sleep forever."

Intercutting quickly, they speak almost interchangeable prayers: "For You are the God of retribution," and then "For the Lord crushes the wicked," while the wealthy merchant prays with sweet maxims: "The Lord is merciful and His love endures forever." Each concludes with an "Amen." Two go out to war, but the merchant's house is invaded, his family attacked, and he is killed.

The competition of prayers recalls the old saw about a hunter encountering a charging lion. When his gun fails to discharge, he falls to his knees and prays desperately. To his amazement, the lion stops and imitates his posture, kneeling with paws clasped. "O Lord," exclaims the relieved hunter, "thank You for sparing this sinner's life. Whatever You ask of me in the future, I shall obey." The lion, surprisingly, also speaks a prayer: "O Lord, I thank You for providing this bounteous meal; may it strengthen and nourish me to do Your will. Amen."

Each of the prayers in Scorsese's drama complement and contradict each other. The three men of faith share the same God, sensing His call upon their paths, and yet stand diametrically opposed to one another. Even as mainline denominations like the Episcopalians split over doctrinal and ethical issues, they battle one another for property rights. Scorsese revealed such political machinations and disputes for what they are.

The saying of grace in films of this era could also reveal political agendas. In *Munich* (Steven Spielberg, 2005), after Black September, in which Israeli Olympic athletes were assassinated by PLO members, a retribution team sets out for either justice or vengeance against those who murdered the Olympic athletes. Louis's (Mathieu Amalric) version of the Lord's Prayer becomes memorable. Said as grace at the dinner table, it delivers a shot at mercenaries. Grandmother interprets it as "blasphemy," crossing herself as he prays, "Our Father who gives us obedient and respectful clients, who obey the rules through which our business thrives, forgive transgressions and prevarications . . ." Ignorant of its meaning, the children still cross themselves when the grace is pronounced.

In *Bridge of Spies* (Steven Spielberg, 2016), the family of lawyer James Donovan (Tom Hanks), who has been approached about defending a Soviet spy in a trade for downed pilot Francis Gary Powers during the Cold War in 1957, assembles at the dinner table. The daughter is quite hungry, but her father insists, "Wait until we say grace." Suddenly, his adjutant arrives and blurts out that Donovan has taken the case. Trying to explain to his wife that everyone deserves a defense, Donovan pauses and prays, "Lord, we thank Thee for the blessings we are about to receive from Thy bounty, through Christ our Lord. Amen." The blessings will extend beyond that one meal as Donovan will succeed in engineering the release of Powers, and in making a friend.

The true story of Seventh-day Adventist, conscientious objector, and medic Desmond Doss (Andrew Garfield) in *Hacksaw Ridge* (Mel Gibson, 2016) highlighted the horrors and brutality of Allied fighting in the Pacific theatre. The film opens with Doss reading Isaiah 40, about the everlasting God who will not grow tired, who gives strength to the weary and increases the power of the weak. "Even youths grow tired and weary, and young men stumble and fall. But those who hope in the Lord will renew their strength. They will soar on wings like eagles. They will run and not grow weary. They will walk and not be faint." The scripture takes on special resonance during the final battle scenes.

Earlier, however, Doss beats his brother with a brick. He repents, reciting the Lord's Prayer. Praise, confession, thanksgiving, and supplication rise from his lips. As he leaves for basic training, his girlfriend, Dorothy, gives him a Bible, bookmarked at the story of David and Goliath in I Samuel 17.

Fighting prejudice against pacifists, Doss must answer questions about whether God talks to him. "I'm not crazy. I pray to God." One of the unique aspects that the film teases out is that praying is as much listening and seeking God's will as telling God what one wants. However, in the heat of battle, when a comrade dies, Doss cries out, "What do You want of me? I don't understand. I can't hear You." Suddenly, he hears screams in the flames. "All right!" he says, and puts on his helmet, returning to the inferno of war. As he rescues man after man, he pleads, "Please, Lord, help me get one more. . . . Help me get one more. . . . One more, help me get one more." His labors are nothing short of a miracle. His fellow soldiers, about to go into the breach once more, will not advance until Private Doss finishes praying for them.

Allegedly, President John Quincy Adams never went to rest at night until he said the familiar little prayer he learned in childhood. Teaching children how to pray was to prepare them for dependence upon God and independence from the opinions of others.[2] Based on a true story, *Evelyn* (Bruce Beresford, 2002) concerns the efforts of one father, Desmond Doyle (Pierce Brosnan), challenging an Irish law regarding the custody of children that was biased against fathers. As the government would place children unwanted by their mothers into Roman Catholic orphanages, fathers had no right of securing their guardianship. Doyle takes the case to the Irish High Court to win back his daughter Evelyn (Sophie Vavasseur).

Abused by one of the nuns, Evelyn goes to church before the trial and sits alone in the cavernous cathedral, praying, "Dear Jesus, I have to go there and answer questions. Help my daddy win. I know You're testing him, but I think he is getting very tired. Please and amen." Her grandfather, who had recently passed away, had told her that God communicates through light, and that light was always a sign of His presence and a reminder of her grandfather's care.

When she is called to the witness stand in the High Court, the prosecuting attorney informs Evelyn what a nun has claimed about her falling down stairs, rather than being knocked about.

"Now, Evelyn Doyle, do you remember the time in Saint Joseph's when you tripped on the stairs and bashed your face? Think, last month, she gave you some aspirin, as your face was all black and blue. That's what Sister Bridget said. You didn't say otherwise, did you? What really happened was what Sister Bridget exactly said, because you wanted to get out of the orphanage and so you made up a story and sent your father a little lie?"

"I didn't lie. I didn't make it up."

The judge looks down at her and reassures her that this is a frightening experience but to try not to be scared, as being a little girl in a big court like this can be intimidating when you are alone. When sun rays hit her hand, she remembers her grandfather, and says, "I'm not scared. I'm not alone. My grandpa is here with me."

The prosecutor disparages her by saying, "She has a very vivid imagination. Her grandfather died some months ago." He continues with his heavy-handed questioning: "Now child, let me ask you one last time. Do you remember falling in the corridor?"

"I didn't fall on the stairs. I was going to tell Sister Felicity what really happened, but it would get Sister Bridget into trouble. So I prayed that God will forgive Sister for hitting me. I forgave her."

"This is preposterous. Why on earth would the good Sister hit you?" Evelyn tells him it was because she told the nun that she shouldn't hit one of the children for getting her catechism wrong. The lawyer gasps, "Do you expect this court to believe that after she did that to you, you prayed for her? I put it to you, you are lying."

Evelyn responds with fervor, "Oh, lying is a sin against the Eighth Commandment, 'Thou shalt not bear false witness against thy neighbor.' I am surprised you don't know that if you are a lawyer."

After the courtroom erupts in laughter, the lawyer says, "Sister Bridget told this court the truth of the matter is that she picked you up when you fell down the stairs."

"Oh, no, that's not true! Hope she goes to confession soon." Amidst more laughter in the courtroom, she asks the lawyer, "Do you want to hear the prayer I said last night?"

"No, we do not."

But the judge interrupts, "Not so fast, Mr. Wolfe. It is material to the court's evaluation of the child's character. Evelyn, let us hear your prayer, please."

She begins quietly, "Lord God, You guide the universe with wisdom and love; hear the prayer we make to You for our country, the beautiful country of Ireland. Through the honesty of our citizens and the wisdom of those who govern us, may lasting peace be delivered and truth and justice flourish. Amen." The court decides in favor of the Doyles.

Historical prayers occur frequently in aid of underdogs. The prayers of the people hope for a David to champion their cause against a Goliath. The underdog story of real boxer Joe Braddock (Russell Crowe) is dramatized in the inspirational *Cinderella Man* (Ron Howard, 2005). Braddock's wife, Mae (Renee Zellweger), enters the church and meets Father Rorick (Chuck Shamata) before the big fight. She confesses that "I came to pray for Jim." The good father smiles and points to a church crowded with all kinds of people. "So did they. They all think that Jim is fighting for them." She joins the great throng of witnesses and intercessors as the brutal match begins, and the challenger Braddock proves to be a true Cinderella.

After the fight, when the announcer proclaims the "unanimous winner and the *new* world champion," the congregation all cheers, crying and jumping, celebrating, with numerous people in the church weeping with joy. Father Rorick looks heavenward and whispers, "Thank You."

Overcoming insurmountable odds in the face of adversity underlies *The Great Debaters* (Denzel Washington, 2007). What makes the story uniquely inspirational, however, is that it is not sheerly through grit and resilience that these underdog debaters will win. The power of prayer buttresses their humble efforts. During the opening, as a camera glides across the bayou, a voice speaks.

> Heavenly father, we came before Thee, knee bent, and body bowed, the way as we know how. Father who controls and knows all things, both the living and the dying of all creatures, give us the strength and the wisdom to do Thy work. In God's name we pray. And all God's people say, "Amen."

The dramatic story of small Wiley College, a black college in Texas, debating Harvard University, traces the lives of those who contribute to the rhetorical training of the team that will triumph. As the radio broadcasts the great debate, various groups pray. Finally, when the winner is announced, great cheering, rejoicing, and hugging explode from those who were diligent in prayer.

In an interview, Denzel Washington acknowledged, "I open the film with a prayer and end it with praise. The spiritual aspects of the film weren't even necessarily in the screenplay, but I added those. It was my desire to start the film with a prayer." His prayer expressed humility and hope, with "knee bent and body bowed."[3] Like *Cinderella Man*, the film ends with resonating expressions of gratitude to God.

Faith and overcoming adversity are also featured in *Hidden Figures* (Theodore Melfi, 2016). The triumph of three brilliant black female mathematicians working for the 1960s space program at NASA's Langley Research Center reflects a true underdog story. The churchgoing, persevering women show their faith and grit in their struggle against racism and sexism. Yet they are ever ready to praise the Lord, as when Mary Jackson (Janelle Monáe) receives a surprising opportunity ("Thank You, Jesus!") or the church minister sings the praise of the women from the pulpit. Grace at dinner time ends in Jesus's name. Yet a prayer at dinner takes on special significance as Colonel Jim Johnson (Mahershala Ali), who has been romancing Katherine (Taraji P. Henson), comes to the table with a plate of food and an engagement ring. Prayers of all sorts are answered, even when Mr. Al Harrison (Kevin Costner) asks for more dedicated commitment from his leading scientists, saying, "Let's have an 'Amen,' dammit."

The prayers depicted in these historical films had a natural quality to them, even humorous at times. Hollywood situated such practices in historical contexts, enhancing past narratives with a quality of authenticity and indirectly reminding contemporary audiences of sacred rituals.

Saying Grace

While the twenty-first century has seen renewed interest in traditional liturgy, individual utterances of familiar prayer forms have also been featured in films. One form that has endured across the decades was the expression of gratitude at meals, with *Christianity Today* highlighting a 2010 magazine cover with "Eat, Pray, Think."[4] Saying grace before meals was as ubiquitous in films as in Norman Rockwell Thanksgiving illustrations. A quintessential moment occurs in *Driving Miss Daisy* (Bruce Beresford, 1989), pitting the loneliness of the wealthy Daisy Werthan (Jessica Tandy) against the devout simplicity of her African American chauffeur, Hoke Colburn (Morgan Freeman). After he serves her food at her long formal table, she says, "Thank you, Hoke." He replies kindly, "Hope you enjoy it." Hoke then goes back into the kitchen with his plate of chicken, green beans, and rice, and prays silently.

Because of Winn Dixie (Wayne Wang, 2005) deposits a ten-year-old girl, Opal (AnnaSophia Robb), abandoned by her mother, with her father, Preacher (Jeff Daniels), of the Open Arms Baptist Church. His small, odd congregation meets in a convenience store. When they catch a mouse during a church service, Preacher simply says, "Let us pray . . . for this mouse."

Opal befriends Winn Dixie, a churchgoing dog who finds and chooses her at the grocery store. By the end of the film, a peculiar family assembles with the mother figure, Gloria (Cicely Tyson), who brings them together for a common meal. As the little community gathers during a spell of inclement weather, Gloria says, "Let's just hold hands and give thanks." She prays, "Dear Lord and heavenly Father, we have egg salad sandwiches, we got pickles and we got doggie and sausages, but most importantly we got good friends, we got good friends to share this warm summer night. Teach us, Lord, to love one another. This we ask in Your name. Amen. Amen." An endearing miracle of friendship among broken people occurs because of Grace and Winn Dixie.

After sharing a series of wild experiences with his terminally ill friend, billionaire Ed Cole (Jack Nicholson), Carter Chambers (Morgan Freeman) fulfills his own set of wishes in *The Bucket List* (Rob Reiner, 2007). Before he dies, he returns to his wife, Virginia (Beverly Todd), and his family for a sumptuous and happy meal. Virginia prays, "Dear heavenly Father, we just want to thank You for this day, for having our family together once again, and for returning our father and husband."

After a seizure, Chambers goes to the hospital, where he crosses off "laugh till I cry" with his friend. Eight members of his family sit on sofas in the waiting room, praying and holding hands, but Chambers goes on to meet his maker. He had not only shared adventures with Cole, but encouraged him to reconcile with his estranged daughter and grandchild.

At the dinner table where Dom (Vin Diesel), Bryan (Paul Walker), and friends gather to eat in *The Fast and the Furious* (Rob Cohen, 2001), Dom makes Jesse (Chad Lindberg) pray because he grabbed food before grace. Jesse must be told whom to address in prayer. He thanks God for car parts, and they eat. In *Fast and Furious 6* (Justin Lin, 2013), when the crew once again gathers around a dinner table, Roman (Tyrese Gibson) thanks God for friends and family and for everything they've been through and done in their lives, because that's what made them who they are. The remarkable aspect of the *Fast and Furious* series is how frequently they stop to give prayers of thanksgiving, and prayers that strive to show both the authenticity and heart of the characters.

The Civil War provides the backdrop for *Cold Mountain* (Anthony Minghella, 2003). It begins with the building of a new church structure and ends with grace said at the end of the tragedy as a new communion of saints, bloodied by the war, gathers to offer thanks. At the end of the film, a remnant, even an emerging matriarchy, congregates around a table laden with good food, laughing and playing the fiddle. Ada Monroe (Nicole Kidman) and Ruby Thewes (Renee Zellweger) usher in a new life with a prayer: "For good friends, good food, good family, for all our blessings, Lord, we thank Thee. Amen. Amen. *Amen!*" In the aftermath of war, grace creates a grateful community.

Farther out west, in *3:10 to Yuma* (James Mangold, 2007), a family hosts the captured outlaw Ben Wade (Russell Crowe) as they await a train that will take him to trial. The father, rancher Dan Evans (Christian Bale), is to accompany him to the train. Wade is a smart man, even recognizing the value of being taciturn as he quotes Proverbs 13:3: "He that keepeth his mouth, keepeth his life. He that opens his lips too wide shall bring on his own destruction."

As they stop to eat at Evans's home, Wade starts gobbling his food down. The younger son admonishes him, "We always wait to say grace."

His mother (Gretchen Mol) corrects her son, "We don't presume to teach other people manners." He replies, "Aren't we supposed to say grace for murderers too?"

With a profound insight, she answers, "Grace is for everyone, dear." To which he persists, "Then why don't we say it?" The worldly Wade says, "I'd like to hear it."

Wade holds a piece of meat up on a fork and watches as the mother prays, "God our Father, Lord and Savior, thank You for Your love and favor. Please bless this food and drink, we pray. Bless all who share with us today." "Amen," says Wade. Here, the criminal is invited into the sacred community of family in a simple expression of thanksgiving. The inclusive prayer stands as an invitation for the sinner to be a part of a community of goodness.

However, in the new millennium, giving thanks for one's blessings often took on a hipster tone. Early in *Catch Me if You Can* (Steven Spielberg, 2002), Frank Abagnale Sr. (Christopher Walken) tells his son Frank Jr. (Leonardo DiCaprio) a little Pelagian parable: "Two little mice fell in a bucket of cream. The first mouse quickly gave up and drowned.

The second mouse wouldn't quit. He struggled so hard that eventually he churned that cream into butter and crawled out. Gentlemen, as of this moment, I am that second mouse."

Later, Frank Jr. meets his girlfriend Carol's respectable lawyer parents, who are Lutheran. They expect their daughter to marry a fine Christian man, and, as usual, he hoodwinks the gullible pair. When they sit down to dinner, the father asks Frank to say grace. After a long pause in which it seems he doesn't know what to say, the father says, "Unless you're not comfortable." Frank borrows the same inspirational tale his father often told at Rotary Club meetings.

> Absolutely. Two little mice fell into a bucket of cream. The first mouse quickly gave up and drowned, but the second mouse, he struggled so hard that he eventually churned that cream into butter and he walked out. Amen.

After they all say "Amen," Carol says with superficial amazement, "Oh, that was beautiful. The mouse, he churned that cream into butter." The clever mix of parable and prayer works well on the gullible family, hinting that the lawyers do not comprehend either.

When Finbar McBride (Peter Dinklage), a man with dwarfism, takes up residence in an abandoned train depot to escape other people in *The Station Agent* (Thomas McCarthy, 2003), he meets a lively hot dog vendor and a struggling artist, who become family. Sitting at a table, he is told to "Bring 'em in." He asks, "What?"

"Grace."

"Really?"

"Really, we got to give thanks. C'mon, bring 'em in. Hands around. God, thank You for letting us sit here and enjoy this meal. Please watch over everybody. Please let my Dad heal; he's driving me fucking crazy. Anybody you guys want to mention? No. Amen. Let's dig in!" Here, grace serves to illuminate a less traditional approach to expressing gratitude. A casual, less solemn conversation with God allowed people to express themselves without religious posturing. They could be themselves.

In *Manchester by the Sea* (Kenneth Lonergan, 2016), Patrick (Lucas Hedges) has an awkward lunch with his estranged mother, Elise (Gretchen Mol), and her born-again fiancé, Jeffrey (Matthew Broderick). His mother, a former alcoholic, has sobered up, and Patrick notices Christian paraphernalia around the house. When Jeffrey pronounces grace over the meal, Elise chastises Patrick for his failure to say "amen," which he said he did, but quietly. The boy feels that he has been judged and found wanting as a religious person. When he and his guardian uncle Lee (Casey Affleck) leave, Lee emphasizes that even though they are Roman Catholic, they are Christians too. The film confirms a growing sense of the Christian orthodoxy among various traditions, even if some fundamentalists do not celebrate it.

In *Eat Pray Love* (Ryan Murphy, 2010), Liz Gilbert (Julia Roberts) is disturbed. Before setting out on a spiritual journey to India and Bali, she desperately prays for guidance, and immediately gets a divorce. "Nice to meet You," she says to God, weeping. "O God, tell me what to do and I'll do it." She finds a parable in an Italian joke about a poor man going to the statue of a saint and begging that he "please let me win the lottery." After many such prayers, the saint finally comes to life and says, "Please, please, please buy a ticket." At a "thanksgiving" meal in Italy with adopted family members eating and expressing their gratitude, Liz tearfully expresses her thanks for just being among them. "Let us thank God. I am grateful to you, Liz," says her Swedish friend. "I thank God for fear. I am afraid the person next to me will leave me. This all makes me so grateful, the love and care you have for each other." They toast each other with a salute of gratitude. In India, Liz tries praying to a Hindu guru (who happens to be visiting New York City), but falls asleep, suggesting that this search around the world may not have been necessary. The film suggests the "Acres of Diamonds" sermon of Philadelphia Baptist minister Russell Conwell, whose message is that she could discovered the treasures in her own backyard.

Some cinematic prayers seek to teach indirectly about saying grace. They are not intended as exemplars for living, but as revelations about how we actually live. In *American Hustle* (David Russell, 2013), the overzealous FBI agent Richie DiMaso (Bradley Cooper) sits down to dinner with a harridan mother (worried about the filter in the fish tank) and his fiancée, on whom he is too ready to cheat. His mother demands that they say a prayer: "Please help Richard marry Diane that I may have grandchildren and that the pope may have more followers. And please bless this food that we are about to eat." A con woman who is playing

Richie calls to summon him away from the family. The phone rings, but his mother insists that he "sit down and pray properly." The superficial prayer exposes the selfishness of the mother, but does interfere with his sinful intentions.

Seeking to understand the existential coincidence or providential appearance of a Sudanese exchange student in his life, Albert Markovski (Jason Schwartzman) comes upon the Hootens, a Christian family, at meal time in the quite muddled *I Heart Huckabees* (David Russell, 2004). A stiff recitation of the Lord's Prayer follows, uttered by the daughter in the smugly middle-class family as a sort of emblem for their sanctimonious status. As they hold hands to pray, Albert's friend, an eco-conscious fireman, Tommy Corn (Mark Wahlberg), accuses them of an allegiance to international exploitation of oil that led to the crises in the Sudan. Fundamentalist Mr. Hooten (Richard Jenkins) defends their position with "God gave us oil. He gave it to us. How can God's gift be bad?" Corn responds, "I don't know. He gave you a brain too, but you messed that up pretty damn good." When the daughter Cricket (Sydney Zarp) says, "Jesus is never mad at us if we live with Him in our hearts!" Corn counters, "I hate to break it to you, but He is—He most definitely is." In this film, the conversation over grace exposes an underlying crisis, hinting that a superficial theology may inform the practice of prayer.

While saying grace in the new millennium showed traditional modes of prayer, it also revealed underlying tensions in such a simple form of gratitude. The ordinary routine of thanking God for food or friends could also expose attitudes of confusion, anger, or trauma.

Comic Grace

Expressing gratitude in the saying of grace also provided fodder for comedy. This kind of thanksgiving in an increasingly secular culture could be used to demonstrate that churches had lost the heart of the Gospel. At the general conference of the United Methodists in 2012, *United Methodist Reporter* contributor Elaine Robinson reminded her readers of John Wesley's warning that the Methodists would become "a dead sect, having the form of religion without the power."[5] Mainline denominations continued to decline not only in numbers but also in

Greg Focker (Ben Stiller) learns a prayer from the movie/stage play *Godspell*, which enables him to impress his potential in-laws in *Meet the Parents* (Jay Roach, 2000).

their ability to adhere to the doctrine, spirit, and discipline of their traditions. As such, the decline of vibrant religious practices, coupled with the religious posturing of those who would say long prayers and parade their religiosity, provided raw material to those who would make fun of such behaviors, especially those who pompously say grace.

The Wedding Crashers (David Dobkin, 2005) revives old jokes about grace at the dinner table, with mischief abounding. In an homage to the prayer scene in Buster Keaton's *Our Hospitality*, old, befuddled Father O'Neil (Henry Gibson) rings his glass and says, "Let us bow our heads in prayer. Heavenly Father, we thank You for the bounty on this table and ask that You bless all the Cleary family and all the friends gathered. Amen." During the prayer with all eyes shut, however, John Beckwith (Owen Wilson) pours a laxative into his rival's glass.

Meet the Parents (Jay Roach, 2000) plays with a running gag that male nurse "Greg" Focker (Ben Stiller) is Jewish, trying to assimilate into a Gentile family. He meets his fiancée's former boyfriend, Kevin Rawley (Owen Wilson), and asks who inspired him to be a woodworker. Kevin responds, "I guess I would have to say Jesus. He was a carpenter, and I just figured if you're going to follow in someone's footsteps, who better than Christ?"

The potential father-in-law, CIA interrogator Jack Byrnes (Robert De Niro), tells Kevin, "Greg's Jewish." Greg confirms it and Kevin quips, "Well, so was J.C. Wow. You're in good company." When the fumbling Greg joins the Protestant family for dinner, Jack asks whether he would like to say grace. His daughter Pam (Teri Polo) reminds her dad again, "Well, Greg's Jewish." "You're telling me Jews don't pray?" Jack replies. Then he addresses Greg: "Unless you have some objection."

Greg quickly acquiesces. "It's not like I'm a rabbi or something. I've said grace at many a dinner table." Having just heard Stephen Schwartz's lyrics for "Day by Day" from the Broadway play and film *Godspell* in a store, Greg proceeds.

> O dear God, thank You. You are such a good God to us. A kind and gentle and . . . accommodating God. And we thank You, O sweet, sweet Lord of hosts, for the . . . smorgasbord You have so aptly lain at our table this day, and each day . . . by day. Day by day . . . by day. O dear Lord, three things we pray [the family members open their eyes in curiosity]: to love Thee more dearly, to see Thee more clearly, to follow Thee more nearly, day by day . . . by day. Amen.

Jack's wife, Dina (Blythe Danner), commends him, "Oh, Greg, that was lovely." Jack simply says, "Interesting."

Greg's grace illustrates how the media shape prayers: not only in giving them form, but in providing the words as well. One can learn to pray by hearing cinematic prayers and imitating them, rather than by studying the scriptures or reading a prayer book. However, the comedy relies upon the biblical illiteracy of both Jew and Gentile, of how ignorant spectators have become and how susceptible we are to mediated prayers.

A joke about blasphemy in taking the Lord's name in vain is exploited in *Miss Congeniality* (Donald Petrie, 2000). As an FBI agent investigating a threat to the Miss America contest, Gracie Hart (Sandra Bullock) has a transmission device plugged into her ear. As the technicians turn the microphone on during a luncheon, it screeches painfully in her ear and she shrieks "Oh, Jesus Christ. Ow. Ooh."

In an archetypal example of making God in one's own image, Ricky Bobby (Will Ferrell) prays to the "eight-pound, six-ounce" baby Jesus in *Talladega Nights* (Adam McKay, 2006).

The other contestants and beauty pageant officials are stunned, but she rises and says she make a mistake. "Oh, I'm sorry, I had a bite of my bagel and forgot to pray." She then folds her hands and improvises, "Dear Jesus, please forgive me for not praying before I had a bit of my bagel and thank You very much." The guys in the truck echo her "Amen." This use of humor points to the adherence to superficial forms of religion, forms that can hoodwink ostensibly devout people.

Talladega Nights (Adam McKay, 2006) earned its legendary comic reputation primarily from an incomparable lunch scene dealing with prayer. While dining on Domino's pizza and Coca-Cola, Ricky Bobby (Will Ferrell), his wife, Carley (Leslie Bibb), his young sons, his father-in-law, and his best friend, Cal Naughton Jr. (John Reilly), provided one of the most revelatory and hilarious parables of how people create God in their own image. Carley calls the clan to the supper of fast food, which she had been "slaving over for hours."

Ricky bows his head.

Dear Lord Baby Jesus, or as our brothers to the south call You, Hesus, we thank You so much for this bountiful harvest of Domino's, KFC, and the always delicious Taco Bell. I just want to take time to say thank You for my family, my two beautiful, beautiful, handsome, striking sons, Walker and Texas Ranger, or T.R., as we call him, and of course, my red-hot smoking wife, Carley, who is a stone-cold fox, who if you were to rate her ass on a hundred, it would easily be a 94. Also wanna thank You for my best friend and teammate, Cal Naughton Jr., who's got my back no matter what. [Ironically, Cal will later have Ricky's wife as well.] Dear Lord Baby Jesus, we also thank You for my wife's father, Chip. We hope that You can use Your Baby Jesus powers to heal him and his horrible leg. And it smells terrible and the dogs are always bothering with it. Dear tiny, infant Jesus, we—

Carley interrupts and says, "Hey, you know, sweetie, Jesus did grow up. You don't always have to call Him 'baby.' It's a bit odd and off-putting to pray to a baby."

Ricky defends his address: "Well, I like the Christmas Jesus best and I'm saying grace. When you say grace you can say it to grownup Jesus, or teenage Jesus, or bearded Jesus or whoever you want."

Carley closes the topic, envisioning God as an idol to be appeased. "You know what I want? I want you to do this grace good so that God will let us win tomorrow." Ricky continues, "Dear tiny Jesus, in Your golden-fleece diapers, with Your tiny, little, fat, balled-up fists—"

Exasperated, Chip objects, "He was a man! He had a beard!" Ricky disregards his father-in-law and states, "Look, I like the baby version the best, do you hear me? I win the races and I get the money." Carley barks, "Ricky, finish the damn grace."

Then Cal (who, at various points, says he likes to think of Jesus as a mischievous badger, a dirty old bum, or a figure skater who wears "like a white outfit" and does "interpretive ice dances of my life's journey") and the boys interject. "I like to picture Jesus in a tuxedo T-shirt, 'cause it says, like, 'I wanna be formal, but I'm here to party, too.' 'Cause I like to party, so I like my Jesus to party." Walker adds, "I like to picture Jesus as a ninja fighting off evil samurai." Then Cal extends his description of partying Jesus: "I like to think of Jesus, like, with giant eagle's wings. And singing lead vocals for Lynyrd Skynyrd, with, like, an angel band. And I'm in the front row, and I'm hammered drunk."

Ricky finishes his long grace:

Okay. Dear eight-pound, six-ounce newborn infant Jesus, don't even know
a word yet, just a little infant and so cuddly, but still omnipotent, we just
thank You for all the races I've won and the 21.2 million dollars—Woo!
[The others chime in with "Woo!" or "Ow!"] Love that money that I have
accrued over this past season. Also, due to a binding endorsement contract
that stipulates I mention Powerade at each grace, I just want to say that
Powerade is delicious and it cools you off on a hot summer day. And we
look forward to Powerade's release of Mystic Mountain Blueberry. Thank
You for all Your power and Your grace, dear baby God. Amen.

For the Bobby family, prayer not only equates to a form of incanta-
tion, but requires the right words, at least from contractual obligations.
The comic idolatry of the scene indicts those who re-create God in their
own image. C. S. Lewis once noted that God is the great iconoclast; He
continually shatters our images of Him by revealing something else. The
revelatory prayers in *Talladega Nights* also demolish any vain and idola-
trous images of God practiced by the rest of us.[6]

Today's preachers are more open to comedy in their prayers. Solemnity has given way to more comic presentations. One tongue-in-cheek
sidelight of the *Talladega Nights* prayers is that an actual pastor, Joe
Nelms, delivered the invocation at NASCAR's Nationwide Series 300 in
New Hampshire on July 23, 2011, using words from the film. He thanked
God not only for the Dodges, Toyotas, and Fords, but for his "smoking
hot wife, Lisa," and then ended it with the film's catchy "boogity, boogity,
boogity, amen." The irreverent prayer captured the delight of race winner Carl Edwards, who requested Nelms for his funeral.

Humor in prayer in the new millennium reflects a more informal
approach to faith. The stigma of religious practices makes many wary,
and so comic relief comes as a welcome distancing mechanism. In the
age of the rise of the nones, more skeptical and agnostic than their pre-
decessors and informed by the predominance of Comedy Central, *The
Simpsons*, and *South Park*, such practices are looked upon with both ignorance and bemusement. Laughter in prayer, both as recognition of the
incongruities of life and as caustic responses to religion itself, became a
new norm.

Laughter Redux

Humor permeated praying beyond the saying of grace in the early years of the new millennium. While forbidding laughter from entering the Holy of Holies, theologian Reinhold Niebuhr suggested that "laughter is the beginning of prayer." Poet W. H. Auden echoed his sentiment in arguing for a liturgical dimension of laughter, finding a place for it in worship, pointing out that the "world of laughter is much more closely related to the world of prayer than either is to the everyday secular world of work." In laughter and prayer one begins to move away from obsession with the self and move into an appreciation of something outside the self. Honest prayers can lead to a recognition of the comic incongruities of being human, of being such an oxymoron as a "spiritual animal" that laughs.[7]

As four old astronauts prepare to soar into space in *Space Cowboys* (Clint Eastwood, 2000), they joke that they've waited forty years, a good biblical number. In the capsule, Frank Corvin (Clint Eastwood) asks Tank Sullivan (James Garner), "Well, what do you say, Reverend? You think a prayer's in order?"

Sullivan responds, "I was just reciting the Shepard's Prayer. Alan Shepard's prayer: 'O Lord, please don't let us screw up. Amen.'"

Olive Penderghast (Emma Stone) goes into a confessional in *Easy A* (Will Gluck, 2010), unaware that no one is there.

> Forgive me, father, for I have sinned. I think that's how you're supposed to start these things. *I'm only going on what I've seen in the movies.* Where do I even start? I've been pretending to be a—how would one phrase it in Catholic words? A harlot. It's not like I've actually been doing the things that people are saying I'm doing, but—then again—I'm not denying them, so I've just been wondering: Is that wrong? . . . It was make-believe and no one was getting hurt. But a lot of people hate me now.

Tearing up, she confesses that she hates herself as well. Then she asks, "I could be wrong, but aren't you supposed to say something or ask me questions? Tell me to say 'Hail Mary'? Hello?" Seeing that the priest's box is empty, she exclaims in exasperation, "Oh, come on!" As a millennial, Olive looks for concrete and practical answers, even from the church. However, the church is not there for her and she hears nothing from

God's representatives. Seeking answers to religious questions in a secular age, Olive looks to the movies for guidance, even on how to pray.[8]

The church does teach how to pray in *St. Vincent* (Theodore Melfi, 2014), where Oliver (Jaeden Lieberher) attends a new school at Saint Patrick's as his parents are going through a divorce. Brother Geraghty (Chris O'Dowd) welcomes him and asks him to lead the class in morning prayers. The students bow their heads, except Oliver, who whispers, "I think, I think I'm Jewish." "Good to know," sighs the priest. "Oliver thinks he's Jewish." The class then clamors to express their own traditions. "So am I," says one. "I'm Buddhist," says another. Brother Geraghty rejoins,

> I'm a Catholic, which is the best of all the religions, really, because we have the most rules and the best clothes. [He is dressed in black with a clerical collar.] Among us we have a Buddhist, an agnostic; we have a Baptist, and we have an "I don't know," which seems to be the fastest-growing religion in the world. And now we have an "I think I'm Jewish," which is a new one for the class, Oliver, so thanks for that. But it does not preclude you from giving us a morning prayer. Let us bow our heads and pray.

Oliver tries, "Dear . . ."
The priest whispers, "God, etcetera, etcetera."
"Dear, dear God . . . thank You?"
Geraghty whispers, "Amen." And the class resounds with a communal "Amen." The priest exclaims, "Amen, thanks be to God" and claps his hands. "All right, stirring stuff. Well done, Oliver. Go grab yourself a seat." Oliver makes friends with a curmudgeonly veteran living next door, Vincent (Bill Murray). At a final scene, after having made the begrudging Vincent a local, albeit reluctant, saint, the family sits around the table eating spaghetti. When someone asks, "Shouldn't we say something, a blessing or a prayer?," all bow their heads again, and Vincent finally says, "No, I'd better not." However, Oliver's friend teaches him how to cross himself. Oliver's prayer reflects a general inability of American culture to pray. Many people do not know how to pray and feel uncomfortable in being asked to pray publicly. It is Brother Geraghty and Oliver's friend who gently, and comically, strive to teach him.

When a Buffalo, New York, television reporter, Bruce Nolan (Jim Carrey), first receives an opportunity to play God in *Bruce Almighty* (Tom Shadyac, 2003), he exploits it for all it's worth, causing havoc to foes and friends alike. Earlier he had raged against God (Morgan Freeman), "God, why do You hate me?" and compiled a laundry list of complaints: "The gloves are off, God." "God has taken my bird and my bush." "God is a mean kid with a magnifying glass." "Smite me, O Mighty Smiter."

God muses, "Now, I'm not big on blasphemy, but that last one made me laugh." God grants His divine powers to Bruce to see whether he can do any better. What Bruce learns is a lesson in humility. However, he begins with arrogance, standing on top of a skyscraper in a storm prating, "I am Bruce Almighty! My will be done!" "Bruce giveth and Bruce taketh away. Don't like it? Megabyte me."

His aptly named girlfriend, Grace (Jennifer Aniston), plays a crucial role in opening his eyes. A mutual friend tells Bruce, "You know what I do every night before I go to bed? Tuck my kids in, maybe have a scoop of ice cream, watch Conan. . . . You know what Grace does? She prays, most of the time for you."

Bruce goes to his Yahweh computer to google "Grace" and is stunned by what he finds. "That woman does pray a lot!" He notices how her prayers are for others: "Please help the daycare kids listen better." "Please guide our president's decisions." "Please be with Mom during this time." "Please help the blood drive reach their goal." "Please help Bruce to be happy." "Please help my relationship with Bruce." "Please watch over Mom." "Please, God, give Bruce strength; he's struggling to find meaning." "Dear God, bless him." "Bruce, Bruce, Bruce!" Suddenly he sees her praying in bed, crying, "It's her! She's logging on."

Her new prayer is different. She is despondent and sad. "Please, God, please. I still love him, but I don't wanna love him anymore. I don't want the hurt anymore, please. Help me forget, please. Help me let him go. Please, help me let him go."

The abrupt realization of the pain he causes drives Bruce out into the night. Thunder rumbles as he walks down the highway in the dark and rain. "You win. I'm done. Please, I don't want to do this anymore. I don't want to be God. I want You to decide what's right for me. I surrender to Your will."

Given the powers of God, Bruce (Jim Carrey) learns the depths of praying when he hears Grace (Jennifer Aniston) pleading with God in *Bruce Almighty* (Tom Shadyac, 2003).

Immediately, a bright light shines on him as he kneels and looks up. Then we find him standing before God, asking whether he's dead. God replies, "You can't kneel down in the middle of a highway and live to talk about it, son."

Questioned about why he died and why now, God responds, "Bruce, you have the divine spark, you have the gift for bringing joy and laughter to the world. I know, I created you." Bruce quips, "Quit bragging." "See, that's what I am talking about. That's the spark."

God gives him prayer beads and instructs him, "I want you to pray, son. Go ahead. Use them."

He offers, "Well, Lord, feed the hungry, and bring peace to all of mankind. How's that?"

"Great," says God, "if you wanna be Miss America. Ah, come on. What do you really care about?"

"Grace."

"Grace. You want her back?"

"No, I want her to be happy. No matter what that means. I want her to find someone who will treat her with all the love she deserved from me. I want her to meet someone who'll see her always as I do now, through Your eyes."

"Now *that's* a prayer."

"Yeah?" "Yeah!"

"It's good?" "It's good." "Goooood," they say in unison.

Bruce's back-and-forth conversations with God capture a twenty-first-century model for praying, born out of the seeker-friendly independent churches that proliferated while staid mainline churches suffered a decline in attendance.

Prayer bits decorated numerous comedy films of the new millennium. One example is *School of Rock* (Richard Linklater, 2003), written by Mike White, in which Dewey Finn (Jack Black) forges a formal class of elementary school kids into a rock band. Just before they are going on to play, Dewey asks them, "Who else is with me?" They all shout, "Yeah!," so Dewey says, "All right, let's pray. God of Rock, thank You for this chance to kick ass. We are Your humble servants. Please give us the power to blow people's minds with our high-voltage rock. In Your name we pray. Amen." And all the kids say, "Amen." Then Dewey concludes, "Now let's get out there and melt some faces! Yeah!"

Susan Stroman's remake of Mel Brooks's *The Producers* (2005) shows Max Bialystock (Nathan Lane) praying desperately at the city fountain for his disastrous play *Springtime for Hitler*. "O Lord, dear Lord, I want that *money!*" Unexpectedly, Leo Bloom (Matthew Broderick) appears. "Mr. Bialystock! I'm back, I changed my mind."

Max looks to heaven and spurts, "Boy, You *are* good!"

Praying is, remarkably, quite effective throughout humorous films. God functions as a sort of arbitrary vending machine who answers the most selfish and stupid of prayers. Certain films attack the prevailing culture of consumerism in Christendom, of those who go to God to get something. But comedy films also show the importance of listening as a central component of praying.

Nacho (Jack Black) approaches the altar of burning candles, genuflects, kneels, and prays in *Nacho Libre* (Jared Hess, 2006), also written by Mike White. He chats with God. "Precious father, why have You given me these desires to wrestle and made me such a stinking warrior?

Have I focused too much on my boots and my fame and my stretchy pants?" Listening to God, he experiences an epiphany that he is to fight and give everything to the little orphans. Nacho finds that God answers his prayers. The film illustrates the findings of cultural anthropologist Will Gervais that popular religiosity tends to be more practical and intuitive and not always in accordance with religious doctrine. The idea that people act in accordance with church teachings is known as the religious congruence fallacy; scholars argue that in reality, there is often a discrepancy between faith and practice, and, not unsurprisingly, that people don't always practice what they preach. However, Nacho, through his prayers, comically comes to a remarkable theological congruence.

In *We're the Millers* (Rawson Thurber, 2013), David Clark (Jason Sudeikis), pretending to be part of a normal family as a cover for running drugs from Mexico, hires stripper Rosie (Jennifer Aniston) and two kids to make up his pretend family. Trying to demonstrate how WASPish they are, Rosie pulls them together for a prayer on board a plane. "Lord, we thank Thee for the blessing of this family vacation. May David find his bliss and bring us all back home safely. May Kenny and Casey fortify their sibling bond over the warm glow of our devoted hearts. And may this entire airplane find safe passage and a bountiful life. Even the Jews. Amen." An oblivious flight attendant sighs, "Wish my family prayed like that." Film comedies can mirror false piety in a culture that discerns bogus practices; however, such films also perpetuate a stereotype of prayer that is hypocritical posturing.

Ron Burgundy (Will Ferrell) sits desperately in the studio of Global News Network in *Anchorman 2* (Adam McKay, 2013), having made a bet that he would leave news reporting if he didn't beat the ratings of his hotshot competitor. "Dear God," he prays, "please help me pull this off. Help me do this and I swear I'll become a monk, shave my head and become a monk . . . Who am I kidding? I'm not going to do that." In spite of his puny self-centeredness, the prayer is answered.

In the Coen Brothers' *The Big Lebowski* (1998), the Dude (Jeff Bridges) stands with his friend Walter (John Goodman) overlooking the Pacific in Malibu, where Walter utters a few words on their recently departed fellow bowler, Donny (Steve Buscemi). The eulogy becomes a question to God, a flashback, in which he asks why God takes all the good young men. Walter then proceeds to deliver his desultory prayer and tribute, describing Donny as a good bowler and surfer, committing his mortal remains to the "bosom of the Pacific Ocean."

The overblown rhetorical flourishes of Lebowski are expanded with the same wit in *O Brother, Where Art Thou?* (2000), a hybrid of the Gospel and Homer's *Odyssey*, built upon Preston Sturges's suggested title from *Sullivan's Travels*. Escaping a chain gang, Pete Hogwallop (John Turturro), Delmar O'Donnell (Tim Blake Nelson), and lead character Ulysses Everett McGill (George Clooney) begin their odyssey and spiritual journey in 1930s Mississippi. When they come upon a baptismal service, the first two boys get wet, with their sins (including a robbery of a Piggly Wiggly) "warshed away." But, Ulysses points out, "even if that did put you square with the Lord, the State of Mississippi's a little more hard-nosed."

Ulysses suggests that they would need a lot more water for him to be baptized, an ironic prophetic statement considering that they will soon be inundated from the 1933 Tennessee Valley Authority Act of damming and releasing waters. The flood will be the cause of his supplication and a symbolic baptism for the reluctant convert.

The stumblebums continue their theological discussion to get to the identity of the devil and the issue of redemption. A blind seer prophesies that while they are now in chains, they will find a fortune, but not the one they seek. Their road will be long and difficult, fraught with peril, but will provide many startling and wonderful sights, such as a cow on the roof of a cotton house. After this arduous journey, salvation will come.

Having been caught by the devil-with-no-eyes, the three men are about to be hanged. Pete and Delmar look to God and ask, "Good Lord, what do we do?"

The slippery, agnostic Ulysses then kneels and prays,

> O Lord, . . . please look down and recognize us poor sinners. Please, Lord. I just want to see my daughters again. I've been separated from my family for so long. I know I've been guilty of pride and sharp dealing. I'm sorry I turned my back on You. Forgive me. We're helpless, Lord. For the sake of my family, for Tommy's sake. For Delmar's and Pete's. Let me see my daughters again, Lord. Help us, please.

Repenting and pleading with God just before his cataclysmic baptism by the Tennessee Valley Authority, Ulysses (George Clooney) beseeches God for help in *O Brother, Where Art Thou?* (Coen Brothers, 2000).

Workers sing as nooses are wrapped about their necks, "You got to go to the lonesome valley. Yes, sir, you got to go there by yourself. Nobody else can go for you. You got to go there by yourself. Mmmmmm."

When a flood cascades over them, Delmar shouts, "A miracle! It was a miracle!"

No longer in danger, Ulysses corrects him: "Delmar, don't be ignorant. I told you they was flooding this valley."

"No! That ain't it! We prayed to God and He pitied us!"

Ulysses returns to his rationalizations. "Well, it never fails. Again, you hayseeds are showin' you want for intellect. There's a perfectly scientific explanation." But the boys point out that "ain't the tune you was singin' back at the gallows!" Ulysses tries to excuse his actions with the fact that "any human being'll cast about in a moment of stress." But the point of Divine Providence and His response to the puny prayers of hayseeds is indeed miraculous.

Similarly, some prayers reveal a desperate bargaining tactic, often by those ignorant of the Bible. Undertaking a long and dangerous journey to transport three madwomen back to Iowa, Mary Bee Cuddy (Hilary Swank) is prayed for in *The Homesman* (Tommy Lee Jones, 2014). As she sets off, a friend prays, "Heavenly Father, look down upon Thy daughter. Bless her in this undertaking. Grant her Thy strength. Guide her with Thy grace that she might carry home these poor souls. We beg of Thee. Amen." Almost immediately, she comes across George Briggs (Tommy Lee Jones) left hanging in the middle of nowhere. He asks the bossy and plain-looking pioneer whether she is an angel. She retorts, "You're not dead." He begs her to help him, "for God's sake." She bargains with him to help her with the women. Trying to show his religion, he spouts, "Uh, vengeance is mine, sayeth the Lord. And bringing in the sheaves. And do unto others. And if you cut me down from this goddamn tree, I'll do anything you tell me to on God's holy name." "All right," she says. "I'll save you." This prayer shows the comic bartering that one sees not only in Jacob trying to make a deal with God, but with shrewd Americans trying to placate a God who practices grace.

While mainline white denominations have shown a marked decline in the twenty-first century, the Pew Research Center has found that there has been an increasing racial and ethnic diversity in Christian circles. Concomitantly, one finds more African Americans and members of other ethnic groups praying in films.

Tyler Perry makes comic use of prayer in many of his films, particularly with his irascible character Madea (Tyler Perry), an over-the-top African American grandma who rules her roost. In *Diary of a Mad Black Woman* (Tyler Perry, 2005), Madea says she'll go to church when they have a smoking section. Her comedy emerges from a familiarity with the realities of church life, even as she complains that "every time I try to read the Bible . . . and Jesus . . . the one with all the words in red . . . I open my Bible to that New Testimony and see all that red and I just give up. Jesus was talkin' way too much."

In *I Can Do Bad All by Myself* (Tyler Perry, 2009), grandma Madea sits on the porch with a young girl she has taken in for foster care. A distrustful and angry delinquent, Jennifer (Hope Wilson) tearfully shares about how her grandma used to tell her to pray about her problems.

Madea says, "That's what you ought to do. Pray about it. Talk to the Lord about it. That's what you oughta do." Jennifer asks her to teach her to pray.

Tyler Perry underlines the biblical illiteracy of prayers while humanizing conversations with God through Madea (Tyler Perry) in *I Can Do Bad All by Myself* (Tyler Perry, 2009).

Madea gulps, "Show you how to pray? Oooooh Lord, child, I haven't talked to God since the last time I saw a cop in my rearview mirror." She sighs. "I guess I can try. I can try to pray. Do you know the number? To call Him? They say Jesus on the mainline, I don't know. Sit back. Okay, bow your head. First, giving honor to God, to the head of my life. Urmmm."

Fadder, I stretch my hand aaang to Thee. Fadder God, God of Abraham, Isaac, and Jacob. God of Shadrech, Meshit, and de billy goat, who was in the fiery furnace that they barbecued on the day of Pentecost, when the Jewish people returned from the Sabbath day up on the mountain top in, uhh, Ethiopia. Ah, God, Mary, Jableisch.

Jennifer interrupts, "That doesn't sound right. That's not how my mother used to do it."

Madea asks, "You ain't feeling the anointing? Honey, listen, I don't know nothing about praying, but all praying is, is talking to God, having a conversation with Him. And at the end of your conversation, you say 'in the name of Jesus.' That's your stamp to get it up there to Him." Humor emerges from the mingling of diverse stories and from the genuine human tendency to improvise out of bits of knowledge. Madea's behavior is symbolic of all human pretension

Salim Akil's *Jumping the Broom* (2011) ties morality and rewards together. Hooking up with a stud in a non-meaningful one-night stand, Sabrina Watson (Paula Patton) realizes she has messed up again. She barters with God, promising not to show her "boobies" to any other man, but only to the man she will marry.

> O God, I did it again. I gave up the cookie for a cute face, nice body, and some mediocre conversation. I don't even think he can spell "mediocre." I promise, God, again, that if You get me out of this situation with some dignity . . . [She sees the guy laughing on his iPhone with some other woman while she dresses.] Okay, just get me out of here. I promise to only share my cookies with my future husband. No more of this.

Driving away, she continues her prayer: "And God, because it's obvious I don't know how to spot a human being, could You please make it clear who You want me to be with. I mean clear! Clear! The kind of clear—" Not watching where she is driving, she hits a pedestrian, Jason Taylor (Laz Alonso), not realizing that she has just run over her future husband. "Oh my God!" she exclaims. "Are you okay?" The accident will prove to be an immediate answer to a heartfelt prayer. Later, she confesses, "God, did I say how much I love Your sense of humor?" After the bride discovers her true parentage through the arrogant meanness of the religious mother-in-law, she runs away. Jason, the groom-to-be, prays, "I need Your help, God. Bring her back." God does.

Disparaging Words of Prayer

In addition to the comic depiction of prayer as a humorous dialogue with God, filmmakers in the early years of the millennium also constructed more satirical and sarcastic portrayals of religious beliefs and behaviors. The rise of the new atheists, including Sam Harris, Richard Dawkins, and Christopher Hitchens, and a legion of anti-religious comedians like Ricky Gervais and Bill Maher abetted an attack on religion as irrational, superstitious, and dangerous. Their publications and public performances found parallels in negative cinematic depictions of prayers.

In the 2014 Pew Research Center's study on the religious landscape in the United States, data suggest that while about 70 percent of Americans identified with some branch of Christian faith, the percentage of adults, mostly young millennials, describing themselves as Christians had dropped around 8 percent since 2007, with unaffiliated Americans (atheist, agnostic, and so forth) gaining six points. This finding paralleled trends in films of the early 2000s, which, as we have seen, often challenged and subverted the ways cinematic prayers were once constructed, with more disparaging depictions.

Reflecting his customary debunking of religious faith, Woody Allen's *Match Point* (2005) offers a jaundiced description of Chris Wilton's (Jonathan Rhys Meyers) father, who was a bit of a religious fanatic. Chris comments, "After he lost both his legs, he found Jesus." Chloe Hewitt Wilton (Emily Mortimer) retorts, "God. . . . Sorry, but it just doesn't seem like a fair trade." So, too, in *Magic in Moonlight* (Woody Allen, 2014), misanthrope magician Stanley (Colin Firth) quotes Thomas Hobbes's view of life as nasty, short, and brutish. When his aunt is dying, he is told, "All you can do is pray." He disparages the power of prayer as he has exposed séances as part of his job. But hoodwinked into thinking that the spiritual world may indeed exist, he begins a grand monologue with whatever may be out there:

> I don't know if You can hear me. . . . [I've] led an exemplary life, but I've always been a skeptic, a nonbeliever, but much worse, a man with contempt for people who give themselves over to the idea of some kind of benevolent Father up there. I always thought it was childish, wishful thinking for primitives: all this purpose for life, this hope, meaning that our suffering accrued for some greater plan, but if what I see at length is real, then I don't have all the answers, and it's possible, even logical, that we are here by design to serve some higher ideal and that You could be real. I know I have no right to expect anything, but my aunt, whom I love, is in mortal danger and so I ask You, I ask You, . . . wait a minute, this is the stupidest wad of twaddle I've ever heard. My common sense tells me I am falling into a seductive morass of sugarcoated claptrap because I want my aunt to be all right.

Though he begins to pray, he rejects the whole labor as poppycock once he discovers that Sophie (Emma Stone) has conned him. When she seeks reconciliation with him, he tells her, "I can't forgive you, only God can forgive." She responds with his mantra: "But you said there is no God." To which he answers, "Precisely my point." He exposes his own desire to pray as self-delusion, rejecting even the concept of God.

In *Café Society* (Woody Allen, 2016), Bobby Dorfman (Jesse Eisenberg) lives with his parents, Marty and Rose Dorfman (Ken Stott and Jeannie Berlin), in Brooklyn in the 1930s. Marty protests against the angel of death, but he protests in silence, saying, "I pray and pray and I don't hear anything." Rose counters that "no answer is also an answer." The comic conversation of a rational man who encounters the silence of God is juxtaposed with the believing response of his wife. When he questions the nontraditional Jewishness of her brother, she says, "You don't pray; you don't fast; and you don't have a traditional Jewish head."

When Bobby goes to Hollywood to work for his secular uncle Phil (Steve Carell), he falls in love with Vonnie (Kristen Stewart), who grew up in Oklahoma and admits she wasn't allowed to talk to Jews. Rejected, he returns to Brooklyn and begins a restaurant with his gangster brother Ben (Corey Stoll). When his crimes are uncovered and he is sent to death row, Ben converts to Christianity just before his execution. He attributes his conversion to Psalm 6, a prayer of distress. Rose wrings her hands in anguish: "First a murderer! Then he becomes a Christian! I don't know which is worse. What did I do to deserve this?" Bobby suggests that it's "too bad Jewish religion doesn't have any afterlife. They'd get a lot more customers." This jibe digs at the consumerist mentality of contemporary religion.

In *The Campaign* (Jay Roach, 2012), Democrat North Carolina congressman Cam Brady (Will Ferrell) is running for reelection. His campaign stumbles when he leaves an obscene call on the phone of a family about to eat meatloaf and mashed potatoes, with their hands folded, saying dinner prayers: "And Lord, we just pray that You bless the table, this food, this family, and this nation." When the phone rings, the father says to his children, "Let the machine just take one for God." As Brady spouts out explicit sexual epithets, the father tries to explain, "He's not listening to Jesus." Roach's clever satire on the sham religion of politicians exposes how aptly religious congruence fallacy applies to political life.

Having messed up, Brady seeks to restore his image by going to a black church and then a Pentecostal snake-handling church, where a snake bites him. His Republican competition, the naïve Marty Huggins (Zach Galifianakis), sets up Brady with a challenge to recite the Lord's Prayer. The two had earlier gotten into a religious debate over whether Jesus had a moustache. Huggins asks whether he has gone to church. Brady says his relationship with God is not measured by attendance.

Brady accuses Huggins of resorting to accusatory tactics, but agrees to accept the challenge if the "media would mind turning off all their recording devices and closing their eyes." Then he begins to mangle the prayer as an associate tries to mime it out for him in charades.

> Our Father, Art, who is up in heaven. Aloe Vera be Thy name. The thigh . . . Thy kingdom . . . come . . . the magic kingdom. As it is on earth in the helicopter. Give us this day our daily . . . pizza. And let us digest it. Forgive us, forgive our passes we commit with womenfolk who sometimes their dresses are too tight, like that's a nice caboose you got there. I know that's not part of it. Keep your heads bowed, please. Forgive us for trespassing and do not lead us to the Temptations because we are tired of them and their music and dancing. Deliver us from evil with Your mighty sword and falcon. Forever and ever and ever. Amen.

The crowd cheers. The satire on religious practices excoriates those politicians who do not heed Jesus's warning in Luke 20:46, about those narcissistic lawyers who wear flowing robes, love to be greeted in the marketplaces, take the most important seats of honor at banquets, and make long prayers.

Disparaging faith traditions is part-and-parcel of the comedy of *21 Jump Street* (Phil Lord, Chris Miller, 2012). Two incompetent undercover cops, Schmidt (Jonah Hill) and Jenko (Channing Tatum), are assigned to high school undercover work since they look so young. Their training officer, aptly named Captain Dickson (Ice Cube), is a profane bully, calling his trainees to get their asses up and embrace their stereotypes. They are sent to 21 Jump Street for training, the location of the Aroma of Christ Church, a Korean sanctuary that has been transformed into a cluttered warehouse training ground, but with a crucifix of a Korean-looking Jesus and white neon lights proclaiming, "God Is Love" hovering over the space.

The inferior-feeling Schmidt goes to the altar rail and kneels, accepting a new type of Christ:

> Hey, Korean Jesus, I don't know if You only cater to Koreans or if You exist, no offense. I just, ah, am really freaked out about going back to high school. It was so fucking hard the first time. I know we haven't made our first arrest. Maybe I'm not the best cop. Korean Jesus, I just don't want to fuck this up. Sorry for swearing so much. The end. I don't really know how to end the prayer.

The filmmakers exploit this seemingly heartfelt prayer with profane language and outrageous humor. Its subtle recognition of the growth of global manifestations of the Christian faith contrasts with its comic sacrilege. While tipping the hat to the Korean faith, it belittles the faith with comic flourishes as well.

Jonah Hill expresses one of the more hilariously self-absorbed prayers in the mostly improvised *This Is the End* (Seth Rogen, 2013), when a biblical apocalypse hits Hollywood and the actors play bizarre caricatures of themselves. As the world comes crashing down, Jonah kneels down and prays, "Dear God, I'd like to pray for a second. It's me, Jonah Hill . . . from *Moneyball*. I hate Jay so much; I think he might be the worst person You ever created. I don't want to judge You, but what were You thinking that day? I love Seth; I love being his friend; he's an awesome guy. . . . Just do me a favor God. Just kill Jay." Such hatred leads to his own demonic possession.

The film echoed what *Christianity Today* had labelled the "juvenilization of the American church."[9] For millennials, stereotyped as pampered, materialistic, and narcissistic, the satirical prayer strikes at their own image. It both deconstructs them and provides comic distance from the perception that such a prayer represents them.

Public prayers elicit both bemusement and irritation from many, leading to satiric and mocking depictions of those prayers uttered by hypocrites who thank God they are not like other men. Even Jesus rebuked such posturing. Thus perceptive filmmakers have created characters whose self-absorption, ignorance, and pride mark what this generation sees of religious behaviors.

Fantasy Prayers

The new millennium ushered in a marvelous set of movie adaptations of comic book heroes and fantasy tales, many with unexpected references to scripture and prayers. The popularity of this genre reflected the creative fiction of bestselling Christian authors like J. R. R. Tolkien, C. S. Lewis, and J. K. Rowling.[10] Fantasy and horror films explore the sacred and profane spheres of human life, often pointing back to Mircea Eliade's conception of myth.

The mythic quality of fantasy allowed prayers and petitions in fantastical settings with extraordinary characters and heroes. In Sam Raimi's *Spider-Man* (2002), Peter Parker's (Tobey Maguire) Uncle Ben (Cliff Robertson) is the moral anchor in the boy's life. Even when he changes a light bulb, he connects to God with his jests: "And the Lord said, 'Let there be light.' And voilà! There is light. Forty soft, glowing watts of it." His wife, Aunt May (Rosemary Harris), commends him: "Good boy. God will be thrilled. Just don't fall on your ass." Uncle Ben and Aunt May represent tradition, which includes the saying of prayers.

When Aunt May prepares a sumptuous Thanksgiving meal, she asks the villain Norman Osborn (Willem Dafoe) to say grace. Bringing out the turkey, she gives the cutting knives to Osborn, who later becomes the Green Goblin, to do the honors. He licks his fingers in anticipation. Aunt May suddenly notices that Peter is bleeding, a sign that Osborn recognizes his identity as the Spider-Man, his nemesis. Aunt May continues, "We will say grace, as this is the boy's first Thanksgiving and we are going to do things properly." However, Osborn leaves the room. Revenge cannot share the table with grace.

By her bedside later, Aunt May kneels and prays, "Lead us not into temptation, but deliver us—" Just then, the Green Goblin smashes through the window with a burst of fire and Aunt May screams, "Deliver us!" The goblin laughs maniacally, and mockingly urges her, "Finish it. Finish it!" She shouts, "from evil!" We next see Aunt May in a hospital bed, but alive. Her traditional prayer is heard and also exposes the villainy of the Green Goblin as the "evil one."

In *Spider-Man 3* (Sam Raimi, 2007), Eddie Brock (Topher Grace) goes into a church and crosses himself with holy water. Sitting in a pew by himself and gazing on a crucifix, he addresses God formally: "It's Brock, sir, Edward Brock Jr. I'm here humbled and humiliated to ask You for one thing . . . I want You to kill Peter Parker." Prayers reveal the hearts of the supplicants, and Brock, the son of the Green Goblin, holds vengeance in his soul.

In the bell tower of the church, Spider-Man struggles with an enveloping kudzu-like skin of revenge. As he tears at it, Brock moves toward the sounding of a bell. He looks up and sees Parker struggling, ripping off the toxic skin, screaming. Some of it spills onto Brock, covers him, and takes over his person, as he becomes Venom. Spider-Man is now released, but Brock possesses it and it possesses him. Evil has overcome him. His prayer for his foe's death resonated with much American anger toward perceived enemies. Fewer Americans were praying for forgiveness as much as justice.

In Marvel Comics' *X-Men 2* (Bryan Singer, Ralph Winter, 2003), the blue mutant Nightcrawler Kurt Wagner (Alan Cumming) moves with ease. Needing to teleport blindly into an enclosed chamber, he says to Storm (Halle Berry), "I told you if I can't see where I am going . . ." to which she responds, "I have faith in you."

They must transport through faith and not by sight. As they prepare to enter the chamber, where Professor Xavier (Patrick Stewart) is imprisoned, Nightcrawler begins his prayer, "Our Father who art in heaven, hallowed be Thy name. Thy kingdom come. Thy will be done, on earth . . ." At this point they are transferred to the room and he finishes his phrase, "as it is in heaven," with his prayer, uttered sincerely, having effected their safe passage.

After the rescue, the mutants seek to fly away, but their plane malfunctions. Jean Grey (Famke Janssen) sacrifices herself, and while the remnant is devastated, Nightcrawler recites the Twenty-Third Psalm as a prayer: "The Lord is my shepherd. Yea, though I walk through the valley of the shadow of death, I will fear no evil, for Thou art with me." Nightcrawler's prayers reflect an orthodox faith even among marginalized characters. In *Daredevil* (Mark Steven Johnson, 2003), a fearless

Matt Murdock (Ben Affleck) finds his mojo enhanced by his confession with Father Everett. When he says, "Bless me, Father, for I have sinned," the priest responds, "What the hell are you playing at, Matt? You didn't come here for forgiveness. You came for permission, and I can't give you that." Murdock argues that he is seeking justice. The priest, with concern for his parishioner, still blesses him: "May God have mercy on you for your sins and grant you everlasting life. Amen."

One of the oddest fantasy films in the new millennium to include the Lord's Prayer may be *Starship Troopers: Marauder* (Ed Neumeier, 2008), with its mix of tongue-in-cheek patriotism and religion battling against giant insects on a distant planet. The film tracks the survival and spiritual struggles of tough Captain Lola Beck (Jolene Blalock), her agnostic team, and an almost frivolous Christian flight attendant, Holly Little (Marnette Patterson) as they are marooned on Planet OM-1. Arachnids systematically eliminate the team, until only Beck and Little are left.

Surrounded and facing imminent death, the two crouch against the overwhelming odds of the monster insects. Just as they are about to be devoured, Little commands the usually resilient but now resigned captain to pray with her.

"What!?" Beck shouts in disbelief.

Little starts: "Lord, hear my prayer. Deliver us from this evil place. Lola, pray with me!"

"It doesn't make any difference."

Little ignores her and sends up her prayer: "Lord, send us an army of angels. And arm them with Your fire and Your sword that they might smite the evil around us." Just then stars appear in the sky.

Stunned, Beck asks, "What is it?"

"Don't you want to live?" Little inquires. "Yes! I want to live!" Beck says. Then, concludes Little, "Just say it." Together they begin the Lord's Prayer, with Beck echoing Little on each phrase. They recite, "Deliver us from evil" even as insect monsters approach. Suddenly the Federation squad descends from the heavens like metallic angels to destroy the monsters. The efficacy of Little's prayer functions as a wish-fulfillment fantasy of its own, in an apocalyptic setting.

In the midst of disasters, one expects desperate praying. Such prayers occur several times in *2012* (Roland Emmerich, 2009), a date allegedly predicted as the apocalypse by the Mayan calendar. The first incidence occurs with the president of the United States (Danny Glover) kneeling in his private chapel, seeking wisdom. He is interrupted by his chief of staff (a melodramatic villain played by Oliver Platt), who finds no time for such extraneous activity, as they must get to giant arks built in China in order to escape destruction. The president makes the selfless decision to stay with his sinking White House. The Italian president likewise stays in his country to pray, presumably at the Vatican. The pope and a congregation in Saint Peter's Square share in a Mass, while cardinals praying in the Sistine Chapel, under Michelangelo's painting, are the first to see the cracks of an imminent earthquake. Then all collapses. Finally, the most heartfelt prayer occurs as the film's protagonist, novelist Jackson (John Cusack), swimming underwater, tries to unravel a cord causing a mechanical malfunction on the ark. His divorced wife pleads with God, "O Lord, please, please, please." After the requisite dramatic pause, Jackson resurfaces and all is well on the ark as a new earth has been prepared. Yet again, prayers are answered (just in the nick of time). In fantasy worlds, anything is possible.

The Haunting in Connecticut (Peter Cornwell, 2009) follows the horror of a family moving into a Victorian home that was previously a mortuary. The mother, Sara Campbell (Virginia Madsen), struggles with why "bad things happen to good people," particularly as her son Matt (Kyle Gallner) suffers from cancer. While driving him back from a treatment, she argues with God about his recovery. Matt awakes and jokingly warns her that talking to yourself is the first sign of madness; she laughs and says she is just chatting with God. He laughs too and says that she had better not threaten Him.

Sara finds that she must war against the evil in the house. Even as the family says grace before a meal, dark visions attack the son. Sobbing and praying over her son, she resists. "No, You can't have him! You can't take my son." The film employs the children's prayer "Now I Lay Me Down to Sleep" to keep the demons at bay. At the end, all the spirits get to do is burn down the house. As Matt recovers from his cancer, Sara ponders the mysterious ways of God. Her devotion again shows the efficaciousness of prayer.

While based on an actual incident of a priest accused of negligent homicide over an exorcism, *The Exorcism of Emily Rose* (Scott Derrickson, 2005) creeps into the religious horror genre. Prayers become the primary weapon against the demon near the denouement. As Father Moore (Tom Wilkinson) prepares to save Emily Rose (Jennifer Carpenter), he instructs the family and friends participating in the ritual. The focal prayers occur during the exorcism itself, with the Lord's Prayer dominating the liturgy.

"Lord Jesus Christ, have mercy upon us," he begins as Emily leans forward, tied to the bed, opening her eyes. He watches her and then announces, "It has begun. Let us pray."

He entreats God, "Send her help from the holy place, Lord. Give her heavenly protection." Then he calls to the others, "May the Lord be with you," and they respond, "And with your spirit."

As they begin to recite the Lord's Prayer, the rite builds to a crescendo. "Our Father who art in heaven," they begin. The "creature" snarls in German (is this the language of hell?), "You think you can save your little girl." They continue, "Thy kingdom come. Thy will be done," and as they arrive at "and lead us not into temptation," unexpectedly Emily screams, "*and deliver us from evil!*" This dramatic prayer adds the climax to the exorcism, as God does deliver the girl from possession. In a postscript, Emily chooses to be a martyr to demonstrate the power of God over evil. Her prayer is answered fully.

Rarely does the numinous presence of the Father's face appear as good in such a genre, in which the supernatural is usually terrible and even demonic. However, an awesome holy power of prayer unleashes a spiritual tsunami in *Bless the Child* (Chuck Russell, 2000). Maggie O'Connor (Kim Basinger) tends a child, "mankind's last hope just turned six," threatened by Satanists. Thousands of rats transform into a winged and horned demon. A community of nuns intercedes with prayer in unison: "For the girl, Cody, the innocent, that she may one day stand against the dragon. We pray to the Lord." "Lord, hear our prayer." They pray for angels to protect her and the Lord hears their prayers, answering with a dramatic epiphany.

A spiritual battle is waged against what seems to be a less spiritual danger when a plague of deadly snakes attacks a community in *Viper* (Bill Corcoran, 2008). Doctor Nicky Swift (Tara Reid) leads many in reciting the Lord's Prayer. Those who have faith receive protection even in handling venomous snakes, a reference to the last chapter of the Gospel of Mark. Both point to G. K. Chesterton's quip that "fairy tales do not tell children that dragons exist. Children already know that dragons exist. Fairy tales tell children that dragons can be killed." The way that the vipers and dragons are killed in these fantasy films is through prayer.

Signs (M. Night Shyamalan, 2002) introduces the theme of faith lost through personal disaster. When the Episcopal Reverend Hess's (Mel Gibson) wife dies in a freak automobile accident, he discards his faith. He is done with praying. Surfeit with suffering, he identifies "two kinds of people: those who see signs, miracles, and those who see coincidences." Sitting with his emotionally wrought family at the dinner table, he growls, "What's the matter with everyone? Eat!"

His young asthmatic son, Morgan (Rory Culkin), suggests, "Maybe we should say a prayer."

"No," says his father. His son persists: "Why not?"

Hess shouts, "We aren't saying a prayer! Eat. I'm not wasting one more minute of my life on prayer, not one more minute." As a prayer would be a concession that his wife did not die in vain and that Hess needs help, he stubbornly resists. Through various supernatural signs, his family is saved from aliens. Divine help comes to show him the miraculous signs and restore his faith.

In a very odd epic fantasy tale, *The Curious Case of Benjamin Button* (David Fincher, 2008), we read a banner on the wall of a black revival tent pronouncing Acts 14:3: "Many who were paralyzed and lame were healed." The congregation sings, "Just as I am, to God, I come, I come." The Pentecostal preacher comes up to Queenie (Taraji Henson) and asks, "What can I do for you, sister?" She whispers into his ear and he announces, "Her parts are all twisted up inside; she can't have no children." He lays his hand on her belly and prays, "Lord, if You can see clear to forgive this woman her sins so she can bear the fruit of her womb . . . out, damnable flesh!" He pushes her into the arms of nurses. "Praise God! Hallelujah!" he shouts, and the congregation joins in.

"And what's this old man's dereliction?" he asks, looking at the wizened, shriveled Benjamin (Brad Pitt). "He's got the devil on his back trying to ride him to the grave before his time." The preacher looks at Benjamin and asks, "How old are you?" He says, "Seven, but I look a lot older." "God bless you," responds the preacher, laughing. "He's seven. Now this man has optimism in his heart and belief in his soul. We all God's children."

"Out, Beelzebub!" he shouts, and then he says, "We gonna have you out of that chair. We gonna have you walking! In the name of God's glory! Rise up! Come on, now God's gonna see you the rest of the way. He's gonna see this old man without the aid of a crutch or a cane. Now walk. Don't touch him. Rise up, old man! Rise up like Lazarus. I said ri—i-i—se up! Say hallelujah." People clap and praise God. The minister collapses dead as Benjamin says, "Well, the Lord giveth and the Lord taketh away." Here, the revival prayers function both to exorcise, to heal, and to prepare the minister for his own homecoming to heaven.

Prayers in fantasy, horror, and adventure films parallel ordinary lives overcome with danger or fear. As characters shout out prayers for deliverance and protection, Hollywood consistently answers these prayers. C. S. Lewis pointed out how one could smuggle theology into fiction, and fantasy and horror films offered secondary worlds in which anything could happen. What happened in the twenty-first century was that prayers were shown to be remarkably efficacious in every world, however fantastic.

Spiritual Warfare

The question of what constitutes spiritual warfare was ignited by the terrorist attacks on September 11, but the battle has not been simply an interreligious conflict. Rather, more conservative Christians would envision their cultural war as a struggle against the government, with the Supreme Court seemingly restricting religious freedom in voting in 2005 that the display of the Ten Commandments in Kentucky courthouses violated the Constitution (even though the Court simultaneously upheld the constitutionality of the display on the Texas State Capitol as a monument of moral and historical significance). For liberal Christians, an ongoing struggle for justice and against poverty and racism pitted them against a materialistic society. Spiritual warfare in the new millennium also touched what scholar Leigh Schmidt called "restless souls." In an era when spirituality overtook religion, people sought meaning outside the church, with their journeys chronicled in their prayers.[11] Yet sin and death remain the final enemies against which all will battle.[12]

Few filmmakers showcase such a variety of spiritual struggles both as an actor and a director as Denzel Washington, who seeks to "speak the full Gospel" through his films. Conflicts in his films are both external and internal. In Robert Zemeckis's *Flight* (2012), Denzel Washington plays Whip Whitaker, an alcoholic pilot, who miraculously inverts and lands a plane when intoxicated and drugged on cocaine. During the turbulence, his co-pilot prays. The co-pilot prays again, with his fundamentalist wife, Vicky, in the hospital, where they invite Whip to pray with them. Seeking to escape the responsibility of his condition, he feigns religiosity. At the inquest, when confronted with lying about a fellow staff member, who happened to be his alcoholic lover, he mumbles and then prays, "Help me, God." The single plea releases him, as he then confesses to the whole truth of his condition. He ends up in jail, but sobers up, freed of his addiction and his self-deception.

In *The Magnificent Seven* (Antoine Fuqua, 2016), prayers fill the war-torn village as much as dead bodies. The beleaguered community that petitions God with the Lord's Prayer and various other intercessions receives a sevenfold sacrificial intervention when the magnificent gunslingers volunteer to help them. Even the villain, lying in the burned-out church, is given an opportunity to pray before his demise, but justice for his wickedness cuts him short.

Two scenes establish the character and identity of the hero, Eli (Denzel Washington), in the apocalyptic *The Book of Eli* (Hughes Brothers, 2009), both of which involve teaching another person how to pray. In the first, a young woman named Solara (Mila Kunis) comes in to pleasure Eli, a righteous man, who refuses her talents and orders her to sit and give him her hands. When she asks what he is doing, he repeats, "Give me your hands. Close your eyes." He prays.

> Dear Lord, we thank You for this meal. Thank You, Lord, for a warm bed to sleep on, thank You for the food we are about to eat, thank You for a roof over our heads on cold nights such as this, it's been too long. We thank You for the gift of companionship in hard times like these. Amen.

"Now we eat. Now we eat," he says. Solara has been introduced to a spiritual life of companionship, of gratitude, and of prayer, one that astounds her so much that she will repeat the same sacrament without realizing that it will also identify Eli to the villainous Carnegie (Gary Oldman).

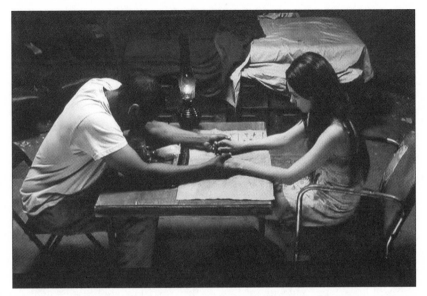

In a pivotal plot point in *The Book of Eli* (Hughes Brothers, 2009), Eli (Denzel Washington) instructs his young charge, Solara (Mila Kunis), in the art of praying.

In a room with Carnegie and her mother, Claudia (Jennifer Beals), food is brought and Claudia tells her daughter to eat. First, however, Solara asks for her Mom's hand. "Close your eyes. Mom, trust me. . . . Dear Lord—" At this point, Carnegie freezes and listens intently. "We thank You for our food. Thank You for my mother. Thank You for the roof over our heads and our new friends. And, uh . . . well, I guess that's all for now."

Carnegie interjects, "Amen. That's the word you're looking for, 'Amen.' That's how you stop." The fact that Eli prayed revealed to Carnegie that the wanderer also possessed a special book of power, an old leather book that he read, emblazoned with an image of a cross on its cover.

As they attempt to escape from Carnegie and his vicious gang, Eli recites, "The Lord is my shepherd; I shall not want. He makes me to lie down in green pastures: He leads me beside the still waters. He restores my soul. He leads me in the paths of righteousness for His name's sake. Though I walk through the valley of the shadow of death, I will fear no evil, for Thou art with me."

Solara responds, "That's beautiful. Did you write that?"

"Yes, I did," he jokes and chuckles. "No, no. No. No, that was around a long time before you and I got here, that's for sure." Yet while Eli descends into his own valley of the shadow of death, he fears no evil.

When Carnegie's posse attempts to capture the book, the tyrant screams, "It's not a book; it's a weapon!"

At the end of his journey, Eli offers his own benediction:

> Dear Lord, thank You for giving me the strength and the conviction to complete the task You entrusted to me. Thank You for guiding me straight and true through the many obstacles in my path. And for keeping me resolute when all around seemed lost. Thank You for Your protection and Your many signs along the way. Thank You for any good that I may have done. I'm so sorry about the bad. Thank You for the friend I made. Please watch over her as You watched over me. Thank You for finally allowing me to rest. I'm so very tired, but I go now to my rest at peace, knowing that I have done right with my time on this earth. I fought the good fight; I finished the race; I kept the faith.

Through the oral tradition of speaking the Bible, *The Book of Eli* teaches one how to pray, how to break bread and be "companions" with grace. Prayer works as the revelatory crux of the film.[13]

The sets of prayers in *We Were Soldiers* (Randall Wallace, 2002) cover both the family left behind and the troops going over to Vietnam. In an early humorous scene of family devotions, Lieutenant Colonel Hal Moore (Mel Gibson) gathers his five children together at bedtime, roughhousing on the bed. He shouts, "Did ya say your prayers?"

Like a disciplined military family, they fall into proper order by their beds. They cross themselves "in the name of the Father, the Son, and Holy Ghost." Then Moore leads them in the Hail Mary.

"Hail Mary, full of grace, blessed are you among women and the fruit of thy womb." Moore looks at his daughter Cecile (Sloane Momsen) and says, "I don't hear you praying, honey."

Little Cecile pouts, "I don't *wanna* be a Catholic! I wanna be a 'Nethodist' like Mommy!"

"You do? And why's that, honey?"

"So I can pray whatever I want." Her older brother cuts in, "That's a sin!"

"Oh no, no, no, that's not a sin. God just made you hardheaded. It's not a sin. Uh, I'll tell you what. You wanna, you wanna pray and thank God for our family?"

"Yes sir," says Cecile. Moore says, "That's good. Well, then, let's do it." Then proceeding as if nothing had happened, he pulls Cecile back into the Roman Catholic tradition with the illusion that she is a Methodist. They all pray, "Hail Mary, full of grace, the Lord is with thee. Blessed art thou among women, and blessed is the fruit of thy womb, Jesus." The inclusive tactic works to give his daughter religious freedom and to teach her to pray the Hail Mary.

The humorous establishment of his beloved family sets the stage for the impending tragedy of the war. Sitting before a stained glass window of the Virgin and Child in a military chapel, Lieutenant Colonel Moore meets a soldier, Second Lieutenant Jack Geoghegan (Chris Klein), who is about to embark for Vietnam and to become a father for the first time. The officer asks his commander what he thinks about being a soldier and a father. Geoghegan tells him that he had helped build a school for orphans because of a warlord's atrocious acts. "I know God has a plan for me. I just hope it's to protect orphans and not make any."

Moore suggests, "Why don't we ask Him? Let's go ask Him." They march up to the altar, and Moore prays,

> Our Father in heaven, before we go into battle, every soldier among us will approach You each in his own way. Our enemies too, according to their own understanding, will ask for protection and for victory. And so, we bow before Your infinite wisdom. We offer our prayers as best we can. I pray You watch over the young Jack Geoghegan that I lead into battle. You use me as Your instrument in this awful hell of war to watch over them. Especially if they're men like this one beside me, deserving of a future in Your blessing and goodwill. Amen.

After the lieutenant says his amen, Moore resumes his prayer: "Oh, yes, and one more thing, dear Lord, about our enemies. Ignore their heathen prayers and help us blow those little bastards straight to hell. Amen again. Thank You." The humor leavens the solemnity of the moment, as Moore will have to wrestle with the death of his soldier.

The epic sea adventure of the H.M.S. *Surprise* in *Master and Commander* (Peter Weir, 2003) chronicles Captain Jack Aubrey's (Russell Crowe) mission to capture a Napoleonic French ship off the coast of South America. Adapted from the Patrick O'Brian novels, the story shows the stark reality of death. Not only must they fight the French, but the heat, stillness of the wind, and lack of water lead the crew to suspect that a Jonah is among them. One officer, Hollom (Lee Ingleby), feels responsible for the distress of the voyage, even throwing himself into the ocean holding a cannonball. Aubrey does not utilize the book of Jonah at his funeral, but inserts the Lord's Prayer, convicting those who had not forgiven him.

Crewmen and cabin boys also die in battle. As bodies are wrapped and prepared for burial at sea in a solemn ritual, Captain Aubrey leads his crew in saying the Lord's Prayer in unison. The crew officers and sailors watch soberly as Aubrey calls their names and offices: bosun's mate, able seaman, quartermaster mate, carpenter's mate, sailing master, and lieutenant. As they finish praying, the captain offers the committal: "We therefore commit their bodies to the deep to be turned into corruption, looking for the resurrection of the body when the sea shall give up the dead for life in the world to come, for our Lord Jesus Christ. Amen." Community stands together in a sacrament of last rites, united against the last enemy of death.

Russell Crowe plays another heroic warrior of the people in Ridley Scott's *Robin Hood* (2010). Returning from the Crusades with King Richard the Lionhearted, Robin comes upon a sword that quickens his memory with its emblem of "Rise and rise again until lambs become lions." He prays over the knight who gave him the sword, "Commit this soldier to Your kingdom, Lord. We ask that You let him through Your gates to eternity, if You will let him in." When he meets up with Lady Marion (Cate Blanchett), she tells him, "I like a quiet church when I pray for a miracle. A miracle I pray for is that the bishop should show some Christian charity." It does not come through the corrupt church, but from Friar Tuck and the outlaw Robin, who supplies the grain that the people might sow and reap and eat. When peasants gather in a hut that is set on fire, one desperately prays, and Marion and her merry men deliver them. The film suggests that God frequently answers prayers by moving His people to act and help others.

Prayers in spiritual battles are also enlisted on the side of evil. A fugitive living on an island off the Mississippi in *Mud* (Jeff Nichols, 2013), Mud (Matthew McConaughey) warns two boys about water moccasin snakes, explaining that God put them here to teach us fear. Mud hides from a vigilante family and their mercenaries hunting him. The revenge-minded family gathers in a dark motel room, conspiring to kill Mud, forming a circle, taking a knee, joining hands, and scratching out an imprecatory prayer. "We are going to pray for the death of the man that killed my son." The director shows their hearts of darkness, which will lead to their own destruction. To those who seek death, even of another, death will come, but not as they expect.

In a spiritual crusade to rescue his daughter, Keller (Hugh Jackson) earnestly recites the complete Lord's Prayer in *Prisoner* (Denis Villeneuve, 2013). His young child wandered off for a "whistle" during a Pennsylvania Thanksgiving celebration and was kidnapped. A serial killer of over sixteen children confessed to a priest that kidnapping and killing children was "the war that I wage with God. Somehow, by taking children away from their parents, people lose their faith."

Keller learns of his missing daughter while in his car as the radio broadcasts a Christian homily: "We should be patient when we are inflicted on, as [God] reminds us that trouble and affliction is what all have reason to expect in this world. Man is born into trouble, not as man, but as sinful man." Keller takes the burden to find his daughter upon himself, while detective Loki (Jake Gyllenhaal, with a tattooed cross on his hand) assures him that he will find her. Keller will take things into his own hands, becoming prisoner to his own vengeance. When one deals with the devil, adapting his own cruel ways, one soon begins to resemble him.

Full of rage and despair, Keller dreams that he hears a whistle blowing and his daughter whispering, "I found it, Daddy." At the depths of his anger and doubt, Keller falls to his knees and prays, "Help me, Lord. I'm relying on Your power, Your mercies, and Your promises. I hope to obtain pardon for my sins." Just as he recites the Lord's Prayer, he stumbles across the maze that leads to his daughter. In response to the prayers, Providence has rescued her, in spite of his own descent through violent means to achieve that end.

In *The East* (Zal Batmanglij, 2013), a prayer brings down a radical terrorist group. Agent Sarah (Brit Marling) infiltrates an anarchist group known as the East, which attacks corporate organizations that damage the environment, hurting those who are "hurting us." Listening to a Christian radio music program, she drives toward her undercover mission and asks God to help her "not be arrogant, but not to be weak." This prayer not only brings about a just ending for all, but also propels the entire narrative to its righteous, sophisticated ending. Critic Patton Dodd keenly observed that the "most unusual aspect of *The East* is that it captures, whether it intends to or not, the very usual, quotidian quality of prayer as it plays out in people's lives. It's quiet, private, personal." While God answers Sarah's prayer, the film focuses more on the character of the woman seeking strength.

The intensity of *There Will Be Blood* (Paul Thomas Anderson, 2007), mixing oil, religion, and greed, is sporadically suspended by prayers that are almost comic. At the opening of an oil derrick, Daniel Plainview (Daniel Day-Lewis) is about to make a simple blessing, and local preacher Eli Sunday (Paul Dano) is expecting to be called upon to give an invocation. Plainview subverts his competitor by flattering the gathered crowd. He suggests that if they stay together and pray together, "and if the good Lord smiles kindly on our endeavor," they will share the profits together. "God bless these honest labors of ours, and, of course, God bless you all."

As the crowd echoes its "Amen," Eli is flummoxed. He will return the slight. He intimates that a horrific accident that occurred at the oil well might never have happened if he had been allowed to give the blessing. Eli's uncharitable character erupts with revenge on Plainview. When Plainview wants to buy a key parcel of land for his drilling, Eli demands that he first get baptized at his Church of the Third Revelation. The conversion scene is relentlessly and ruthlessly harsh. The convert goes through an intense inquisition, forced on his knees to confess his sins such as lusting after women and abandoning his child. Plainview must shout that he is a sinner who wants the blood. Eli slaps him across the face to chase out the devil and coerce his acceptance of Jesus as Lord and Savior.

The congregation begins to sing, "Would you be free from the burden of sin? There's power in the blood" while the baptism ceremony continues. However, the finale of the film will reverse the power relations between the two men, revealing the dangers of playing with the fire of prayer. The coerced prayer reveals the dark hearts of both sinners, their souls torturously entwined in a fierce and deadly spiritual war. Their prayers are merely bloody war cries.

Million Dollar Baby (Clint Eastwood, 2005) focuses upon female boxer Maggie Fitzgerald (Hilary Swank). Her reluctant trainer and manager, Frankie Dunn (Clint Eastwood), estranged from his lost daughter, has attended Roman Catholic Mass for twenty-three years. The cantankerous Frankie's search for redemption and restoration continues to haunt him, even with his ex-boxer friend, Scrap (Morgan Freeman), offering hope.

Frankie's spiritual life is depicted as he kneels to pray at his bedside. Crossing himself and groaning, he reminds God of their previous talks: "Well, do Your best, Lord, to protect Katie, Annie too. Other than that, You know what I want, no use me repeating myself."

At his church, the Bells of Saint Mark, he approaches Father Horvak (Brian F. O'Byrne). "Father, that was a great sermon. Made me weep." The suspicious and hassled priest asks, "What's bothering you this weekend?"

"It about one God, three gods." The priest says, "Frank, most people figure this out in kindergarten. It's about faith." To which Frank quips, "So like Snap, Crackle, and Pop."

Father Horvak explodes, "You comparing my God to Rice Krispies? There is one God!"

"What about the Holy Ghost? About Jesus?"

The exasperated priest shouts, "Don't play stupid. There are no demigods, you fucking pagan. Did you write your daughter?" Frankie says, "Absolutely." "Now you're lying," discerns the priest. "Take a day off. Don't come to mass tomorrow." Frank's playful sarcasm is contradicted by his devout prayers; his wit masks a grieving heart. For him, prayer is the only source of communication he has with a world that has beaten him up.

Director Martin Scorsese upends the traditional hagiography film in *Silence* (2016) as his saints in Japan wrestle with their loss of faith, and cry out, "I pray, but I'm lost. Am I just praying to silence?" Harking back to the existential crises in Ingmar Bergman films, Scorsese's protagonists question the deafening silence.

While such films portend a certain brand of authenticity, another film reaffirms traditional modes and augurs a distinctly countercultural trajectory. In the growing subgenre of Christian films, prayers suffuse the narrative of *War Room* (Alex Kendrick, 2015). The film opens the door to Miss Clara's (Karen Abercrombie) closet of answered prayers that transform the lives of those who meet her. "Guide me to who You want me to help," she intones.

> Raise up more that will call upon Your name. Raise up those that love You and seek You and trust You. Raise them up, Lord, raise them up. . . . I pray for unity among those that love You. I pray that You open their eyes so that they can see Your truth. Raise them up, Lord, that they will proclaim that there is salvation in the name of Jesus Christ.

The entire film demonstrates the dynamic prayer of this one elderly saint, a warrior who "fights on her knees." Miss Clara's strength is echoed in one of the most eloquent warfare prayers in *A Quiet Place* (John Krasinski, 2018), where a family silently holds hands around a dinner table and viewers share in a moment of peace during an alien reign of terror.

The twenty-first century unleashed a sense of existential struggle, not only over the threat of fundamentalist religions and their holy wars, but over homegrown mass shootings, international tensions, global refugees, and a general spiritual malaise. David Frum, senior editor of the *Atlantic*, opined on the present status of prayer:

> Prayer refreshes the soul and clears the mind. It opens the way to repentance and improvement. But prayer alone does not lift from human beings the duty to do what they have the power to do. And that's not my personal opinion. It's also the opinion, emphatically declared, of the God to whom believers in the Bible address their prayers. In the stately words of the King James translation, Isaiah 1:15: "And when ye spread forth your hands, I will hide mine eyes from you: yea, when ye make many prayers, I will not hear: your hands are full of blood."[14]

Cinematic prayers in the first years of the twenty-first century harked back to stories from history, presenting ways people used to pray. Some were inspirational, while others tested what it meant to pray. This new millennium era was marked with various kinds of laughter, laughter that revealed the foibles of flawed humans saying grace or seeking God. Yet some cynical laughter attacked the enterprise of divine communication, indicating a growing divide between belief and unbelief. For many, this augured a sense of the looming judgment of Ichabod over a nation that was losing its way, reflected in the prayers of spiritual warfare dealing with suffering and meaning. But Hollywood was sure to continue to mutter prayers, echoing both human hypocrisy and a genuine quest for dialogue with God.

Conclusion

With the turn of the new millennium, prayers resurfaced in the popular culture with questionable theology, expressing magical requests, sentimental submissions to providence, personal wrestlings with God, and imitations of other mediated prayers. It hardly mattered that the world had seen a century's worth of innovation and advancement; the human heart—and American culture—resumed where it had begun at the dawn of cinema when it came to prayer. *Plus ça change.*

Our analysis of the historical periods of the last century suggests that some eras sprout more prayers than others. For example, the 1930s, with its Production Code warning about ridicule of religion, curtailed the inclusion of religious matters in film scripts. But prayers in films follow the undulating sweep of church history itself. In "The Five Deaths of the Faith," a chapter in his book *The Everlasting Man*, the inimitable British journalist G. K. Chesterton outlined several historical episodes in which the church had "to all appearances been hollowed out from within by doubt and indifference." Yet it rose again with a new vigor, for "in every such case, the sons were fanatical for the faith where the fathers had been slack about it." So Hollywood, quietly keeping prayers in the background during the Depression and uttered mostly by children, revived them during a world war.

However, this study is only a beginning. This volume has collected and categorized numerous prayers embedded in Hollywood films over the last century, proposing pertinent—and hopefully cogent—themes for various historical eras. It has offered breadth, but then, perhaps frustrating to many readers, it necessarily lacks the depth that one might want but that cannot be provided in a single volume. Yet the scope of this study and its extensive documentation provide a heuristic resource for further analysis. Surveying the cinematic landscape, this work has demonstrated the ways films have shaped popular ideas about prayer, even in prescribing its postures and words.

First, over the last century, one can see the pervasive presence of prayers in Hollywood films. Cinematic prayers are more ubiquitous than one has likely realized, serving as strategically designed product advertisements for a divine presence. Some are quietly embedded in scenes, such as the Serenity Prayer whispered in the back of an Uber in *The Equalizer 2* (Antoine Fuqua, 2018), with the immediate efficacy of keeping one from temptation. Others are clearly rooted in human experience. For example, in one of the most inspiring dramas, *Wonder* (Stephen Chbosky, 2017), Isabel Pullman (Julia Roberts), the mother of a child whose face is disfigured with Treacher Collins Syndrome, watches as her son steps tentatively toward a new fifth grade class, praying, "Dear God, please make them [other children] be nice to him." It is a prayer that is more than answered, but one that every parent prays. The Jewish Amidah prayers of Gene Wilder as Avram Belinksi, an orthodox Polish rabbi and virtuous schlemiel, transporting the Torah to a San Francisco synagogue in *The Frisco Kid* (Robert Aldrich, 1979) and Tevye's (Topoi) memorable chats with God in *Fiddler on the Roof* (Norman Jewison, 1971) remind one to celebrate faith traditions and Sabbath prayers (and one for the tsar: "May the Lord bless and keep the tsar . . . far away from us"). Others erupt out of the unfettered imaginations of comic directors like Mel Brooks or Tyler Perry with gusto.

Second, one observes a diversity of prayer types and praying agents. Every genre of film includes prayers that confess, give thanks, or make desperate supplication. Demographically, men and women of all races and ages, saints, sinners, and hypocrites pray. The valence of prayers runs the gamut from sincere, solemn, and impassioned pleas to humorous, ironic, and sacrilegious ones. And one finds a remarkable efficacy of prayers, with the vast majority being answered within the ninety minutes of dramatic development.[1]

Third, while seeking to connect cinematic prayers to historical trends may be a quixotic quest, this volume placed the use of these religious expressions into a general historical context. It has shown that filmmakers often discern the signs of the times and are quick to incorporate religious trends. Some filmic prayers even have an isomorphic correspondence with moments in church history (as we saw with *Easy Rider* and the flowering of the Jesus movement and with *Rosemary's Baby* and the Death of God theology), although most offer more generic indicators of a spiritual climate, connected tangentially to the religious Zeit-geist of their eras.

Fourth, I must acknowledge that some films function as prayers themselves. Critic Roger Ebert began his review of Terrence Malick's *The Tree of Life* (2011) by praising it as a form of prayer. "Some few films evoke the wonderment of life's experience," he wrote, "and those I con-sider a form of prayer."[2] The prayers in films can give voice to deep long-ings, frustrations, guilt, hope, and thanksgiving.

Finally, what these examples of cinematic prayer do more than any-thing is work as parables that invite reflection. Some are exemplary: they model how to talk to God, what to talk about, what it means to engage in prayer. Others are revelatory: they show us something about ourselves, about our culture, or about the narcissism or deepest yearnings of the human soul. They speak to subterranean currents of anxiety, fear, hope, longing, or gratitude. Like jokes, cinematic prayers can be laid alongside some truth or insight that enables them to spark an idea in the one who sees and hears. They are parables. These parables do reveal adjunct in-sights. Films rarely depict people praying in community, except perhaps in saying grace before meals or at funerals. As one would expect in both American culture and Hollywood narrative paradigms, the individual protagonist is privileged over the community. He or she dictates the tra-jectory of the story, seeking to shape his or her destiny. The remarkable aspect of prayer in these films is that they often, as in the case of a classic film like *The African Queen*, alter the very arc of the narrative. Prayers in films do often change people and stories.

Cinematic praying also involves more expression and talking than listening. A recent Pew Research Center report indicated that only 39 percent of respondents said that when they talk to God, God talks back; 56 percent responded that when they talk to God, God does not talk back.[3] The crisis is aptly illustrated in *Mad Max* (George Miller, 2015). As a bevy of young fertile wives flees from the tyranny of Immortan Joe (Hugh Keays-Byrne), one pauses to put her hands together. As she fum-bles, another asks her what she is doing and she says, "Praying." When she is asked to whom, she responds that she's praying to "anyone who's listening." There is doubt whether anyone will speak back. Movies rarely show people hearing from God, a scenario that might lack dramatic ten-sion or would simply be quite boring.

As we have seen, the phenomenon of praying in the movies is more extensive than one might imagine, and perhaps seemingly a miracle in itself in what many people see as a secular industry. Remarkably, filmic prayers also instruct spectators how to pray directly. Movies like *I Can Do Bad All by Myself* and *The Book of Eli* show how the media teach us to pray, with the most direct of connections occurring when Olive in *Easy A* says about her prayers, "I'm only going on what I've seen in the movies!"

One of the most popular twentieth-century authors of Christian apologetics, Ronald Knox, a priest whose concern was to deepen the spiritual life of his flock, emphasized praying. However, a little boy watched the elderly man walking back and forth in the garden, book in hand, and asked,

"What are you doing, Ronnie?"

"I'm praying," Knox answered.

"No, *that's* not how you pray!" Kneeling down, the four-year-old folded his hands and said, "*This* is how you pray."[4]

After a century, the movies seem to look back at saints and sinners trying to pray, and say, "That's not how you pray. *This* is how you pray." Alas, so it is that movies, in aiming at authenticity and verisimilitude or sheer fantasy and satire, indirectly, and mostly unintentionally, provide a primer on how one is to pray.

ACKNOWLEDGMENTS

I would like to thank the Louisville Institute for its generous Project Grant for Researchers to study this project for what feels like the last century. I think we were all praying for it to end. My joyous gratitude also goes to Barbara Newington and Dolly Rasines of the Newington-Cropsey Foundation for their visionary support, cheerful fellowship, and tuna fish sandwiches. New York University Press editor Jennifer Hammer remains the spring of this book's existence; more than anyone, she rescued it from incoherence and guided me away from rabbit trails and cul-de-sacs. Thanks as well to Rosalie Morales Kearns for her meticulous work in cleansing this book of so many silly and careless mistakes. I also thank the staff of the University of Southern California's Warner Bros. Archives for tireless help. And from our own Virginia Wesleyan University library staff, I thank the eagle-eyed Sherry Matis. This work would be languishing on the vine without the research, suggestions, and arguments of many colleagues and former students, especially the keenly incisive Scotty and Joy Sawyer, who could see the eternal in the quotidian, Steve Sylvester, who recognizes cant from thousands of miles away, and Kirsten Powell, who dug up old prayers. I thank many inspirational supporters, the Reverend Andy Buchanan, Craig Wansink, Kelly Jackson, Kathy Merlock Jackson, Lisa Lyon Payne, Ben Fraser, Bill Brown, Dennis Bounds, Gil Elvgren, John Lawing, and the Galilee Friday very early morning men's group. For the film crew adapting this book into a film, Greg Frances, Vickie Bronaugh, Steve Sylvester, Chris Auer, and Stu Minnis, I offer a shout out. I thank my young insightful wife, Karen, who never failed to pray for me or get me outside for long walks, and our tiny children, Chris and Caroline, for humoring me (and for Cary Joseph for choosing to marry Caroline over the period of this book's writing). Mostly, I thank God, from whom all these blessings flow.

NOTES

INTRODUCTION

1 "How We Talk to God," *U.S. News and World Report*, December 20, 2004, 55.
2 Hurley, *Theology through Film*, ix.
3 In this book's analyses I have generally avoided biblical films in which one would most easily find examples of prayers, as well as international films such as those of Dreyer, Bresson, Bergman, and Tarkovsky, upon which one could ruminate endlessly.
4 Zaleskis and Zaleskis, *Prayer*.
5 Thomas, *King Cohn*, 243.
6 Allen, *Only Yesterday*; Ahlstrom, *A Religious History of the American People*; May, *Screening Out the Past*.

CHAPTER 1. SILENT PRAYERS

1 Mark Twain, *The Bible According to Mark Twain* (New York: Touchstone, 1996), 222. This is remarkably similar to C. S. Lewis's *Screwtape Letters* (New York: Macmillan, 1961), where Satan ridicules the "hairless biped" called man, "little brutes" that "make him vomit" (101).
2 Marty, *Modern American Religion*, 17.
3 Ostrander, *Life of Prayer in a World of Science*.
4 James, *Varieties of Religious Experience*, 215; Poloma and Gallup, *Varieties of Prayer*.
5 Lynd and Lynd, *Middletown*.
6 See Morgan, *Protestants and Pictures*.
7 G. K. Chesterton, *Tremendous Trifles* (London: Methuen, 1927), 203.
8 The Men and Religion Forward movement sought to transform society with a brotherhood of muscular spiritual men. See *Advance* 61 (February 23, 1911): 3. It would echo in the 1980s as the Promise Keepers movement. See Gail Bederman on the masculinization of the Protestant middle class in "The Women Have Had Charge of the Church Long Enough," in Juster, *A Mighty Baptism*, 116.
9 Tibbetts, *His Majesty, the American*.
10 Raymond Durgnant and Scott Simmon, *King Vidor, American* (Berkeley: University of California Press, 1990), 31.
11 Larry Holland, "Miracle Man," in *Magill's Survey of Cinema*, ed. Frank Magill (Englewood Cliffs, NJ: Salem Press, 1982), 751–53.

12 Hampton, *History of the American Film Industry*, 217.
13 Sherwood, *Best Moving Pictures of 1922–1923*, 27–30.
14 See Lindvall, *Sanctuary Cinema*.

CHAPTER 2. CENSORED PRAYERS

1 See Elesha Coffman, "Constituting the Protestant Mainline: *Christian Century*, 1908–1947" (PhD diss., Duke University, 2008), http://dukespace.lib.duke.edu (accessed August 30, 2015).
2 Ibid., 45.
3 Wills, *Head and Heart*, 457.
4 Weisenfeld, *Hollywood Be Thy Name*, 30.
5 Blumhofer, *Aimee Semple McPherson*.
6 H. L. Mencken, "Interlude in the Socratic Manner," in Mast, *Movies in Our Midst*.
7 Pastor Wilkins comically shames his penny-pinching congregation with a prayer: "Thou hast put into the hearts and minds of the people here to feed and clothe me and mine. Thou hast given us evidence tonight of their bounty and we thank Thee that Thou, in Thy infinite wisdom, have given me but one child to feed and one wife to clothe."
8 A French auteur's later perspective on the Depression, *The Southerners* (Jean Renoir, 1945), showcases the dirt-poor but hardworking cotton farmer Sam Tucker (Zachary Scott), who chooses to "grow his own crops." He talks straight with the Lord after a good yield, returning thanks: "Much obliged, Lord. Looks like the Tuckers are going to make it after all. Amen."
9 In Steinbeck's novel, religion is useless and impractical. Grandma likes having the preacher with them, as he can say the morning grace. When Grandpa dies, in spite of Casy reciting the Lord's Prayer, Steinbeck shows how deficient prayer is. Later, in the Hooverville camp, Casy confides in Tom, "Use ta rip off a prayer an' all the troubles'd stick to that prayer like flies on flypaper, an' the prayer'd go a-sailin' off, a-taken' them troubles along. But it don' work no more."
10 While viewed with some condescension, the prayers of country hicks could also become subjects of comedy. Buster Keaton's actual family plays the Diltz hillbilly clan in his comic *Palooka from Paducah* (Charles Lamont, 1935), whose family business, moonshining, takes a hit during Prohibition. The hillbilly family tries to grab the food at dinner; the father shouts, "Hey!" They all put their hands, holding forks, up against their foreheads in prayer. When the father finally says, "Amen," they all dig in greedily. Keaton repeats the joke from *My Wife's Relations* of a loutish family's lack of table manners, as they mutter grace and then attack their vittles. They may not be fully civilized, but they would say their prayers.
11 "Religion during the Depression," University of Virginia Department of American Studies, http://xroads.virginia.edu (accessed May 31, 2018); see Robert M. Miller, *American Protestantism and Social Issues, 1919–1939* (Chapel Hill: University of North Carolina Press, 1958); and Herman C. Weber, ed., *Yearbook of American*

Churches: A Record of Religious Activities in the United States for the Years 1933–1934 (New York: Yearbook of American Churches Press, 1939).

12 A 1930s *New Yorker* cartoon showed the insouciance of the upper classes with a wealthy man tipping his hat on the way to heaven.

13 Jerald Brauer, *Protestantism in America* (Louisville, KY: Westminster, 1965).

14 Isabel Leighton, *The Aspirin Age: 1919–1941* (New York: Simon and Schuster, 1963).

15 Bob Watson, who played Pee Wee, the boy struck by the car, would become a Methodist minister, telling Tracy that the actor's portrayal of Father Flanagan as a warm, caring, and praying priest was a major influence on his decision to enter the ministry.

16 General Research Box 1014, 22, Warner Bros. Archives, University of Southern California, Los Angeles (hereafter WB Archives).

17 Crowther, *The Lion's Share*, 257–58.

18 One such "positive" film was Frank Borzage's adaptation of Lutheran minister Lloyd Douglas's spiritual novel *The Green Light* (1937), which paradoxically appeared at an odd time, with the world about to descend into the maelstrom of war. What characterized the melodrama was the semi-mystical performance of Cedric Hardwicke's Anglican minister and radio personality, Dean Harcourt, who preaches that a "Power" puts red lights before a man so that he may learn through his sufferings. That man then evolves, with the "inexorable march to eternity," from the red lights of his life to a green light. Harcourt speaks in vague aphorisms of progressive faith with few references to God (but then, he is a liberal Anglican). He honors "civilization, as a great parade in which many stumble, many are lost, but regardless of individual destiny, the great parade must march on." In contrast to orthodox theology, he solemnly asserts that "we as individuals don't count." Ironically, the hedonist Errol Flynn plays the sacrificial doctor Paige, who as a human guinea pig discovers a vaccine at the Rocky Mountain Public Health Laboratory to save the farmers of Montana. No prayers are said when he is sick, but he survives and the parade marches on. At the ending of the film, Harcourt mounts his pulpit and pontificates from Romans 11: "Oh the depth of the riches of the wisdom and the knowledge of God. How unsearchable are His judgments; His ways past finding out. Who hath known the mind of the Lord? Who hath been His counselor?" With the choir of boys responding with an anthem of "Amen" as the grand dean of the church hobbles out on his canes, the former agnostic doctor sits sublimely in his pew with his beloved. Prayers function as pretty rhetorical prose that secular agents can appreciate, but not embrace. *The Green Light* did not really offer passionate prayers or vigorous conversations with God, but tonics and bromides for the spiritually minded and ethically effete elites. Prayers were simply green lights that directed traffic throughout the cosmos.

CHAPTER 3. FOXHOLE PRAYERS

1 The documentary *MGM: The Lion Roars* shows Mayer as the godfather of family pictures, demonstrating to Andy Hardy (Mickey Rooney) how to pray.

2 The papers in the WB Archives show how the producers investigated correct biblical citations. On giving Caesar his due: "Which commandment is 'Thou shalt not kill'?" Howard Hawks General Research Record, *Sergeant York* 29: 17.40 in File 1017103. On the same page, it asks for Bible quotations "to provide humorous log line for scene 43."

3 Koppes and Black, *Hollywood Goes to War*, 92.

4 Bosley Crowther, "*Susan and God*," *New York Times*, July 12, 1940.

5 C. S. Lewis, *Screwtape Letters* (New York: Macmillan, 1943).

6 Jesse Bader, letter to WB, July 19, 1942, page 1, in *One Foot in Heaven* Research File, WB Archives.

7 W. M. Zink, letter, November 15, 1941, General Research Record 1016 A 2878A, *One Foot in Heaven* Story File, WB Archives.

8 Harry Krieger, letter, October 31, 1941, General Research Record 1016 A 2878A, *One Foot in Heaven* Story File, WB Archives.

9 "Minister Attacks WB Selection of Advisor for *Foot in Heaven*," *Variety*, April 23, 1941, 4.

10 Story file 2143B, #2 of 3, Memos and Correspondences, WB Archives. Hymns played a major role in depicting the life of the Methodist church. A performance of "Abendsegen," or "The Children's Evening Prayer" from *Hansel and Gretel*, by nineteenth-century composer Engelbert Humperdinck, provided partial background instrumental music for the film, which was replete with hymns. A minister's musical medley arranged by Max Steiner is complemented with vocal hymns, such as "What a Friend We Have in Jesus," "Faith of Our Fathers," and the culminating and triumphant "The Church's One Foundation."

11 Robert McIlwaine, *Presbyterian Layman*, January 9, 1942.

12 "The Hospitable Trappists," *Catholic World*, March 1939; "Current Films," *Christian Herald*, October 1945, 59.

13 Casey Robinson, letter to Hal Wallis, February 14, 1940, 4; Inter-Office Communication, January 16, 1940, WB Archives.

14 Memo regarding *All This and Heaven Too*, September 21, 1939, WB Archives.

15 Extract from a burial service, Office of the Chaplain, Fort MacArthur, CA, May 18, 1942, supervised by Herman Lissauer, Head Research, May 15, 1942, File 1010, WB Archives.

16 Don Blanding, "They Speak of God," in *Pilot Bails Out* (New York: Dodd Mead, 1943). Blanding was the poet laureate of Hawaii.

17 Joseph Breen, note to Jack Warner, May 23, 1944, 128, WB Archives.

18 Jack Moffitt, note to Hal Wallis, March 20, 1944, Inter-Office Communication, WB Archives.

19 Bosley Crowther, "*God Is My Co-Pilot*," *New York Times*, March 24, 1945.

20 Lyle Dorsett, *Serving God and Country: U.S. Military Chaplains in World War II* (New York: Dutton Caliber, 2013).

21 R. G. Mensing, American Legion, letter to WB, May 28, 1940, WB Archives.

22 Max Milder, London office of WB, letter to Jack Warner, May 15, 1940, WB Archives.

CHAPTER 4. POSTWAR SECULAR PRAYERS

1 While churchmen praised Warner Bros.' production of *The Silver Chalice* (Victor
Saville, 1954), the censors raised concerns about lascivious scenes of lustful kissing. This was not supposed to be the Song of Solomon. See file 2262, Memos and
Correspondence, WB Archives. Art Linkletter told a joke to Jack Warner (December 21, 1954) during the production of *The Silver Chalice* in which a "fellow
sent his girl a pair of panties with 'Merry Christmas' embroidered on one side and
Happy New Year' on the other. She called him up and thanked him and invited
him to come up and see her between the holidays."

2 Wuthnow, *The Crisis in the Churches*, 5, 10; Wuthnow, *Restructuring of American
Religion*, 17.

3 Herberg, *Protestant-Catholic-Jew*.

4 The film was duly celebrated by the OCIC, the International Catholic Organization for Cinema, in 1948, for contributing to the "revival of the moral and spiritual
values of humanity."

5 Director Goulding asked Tyrone Power to refrain from having sexual relations
until after they had shot the scene with the yogi, and Tyrone thought that his temporary chastity may have enhanced his performance. Power was attracted to his
leading lady, Gene Tierney, who rebuffed him, as she was dating John Kennedy.

6 C. S. Lewis, "Forgiveness," in *Mere Christianity* (New York: Macmillan, 1952).

7 Harold Russell, "Guideposts Classics: Harold Russell on a Soldier's Faith," *Guideposts*, www.guideposts.org (accessed July 6, 2016).

8 Gottlieb, *Alfred Hitchcock Interviews*, 57–58.

9 Wuthnow, *Remaking the Heartland*, 4.

10 Wuthnow, *Red State Religion*.

11 "Synopsis," *Johnny Belinda* Research Record 1014, October 28, 1947, 6, WB Archives. In the research record, WB researcher McLaughlin sought out the order of
service in the Presbyterian Church and suggested hymns for the church service,
including "Rock of Ages" and "Abide with Me." September 16, 1947, 5.

12 Inter-Office Communication to Steve Trilling, October 24, 1947, WB Archives.

13 In an American Film Institute seminar with Frank Capra, one student asked the
director about the balance between the will of a character and the role of faith
in God. Capra reflected and said, "I'm wise enough to know you can't make a
religious tract into a film." He recounts an anecdote in which Jimmy Stewart goes
into "a saloon and prays, 'Show me the way, God. I'm at the end of my rope.' And
he barely says it and he gets punched in the nose. And he says, 'That's what I get
for praying.'" The author thanks his old friend Bob Gazzale, president and CEO of
the AFI, for sharing this clip.

14 Richard Maynard, "Ten Commandments of the Cowboy," in *American West on
Film* (Plymouth, MI: Hayden Book, 1974), 62.

15 When Douglas tells his former lover Josefa (Joan Collins) that he doesn't go to
church anymore, she directs him to the church, saying, "There's a woman inside

you might do well to talk to." He goes in to view the Virgin Mary, who coincidentally looks a lot like Joan Collins.

16 Bosley Crowther, "*Bishop's Wife* Review," *New York Times*, December 10, 1947.

17 Celebrity Bing Crosby appears in a cameo as himself playing golf, sinking a putt,
and saying, "Thanks" to the heavens.

18 Ellwood, *The Fifties Spiritual Marketplace.*

19 At the Christmas service, the men sing Franz Gruber and Joseph Mohr's "Silent
Night" reverently. (Max Steiner received an Academy Award nomination for his
score.) McDermid, Inter-Office Communication to Trilling, March 18, 1954, File
1766A, WB Archives. Censors objected to picture of "a luscious semi-nude" on the
chaplain's billboard.

20 Two "strangely warmed" biopics celebrated the spiritual calling of Methodist
preachers: the joyous trajectory of Methodist minister William Hartzell Spence
(Fredric March) in *One Foot in Heaven* (Irving Rapper, 1941) and Methodist
minister William Asbury Thompson helping the poor in *I'd Climb the Highest
Mountain* (Henry King, 1951), both served with a potluck of prayers.

21 Walter MacEwen, NCC, letter to Warner Trilling, March 2, 1960, WB Archives.

22 Letter dated August 20, 1959, 2204 B File, *Sins of Rachel Cade* (Gordon Douglas,
1961), WB Archives.

23 Breen, MPPDA, letter to Jack Warner, February 11, 1946, *Life with Father* 2043 1/3,
WB Archives. He is told to get in touch with official advisor Episcopal minister
Reverend J. Herbert Smith, Beverly Hills.

24 Breen worried about a reference to "miserable sinner" in the prayer, but decided
not to mention it to the committee as "they will start looking for other faults"
and Bishop Stevens was coming up for election as presiding bishop, with ensuing
politics. Breen memo, November 23, 1946, WB Archives.

25 Reverend Herbert Smith as cited by James Allen from WB, February 19, 1946, WB
Archives. A February 22, 1947, *Los Angeles Times* article, "Hollywood's Vicar Roles
Irk Minister," noted another complaint from England that the Anglican vicar
portrayed was "a bit of a buffoon" and suggested that his church establish a liaison
office in Hollywood like the Roman Catholic one. The Episcopalians opined that
Church of England clergymen are portrayed as "pretty poor fish," while Roman
Catholics are beautifully presented.

26 Eric Johnston and Joseph Breen, memo to Steve Trilling, March 25, 1946, WB
Archives.

27 Robert Buckner, memo to Steve Trilling, March 18, 1946, File 2/3, WB Archives.

28 MPAA, letter to Jack Warner, September 6, 1946, WB Archives.

29 Nathan Levinson, letter to Bill Schaeffer, April 7, 1947; and letter to Howard and
Buck Crouse, April 8, 1947, File *Life with Father*, WB Archives.

30 Letter, *Pathfinder*, October 24, 1947, WB Archives.

31 Maverick filmmaker Luis "Thank God, I'm an atheist" Buñuel celebrated faith
in his films more than many religious filmmakers. He kept to the text of Daniel
Defoe's *Robinson Crusoe* (1954) and showcased the castaway finding a Bible and

reading, "'Come to me in the day of trouble and I will deliver thee. I shall glorify thee.' Yes, it's true, only He can deliver me from this place." In his recognition of his sin and his need, Crusoe continues that he would "now respect the Sabbath and mark that day different from all others," which will lead to Friday's name, marked for the day on which he was found. When he goes to his Valley of Echo, he shouts out, "The Lord is my shepherd," and finds a congregational response in creation that echoes, "The Lord is my shepherd." The worship continues as he leads, "I shall not want. (I shall not want). He leadeth me beside still waters. (He leadeth me beside still waters.) He restores my soul. He restores my soul, my soul, my soul, my soul." It is a beautifully poignant and moving moment in the atheist director's film and a fitting end to an era that prayed, looking for an echo.

32 Warren and Thomas, *Keep Watching the Skies*, 26.
33 Cowan, *Sacred Space*, 202.
34 Joseph Breen, letters to Jack Warner, December 2, 1953, and May 21, 1954, in *East of Eden* 2954, WB Archives.
35 Herberg, *Protestant-Catholic-Jew*.

CHAPTER 5. CYNICAL PRAYERS

1 Joanne Beckman, "Religion in Post–World War II America," n.d., National Humanities Center, http://nationalhumanitiescenter.org (accessed May 25, 2017).
2 Wuthnow, *The Restructuring of American Religion*; Wuthnow, *After Heaven*.
3 Aljean Harmetz, "Burden of Dreams: George Lucas," in *George Lucas: Interviews*, ed. Sally Kline (Jackson: University Press of Mississippi, 1999), 143.
4 Vincent Canby, "*Hawaii*," *New York Times*, October 11, 1966.
5 Bellah et al., *Habits of the Heart*, 221.
6 When Yossarian expresses his doubt about God to a lieutenant's wife with whom he is having an affair, she screams and beats him about the head. He asks why she is getting upset, since she doesn't believe in God. "I don't," she sobs, bursting violently into tears. "But the God I don't believe in is a good God, a just God, a merciful God. He's not the mean and stupid God you make him out to be."
7 Gene Phillips, *Ken Russell* (Boston: Twayne, 1979), 162–66.
8 "What in the Blazes Is Ken Russell Up To Now?," *New York Times*, June 23, 1974, 29.
9 Adam Cohen, "After 30 Years, the Mood of *Nashville* Feels Right Once Again," *New York Times*, June 6, 2005. Altman's skewering satires against religion also slice through his *A Wedding* (1976), in which a doddering old priest, Bishop Martin, forgets how to pray. During a storm, the bride Muffin's (Amy Stryker) family sings "Heavenly Sunlight" in the dark basement.
10 Seydor, *Peckinpah*.
11 In Peckinpah's *Major Dundee* (1965), Waller asks Major Dundee whether he is pursuing the Apache or a promotion. "Whatever my reasons are, Frank," Dundee responds, "you'd better get down on your knees and pray to God I don't take you with me."

12 Raymond Schroth, "The Death and Life of Bishop Pike," *New York Times*, August 1, 1976, www.nytimes.com (accessed May 31, 2018).

13 Mrs. Fenty rebukes Rumson, telling him, "You should read the Bible, Mr. Rumson." Rumson counters, "I have read the Bible, Mrs. Fenty." To which she responds once more, "Didn't that discourage you about drinking?" "No," he says, "but it sure killed my appetite for readin'!"

CHAPTER 6. REVIVAL OF PRAYER

1 Cowan, *Sacred Space*, 88.

2 Pauline Kael, "On Golden Swamp," *New Yorker*, October 3, 1985, 104.

3 James Wall, "On Film," *Christian Century*, November 9, 1983, 1022.

4 Alice Cross, "*Places in the Heart* and *Country*," *Cineaste* 14, no. 1 (1985).

5 Pauline Kael, "Current Cinema," *New Yorker*, October 15, 1985, 170, 171.

6 Pauline Kael, "Current Cinema," *New Yorker*, February 25, 1985, 78–81.

7 Robert Lamm, "Can We Laugh at God? Apocalyptic Comedy in Film," *Journal of Popular Film and Television*, July 14, 2010, 81–90.

8 The words are very similar to George Carlin's mix of church/state relations, "Our Father who art in heaven and to the republic for which it stands."

9 See Robert Webber, *Evangelicals on the Canterbury Trail* (Nashville: Word, 1985).

10 One sketch from *Monty Python's Flying Circus* ("The Bruces") takes a shot at the obligatory prayers uttered in generic settings, beginning with "O Lord, we beseech Thee. Amen."

11 Dan Yakir, "Brazillant," *Film Comment* 20, no. 3 (May–June 1984): 56–59.

12 Jack Kroll, "Faith, Hope and Treasury," *Newsweek*, November 3, 1986, 81.

13 Daniel Berrigan, "*The Mission* Diary," *American Film* 12, no. 2 (November 1986): 20–26, 65; Roland Joffe, "Light Shining in Darkness," *Film Quarterly* 40, no. 4 (Summer 1987): 2–11; Rochelle Ratner, "*The Mission*," *Film Quarterly* 42 (1988): 62–63; F. Sege, "*The Mission*," *Variety*, May 21, 1986, 25–26; M. Buckley, "*The Mission*," *Films in Review* 38, no. 1 (January 1987): 47.

14 Steve Pond, "Paul Schrader," *Rolling Stone*, January 15, 1987, www.rollingstone.com (accessed January 13, 2018).

15 John Simon, "Merciful Heavens," *National Review*, April 29, 1983, 9, 508.

16 Pauline Kael, "*Tender Mercies*," *New Yorker*, May 16, 1983, 119–21.

17 Pollock, *Skywalking*.

CHAPTER 7. POSTMODERN PRAYERS

1 Reid Monaghan, "How to Pray before, during, and after Competition," December 22, 2016, Athletes in Action, https://athletesinaction.org (accessed June 28, 2018).

2 Luckmann, *The Invisible Religion*.

3 Elizabeth McAlister, "The Militarization of Prayer in America," *Journal of Religious and Political Practice* 2, no. 1 (2016): 114.

4 Michael McCullough, Giacomo Bono, and Lindsey Root, "Religion and Forgiveness," in *Handbook of the Psychology of Religion and Spirituality*, ed. Raymond
   Paloutzian and Crystal Park (New York: Guilford, 2005), 398.
5 Uniquely Jewish prayers deserve another book. The prayerful blessings of "Ein
   Keloheinu" ("There is no one like our God") is sung by a black gospel choir
   in *Keeping the Faith* (Edward Norton, 2000). The Kaddish of praise or of mourning occurs frequently, most powerfully in the opening of *Schindler's List* (Steven
   Spielberg, 1993) by Holocaust survivor Emil Katz and then hauntingly at the
   factory. In the film *Yentl* (Barbra Streisand, 1983), the rabbi asks who will say
   Kaddish at Yentl's father's funeral. Though Kaddish is traditionally recited by a
   son, Yentl (Barbra Streisand) replies that she will, to the shock of those assembled.
   The hymn of praise to God also occurs with Italian boxer Rocky Balboa in *Rocky
   III* (Sylvester Stallone, 1982) reciting the Mourner's Kaddish at the funeral of his
   Jewish coach, Mickey Goldmill (Burgess Meredith). The first communal prayer
   service before Yom Kippur, the moving Kol Nidre sequence, is chanted in the
   climactic final scene of both the 1927 version of *The Jazz Singer* (Alan Crosland)
   and again in Neil Diamond's 1980 remake, as the prodigal Yussel Rabinovitch
   returns to New York to sing it and be reconciled with his estranged cantor father.
   Gene Wilder plays Avram Belinski, a Polish rabbi, in *The Frisco Kid* (Robert
   Aldrich, 1979), and recites an obscure Aleinu prayer (the psalm of the day for
   Thursday) in a sing-song mumbling performance. Dressed in tallit and tefillin, the
   rabbi is observed by curious boys who try to understand what seem like unintel-
   ligible ramblings. In one of the more unexpected renditions, Nazi sympathizer
   René Belloq (Paul Freeman) exploits the traditional Aramaic prayer given before
   reading the Torah, the B'rikh Shmei, when he oversees the opening of the Ark of
   the Covenant in *Raiders of the Lost Ark* (Spielberg, 1981), with horrific results for
   the unbelieving Nazis. But the musical prayers of *Prince of Egypt* (Brenda Chapman, Simon Wells, Steve Hickner, 1998) and *Fiddler on the Roof* (Norman Jewison, 1971) linger long in the soul of viewers. One of the most elemental prayers
   that celebrates every moment as a miracle, or *nes*, rings out of the song "Sabbath
   Prayer," which evokes a longing for God and His blessings upon the daughters
   in the midst of crisis, as the parents entreat earnestly, "May the Lord protect and
   defend you!" Chaim Topol, as Tevye, converses with God, complains to Him,
   debates with Him, marked with passion, humor, and a melancholy sort of hope.
   When professor Larry Gopnik (Michael Stuhlbarg) prepares for his son Danny's
   (Aaron Wolff) bar mitzvah in *A Serious Man* (Coen Brothers, 2009), his boy
   gets stoned on weed while his proud father witnesses his son's stumbling prayers.
   Critic David Zvi Kalman discusses a stranger romantic comedy, *Once upon a
   Honeymoon* (Leo McCarey, 1942), in which Cary Grant and Ginger Rogers are
   mistaken as Jewish in Poland during the Nazi invasion. They wait for deportation
   with other Jews, who pray the ancient "Shema Koleinu," "Hear Our Voices," one
   of the core texts of the High Holidays liturgy. Unaware of the horrendous fate of

the Jews, Grant joins in with the cantors and prays in Hebrew, "Accept with mercy and favor our prayer." The screen fades to black.

6 "Trends in Attitudes toward Religion and Social Issues: 1987–2007," Pew Research Center, www.pewresearch.org (accessed June 28, 2018).

CHAPTER 8. MILLENNIAL PRAYERS

1 Wuthnow, *The Crisis in the Churches*; Wuthnow, *America and the Challenges of Religious Diversity*; Wuthnow, *After the Baby Boomers*.

2 Bourne, *Now I Lay Me Down to Sleep*, 3.

3 Michael Kress, "Interview: Denzel Washington's Ministry of Movies," *Beliefnet*, December 2007, www.beliefnet.com (accessed February 24, 2018).

4 See Paul Boers, "Learning the Ancient Rhythms of Prayer," *Christianity Today*, January 8, 2001; and Stan Guthrie, "The Blessing of Gratitude," *Christianity Today*, November 24, 2010.

5 "A View of General Conference, from the 'Muddled Middle,'" *United Methodist Reporter*, May 8, 2012, http://unitedmethodistreporter.com (accessed June 30, 2018).

6 Ostensibly a southern religious man, Ricky cries out in panicked prayer when he runs around with his underwear on fire. He calls for help from Jesus, the Jewish God, Allah, and finally from Tom Cruise to "use your witchcraft on me to get the fire off me," a sly dig at the Scientology practiced by the star. Will Ferrell's movies incorporate prayers as comic relief. In *Winter Passing* (Adam Rapp, 2005), Ferrell plays a minor character, Corbit, an amateur Christian musician who has come to stay with a reclusive novelist, Don Holden (Ed Harris). At one point Holden's estranged daughter, Reece (Zooey Deschanel), comes home to research him. She sits with them and an ex-graduate student at dinner. When someone asks, "Would you like to say grace?," she scoffs, "Since when does anyone in this house say grace? I thought you were an atheist." Her father responds, "Grace is okay." "Wow," she says caustically. "I can't believe that this is the same man who told his six-year-old daughter that Christmas was a Republican capitalist conspiracy created by the Hallmark Corporation and that if Jesus was alive today, he'd be down in Nicaragua, rallying the Sandinistas. Grace away." Corbit waits until all heads are bowed, then with simplicity, speaks. "Dear God, thank You for food and for the company. Reece seems pretty cool. It's nice to have her here. And thank You for a nice home."

7 See Terry Lindvall, *Surprised by Laughter: The Comic World of C. S. Lewis* (Nashville: Thomas Nelson, 1996).

8 Looking for a Bible in a bookstore, Olive asks for the religion section and is told that it is in "bestsellers, right next to *Twilight*."

9 See "Forever Young: The Juvenilization of the American Church," *Christianity Today*, June 8, 2012.

10 In regard to superheroes, *Christianity Today* even identified C. S. Lewis as a "superstar" on the cover of its December 2013 issue.

11 Leigh Schmidt, *Restless Souls: The Making of American Spirituality* (New York: HarperOne, 2005).

12 Kathryn Jean Lopez, "To Hell with Satan: Interview with Paul Thigpen, Author of *Manual for Spiritual Warfare*," *National Review*, March 21, 2015.

13 Russ Breimeier, "*Book of Eli*," *Christianity Today*, January 15, 2010; Manohla Dargis, "In This World, It Pays to Be a Loner: *The Book of Eli*," *New York Times*, January 14, 2010; Denzel Washington, *A Hand to Guide Me* (Des Moines: Meredith Books, 2006).

14 David Frum, "When Prayer Alone Does Not Suffice," *Atlantic*, June 4, 2017, www.theatlantic.com (accessed July 1, 2018).

CONCLUSION

1 William Brown, Benson Fraser, and Terry Lindvall, "Hollywood Teach Us to Pray: A Content Analysis of Feature Film Portrayals of Prayers as Models for Spiritual Practice," paper presented at the Popular Culture Association national conference, Boston, April 13, 2012.

2 Roger Ebert, "A Prayer Beneath the Tree of Life," *Chicago Sun-Times*, May 17, 2011, www.rogerebert.com (accessed December 1, 2018). See Josh Larsen, *Movies Are Prayers: How Films Voice Our Deepest Longings* (Westmont, IL: InterVarsity Press, 2017).

3 "We Believe in God," editorial, *Christianity Today*, June 2018, 15.

4 Walsh, *Second Friends*, 263.

FILMOGRAPHY

3:10 to Yuma (James Mangold, 2007)
21 Jump Street (Phil Lord, Chris Miller, 2012)
976-EVIL (Robert Englund, 1988)
2012 (Roland Emmerich, 2009)

Ace in the Hole (Billy Wilder, 1951)
The Adventures of Huckleberry Finn (Michael Curtiz, 1960)
An Affair to Remember (Leo McCarey, 1957)
The African Queen (John Huston, 1951)
Air Force (Howard Hawks, 1943)
The Alamo (John Wayne, 1960)
Alfie (Lewis Gilbert, 1966)
Alfie (Charles Shyer, 2004)
Alice in Wonderland (Tim Burton, 2010)
Alien 3 (David Fincher, 1992)
All Night Long (Harry Langdon, 1924)
All This and Heaven Too (Anatole Litvak, 1940)
Amadeus (Milos Forman, 1984)
American Hustle (David O. Russell, 2013)
Amistad (Steven Spielberg, 1997)
Anchorman 2 (Adam McKay, 2013)
Angela's Ashes (Alan Parker, 1999)

Angels in the Outfield (Clarence Brown, 1951)
Angels in the Outfield (William Dear, 1994)
Angels with Dirty Faces (Michael Curtiz, 1938)
Apocalypse Now (Francis Ford Coppola, 1979)
The Apostle (Robert Duvall, 1997)
Appaloosa (Sidney Furie, 1967)
Argo (Ben Affleck, 2012)
At Play in the Fields of the Lord (Hector Babenco, 1991)

Back from Eternity (John Farrow, 1956)
Back to Bataan (Edward Dmytryk, 1945)
Bad Little Angel (Wilhelm Thiele, 1939)
The Bad Sick (Judd Apatow, 2017)
Ballad of Cable Hogue (Sam Peckinpah, 1970)
Barcelona (Whit Stillman, 1994)
Bardelys the Magnificent (King Vidor, 1926)
Bataan (Tay Garnett, 1943)
Battle Cry (Raoul Walsh, 1955)
Battleground (William Wellman, 1949)
Battle Hymn (Douglas Sirk, 1957)

Because of Winn Dixie (Wayne Wang, 2005)

Becket (Peter Glenville, 1964)

Bedazzled (Stanley Donen, 1967)

Bedevilled (Mitchell Leisen, 1956)

The Best Years of Our Lives (William Wyler, 1947)

Beyond the Rocks (Sam Woods, 1922)

Big Bad Mama (Steve Carver, 1974)

The Big Lebowski (Coen Brothers, 1998)

Bird in a Cage (Antonio Zarro, 1987)

The Birth of a Nation (D. W. Griffith, 1915)

The Bishop's Wife (Henry Koster, 1947)

Black Narcissus (Michael Powell, E. Pressburger, 1947)

Black Robe (Bruce Beresford, 1991)

Blazing Saddles (Mel Brooks, 1974)

Bless the Child (Chuck Russell, 2000)

Body and Soul (Oscar Micheaux, 1925)

The Book of Eli (Hughes Brothers, 2009)

Boomerang (Elia Kazan, 1947)

Boondock Saints (Troy Duffy, 1999)

Boys Town (Norman Taurog, 1938)

The Bravados (Henry King, 1958)

Breaking the Waves (Lars von Trier, 1996)

Bride of Frankenstein (James Whale, 1935)

Bridge of Spies (Steven Spielberg, 2016)

A Bridge Too Far (Richard Attenborough, 1977)

Brigadoon (Vincente Minnelli, 1954)

Bring It On (Peyton Reed, 2000)

Broken Arrow (Delmer Daves, 1950)

Brother Orchid (Lloyd Bacon, 1940)

Brother Sun, Sister Moon (Franco Zeffirelli, 1972)

Bruce Almighty (Tom Shadyac, 2003)

The Bucket List (Rob Reiner, 2007)

Bumping into Broadway (Hal Roach, 1919)

Butch Cassidy and the Sundance Kid (George Roy Hill, 1969)

Butter (Jim Field Smith, 2011)

Cabin in the Sky (Vincente Minnelli, 1943)

Café Society (Woody Allen, 2016)

The Campaign (Jay Roach, 2012)

Captain Eddie (Lloyd Bacon, 1945)

Captain from Castile (Henry King, 1947)

Captains Courageous (Victor Fleming, 1937)

Cardinal Richelieu (Rowland Lee, 1935)

Carrie (Brian De Palma, 1976)

Car Wash (Michael Schultz, 1976)

Catch Me if You Can (Steven Spielberg, 2002)

Catch-22 (Mike Nichols, 1970)

Chariots of Fire (Hugh Hudson, 1981)

Chato's Land (Michael Winner, 1972)

Children of the Corn (Fritz Kiersch, 1984)

A Child's Faith (Biograph, 1910)

Chisum (Andrew McLaglen, 1970)

Chocolat (Lasse Hallstrom, 2000)

Cimarron (Wesley Ruggles, 1931)

Cinderella Man (Ron Howard, 2005)

The Cleaner (Renny Harlin, 2007)
Close Encounters of the Third Kind (Steven Spielberg, 1977)
The Cohens and the Kellys (Harry A. Pollard, 1926)
Cold Mountain (Anthony Minghella, 2003)
The Color Purple (Steven Spielberg, 1985)
Come Back, Little Sheba (Daniel Mann, 1952)
The Comedians (Peter Glenville, 1967)
Coming to America (John Landis, 1988)
The Company of Wolves (Neil Jordan, 1984)
The Confession (David Hugh Jones, 1999)
The Conversation (Francis Ford Coppola, 1974)
The Converts: Strange Transformation of Two Souls (D. W. Griffith, 1910)
Cool Hand Luke (Stuart Rosenberg, 1967)
Country (Richard Pearce, 1984)
Count Three and Pray (George Sherman, 1955)
Courage under Fire (Edward Zwick, 1996)
Cronos (Guillermo del Toro, 1993)
Cross Creek (Martin Ritt, 1983)
The Curious Case of Benjamin Button (David Fincher, 2008)

Damsels in Distress (Whit Stillman, 2011)

Dangerous Minds (John N. Smith, 1995)
Daredevil (Mark Steven Johnson, 2003)
Darling (John Schlesinger, 1965)
David Copperfield (George Cukor, 1935)
The Day the Earth Stood Still (Robert Wise, 1951)
Dead Man Walking (Tim Robbins, 1995)
Deal of the Century (William Friedkin, 1983)
Death Wish (Michael Winner, 1974)
Death Wish II (Michael Winner, 1982)
The Deer Hunter (Michael Cimino, 1978)
Deliver Us from Evil (Scott Derrickson, 2013)
Desperado (Robert Rodriguez, 1995)
Despicable Me (Pierre Coffin, Chris Renaud, 2010)
Destination Tokyo (Delmer Daves, 1943)
The Detective (Robert Hamer, 1954)
Detective Story (William Wyler, 1951)
The Devil (James Young, 1921)
The Devil at Four o'Clock (Mervyn LeRoy, 1961)
The Devil's Disciple (Guy Hamilton, 1959)
Devotion (Curtis Bernhardt, 1946)
Diary of a Country Priest (Robert Bresson, 1951)
Diary of a Mad Black Woman (Tyler Perry, 2005)
The Dilemma (Ron Howard, 2011)

Dimples (William Seiter, 1936)
The Dirty Dozen (Robert Aldrich, 1967)
Dirty Harry (Don Siegel, 1971)
Divine Secrets of the Ya-Ya Sisterhood (Callie Khouri, 2002)
Dogma (Kevin Smith, 1990)
Dragnet (Tom Mankiewicz, 1987)
Dragonheart (Rob Cohen, 1996)
Driving Miss Daisy (Bruce Beresford, 1989)
Dr. Jekyll and Mr. Hyde (Rouben Mamoulian, 1931)
Dr. Strangelove (Stanley Kubrick, 1964)
The Drunkard's Reformation (D. W. Griffith, 1909)
Duel in the Sun (King Vidor, 1946)

The East (Zal Batmanglij, 2013)
East of Eden (Elia Kazan, 1955)
Easy A (Will Gluck, 2010)
Easy Rider (Dennis Hopper, 1969)
Easy Street (Charlie Chaplin, 1917)
Eat Pray Love (Ryan Murphy, 2010)
Eighth Grade (Bo Burnham, 2018)
Election (Alexander Payne, 1999)
Eleni (Peter Yates, 1985)
The Elephant Man (David Lynch, 1980)
Elmer Gantry (Richard Brooks, 1960)
The End (Burt Reynolds, 1978)
End of Days (Peter Hyams, 1999)
The End of the Affair (Neil Jordan, 1999)
The Equalizer 2 (Antoine Fuqua, 2018)
Escape Plan (Mikael Håfström, 2013)

Evan Almighty (Tom Shadyac, 2007)
Evelyn (Bruce Beresford, 2002)
The Exorcism of Emily Rose (Scott Derrickson, 2005)
The Exorcist (William Friedkin, 1973)

The Fall of the House of Usher (Roger Corman, 1960)
Family Plot (Alfred Hitchcock, 1976)
Far and Away (Ron Howard, 1992)
A Farewell to Arms (Frank Borzage, 1932)
Fast and Furious 6 (Justin Lin, 2013)
The Fast and the Furious (Rob Cohen, 2001)
Faster (George Tillman Jr., 2010)
The Fault in Our Stars (Josh Boone, 2014)
The FBI Story (Mervyn LeRoy, 1959)
Fiddler on the Roof (Norman Jewison, 1971)
Fighting 69th (William Keighley, 1940)
Five Came Back (John Farrow, 1939)
Five Card Stud (Henry Hathaway, 1968)
Fletch Lives (Michael Ritchie, 1989)
Flight (Robert Zemeckis, 2012)
Flirting with Fate (Christy Cabanne, Douglas Fairbanks, 1916)
The Floorwalker (Charlie Chaplin, 1916)
The Fog (John Carpenter, 1980)
Fools' Parade (Andrew W. McLaglen, 1971)
Footloose (Herbert Ross, 1984)
Forgive Us Our Trespasses (George Melies, 1912)

For Heaven's Sake (Sam Taylor, 1926)

For Love of the Game (Sam Raimi, 1999)

Forrest Gump (Robert Zemeckis, 1994)

For Richer or Poorer (Bryan Spicer, 1997)

Frailty (Bill Paxton, 2001)

Freeway (Matthew Bright, 1996)

Friday Night Lights (Peter Berg, 2004)

Friday the 13th VI (Tom McLoughlin, 1986)

Friendly Persuasion (William Wyler, 1956)

The Frisco Kid (Robert Aldrich, 1979)

Frost/Nixon (Ron Howard, 2008)

The Fugitive (John Ford, 1947)

A Funny Thing Happened on the Way to the Forum (Richard Lester, 1966)

The Furies (Anthony Mann, 1950)

Gangs of New York (Martin Scorsese, 2002)

The Gaucho (Richard Jones, 1927)

Ghost (Jerry Zucker, 1990)

Giant (George Stevens, 1956)

Glory (Edward Zwick, 1989)

God Is My Co-Pilot (Robert Florey, 1945)

Gods and Generals (Ronald Maxwell, 2003)

God's Little Acre (Anthony Mann, 1958)

Gone with the Wind (Victor Fleming, Sam Wood, George Cukor, 1939)

The Good, the Bad and the Ugly (Sergio Leone, 1966)

The Grapes of Wrath (John Ford, 1940)

The Great Bank Robbery (Hy Averback, 1969)

The Great Debaters (Denzel Washington, 2007)

The Great Sinner (Robert Siodmak, 1949)

The Green Mile (Frank Darabont, 1999)

Green Pastures (Marc Connelly, 1936)

Gunfight at the OK Corral (John Sturges, 1957)

The Gunfighter (Henry King, 1952)

Hacksaw Ridge (Mel Gibson, 2016)

Hallelujah (King Vidor, 1929)

Hang 'Em High (Ted Post, 1968)

Hannah and Her Sisters (Woody Allen, 1986)

Happy, Texas (Mark Illsley, 1999)

Hard to Kill (Bruce Malmuth, 1990)

The Haunting in Connecticut (Peter Cornwell, 2009)

Hawaii (George Roy Hill, 1966)

Heathers (Michael Lehmann, 1988)

Heaven (Tom Tykwer, 2002)

Heaven Knows, Mr. Allison (John Huston, 1957)

Heaven with a Gun (Lee H. Katzin, 1969)

Heidi (Allan Dwan, 1937)

Hell's Hinges (Charles Swickard, 1916)

Hidden Figures (Theodore Melfi, 2016)

The Hiding Place (James Collier, 1972)

High Fidelity (Stephen Frears, 2000)

High Plains Drifter (Clint Eastwood, 1973)
Home Alone (Chris Columbus, 1990)
The Homesman (Tommy Lee Jones, 2014)
Hook (Steven Spielberg, 1991)
Hoosiers (David Anspaugh, 1986)
How Green Was My Valley (John Ford, 1941)
The Howling II (Philippe Mora, 1985)
How the West Was Won (John Ford et al., 1963)
Hudson Hawk (Michael Lehmann, 1991)
The Human Comedy (Clarence Brown, 1943)
The Hunchback of Notre Dame (William Dieterle, 1939)
The Hypocrite (Lois Weber, 1915)

I Can Do Bad All by Myself (Tyler Perry, 2009)
I Confess (Alfred Hitchcock, 1953)
I'd Climb the Highest Mountain (Henry King, 1951)
The Idol Dancer (D. W. Griffith, 1920)
I Heart Huckabees (David O. Russell, 2004)
I'm Gonna Git You Sucka (Keenen Ivory Wayans, 1988)
The Incredible Shrinking Man (Jack Arnold, 1957)
Independence Day (Roland Emmerich, 1996)
Inherit the Wind (Stanley Kramer, 1960)

Invaders from Mars (Tobe Hooper, 1986)
Invasion of the Body Snatchers (Don Siegel, 1957)
The Iron Giant (Brad Bird, 1999)
It's a Wonderful Life (Frank Capra, 1946)
I Walked with a Zombie (Jacques Tourneur, 1943)

Jack the Giant Killer (Bryan Singer, 2013)
Jane Eyre (Robert Stevenson, 1943)
Jaws (Steven Spielberg, 1975)
The Jazz Singer (Alan Crosland, 1927)
The Jazz Singer (Richard Fleischer, 1980)
The Jerk (Carl Reiner, 1979)
Joe versus the Volcano (John Patrick Stanley, 1990)
The Jolly Monks of Malaba (1906)
Johnny Be Good (Bud Smith, 1998)
Johnny Belinda (Jean Negulesco, 1948)
Johnny Got His Gun (Dalton Trumbo, 1971)
Judge Hardy and Son (George Seitz, 1939)
Jumping the Broom (Salim Akil, 2011)
Just Cause (Arne Glimcher, 1995)

Keeping the Faith (Edward Norton, 2000)
Key Largo (John Huston, 1948)
The Kid (Charlie Chaplin, 1921)
Kidnapped (Robert Stevenson, 1960)
The Killers (Robert Siodmak, 1946)

Knute Rockne, All American (Lloyd Bacon, 1940)

Lakeview Terrace (Neil Labute, 2008)

Last Days of Disco (Whit Stillman, 1998)

A League of Their Own (Penny Marshall, 1992)

Leap of Faith (Richard Pearce, 1992)

Left Behind: The Movie (Vic Sarin, 2000)

The Left Hand of God (Edward Dmytryk, 1955)

Les Miserables (Tom Hooper, 2012)

Lethal Weapon 3 (Richard Donner, 1992)

License to Wed (Ken Kwapis, 2007)

Lifeboat (Alfred Hitchcock, 1944)

The Life of Pi (Ang Lee, 2012)

Life with Father (Michael Curtiz, 1947)

The Light of Day (Paul Schrader, 1987)

Lilies of the Field (Ralph Nelson, 1963)

Little Annie Rooney (William Beaudine, 1925)

Little Big Man (Arthur Penn, 1970)

Little Daddy (Robert McGowan, 1931)

The Little Minister (Richard Wallace, 1934)

Little Miss Broadway (Irving Cummings, 1938)

The Little Princess (Walter Lang, 1939)

The Littlest Rebel (David Butler, 1935)

Lolita (Stanley Kubrick, 1962)

The Lone Ranger (Gore Verbinski, 2013)

Lust for Life (Vincente Minnelli, 1956)

Madame Bovary (Vincente Minnelli, 1949)

Mad Max (George Miller, 2015)

Magic in Moonlight (Woody Allen, 2014)

The Magnificent Seven (Antoine Fuqua, 2016)

Magnolia (Paul Thomas Anderson, 1999)

Major Dundee (Sam Peckinpah, 1965)

Major League (David Ward, 1989)

Manchester by the Sea (Kenneth Lonergan, 2016)

A Man for All Seasons (Fred Zinnemann, 1966)

Man on Fire (Tony Scott, 2004)

Manslaughter (Cecil B. DeMille, 1922)

Marjoe (Sarah Kernochan, Howard Smith, 1972)

The Mark of Zorro (Rouben Mamoulian, 1940)

Mary, Queen of Scots (Charles Jarrott, 1971)

M*A*S*H* (Robert Altman, 1970)

Masque of the Red Death (Roger Corman, 1964)

Master and Commander: The Far Side of the World (Peter Weir, 2003)

Match Point (Woody Allen, 2005)

Matewan (John Sayles, 1987)

Meet the Parents (Jay Roach, 2000)

Million Dollar Baby (Clint Eastwood, 2005)

The Minus Man (Hampton Fancher, 1999)

Miracle at St. Anna (Spike Lee, 2008)

The Miracle Man (George Loane Tucker, 1919)

The Miracle Woman (Frank Capra, 1931)

The Miracle Worker (Arthur Penn, 1962)

Miss Congeniality (Don Petrie, 2000)

The Mission (Roland Joffe, 1986)

The Missionary (Richard Loncraine, 1982)

Mission Impossible 3 (J. J. Abrams, 2006)

Mississippi Burning (Alan Parker, 1988)

Miss Sadie Thompson (Curtis Bernhardt, 1953)

Moneyball (Bennett Miller, 2011)

Monty Python and the Holy Grail (Terry Gilliam, Terry Jones, 1975)

Monty Python and the Meaning of Life (Terry Jones, Terry Gilliam, 1983)

Morning Departure (Roy Baker, 1950)

The Mosquito Coast (Peter Weir, 1986)

Mrs. Miniver (William Wyler, 1942)

Mud (Jeff Nichols, 2013)

Munich (Steven Spielberg, 2005)

The Murderer Lives at Number 21 (Henri-Georges Clouzot, 1942)

Must Love Dogs (Gary David Goldberg, 2005)

Mutiny on the Bounty (Frank Lloyd, 1935)

My Fair Lady (George Cukor, 1964)

My Six Loves (Gower Champion, 1963)

Mystic Pizza (Donald Petrie, 1988)

Nacho Libre (Jared Hess, 2006)

The Naked and the Dead (Raoul Walsh, 1958)

The Name of the Rose (Jean-Jacques Annaud, 1986)

Nashville (Robert Altman, 1975)

National Lampoon's Christmas Vacation (Jeremiah Chechik, 1989)

National Lampoon's Vacation (Harold Ramis, 1983)

Necessary Roughness (Stan Dragoti, 1991)

Nevada Smith (Henry Hathaway, 1966)

New Wives for Old (Cecil B. DeMille, 1918)

A Nightmare on Elm Street (Wes Craven, 1984)

A Nightmare on Elm Street 4: The Dream Master (Renny Harlin, 1988)

Night of the Hunter (Charles Laughton, 1955)

Night of the Iguana (John Huston, 1964)

Night of the Living Dead (George Romero, 1968)

Noah's Ark (Michael Curtiz, 1928)

Nothing but Trouble (Dan Aykroyd, 1991)

Notorious Bettie Page (Mary Harron, 2005)

The Nun's Story (Fred Zinnemann, 1959)

O Brother, Where Art Thou? (Coen Brothers, 2000)

Of Human Bondage (Ken Hughes, Henry Hathaway, 1964)

Of Human Hearts (Clarence Brown, 1938)

Once upon a Honeymoon (Leo McCarey, 1942)

One Foot in Heaven (Irving Rapper, 1941)

On Golden Pond (Mark Rydell, 1981)

On the Waterfront (Elia Kazan, 1954)

Our Hospitality (John Blystone, Buster Keaton, 1923)

Our Man in Havana (Carol Reed, 1959)

The Outlaw Josey Wales (Clint Eastwood, 1976)

Out of Towners (Arthur Hiller, 1970)

The Outsiders (Francis Ford Coppola, 1983)

The Pagan (W. S. Van Dyke, 1929)

Paint Your Wagon (Joshua Logan, 1969)

Paisan (Roberto Rossellini, 1946)

Pale Rider (Clint Eastwood, 1985)

The Palm Beach Story (Preston Sturges, 1942)

Paper Moon (Peter Bogdanovich, 1973)

Passion Flower (William DeMille, 1930)

Patton (Franklin Schaffner, 1969)

Peyton Place (Mark Robson, 1957)

Pinocchio (Roberto Benigni, 2002)

Places in the Heart (Robert Benton, 1984)

Plymouth Adventure (Clarence Brown, 1952)

Polly of the Circus (Alfred Santell, 1932)

Pray TV (Rick Friedberg, 1980)

Priest (Scott Stewart, 2011)

Prince of Egypt (Brenda Chapman, Simon Wells, Steve Hickner, 1998)

Prisoner (Denis Villeneuve, 2013)

The Prisoner of Zenda (Rex Ingram, 1922)

The Producers (Susan Stroman, 2005)

The Prophecy (Gregory Widen, 1995)

Psycho (Alfred Hitchcock, 1960)

Pulp (Michael Hodges, 1972)

The Quiet Man (John Ford, 1952)

A Quiet Place (John Krasinski, 2018)

Raiders of the Lost Ark (Steven Spielberg, 1981)

Rain (Lewis Milestone, 1932)

Raising Helen (Garry Marshall, 2004)

Rambo 4 (Sylvester Stallone, 2008)

The Razor's Edge (Edmund Goulding, 1946)

Rebecca of Sunnybrook Farm (Marshall Neilan, Mary Pickford, 1917)

Rebecca of Sunnybrook Farm (Allan Dwan, 1938)

Red Light (Roy Del Ruth, 1949)

Rented Lips (Robert Downey Sr., 1988)

Repentance (Tengiz Abuladze, 1984)

Resurrection (D. W. Griffith, 1909)

The Revenant (Alejandro González Iñárritu, 2015)

The River (Mark Rydell, 1984)

A River Runs through It (Robert Redford, 1992)

Robin Hood (Ridley Scott, 2010)

Robin Hood: Prince of Thieves (Kevin Reynolds, 1991)

Robinson Crusoe (Luis Buñuel, 1954)

Rocky (John Avildsen, 1976)

Rocky III (Sylvester Stallone, 1982)

Rome, Open City (Roberto Rossellini, 1945)

Rooster Cogburn (Stuart Millar, 1975)

Rosemary's Baby (Roman Polanski, 1968)

Rudy (David Anspaugh, 1993)

Russian Ark (Alexander Sokurov, 2002)

Sadie Thompson (Raoul Walsh, 1928)

Salvation Army Lass (D. W. Griffith, 1909)

The Sandpiper (Vincente Minnelli, 1965)

San Francisco (W. S. Van Dyke, 1936)

Saving Private Ryan (Steven Spielberg, 1998)

Saving Silverman (Dennis Dugan, 2001)

Scaramouche (George Sidney, 1952)

Schindler's List (Steven Spielberg, 1993)

School of Rock (Richard Linklater, 2003)

Sea Bat (Lionel Barrymore, 1930)

The Searchers (John Ford, 1956)

Season of the Witch (Dominic Sena, 2011)

The Secret Life of Bees (Gina Prince-Bythewood, 2008)

Selma (Ava DuVernay, 2014)

Sergeant York (Howard Hawks, 1941)

A Serious Man (Coen Brothers, 2009)

Seven Brides for Seven Brothers (Stanley Donen, 1954)

The Seventh Seal (Ingmar Bergman, 1957)

The Seventh Victim (Mark Robson, 1943)

Seven Women (John Ford, 1966)

Shadowlands (Richard Attenborough, 1993)

Shadows (Tom Forman, 1922)

Shakespeare in Love (John Madden, 1998)

Shane (George Stevens, 1953)

Shanghai Express (Josef von Sternberg, 1932)

Shawshank Redemption (Frank Darabont, 1994)

Shenandoah (Andrew V. McLaglen, 1965)

The Shepherd of the Hills (Henry Hathaway, 1941)

Signs (M. Night Shyamalan, 2002)

Silence (Martin Scorsese, 2016)

Silent Movie (Mel Brooks, 1976)

Silver Bullet (Daniel Attias, 1985)

Silver Chalice (Victor Saville, 1954)

Simon Birch (Mark Steven Johnson, 1998)

Since You Went Away (John Cromwell, 1944)

Sins of Rachel Cade (Gordon Douglas, 1961)

Sister Act (Emile Ardolino, 1992)

Skin Game (Paul Bogart, 1971)

Sky Pilot (King Vidor, 1921)

Slaughterhouse Five (George Roy Hill, 1972)

Sleepers (Barry Levinson, 1996)

Smokey and the Bandit (Hal Needham, 1977)

Snows of Kilimanjaro (Henry King, 1952)

Snow White and the Huntsman (Rupert Sanders, 2012)

Snow White: A Tale of Terror (Michael Cohn, 1997)

The Soloist (Joe Wright, 2009)

Song of Bernadette (Henry King, 1943)

Song without End (Charles Vidor, George Cukor, 1960)

Sophie Scholl: The Final Days (Marc Rothemund, 2005)

So Proudly We Hail (Mark Sandrich, 1943)

Sorrowful Jones (Sidney Lanfield, 1949)

The Sound of Music (Robert Wise, 1965)

Spaceballs (Mel Brooks, 1987)

Space Cowboys (Clint Eastwood, 2000)

Sparrows (William Beaudine, Mary Pickford, 1926)

Spencer's Mountain (Delmer Daves, 1963)

Spider-Man (Sam Raimi, 2002)

Spider-Man 3 (Sam Raimi, 2007)

Spitfire (John Cromwell, 1934)

Splendor in the Grass (Elia Kazan, 1961)

Stardust Memories (Woody Allen, 1980)

Starship Troopers: Marauder (Ed Neumeier, 2008)

Stars in My Crown (Jacques Tourneur, 1950)

The Station Agent (Thomas McCarthy, 2003)

Steel Magnolias (Herbert Ross, 1989)

The Story of Dr. Wassell (Cecil B. DeMille, 1944)

Story of G.I. Joe (William Wellman, 1945)

Strange Cargo (Frank Borzage, 1940)

The Strong Man (Frank Capra, 1926)

St. Vincent (Theodore Melfi, 2014)

Susan and God (George Cukor, 1940)

Sweet Bird of Youth (Richard Brooks, 1962)

Talladega Nights: The Ballad of Ricky Bobby (Adam McKay, 2006)

The Temptation of St. Anthony (American Mutoscope and Biograph, 1902)

The Ten Commandments (Cecil B. DeMille, 1923)

Tender Mercies (Bruce Beresford, 1982)

The Tender Years (Harold Schuster, 1948)

Tess of the Storm Country (John Robertson, 1922)

Theatre of Blood (Douglas Hickox, 1973)

There Will Be Blood (Paul Thomas Anderson, 2007)

They Call Me Mister Tibbs! (Gordon Douglas, 1970)

They Came to Cordura (Robert Rossen, 1959)

The Three Musketeers (Stephen Herek, 1993)

Tightrope (Richard Tuggle, 1984)

Titanic (James Cameron, 1997)

Tommy (Ken Russell, 1975)

To Save Her Soul (Mary Pickford, 1909)

Trading Places (John Landis, 1983)

Training Day (Antoine Fuqua, 2001)

The Tree of Life (Terrence Malick, 2011)

Trinity Is Still My Name (Enzo Barboni, 1972)

Trouble along the Way (Michael Curtiz, 1953)

The Trouble with Angels (Ida Lupino, 1966)

The Turn in the Road (King Vidor, 1918)

The Twelve Chairs (Mel Brooks, 1970)

The Twinkle in God's Eye (George Blair, 1955)

Unbroken (Angelina Jolie, 2014)

Under the Volcano (John Huston, 1984)

United 93 (Paul Greengrass, 2006)

Valerian (Luc Besson, 2017)

Varsity Blues (Brian Robbins, 1999)

Viper (Bill Corcoran, 2008)

Waking Ned Devine (Kirk Jones, 1998)

A Walk to Remember (Adam Shankman, 2002)

War and Peace (King Vidor, 1956)

War of the Worlds (Byron Haskins, 1953)

War Room (Alex Kendrick, 2015)

We Are Marshall (McG, 2006)

A Wedding (Robert Altman, 1976)

Wedding Crashers (David Dobkin, 2005)

We're the Millers (Rawson Thurber, 2013)

The Westerner (William Wyler, 1940)

West Side Story (Robert Wise, 1961)

We Were Soldiers (Randall Wallace, 2002)

Whispering Chorus (Cecil B. DeMille, 1918)

White Cargo (Richard Thorpe, 1942)

Who's Afraid of Virginia Woolf? (Mike Nichols, 1966)

The Wicker Man (Robin Hardy, 1973)

The Wild Angels (Roger Corman, 1966)

The Wild Bunch (Sam Peckinpah, 1969)

The Wild Rovers (Blake Edwards, 1971)

Winter Passing (Adam Rapp, 2005)

Witchfinder General/The Conqueror Worm (Michael Reeves, 1968)

Witness (Peter Weir, 1985)

The Wolfman (George Waggner, 1941)

Wonder (Stephen Chbosky, 2017)

The Wonderful World of the Brothers Grimm (Henry Levin, Georg Pal, 1962)

World Trade Center (Oliver Stone, 2006)

Wrath of God (Ralph Nelson, 1972)

The Wrong Box (Bryan Forbes, 1966)

The Wrong Man (Alfred Hitchcock, 1956)

Wuthering Heights (William Wyler, 1939)

X-Men 2 (Bryan Singer, Ralph Winter 2003)

The Yearling (Clarence Brown, 1946)

The Year of Living Dangerously (Peter Weir, 1982)

Yentl (Barbra Streisand, 1983)

You Can't Take It with You (Frank Capra, 1938)

Young Frankenstein (Mel Brooks, 1974)

SELECTED BIBLIOGRAPHY

Ahlstrom, Sydney. *A Religious History of the American People.* New Haven: Yale University Press, 1972.

Allen, Frederick. *Only Yesterday: An Informal History of the 1920s.* New York: Harper, 1931.

Ayo, Nicholas. *The Lord's Prayer: A Survey Theological and Literary.* Notre Dame: University of Notre Dame Press, 1992.

Bellah, Robert, Richard Madsen, William M. Sullivan, Ann Swidler, and Steven M. Tipton. *Habits of the Heart: Individualism and Commitment in American Life.* Berkeley: University of California Press, 2007.

Blumer, Herbert. *Movies and Conduct.* New York: Arno, 1970.

Blumhofer, Edith L. *Aimee Semple McPherson: Everybody's Sister.* Grand Rapids, MI: Eerdmans, 1993.

Bourne, William. *Now I Lay Me Down to Sleep: The Prayer of Childhood.* New York: Randolph, 1881.

Brennan, Mary C. *Turning Right in the Sixties: The Conservative Capture of the GOP.* Raleigh: University of North Carolina Press, 1995.

Butler, Jon, Grant Wacker, and Randall Balmer. *Religion in American Life: A Short History.* New York: Oxford University Press, 2011.

Cowan, Doug. *Sacred Space: The Quest for Transcendence in Science Fiction Film and Television.* Waco: Baylor University Press, 2010.

Crowther, Bosley. *The Lion's Share: The Story of an Entertainment Empire.* New York: Dutton, 1957.

Ellwood, Robert. *The Fifties Spiritual Marketplace: American Religion in a Decade of Conflict.* New Brunswick: Rutgers University Press, 1997.

Gottlieb, Sydney. *Alfred Hitchcock: Interviews.* Jackson: University Press of Mississippi, 2003.

Hampton, Benjamin B. *History of the American Film Industry: From Its Beginnings to 1931.* Mineola, NY: Dover, 1970.

Harvey, Paul. *Freedom's Coming: Religious Cultures and the Making of the South.* Chapel Hill: University of North Carolina Press, 2005.

Herberg, Will. *Protestant-Catholic-Jew: An Essay in American Religious Sociology.* New York: Doubleday, 1960.

Hurley, Neil. *Theology through Film.* New York: Harper and Row, 1970.

James, William. *Varieties of Religious Experience: A Study in Human Nature.* New York: Penguin, 1994.

Johnston, Robert K. *Reel Spirituality: Theology and Film in Dialogue.* Grand Rapids, MI: Baker Academic, 2006.

Juster, Susan, ed. *A Mighty Baptism: Race, Gender, and the Creation of American Protestantism.* Ithaca: Cornell University Press, 1996.

Keyser, Les, and Barbara Keyser. *Hollywood and the Catholic Church: The Image of Roman Catholicism in American Movies.* Chicago: Loyola Press, 1984.

Koppes, Clayton, and Gregory Black. *Hollywood Goes to War: How Politics, Profits and Propaganda Shaped World War II Movies.* Berkeley: University of California Press, 1990.

Lindvall, Terry. *Sanctuary Cinema: Origins of the Christian Film Industry.* New York: New York University Press, 2007.

Luckmann, Thomas. *The Invisible Religion: The Problem of Religion in Modern Society.* New York: Macmillan, 1971.

Lynd, Robert, and Helen Lynd. *Middletown: A Study in Modern American Culture.* San Diego: Harcourt Brace Jovanovich, 1959.

Marty, Martin. *Modern American Religion.* Chicago: University of Chicago Press, 1986.

Mast, Gerald, ed. *Movies in Our Midst: Documents in the Cultural History of Film in America.* Chicago: University of Chicago Press, 1983.

Morgan, David. *Protestants and Pictures: Religion, Visual Culture, and the Age of American Mass Productions.* New York: Oxford University Press, 1999.

Ostrander, Rick. *The Life of Prayer in a World of Science: Protestants, Prayer, and American Culture, 1870–1930.* New York: Oxford University Press, 2000.

Pickford, Mary. *Sunshine and Shadow.* New York: Doubleday, 1955.

Pollock, Dale. *Skywalking: The Life and Films of George Lucas.* Boston: Da Capo, 1999.

Poloma, Margaret, and George Gallup Jr. *Varieties of Prayer: A Survey Report.* Philadelphia: Trinity Press International, 1991.

Romanowski, William. *Reforming Hollywood: How American Protestants Fought for Freedom at the Movies.* New York: Oxford University Press, 2012.

Schweiger, Beth Barton, and Donald Mathews, eds. *Religion in the South: Protestants and Others in History and Culture.* Chapel Hill: University of North Carolina Press, 2004.

Seydor, Paul. *Peckinpah: The Western Films.* Urbana: University of Illinois Press, 1997.

Shelley, Bruce. *Church History in Plain Language.* Nashville: Thomas Nelson, 2012.

Sherwood, Robert. *Best Moving Pictures of 1922–1923.* Boston: Small, Maynard, 1923.

Thomas, Bob. *King Cohn: The Life and Times of Harry Cohn.* New York: Putnam's, 1967.

Tibbetts, John. *His Majesty, the American: The Cinema of Douglas Fairbanks, Sr.* New York: A. S. Barnes, 1977.

Vidor, King. *A Tree Is a Tree.* London: Longmans, Green, 1954.

Walsh, Milton. *Second Friends: C. S. Lewis and Ronald Knox in Conversation.* San Francisco: Ignatius Press, 2008.

Warren, Bill, and Howard Thomas. *Keep Watching the Skies.* Jefferson, NC: McFarland, 1982.

Weisenfeld, Judith. *Hollywood Be Thy Name: African American Religion in American Film.* Berkeley: University of California Press, 2007.

White, James F. *Protestant Worship: Traditions in Transition.* Westminster, TN: John Knox Press, 1989.

Wills, Garry. *Head and Heart: American Christianities.* New York: Penguin, 2007.

Wuthnow, Robert. *After Heaven: Spirituality in America since the 1950s.* Berkeley: University of California Press, 1998.

———. *After the Baby Boomers: How Twenty- and Thirty-Somethings Are Shaping the Future of American Religion.* Princeton: Princeton University Press, 2007.

———. *America and the Challenges of Religious Diversity.* Princeton: Princeton University Press, 2005.

———. *The Crisis in the Churches: Spiritual Malaise, Fiscal Woe.* New York: Oxford University Press, 1997.

———. *Red State Religion: Faith and Politics in America's Heartland.* Princeton: Princeton University Press, 2012.

———. *Remaking the Heartland: Middle America since the 1950s.* Princeton: Princeton University Press, 2012.

———. *The Restructuring of American Religion: Society and Faith since World War II.* Princeton: Princeton University Press, 1988.

Zaleskis, Philip, and Carol Zaleskis. *Prayer: A History.* Boston: Houghton Mifflin Harcourt, 2006.

INDEX

Tolkien, J. R. R., 147, 268, 307
Tolstoy, Leo, 112, 230
Tracy, Spencer, 49, 50, 54–55, 113–114, 121, 141
Trumbo, Dalton, 164, 169
Twain, Mark, 7–8, 87, 147, 218

Varieties of Religious Experience (James), 8
Vatican II, 98, 105, 137, 182
Vidor, King, 28–29, 34–35, 103–104, 112
Voltaire, 104
Vonnegut, Kurt, Jr., 172
Von Sydow, Max, 164, 186, 222
Von Trier, Lars, 265

Walken, Christopher, 201, 269, 283–284
Walker, Alice, 204
Wallace, Randall, 316–317
Walsh, Raoul, 26, 133
Warren, Rick, 246, 252, 256
Washington, Denzel, 244, 280, 313, 314–316
Waters, Ethel, 74
Watson, Emily, 258, 265
Wayans, Keenen Ivory, 219
Wayne, John, 78–79, 124, 125, 136–137, 155–156, 192, 194–195
Weaver, Richard, 6
Weaver, Sigourney, 230, 270
Weir, Peter, 207, 224, 230, 318
Weisenfeld, Judith, 35
Welles, Orson, 65
Wellman, William, 89, 92

Wells, H. G., 148
Werfel, Franz, 84
Wesley, Charles, 180
Wesley, John, 57, 114
West, Mae, 32
Westminster Catechism, 213
Whale, James, 60
Wilde, Oscar, 39
Wilder, Gene, 198, 326, 339n5
Wilder, Laura Ingalls, 114
Williams, Tennessee, 143
Willis, Bruce, 214
Wilson, Owen, 262, 287
Winter, Ralph, 308
Winters, Shelley, 137–138, 154
Wise, Robert, 148, 173, 174
Witherspoon, Reese, 217
World Council of Churches, 114, 118, 123
Wuthnow, Robert, 5, 98–99, 114, 158, 273
Wyler, William, 64, 69, 82, 102, 103, 142
Wyman, Jane, 76, 115–116

Yancey, Philip, 249
Yates, Peter, 231
Young, Loretta, 128

Zaleskis, Philip and Carol, 3
Zanuck, Daryl F., 84
Zeffirelli, Franco, 161
Zemeckis, Robert, 264–265, 314
Zinnemann, Fred, 111, 160
Zwick, Edward, 243, 244

ABOUT THE AUTHOR

Terry Lindvall is C. S. Lewis Chair of Communication and Christian Thought at Virginia Wesleyan University in Virginia Beach, Virginia. Previously he taught at Duke University's Divinity School and was the Walter Mason Fellow of Religious Studies at the College of William and Mary. He is the former "Peck's bad boy" president of Regent University, where he served on the original faculty as a professor of film and communication and the arts. He is the author of *God Mocks: A History of Religious Satire from the Hebrew Prophets to Stephen Colbert*; *Divine Film Comedies*; *Surprised by Laughter: The Comic World of C. S. Lewis*; *The Mother of All Laughter: Sarah and the Genesis of Comedy*; and *The Silents of God: Selected Issues and Documents in Silent American Film and Religion, 1908–1926*, among other works. He is married to Karen Lindvall, a musician with Guava Jam. They have two children, Chris, a comedy writer in Hollywood with Andrew Jay Cohen, and Caroline, a seventh grade English teacher, who recently married Cary Joseph, another middle school English teacher.